COMMUNICATIVE COMPETENCE: THEORY AND CLASSROOM PRACTICE

Texts and Contexts in Second Language Learning

SANDRA J. SAVIGNON

ADDISON-WESLEY PUBLISHING COMPANY

Reading, Massachusetts • Menlo Park, California
Don Mills, Ontario • Wokingham, England • Amsterdam
Sydney • Singapore • Tokyo • Madrid • Bogota
Santiago • San Juan

THE ADDISON-WESLEY SECOND LANGUAGE
PROFESSIONAL LIBRARY SERIES

Sandra J. Savignon
Consulting Editor

HIGGINS, John and JOHNS, Tim
Computers in Language Learning

MOHAN, Bernard A.,
Language and Content

SAVIGNON, Sandra J., BERNS,
Margie S.
*Initiatives in Communicative
Language Teaching: A Book of Readings*

SMITH, Stephen M.
*The Theater Arts and the
Teaching of Second Languages*

VENTRIGLIA, Linda
Conversations of Miguel and Maria

WALLERSTEIN, Nina
Language and Culture in Conflict

Library of Congress Cataloging in Publication Data

Savignon, Sandra J.
    Communicative Competence

    Includes bibliographies and index.
    1. Languages, Modern--Study and teaching.
2. Communicative Competence. I. Title.
PB36.S27   1983   418'.007'11   83-2605
ISBN 0-201-06503-7

Illustrations: Art Ciccone, Judy Filippo and Patricia O. Williams

ISBN: 0-201-06503-7
    EFGHIJKL-AL-89876

To my students,
for giving meaning to the words of Chaucer I learned as a girl,
"And gladly wolde he lerne and gladly teche."

Preface

For the second language teaching profession the past decade has been a period of growing concern with *meaning*. The importance of meaningful language use at all stages in the acquisition of second language communicative skills has come to be recognized by language teachers around the world, and many curricular innovations have been proposed in response. "Real communication"—as opposed to the drill-like pseudocommunication to which teachers and learners have been accustomed—"meaningful activity," and "spontaneous expression" are now familiar terms in discussions of what should go on in a language classroom.

The term *communicative competence* itself has received widespread interpretations. Coined by a sociolinguist (Hymes 1971) to include knowledge of sociolinguistic rules, or the appropriateness of an utterance, in addition to knowledge of grammar rules, the term has come to be used in language teaching contexts to refer to the ability to convey meaning, to successfully combine a knowledge of linguistic and sociolinguistic rules in communicative interactions (Savignon 1971). Those theorists who have extended to communication the distinction that has been made in theoretical linguistics between (grammatical) competence and performance (Chomsky 1965) have coined yet another term, *communicative performance*.

As the discussion of definitions continues among the more theoretically minded, language teachers have proceeded to develop teaching strategies and techniques that put a proper focus on meaning. These strategies offer a range of alternatives, reflecting the imaginative richness of a profession free to follow its many intuitions and convictions about what works best in a particular setting. In fact, the one word that best characterizes second language teaching methods today is *diverse*. Moreover, the emphasis is no longer so much on methods as it is on the *contexts* in which a second language is being learned and the needs and interests of those who are learning it. That is, there is now general agreement that no one method is adequate to meet the needs of all learners in all contexts.

Along with the attention being given to the contexts of language learning, and corresponding to the focus on meaning, there has been a movement away from the analysis and drill of isolated grammatical structures and toward the analysis and use of *language in setting*, or *texts*. The development of the learners' communicative abilities is seen to depend not so much on the time they spend rehearsing grammatical patterns as on the opportunities they are given to interpret, to express, and to negotiate meaning in real-life situations.

Communicative Competence Theory and Classroom Practice is a book about texts and contexts in second language learning. It is intended for classroom teachers and teachers in training as an introduction to the theoretical bases of communicative language teaching and as a guide to building a second language program consonant with those theories.

Chapter 1 begins with an examination of the theoretical and pedagogical issues underlying recent developments in second language teaching. Chapter 2 provides an overview of the relatively new research field of second language acquisition and its potential for making a contribution to classroom teaching. Chapter 3 addresses the issue of attitudes—those of the teacher as well as the learner—and recommends ways of assessing learner needs in different contexts. Chapter 4 illustrates different approaches to syllabus design—structural, notional-functional, and situational—and provides guidelines for materials development and evaluation. Chapter 5 is a collection of learning activities based on the principles of communicative language teaching introduced in earlier chapters. These activities are organized into components that correspond to different facets of the language acquisition process: Language Arts, Language for a Purpose, Personal Language Use, Theater Arts, and Beyond the Classroom. A discussion of learner errors and their treatment is also included. In conclusion, Chapter 6 provides a basic introduction to language test theory, with examples of test items and suggestions for ways in which tests can be made more reflective of communicative language use.

Each chapter includes a section entitled *Suggested Readings*, an annotated list of recommended books and articles for further reading, followed by a section entitled *Research and Discussion*, a series of questions and projects intended to promote discussion and exploration of the major issues that have been presented. The *Glossary* at the back of the book provides brief definitions of specialized terms or terms that have taken on special meaning in discussions of language and language learning and may be unfamiliar to some readers.

Throughout each chapter there are suggestions for ways in which programs can be made more responsive to the communicative goals of both learners and teachers. Underlying these suggestions is the view that a successful second language program consists of more than a textbook and classroom study. Once the goal is communication, a second language program must be seen as one that encourages students to move from the classroom to the second language world beyond and back again to the classroom. In this age of linguistic diversity *within* nations and an ever increasing communication *among* nations, many if not most learners will at some time have access to second language use outside the classroom. Air travel, radio, television, cinema, newspapers and magazines, and the presence of a variety of ethnic communities in most large cities of the world all bring the second language closer to learners and can provide an ongoing learning environment once classes are over. Moreover, the learner's second language proficiency will wax and wane as this learning environment, or the nature of the learner's interaction with it, changes. Second language (L2) skills, like first language (L1) skills, are seldom static and can be increased through training and experience.

The decision of how best to use the available classroom hours in a second language program rests ultimately, then, on the analysis of the context in which the learning is taking place. For example, what are the immediate opportunities for outside-of-class interaction in the second language? What are the short-range opportunities? Long-range? How do the three interrelate? The appropriateness of a particular program depends, further, on an assessment by the teachers involved of the best use of their personal strengths. With the understanding that teaching itself involves two-way communication comes the awareness that not only learner needs but teacher needs must be met. Language teachers are short and tall, quiet and loud, native speakers and non-native speakers. A teaching style adopted with great success by one may ill suit another. We may learn from the experiences of colleagues, but each of us must ultimately discover what fits him or her best, what particular combination of methods and materials is most appropriate in the context in which it will be used. The more we know about the changes that are taking place in second language teaching around the world, and the better we understand the nature of the goals we are trying to achieve, the greater our chances of success in developing our own second language program—one that will meet the communicative needs of a new generation of learners.

Acknowledgments

The support and encouragement of many people have been important to me in the preparation of this book. I am indebted first and foremost to the many students and teachers of second languages whom I have been privileged to know. Their interest, imagination, and dedication to the goals of interpersonal communication have been an enduring source of inspiration in my research and writing.

A professional debt of a very special kind is owed those who have given generously of their time to read preliminary versions of all or parts of the manuscript. They include Lyle Bachman, Michael Canale, Lonna Dickerson, Lu Doyle, Pearl Goodman, Braj Kachru, Diane Larsen-Freeman, Frank Medley, Sally Sieloff Magnan, Lucy Schmidt, Tony Silva, John Upshur, and the English as a second language and foreign-language methods students in my undergraduate and graduate classes at the University of Illinois. Their reactions and insights have contributed a valuable perspective to the views expressed herein.

To Margie Berns, my research assistant, I am grateful not only for her scrupulous attention to details but, more especially, for listening to me and thinking with me these many months.

A word of thanks is also due Byron Bush, my editor at Addison-Wesley, who has made my task of writing all the more pleasant, and to Albert-John Kelly and Cynthia Kuzman for their creative attention to the many details of manuscript preparation.

Last but not least, I wish to acknowledge the Research Board at the University of Illinois, Urbana-Champaign, without whose generous support this book may well have remained but an idea.

Urbana, Illinois   Sandra J. Savignon
September 1982

Contents

Chapter 1

Definitions of Communicative Competence

I am not a good mimic and I have worked now in many different cultures. I am a very poor speaker of any language, but I always know whose pig is dead, and when I work in a native society, I know what people are talking about and I treat it seriously and I respect them, and this in itself establishes a great deal more rapport, very often, than the correct accent. I have worked with other field workers who were far, far better linguists than I, and the natives kept on saying they couldn't speak the language, although they said I could! Now, if you had a recording it would be proof positive I couldn't, but nobody knew it! You see, we don't need to teach people to speak like natives, you need to make the other people believe they can, so they can talk to them, and then they learn.

—Margaret Mead

Collecting definitions of *communicative competence* is fun. Teachers, methodologists, and textbook writers have used the term in many interesting if confusing ways. Some use it assuredly, some tendentiously, others cautiously. Some still have trouble pronouncing it!

The confusion is no doubt inevitable. As the term began to appear with increasing frequency in discussions of second language learning, it came to be a symbol for everything that *audiolingualism* could not be—flexible, creative, responsive to learner needs. As such, it served as a focus for the pent-up frustration that resulted from the failure of audiolingualism to keep the promises made in the optimism of the 1960s. Once communicative competence appeared to have become synonymous with progressive, innovative teaching, everyone wanted to use the term to describe what he or she was doing—everyone, that is, except those who saw in it a disregard for *grammar*, an "anything-goes-as-long-as-you-get-your-meaning-across" approach to second language teaching. This latter group sought, rather, to identify with those who preserved "grammar" as the cornerstone of language study and scorned communicative competence as an unfortunate yet passing fad.

The feeling is now generally shared that it is time to sort out the pieces and put them together in a meaningful, coherent way. What, in fact, does the concept communicative competence mean? What does it imply for the shape of second language teaching in the years ahead? Is there sufficient agreement among professionals so that a coherent classroom model can be defined for others to follow? What skills does communicative language teaching call for on the part of the teacher? What preparation should be given to language teachers now in training?

This chapter will consider definitions of competence and communication in language and the ways in which the term communicative competence has been interpreted by second language teachers and methodologists. Section 1.1 is a statement of general premises. Section 1.2 looks at both theoretical and pedagogical issues in the recent history of linguistics and second language teaching. Section 1.3 proposes a classroom model of communicative competence as a basis for further discussion and research. In conclusion, Section 1.4 shows that the concept of communicative competence is not entirely a twentieth-century invention.

1.1 PREMISES

Competence

A helpful perspective on the term *competence* comes from *outside* the language teaching field. David McClelland, a Harvard psychologist, has gained recognition in the business world for his work in defining and assessing competence for a particular job. McClelland's competency theory asserts that standard aptitude tests are crude measures, irrelevant, in the main, to real-life job success. He has shown the incongruity between the kinds of aptitude tests typically administered by prospective employers—standard intelligence and aptitude tests similar to those required of applicants to college and professional schools—and the job itself. These tests are undoubtedly helpful in predicting academic success, acknowledges McClelland, since academic success is based in large part on more tests of a similar nature. As he puts it, "The games people are required to play on aptitude tests are similar to the games teachers require in the classroom" (1973:1). There is no evidence, however, that students who do well on the aptitude tests and earn good grades will excel in their careers. Evidence is to the contrary. The poorer students have just as much chance of success in life as their straight-A peers, *provided they have attained the same level of education and have earned the same qualifying diplomas.*

Some psychologists have attempted to justify the continued use of aptitude tests as predictors of success by pointing to significant correlations between scores on the test, job prestige, and even mental health. The problem with these correlations is that they have been artificially introduced. The test scores serve as a selection device, providing access to the more prestigious jobs whose holders are likely to be happier and better adjusted in general than those who fail to get the jobs. Thus the aptitude tests can no longer be said to be independent; they have become part of the criterion itself.

> To make the point even more vividly, suppose you are a ghetto resident in the Roxbury section of Boston. To qualify for being a policeman you have to take a three-hour-long general intelligence test in which you must know the meaning of words like "quell," "pyromaniac," and "lexicon." If you do not know enough of those words or cannot play analogy games with them, you do not qualify and must be satisfied with some such job as being janitor for which an "intelligence" test is not required yet by the Massachusetts Civil Service Commission. You, not unreasonably, feel angry, upset and unsuccessful. Because you do not know those words, you are considered to have low intelligence and since you consequently have to take a low status job and are unhappy, you contribute to the celebrated correlations of low intelligence with low occupational status and poor adjustment. [McClelland 1973:4]

A more meaningful approach to assessing competence, in McClelland's view, is to give tests of skills that are reflected in proficiency on the job. Identify top performers, and describe those behaviors that set them apart from the others. "If you want to test who will be a good policeman, go find out what a policeman does. Follow him around, make a list of his activities, and sample from that list in screening applicants" (1973:7). Valid criterion sampling of this kind requires testers to get out from behind their desks and their "endless word and pencil and paper games" and into the field to record and analyze actual performance. This is admittedly not an easy task. Success depends on both the theoretical sophistication of the testers and their practical ability to gather the needed observations. Once the criterion behaviors have been established, these can be made explicit to those who will take the resulting performance test.

Perhaps the most important point that McClelland makes is that the characteristics tested and the ways of improving on these characteristics should be made *public and explicit*. This principle is in sharp contrast to the long tradition in psychometrics of keeping test items a secret. This secrecy is maintained ostensibly for reasons of test security. But it is motivated in large part by the fear that if applicants have prior knowledge of the nature of the items they will be able to practice and earn a high score, one that may no longer correlate with subsequent performance, and thereby destroy the predictive power of the test. This has resulted in another flourishing tradition: the numerous and successful commercial schools, workshops, and self-help materials that provide practice in testlike tasks for enterprising applicants. How much simpler it would be, concludes McClelland, to make explicit to the learner the criterion behavior that will be tested. The psychologist, teacher, and learner may then collaborate openly in working to improve the applicants performance on directly observable job-related skills.

We may take, then, as our starting point for defining communicative competence, the identification of behaviors of those considered successful at what they do, specifically, the identification of the characteristics of good communicators. This leads us in turn to the *communication* part of our concern. What is communication? What determines success in communication? Are some people better communicators than others?

Communication

Communicating—or getting our message across—is the concern not only of second language teachers but of us all in our daily lives in whatever language we happen to use. Our successes are a continual source of jubilation—*This time he got the message!*—and comfort—*You really do understand, don't you?* Our failures are a source of frustration—*I wonder what he meant by that?*—and discouragement—*Somehow I can never seem to make them understand.* Learning how to be better communicators is important to all of us in both our private and public lives. Better communication means better understanding of ourselves and others; less isolation from those around us; and more productive, happy lives.

We begin at birth by interacting with those around us to keep warm, dry, and fed. We learn very soon that the success of a particular communication strategy depends on the willingness of others to understand and on the interpretation they give to our meaning. Whereas a whimper will suffice to bring a mother running with a clean diaper and warm milk in one instance, sustained screaming over long stretches of time will be ineffectual in another. We learn, then, that meaning is never one-sided. Rather, it is *negotiated* between the persons involved.

As we grow up our needs grow increasingly complex and, along with them, our communication efforts. Different words, we discover, are appropriate in different settings. The expressions we hear on the playground or through the bedroom door may or may not be acceptable at the supper table. We may decide to use them anyway to attract attention. Along with words we learn to use intonation, gestures, facial expression, and many other features of communication to convey our meaning to persons around us. Most of our repertoire of communication strategies develops unconsciously, through assimilation of role models—persons we admire and would like to resemble to some extent—and the success we experience in our interactions. In childhood, peer as well as adult reactions are usually quite spontaneous and direct; they give immediate feedback on the way our meaning has been interpreted: *That's no way to talk to your father!—Just for that, I'm not going to play with you anymore.—All you ever do is talk about how great you are. You think you're so smart!*

Formal training in the classroom affords an opportunity to gain systematic practice in an even wider range of communicative activities. Show and Tell, an activity that has become an integral part of most preschool programs, provides an early opportunity to report to a group in a formal setting on a previously prepared topic. Group discussions, moderated by the teacher, give young learners important practice in taking turns, getting the attention of the group, stating one's views, and perhaps disagreeing with others in a setting other than the informal family or playground situations with which they are familiar. Classrooms also provide practice in written communications of many kinds. Mother's Day cards are an early writing task for many children. Reports, essays, poems, business letters, and job application forms are routinely included in many school curricula and provide older learners with practical writing experience.

A concern for communication extends beyond school years and into adult life. Assertiveness training, the development of strategies for conquering stage fright, and an awareness of *body language*—the subtle messages conveyed by posture, hand movement, eyes, smile—are among the many avenues to improved communication as adults. The widespread popularity of guides to improving communication within couples and between parents and children attests to our ever present concern with learning to communicate more effectively in our most intimate relationships, to understand and to be understood by those closest to us.

Training of an even more specialized nature is available for those whose professional responsibilities or aspirations require it. Advice on how to dress and appear "businesslike," including a recommendation for the deliberate use of technical jargon to establish authority, is available for professional women who want to be taken seriously in what has historically been considered a man's world. Specialized courses in interviewing techniques are useful for employers and others who interview people frequently in their professional lives. Practice includes learning how to ask the right questions in order to elicit the needed information, listening for implied as well as spoken responses, and watching for nonverbal cues to meaning. Persons who find themselves a focus of public controversy have discovered they need to learn how to be interviewed, to develop strategies for dealing with hostile as well as friendly questioning without appearing angry or embarrassed. *Newsweek* magazine (23 March 1981) reports on the success of Arnold Zenker, a former manager of news programming at Columbia Broadcasting System (CBS) and a one-time substitute for retired CBS anchorman Walter Cronkite. Zenker now runs his own consulting company in Boston. He teaches businesspersons how to cope with a hard-hitting television interview and does a lot of what he calls "crisis work," helping executives who are under fire from the media or government investigators. One technique he uses involves *acting out* what is for many executives their worst nightmare, being questioned by CBS reporter Mike Wallace. Zenker plays the role of Wallace. "I get even nastier and more vindictive than Mike Wallace would be." His coaching includes every detail of the interview, including "right down to when they should stroke their right eyebrow."

One of the important lessons to be learned here, as in other communicative contexts, is that what matters is not the intent but the *interpretation* of the communicative act. Conveyance of meaning in unfamiliar contexts requires

CONCERN FOR IMPROVING COMMUNICATION SKILLS IS ALL AROUND US

Part-time

Be a Communiversity Instructor

Learn valuable communication
and leadership skills
while meeting people with similar
interests

UNDERSTANDING YOUR PSYCHOLOGIST

Therapy is most effective when the lines of communication are open and operating in two directions. The key is asking for an explanation.

FORD'S
Insider
A CONTINUING SERIES OF
COLLEGE NEWSPAPER SUPPLEMENTS

COMMUNICATING
A Guide to Getting Your Message Across

WHY DID I SAY THAT?

College Doublespeak:
How To Read Between the Lines
PAGE 3

You CAN Maximize Your Memory
(And Don't You Forget It!)
PAGE 12

Those Lips, Those Eyes:
What Your Face Communicates
PAGE 4

Winning the Battle
Of the Blue Book
PAGE 16

And much more, including strategies for
conquering stage fright, complaining with panache,
and building better body language

CAMPUS BRIEFS

Special English class

A special course is available this semester for teaching assistants from other lands who may have difficulty speaking or understanding English.

The class, offered by the Division of English as a Second Language, is designed to help foreign teaching assistants communicate with their students and colleagues.

Source: Ford's Insider, Knoxville, Tn.: 13–30 Corporation 1981.

practice in the use of the appropriate *register* or *style* of speech. If a woman wants to sound like a business executive, she has to talk the way business executives talk when they are on the job. The same register would of course be inappropriate when talking of personal matters with a spouse or an intimate friend. Similarly, executives who must cope with an investigative reporter may be helped to develop an appropriate style. They need to learn how to convey a sense of calm and self-assurance. Effective communication in this particular context may require the use of language to avoid a direct answer or to hide one's intent while appearing to be open and forthright. In both instances an understanding of what is *really* happening, as opposed to what one would *like* to see happening, is the first step toward improved communication.

Communication, then, is a continuous process of *expression, interpretation,* and *negotiation.* The opportunities for communication are infinite and include systems of signs and symbols (which we cannot begin to classify or even identify), of which language is but a part. The color of our skin, the way we dress, the way we wear our hair, the way we stand, smile, listen, nod, and pause all communicate to others along with the sound of our voice and the words we speak. We are concerned with communication from birth, and we learn to respond in new contexts as we accumulate life experiences. The meaning we *intend* and the meaning we *convey* are often not the same. In going from thoughts and feelings to their symbolic representation—in written or spoken words, gesture, design, color, movement, or sound—choices must be made. We make the best use we can of the symbolic systems we know. The meaning we convey depends on others who share an understanding of these symbols and who may or may not interpret them as we intend.

Competence in Communication

From the preceding considerations the following characteristics of competence in communication seem to emerge.

1. Communicative competence is a *dynamic* rather than a static concept. It depends on the negotiation of meaning between two or more persons who share to some degree the same symbolic system. In this sense, then, communicative competence can be said to be an *interpersonal* rather than an intrapersonal trait.

2. Communicative competence applies to *both written and spoken language, as well as to many other symbolic systems.*

3. Communicative competence is *context specific.* Communication takes place in an infinite variety of situations, and success in a particular role depends on one's understanding of the context and on prior experience of a similar kind. It requires making appropriate choices of *register* and *style* in terms of the situation and the other participants.

4. There is a theoretical difference between *competence* and *performance*. Competence is defined as a *presumed underlying ability*, and performance as the *overt manifestation* of that ability. Competence is what one *knows*. Performance is what one *does*. Only performance is observable, however, and it is only through performance that competence can be developed, maintained, and evaluated.

5. Communicative competence is *relative*, not absolute, and depends on the cooperation of all the participants involved. It makes sense, then, to speak of *degrees* of communicative competence.

These characteristics and the terms used to describe them—*register, style, context*, and the distinction between *competence* and *performance*—will be explored more fully, with additional examples, in Section 1.2.

Our concern in Section 1.1 has been with general premises of competence and communication. There has been no mention of *grammar, vocabulary*, and *pronunciation*—the building blocks of second language teaching as we have known it. Now we turn our attention to the concepts of competence and communication within the context of second language learning and teaching.

1.2 COMMUNICATIVE COMPETENCE IN LANGUAGE TEACHING

The course of second-language teaching methodology has never run smooth, and the development of communicative language teaching in recent years is no exception. The temptation has been to look for theoretical developments as the basis for new methodologies, which are then defined, tested, and refined to meet program goals. In fact, teaching methodologies respond to a variety of economic, political, social, and intellectual influences, only one of which is theoretical developments in related disciplines such as linguistics, psychology, and anthropology. Pressures in the marketplace, on the political front, and in society at large work along with dissatisfaction with the old ways to effect changes that, given the proper leadership and encouragement, result in the redefinition of methods and goals. Teaching always has been and always will be as much art as it is science. That this is so, however, should not deter us from elaborating methods, systematically trying them out, and judging the results. The theoretical support for what may or may not work in practice is of interest insofar as it provides a broader view of the directions we are pursuing.

LANGUAGE TEACHING METHODS RESPOND TO A VARIETY OF INFLUENCES

The development of the concept of communicative competence as it relates to language teaching can be traced to two sources, one theoretical, the other practical. The former comes from discussions in psychology, linguistics, and communication theory; the latter comes from pedagogical needs and concerns. In both theory and practice the perspective provided by the concept of communicative competence is broader than the narrowly descriptive linguistic view that characterized L2 methodologies prior to the mid-twentieth century. It is broader, too, than the structuralist approach to language description that combined with behaviorist psychology to provide theoretical justification for audiolingual methodology in the 1940s and 1950s. The notion of communicative competence goes *beyond* narrowly defined linguistics and learning psychology to the fields of anthropology and sociology. It looks at language not as individual behavior but as one of many symbolic systems that members of a society use for communication among themselves. People and the languages they use are viewed not in isolation but in their social contexts or settings.

Theoretical Issues

Language as Social Behavior

In the mid-twentieth century M.I.T. linguist Noam Chomsky directed linguistic studies away from structuralist concerns with procedures for isolating phonemes and morphemes in linguistic descriptions. Whereas structural linguists like Bloomfield (1933) and others had focused on "surface" features of phonology and morphology, Chomsky concerned himself with "deep" *semantic* structures, or the way in which sentences are understood. Transformational-generative grammar focused on the underlying grammatical *competence* assumed to be common to all native speakers. The distinction made by Chomsky between this underlying grammatical competence and its overt manifestation in language *performance* is important to an understanding of Chomskyan linguistics and the reactions it provoked. Although structural linguists, interested in the surface forms of language, had relied on native speakers' speech and writing samples for their data, Chomsky considered such samples not only *inadequate*—they can never contain examples of all the possible structures of a language—but actually *misleading* since they include errors in performance:

> Linguistic theory is concerned primarily with an ideal speaker-listener, in a completely homogeneous speech community, who knows its language perfectly and is unaffected by such grammatically irrelevant conditions as memory limitation, distractions, shifts of attention and interest, and errors (random or characteristic) in applying his knowledge of the language in actual performance. [1965:3]

The assumption of an underlying competence common to all native speakers allowed generative grammarians to check their assumptions of grammaticality against the intuitions of a single informant; in most cases this informant was simply the linguist. Coulthard (1977:3) summarizes the situation in linguistic studies in the 1960s thus: "The insights achieved by transformational grammarians were enormous but as time passed the problems became more serious. It became necessary to talk of degrees of grammaticality or acceptability; crucial examples were attacked as ungrammatical and defended as 'acceptable in my idiolect.' Meanwhile the timebomb *meaning* was ticking away."

It was the concern with meaning that led the anthropologist and linguist Dell Hymes to take issue with the formulation of *linguistic competence* proposed by Chomsky. In opposition to Chomsky's view of the "ideal speaker-listener" as a nonexistent abstraction, Hymes looks at the *real* speaker-listener in that feature of language of which Chomsky gives no account: *social interaction.* It is precisely on language in actual performance that Hymes focuses. Much of what, for Chomsky, is extraneous to a theory of *linguistic competence* and relegated to a theory of *performance,* or *language use,* is, for Hymes, an integral part of a theory of *communicative competence*:

> The linguist's problem is to explain how a child comes rapidly to be able to produce and understand (in principle) any and all of the grammatical sentences of a language. If we consider a child actually capable of producing all possible sentences he would probably be institutionalized, particularly if not only the sentences but also speech or silence were random or unpredictable. We then have to account for the fact that a normal child acquires knowledge of sentences not only as grammatical but also as appropriate. This is not accounted for in a transformational grammar, which divides linguistic theory into two parts: linguistic competence and linguistic performance. [1971:5]

Hymes's concern is with the *integration* of linguistic theory with a more general theory of *communication* and *culture*. Members of a community will behave and interpret the behavior of others according to the knowledge of the communicative systems they have available to them. This knowledge *includes, but is not limited to*, the formal possibilities of the *linguistic code*. "The grammatical factor is one among several which affect communicative competence." An adequate theory of competence must be sufficiently general to account for *all* forms of communication. With that goal in mind, Hymes proposes four parameters to the systems of rules that underlie communicative behavior:

1. Whether (and to what extent) something is formally *possible*;
2. Whether (and to what extent) something is *feasible*;
3. Whether (and to what extent) something is *appropriate* (adequate, happy, successful) in relation to a context in which it is used and evaluated;
4. Whether (and to what extent) something is in fact done, actually *performed*, and what its doing entails. [1971:12]

Included in his concept of competence is both tacit *knowledge* and *ability for use*. That is, knowledge of each of the parameters listed above is only a *part* of communicative competence. Ability for use also relates to all four parameters and includes noncognitive factors such as motivation, attitude, and general interactional competence, that is, composure, courage, and sportsmanship. People vary in both their knowledge and their ability to use that knowledge. The performance of a person in any one context reflects, moreover, the *interaction* between that person's competence, the competence of others, and the nature of the event itself as it unfolds.

Functions of Language

The work of British linguist M.A.K. Halliday adds another perspective to the elaboration of a theory of communicative competence, that of the *functions* of language. Noting that language has evolved in the service of social functions, Halliday has been concerned with moving away from the purely formal or structural preoccupations that have dominated linguistic theory toward a synthesis of structural and *functional approaches* in the study of language. Only by looking at language in use or in its *context of situation* are we able to understand the functions served by a particular grammatical structure. "Linguistics . . . is concerned . . . with the description of speech acts or texts, since only through the study of language in use are all the functions of language, and therefore all components of meaning, brought into focus" (1970:145).

An understanding of the importance of Halliday's observations for linguistic inquiry involves an understanding of the terms he uses. Since they appear with increasing frequency in discussions of language and language teaching, these terms will be defined and their meanings explored in some detail. The interrelatedness of the concepts they represent will be obvious.

Context of situation was first used by Bronislaw Malinowski (1923, 1935), an anthropologist who worked with primitive languages and the problems of meaning equivalence in translation. It was Firth (1930, 1937), a British historian-turned-linguist and colleague of Malinowski, who subsequently used the term to identify those environmental features—the people, their behavior, the objects involved, the words used, and so forth—that are relevant to the interpretation of a particular communicative act. Firth and Malinowski differed in their use of the term, however, and these differences are reflected in current sociolinguistic views. Malinowski used the term context of situation only in relation to primitive languages; Firth viewed it as part of a more general linguistic theory. Malinowski looked primarily at the *environmental reality*, whereas Firth focused on *text* (discourse in both spoken and written form, as we shall see more fully later in this chapter). For Malinowski context of situation referred to the *physical* environment; for Firth it represented an *abstract* concept.

Both Halliday and Hymes owe a debt to the theories advanced by Malinowski and Firth. In his attention to the environmental reality of *speech acts*, Hymes reflects the particular influence of Malinowski. Halliday, on the other hand, has pursued the more abstract, theoretical aspects of context of situation advanced by Firth. Although both Halliday and Hymes are concerned with language in a social setting, Halliday goes even further than Hymes in his rejection of Chomsky's distinction between competence and performance. Whereas Hymes redefines competence to include ability for use, Halliday rejects the distinction itself as either unnecessary or misleading: It is "unnecessary if it is just another name for the distinction between what we have been able to describe in the grammar and what we have not, and misleading in any other interpretation" (1970:145).

Function is the *use* to which language is put, the *purpose* of an utterance rather than the particular grammatical form an utterance takes. A language function has to do with *what* is said as opposed to *how* something is said. Language is used for an infinite number of purposes: to command, to describe, to request, to agree, to report, to avoid, to hide intent, to attract attention, etc. The function of a particular utterance can be understood only when the utterance is placed in its context of situation. *Speech act* theory (Austin 1962; Searle 1970) is concerned with the functional units of speech and the ways in which they derive their meaning not from grammatical form but from the *rules of interpretation* that prevail in a given *speech community*.

If we look at the *function* of an utterance from the speaker's point of view, we soon see that the grammatical categories we learned in school—

The imperative is for giving orders.

The interrogative is for asking questions.

The declarative is for making statements.

—simply do not apply. Around a family supper table, for example, a command to the forgetful child who set the table is likely to be in the form of anything but the imperative. *Where's the bread? Who set the table? I don't see the bread!* are among the possibilities. Children understand well the intent of such "questions" or "statements" and are quick to respond. They are also aware of the inappropriateness of a similar command form on their part. If they want bread, they request it politely, *May I please have some bread?* This is also the form an adult might use with a guest at a formal dinner.

The indirectness with which we make requests, deny permission, express disagreement, etc. as adults is sometimes perplexing to children. Young children are very direct in their requests, denials, and disagreements and may find adult subterfuge puzzling or even annoying:

Julie: Are you going to come with me to the concert tonight?

Mom: I think maybe I should stay home and do some reading.

Julie: Why don't you just say "no"!

In time, of course, children, too, develop subtle ways of refusing an invitation, making a request, expressing disagreement, and showing interest. They learn to use a variety of forms for realizing the many social functions of language. These social functions together constitute but one of three *basic* functions of language defined by Halliday, basic functions that correspond to general categories of needs met by language:

1. Language serves for the expression of 'content': that is, of the speaker's experience of the real world, including the inner world of his own consciousness. We may call this the *ideational* function. . . . In serving this function, language also gives structure to experience, and helps to determine our way of looking at things, so that it requires some intellectual effort to see them in any other way than that which our language suggests to us.

2. Language serves to establish and maintain social relations . . . through this function, which we may refer to as *interpersonal*, social groups are delimited, and the individual is identified and reinforced, since by

enabling him to interact with others language also serves in the expression and development of his own personality.

3. Finally, language has to provide for making links with itself and with features of the situation in which it is used. We may call this the *textual function*, since this is what enables the speaker or writer to 'construct' texts, or connected passages of discourse that is situationally relevant; and enables the listener or reader to distinguish a text from a random set of sentences. [Halliday 1970:143]

Halliday's description of the textual function of language uses the word *text* to refer to *connected discourse in both written and spoken language*. A text, accordingly, establishes a *situation* as distinguished from a random set of sequential sentences.

In subsequent work Halliday has pursued his analysis of the social or interpersonal aspects of language to show the systematic relationship between patterns of behavior and linguistic expression. An analysis of this kind requires looking first at the social context within which meaning takes place to describe the relevant extralinguistic features. Behavior patterns or "social meanings" are derived from the social context and are, in turn, expressed in language.

Halliday divides these patterns of behavior into two categories: *social* and *situational*. *Social patterns* include the social aspects of language use, such as establishment of boundaries in interpersonal relations, as well as the definition of *social roles*—parent to child, classmate to classmate, teacher to student, employer to employee, stranger to stranger, etc. *Situations* are the settings in which language is used. It is the situation that permits us to speak of a *text* or *language in setting*. "Here we are concerned not with behavior patterns that are socially significant in themselves but with socially identifiable units—transactions of various kinds, tasks, games, discussions and the like—within which the behavior is more or less structured" (1973:80).

In sum, for Halliday as for Hymes, we need to look at what people say (that is, the text) in *context* rather than at the possible linguistic production of an "ideal" speaker who knows all the formal rules. A focus on social meaning within a broad definition of communication provides a basis for the interpretation of language.

A Speaker's Intent

To appreciate the complexities of linguistic interaction in context and the difficulty in judging speaker's intent, we have only to look at one small example, a seemingly straightforward telephone conversation. What should you say when someone says, "Hello. Mrs. Savignon?" My ten-year-old daughter asked me this. Her concern was not pronunciation, vocabulary, or grammar. It was the *interpretation* of the caller's intent and the *appropriateness* of her response.

Telephone transactions are but one of the contexts of spoken discourse, a relatively well-defined one wherein visual cues to meaning are absent, and there is consequently more reliance on language itself to infer meaning. Other cues include, of course, the *time* of day or night and the *frequency* and *nature* of telephone use in a particular setting. Among the responses that my daughter herself proposed to the utterance were:

No, (it isn't);

No, this is Julie;

No, this is her daughter;

Just a minute, (I'll call her);

(I'm sorry) she's not at home right now;

Who's calling please?

The first step in determining a response is of course the interpretation of the caller's intent. What appears to be a query may not be a query at all: It may be a greeting, a statement, or a command. Or it may serve more than one of these functions. Some possible meanings are:

I want to speak with Mrs. Savignon and think this is she;

I want to speak with another member of the household but think I recognize the voice of Mrs. Savignon and want to be polite;

This is a call for the "lady of the house";

I want to speak with Mrs. Savignon and am not sure this is she.

Intonation might provide a cue. Is the utterance questioning? indifferent? assertive? friendly? On the other hand, telephone solicitors have learned, for good reason, to sound deceptively friendly. Voice quality may be another cue. Does it sound familiar? But these are only a few cues on which to base one of a wide choice of responses. It was thus impossible to conclude what was the best "all around" response, even for this simple, almost daily occurrence.

Classroom Issues

A theory of communicative competence rests, then, on a broad perspective of all culture as communication or meaning, on the one hand, and the description of the patterned relationship of social role and social setting to linguistic expression, on the other. While philosophers, linguists, and anthropologists have explored theoretical models of the relationship between communication and language, language teaching methodologists have pursued the development of strategies that respond in their own way to the distinction between *language form* and *language function*, between *language usage* and *language use*. This development has been led by teachers, curriculum coordinators, and learners who have sought to make *communication* not only a stated goal but an *attained goal* of L2 programs. The following firsthand account will serve perhaps to make the story of that development all the more vivid.

My interest in communicative competence began with my experience as a teacher of French during the 1960s when audiolingualism was sweeping the United States and having an influence on language programs around the world. It is an experience shared, no doubt, by many teachers of my generation, as well as by older and younger colleagues. My first teaching assignment was at one of the N.D.E.A. (National Defense Education Act) institutes funded by the U.S. government following the Russians' launching of Sputnik in 1957. The summer language institutes were part of a larger effort to provide advanced training for secondary school teachers in disciplines deemed critical to national defense—mathematics, science, and foreign languages.

Institutes concerned with foreign languages were established according to the general language proficiency of the participants; Level 1 represented the top level, and Level 4 was for those whose skill was virtually nonexistent (teachers with two or three years of study in French, Spanish, or German somewhere in their past who were being pressed into service to meet the needs of a rapidly increasing foreign language enrollment in American schools). My particular assignment was the pattern drill sections at a Level 4 French institute.

Audiolingual Methods: Forms Without Functions

Regardless of level, all language institutes shared a core program in applied linguistics. This core provided the rationale for the audiolingual method that we were promoting. It was called the *New Key*. Existing grammar-translation and reading methods of L2 teaching were described as rusty old keys that had been replaced by a new, scientific method based on the structural analysis of spoken language. A daily seminar introduced concepts, such as *phonemes*, *allophones*, *morphemes*, and *allomorphs*, on which this analysis was built. Participants at our Level 4 institute spent their evenings studying these new terms and memorizing the dialogues in *Audio-Lingual Materials (A-LM)* textbooks.

I cannot say I was unhappy there. There was a marvelous spirit of cooperation among the staff, a capable director, and a congeniality within the group of participants with whom we spent a good part of each day. I liked my job because it was neat and well defined. There was no need to worry about what to do in class. The pattern was there; all I had to do was follow it. I knew what to expect, and the participants knew what to expect. Time was used well. None was "wasted" on discussions of *why* or *how*. I recall having been particularly happy not to have had to entertain the questions of one participant in particular, a veteran Latin teacher, who was uncomfortable with the emphasis on rapid drill and sought to digress into discussions of grammar. Moreover, I proved a good pattern drill leader and the following summer was given the more prestigious responsibility of introducing the dialogues.

AUDIO-LINGUAL MATERIALS

The accepted *A-LM* procedure of dialogue presentation was to draw stick figures on the board to represent each person in the dialogue. Dialogues were introduced two or three lines at a time and drilled through the use of backward buildup. The teacher's manual directed teachers to "insist on normal speed and high quality intonation and pronunciation at all times." Learners were not to look at written material of any kind.

Marie

Louis

Marie: Ça y est! Des saucisses!
Louis: Mais il y a du riz aussi!
                         aussi!
                du riz aussi!
          il y a du riz aussi!
      Mais il y a du riz aussi!

Source: Unit 3, *A-LM French: Level One* (New York: Harcourt Brace & World, 1961).

These dialogue presentations were rather pleasant. The class met first thing in the morning and was limited to ten participants. Participants sat in a semicircle and repeated after me both as a group and individually. Repeating sounds, words, groups of words, and finally entire utterances, everyone in the class tried to imitate my pronunciation and pattern of intonation. We then began to combine utterances. I would repeat the first line, and the class would respond with the second. One half of the class would repeat the first line, and the other half of the class would respond with the second. We continued like this until we reached the point later in the week where individuals could take the role of Marie or Louis interchangeably and recite the entire dialogue.

The New Key, as I have said this audiolingual or behaviorist approach came to be known, won the day and was popular for many years. The story of the development of the New Key and the rapid innovations it brought to language teaching is well known. Although the method itself was not the direct result of linguistic theory, its advocates sought support from structural linguistics. The prestige enjoyed by linguistic science among members of the language teaching profession was reflected in claims for a "scientific" approach to language teaching. This approach included comparison of the structures of the L2 with those of the L1 to reveal the problems that would be encountered by the learner. A *contrastive analysis* of the differences in sound systems, structures, and vocabulary would provide the basis for developing the most effective teaching materials (Fries 1945). Basically, however, the reliance on active drill of the structural patterns of language found support *not* in linguistic theory but in the behaviorist theory of language acquisition. Mimicry and memorization were considered the most efficient route to L2 use. The teacher's manual for *A-LM French: Level One* summed up this view by citing Nelson Brooks, the Yale professor who served as general editor for the materials: "Language behavior is not a matter of solving problems but of performing habits so well learned that they are automatic" (1961:3).

HABIT FORMATION

The following introduction to a beginning-level Spanish textbook is representative of instructional materials developed in the 1960s. Some of these same materials are still in use today.

Throughout Levels I and II of *Learning Spanish the Modern Way* students are introduced to Spanish in a natural cultural context through situational dialogs or narratives. They master the vocabulary and structures in the dialogs and narratives by means of a wide variety of drills. This mastery is achieved through a fixed progression of learning steps consisting of: (1) listening comprehension, (2) model imitation, (3) repetition, (4) substitution, (5) self-expression.

The general procedure for using each unit is as follows:

1. The students are exposed to dialogs and narrations by means of filmstrips and motion pictures.

2. In order to master the phonology of Spanish, the students memorize the dialogs, using the native voices on the tapes as models.

3. The students practice to the point of mastery the structure drills based on patterns taken from the dialogs or narrations.

4. Tapes for language laboratory work or machine drill in the classroom enable the students to reinforce what they have learned. By practicing in the laboratory the same drills presented in class, the students establish speech habits which will become natural and automatic. In other words, they *overlearn* the material.

5. The students then learn to read the material that they can already understand and say.

6. Written exercises in the textbook provide another opportunity for reinforcement.

Source: E. Brenes et al., *Learning Spanish the Modern Way* (New York: McGraw-Hill, 1963), pp. 10–11.

In audiolingual teaching practice and curriculum development the primacy of the oral language was unquestioned regardless of the goals of the learner:

> The practice which the student contributes must be *oral practice*. No matter if the final result desired is only to *read* the foreign language the mastery of the fundamentals of the language—the structure and the sound system with a limited vocabulary—must be through speech. The speech *is* the language. The written record is but a secondary representation of the language. [Fries 1945:6]

The basic tenets of the audiolingual methodology, then, claimed theoretical support both in structural linguistics and behaviorist learning psychology. These tenets were elaborated in the intensive programs developed in the Army Specialized Training Program (ASTP) and at the centers established for the teaching of English as a foreign language in the 1940s, especially at the English Language Institute at the University of Michigan. Eventually they found their way to second language classrooms throughout the United States and around the world. The list below summarizes these tenets.

1. Language learning is habit formation.
2. Language performance consists of four basic skills: listening, speaking, reading, and writing.
3. L2 learning, like L1 learning, should begin with listening and speaking, regardless of the end goal of the learner.
4. A contrastive analysis of the phonological and structural differences between L1 and L2 provides the most effective basis for materials development and sequence.
5. The basic unit of practice should always be a complete structure. Production should precede from repetition to substitution and continue until responses are automatic. Spontaneous expression should be delayed until the more advanced levels of instruction. Production errors in structural or phonological features mean that the patterns have not received sufficient prior drilling.
6. The teacher is the center of all classroom activity and is responsible for maintaining attention and a lively pace.

Language teaching, like any other profession, has developed a vocabulary of its own. The following terms are among those that have come to be associated with teaching practices reflecting the structuralist/behaviorist view of language: *mastery, skills, the four skills, aural-oral, patterns, drills, mim-mem (mimicry-memorization), stimulus, automatic, habit*.

Functional Proficiency: An Elusive Goal

What was troubling in the otherwise three pleasant summers I spent at the

Level 4 French institute was the discernible disjuncture between mimicry, memorization, and pattern manipulation, on the one hand, and the spontaneous use of French for communication, on the other. It was not that opportunity for informal conversation was not provided in our program. It was. One of our initial plans was to establish language tables at lunch with one instructor assigned to each table of six participants. This was to give us the chance to get to know one another outside class as well as to expand participants' L2 vocabulary beyond that which was included in the textbook. It soon became apparent, however, that if participants and staff were to relax enough to enjoy their lunches, the language tables would have to be disbanded. The participants sat awkwardly silent with their classmates, too uneasy to eat, while the instructor attempted a monologue to keep up the appearance of conversation and directed a question now and again at some unlucky companion—time enough to take a hurried bite of salad or stew. Instead of the lunch tables, we ultimately established conversation tables at coffee breaks—twenty minutes every morning and afternoon. These did not work much better. There continued to be a good deal of tension and little conversation. And the consumption of doughnuts decreased markedly!

What these coffee breaks taught me was that if our goal was the *communication of ideas*, the *sharing of information* about oneself and others, then the hours we were spending in memorization and drill of structures were of questionable value. Moreover, we had conveyed to our participants the impression that when they did speak out, it should be with accuracy and ease.

How, then, were they to achieve this accuracy and ease when they were thinking about the families they had left at home and we were rehearsing dialogues between Louis and Marie about sausages and rice? What was my role during these "conversations"? Was I to "direct" the discussions to sausages and rice and meat and potatoes, encouraging the use of the structures we had been drilling—des *saucisses*, du *riz*, de la *viande*, des *pommes de terre*. If I was successful in getting participants to talk about what they liked to eat or about what Louis and Marie liked to eat, and then they said *du saucisse*, was I then to correct them? Or was I, on the other hand, to find out what everyone at the table *wanted* to say, whether or not it fit the structures we had been drilling, and give them the French equivalent to repeat? We were in a dilemma. There had been no provision in our program for learning how to learn, for *coping* with the inevitable linguistic disadvantage one faces when expressing oneself in a second language. It was little wonder few ventured forth.

What would happen, I asked myself, if we were to *begin with meaning* rather than with grammatical structures? How could we provide learners with the *coping strategies* they needed to get information from native speakers, to make the best use of what knowledge of language and other communicative means they did have to get their message across? How would native speakers respond to the way learners used the language to get or to give information? What would determine the success of their attempts to communicate in a real-life setting? And how would the learners themselves feel about the change in emphasis?

The teaching and research project to which the experiences recounted above eventually led (Savignon 1971, 1972a, 1972b) was designed to explore the disjuncture between the control of linguistic structure in classroom drills and on standardized tests and the use of language for a communicative purpose. What would happen if systematic practice in trial-and-error communication were provided as part of a beginning level adult L2 program? What would be the nature of such practice? How could its value be assessed? For the purposes of research the following distinctions were made between *linguistic competence* and *communicative competence*:

> Current audiolingual methodology, with its attendant testing concepts, reflects little concern for the distinction between communicative competence and linguistic competence. The latter may be defined as the mastery of the sound system and basic structural patterns of a language. It is typically measured by discrete-point tests consisting of discrete or separate measures of achievement in terms of the elements of language: pronunciation, grammar and vocabulary. *Communicative competence* may be defined as the ability to function in a truly communicative setting—that is, in a dynamic exchange in which *linguistic competence* must adapt itself to the total informational input, both linguistic and paralinguistic, of one or more interlocutors. . . . Success in . . . communicative tasks depends largely on the individual's willingness to express himself in the foreign language, on his resourcefulness in making use of the lexical and syntactical items which he has at his command, and on his knowledge of the paralinguistic and kinesic features of the language—intonation, facial expression, gestures, and so on—which contribute to communication. Linguistic accuracy in terms of pronunciation, grammar and vocabulary is but *one* of the major constituents in this complex interaction. [Savignon 1972b:8–9]

It is no doubt a reflection of the researcher's own audiolingual training, as well as the teaching program in which she found herself, that the focus of the study was on *oral* communication. In fact, this has been the focus of most recent methodological research. We are clearly in a time when the spoken language occupies our attention—a needed correction, perhaps, to a long tradition wherein *reading* was the major if not the sole aim of L2 teaching. (One exception to this current trend, as we shall see in Chapter 3, is an interest in the development of specialized courses in reading for academic or professional purposes.)

An important potential criticism of the trial-and-error approach to language teaching being proposed was that it would encourage structural errors. Audiolingual methodology held that avoidance of error was essential lest the learner develop "bad habits." This necessitated our remaining within the confines of structures presented and drilled in the textbook or method. Evaluation of the communicative approach had therefore to include measures of both communicative *and* linguistic competence. The end results of the study showed communicative activities of a trial-and-error nature, where the emphasis was on getting meaning across, to be just as effective as structure drills in developing grammatical competence. And these activities were a good deal *more effective* than drill in developing communicative competence. A summary of the research project, including a description of the teaching activities and test formats used, is included in Chapter 2.

Throughout the audiolingual era there could be heard a strain of dissent to the scientific analysis of discrete phonological and structural features as a basis for language test construction. Respected voices pointed out that language was more than the sum of its parts, that language proficiency could not be measured by adding up scores on discrete-point items of the elements of language. As early as 1961, John Carroll recommended tests "in which there is less attention paid to specific structure points or lexicon than to the total communicative effect of an utterance" (Carroll [1961] 1972:318). Upshur (1968) and Spolsky (1968) voiced similar views on the failure of tests of language mechanics to assess language use for communicative purposes. Jakobovits talked about what it is to know a language:

> Everyone accepts the notion that language is a means of communication, but there is much less agreement about just what is involved in the ability to communicate. The distinction between "linguistic competence" and "communicative competence" is either not explicitly taken into account in the majority of FL courses or it is tacitly assumed that the former must precede the latter in such a way that a certain high level of linguistic competence must be achieved before attempting the functional use of the FL. [1968:184]

These views went unheeded in the mainstream of language pedagogy in the 1960s. This mainstream was not to be deterred from its goal of bringing "objectivity" to language teaching and testing. To be sure, the testing and teaching practices that prevailed were never as pure in practice as in theory. Numerous examples can be cited of test items that were integrative in many respects. What's more, there were classroom teachers who, in spite of the popularity of audiolingual methods, claimed success with other methods or with a combination of methods. Yet the mood was clearly one of teaching and testing language "scientifically" through the isolation of its parts.

Views of language as context, language as interaction, and language as negotiation were nonetheless developed, both by the researchers and theorists cited above and by classroom teachers. They were to nourish the philosophy of the quiet revolution in language teaching that would find its beginnings in the 1970s. The list that follows summarizes the guiding tenets of the communicative approach to second language teaching.

1. Language use is creative. Learners use whatever knowledge they have of a language system to express their meaning in an infinite variety of ways.

2. Language use consists of many abilities in a broad communicative framework. The nature of the particular abilities needed is dependent on the roles of the participants, the situation, and the goal of the interaction.

3. L2 learning, like L1 learning, begins with the needs and interests of the learner.

4. An analysis of learner needs and interests provides the most effective basis for materials development.

5. The *basic* unit of practice should always be a text or a chunk of *discourse*. Production should begin with the conveyance of meaning. Formal accuracy in the beginning stages should be neither required nor expected.

6. The teacher assumes a variety of roles to permit learner participation in a wide range of communicative situations.

The descriptive vocabulary that has come to be associated with communicative language teaching includes the following terms: *learner needs, approximation, functions, abilities, discourse, interpretation, interaction, negotiation, contexts,* and *appropriateness*.

Interpretations of Communicative Competence

Since the introduction of the term communicative competence into the language teaching literature there have been numerous interpretations of its meaning. Methodologists have tended to focus on one or another facet of what can best be called a *philosophy* of language rather than a method, which brings an unintended but inevitable confusion to those who are unfamiliar with the evolution in theory and in practice of that philosophy. The term has become even more confused through its use to describe methodologies that have remained essentially audiolingual in practice. None of these interpretations is necessarily all wrong; each is only partially right. Without attempting to survey the many interpretations that have been lent to communicative competence in the writings of language teaching methodologists, it seems useful for purposes of charting a course for the future development of communicative language teaching to identify those interpretations that have had a widely felt influence on our present understanding of the concept.

Most discussions of communicative competence in language programs appear to reflect one of three general interpretations. Discussions that propose communicative activities as something to be *added* to existing programs reflect a view of language learning as going *from surface grammatical structures to meaning*. The grammatical progression we were following in audiolingual methods as well as in earlier methods, was fine; we simply were not going far enough soon enough. An *alternative* view is that grammar should not be the initial focus at all. One first learns how to convey meaning, how to participate in speech events. The experience of communication may lead, in turn, to a structural or functional analysis of the language, but this experience is not dependent on prior analysis. In this way, then, language acquisition is seen as proceeding *from meaning to surface structure*.

A third interpretation of communicative competence has set aside explicit discussion of learning strategies in order to focus, rather, on syllabus content, that is, on the selection of items to be taught. An analysis of language in terms of the *situations* or settings in which it is used and of the meanings or *functions* it serves in these settings provides the basis for establishing a communicative syllabus. The inclusion of specific structures depends on the *specification of context* within which the learner will use the L2. We shall look now at each of these interpretations in turn.

From Surface Structure to Meaning

In her discussion of the implications of communicative competence for language teaching, Paulston has emphasized Hymes's elaboration of the social rules of language use "rather than taking it to mean simply linguistic interaction in the target language" (1974:374). She points out that many "communicative activities" in language classrooms, though they provide useful practice in the manipulation of linguistic forms, are devoid of "social meaning" in the sense that they are not an accurate reflection of L2 culture. In her view it is possible to engage successfully in a variety of interaction activities (for example, problem solving, role playing, and games such as Twenty Questions) with no knowledge of the L2 rules of social use. Role playing that is culturally situated may be useful in developing communicative competence *only if* the teacher gives attention to the appropriateness in the second culture of alternative responses. If not, these activities do nothing to reveal the cultural biases of the learners and may, in fact, strengthen them. Focus on L2 social rules, moreover, puts a tremendous burden on the teacher who must become an anthropologist of sorts, discovering and interpreting cultural behavior for which there are no explicit rules.

Communicative competence, as Paulston defines it, is not a necessary goal of every language program. In her words, "It is valid to ask how much communicative competence one needs to teach in foreign language teaching" (1974:352). Where successful interaction in an L2 culture *is* the goal, however, she points out that care must be taken to provide an authentic L2 cultural context for the interpretation of meaning. Where this care is absent, the goal of communicative competence is an illusion.

Paulston's concern for cultural context strikes a proper note of caution in a discussion of the implications of the concept of communicative competence for L2 programs. Considerations of social meaning are not only important, they are at the very heart, as we have seen, of a definition of communicative competence. All language is interpreted in a *social framework* of some kind, even if it is only "French for the classroom" or "Spanish for pattern practice." Within a *classroom context*, for example, the *meaning* of a particular utterance may be no

more than the demonstration of formal accuracy to earn an A on a test. The
meaning, whatever it might be, depends on a *common understanding* among the
participants involved in a given transaction. This understanding will grow
from shared experiences, with participants *moving toward one another* until they
know what others *mean*—sometimes without their saying even a word! By its
very nature a cohesive classroom creates its own *community* wherein the participants have their individual roles and learn to understand one another. Teachers, too, whether they are native or nonnative speakers of the language they
are teaching, move toward the learners and come to understand them. The
result may be a speech community with not only a *sociolinguistic* code but also
a *linguistic* code of its own, one that may not be understood in another context.

Paulston's concern for authenticity in classroom attempts to duplicate an
L2 culture is valid. However, to define communicative competence *solely* in
terms of the sociolinguistic norms of a particular speech community seems too
restricted a view and contrary to the characteristics of communicative competence set forth in Section 1.1 of this chapter. In the first place there may exist *not
one* but *several* L2 cultures, each with a different set of rules. More important,
the L2 may be widely used as a means of communication among nonnative
speakers *outside a community to which it is native.* Almost half the English
speakers in the world, for example, are nonnative speakers who use *varieties* of
English in a world context. These varieties have distinctive linguistic, sociolinguistic, and communicative features. Indian English is but one example of a
nonnative variety of English that is distinct from British English, American
English, Canadian English, and Australian English. Numerous other L1 language groups have adopted English as a means of communication not only
with native speakers but among themselves. In some instances, English,
Spanish, French, or some other written code has been adopted as a language of
literacy in speech communities where there exists no written form of the L1. In
all the above contexts, intelligibility, once again, depends not on the aping of
native-speaker linguistic and sociolinguistic patterns but on the *negotiation of
meaning* between those involved. Communication is a two-way street. In the
words of one respected Third World linguist, "A little effort on the part of the
native speakers to understand Indians is as important as a little effort on the
part of Indians to make themselves understood to those who use English as
their first language. The result will be a desirable variety of English . . . intelligible, acceptable and at the same time enjoyable. Let us not make almost
eighteen million Indian English speakers sound like WASPs lost in the tropical
terrain of India" (Kachru 1976:235).

WHOSE MODEL?

Discussions of which language model to follow in L2 teaching have led to heated debate, not to mention ridicule and insult, between lay persons and language teachers alike. Proponents of local varieties of English, for example, have met with staunch opposition from those who seek to impose "standard"—that is, colonial—models, which, in turn, are not nearly as uniform as those who support them seem to suggest. The following news item from the francophone province of Quebec in Canada sums up the tension between language varieties that is found around the world.

Quebec Dictionary Gives Horse Laugh to Snobbery

By STANLEY MEISLER
Los Angeles Times

MONTREAL — For years, those who spoke "proper French" have ridiculed the kind of French used by the ordinary people of Quebec. The language of the farms and the streets has been dismissed as "Joual" — the Quebec French word for horse.

"It is the most derogatory term you can think of," says Leandre Bergeron, who has just published a "Dictionary of the Quebec Language."

Bergeron, 47, is a former professor of French literature who lives on an isolated farm in northwestern Quebec. His dictionary contains 15,000 French words and expressions never used by French speakers in France.

Each dictionary comes wrapped in a blue band that warns, "Forbidden to those under 18, to professors of French, to linguists and to announcers of Radio Canada."

"It's caused quite a stir," he said. "A polemic is going on. There are defenders of French French who say this dic-

"There are people who are spending weekends with it and having parties with it," Bergeron said. "It's a political book. It represents the right of a people to their own language."

Most French-speaking Quebecers are descended from settlers who arrived in the 16th and 17th centuries and their language, like the language of their American neighbors, reflects centuries of experience far different from the experience of people who remained in Europe.

To an outsider the most surprising feature of Bergeron's dictionary is the number of vulgarisms deriving from religion. One of the most vulgar words in Joual is the expletive "tabernac," a word that would not find its way into a family newspaper in Quebec. At its most literal, the word means what it suggests to an English speaker — tabernacle. Yet it is so strong a vulgarism here that Quebecers sometimes fudge the word into "tabernouche" just as

jeans, la deadline, and le dill picule.

Other anglicisms, however, need explanation. The word "Pepsi," for example, is defined by Bergeron as an insulting word used by English-speaking Quebecers to belittle French-speaking Quebecers. When Pepsi-Cola was introduced, Bergeron said, its producers, trying to enter a market dominated by Coca-Cola, sold their drink in larger bottles for the same price. The bargain appealed to members of the working class of Quebec who were mainly French speakers. As a result, the snobbish, English-speaking Coke drinkers began to refer to the French speakers as "Pepsis."

In the great part of the language that has no hint of English, some of the phrases are very descriptive. To be "Jeanne d'Arc" is to be a woman who has sworn never to take an alcoholic drink.

Joual is full of naughty and irreverent puns and euphemisms. The French word for a woman's breasts — seins — has the same pronounciation as the word "saint." So Quebecers refer to a woman's breasts as her "Saint-Joseph."

Most of the words in the dictionary are neither English nor naughty and much harder to explain to an English reader. Many are like the word joual itself, which may be derived from a change in pronounciation over centuries of cheval, French for horse.

The meanings of many of these words are obvious to an English speaker. Among them are le background, la blind-date, baille-baille (pronounced bye-bye), jumbo, le black-eye, les blue jeans, la deadline, and le dill picule.

---

tionary should not have been written."

A university and a junior college recently canceled his scheduled talks. Bergeron said Quebec educators still demand that their students stop using Quebec French.

There also have been objections to the vulgarity of many of the words.

Yet the dictionary has already sold 10,000 copies, a best-seller in this Canadian province of 6.3 million people. In an era of intense French-Canadian nationalism, the book has become a source of pride.

Americans alter a vulgarism into the word "shoot."

Bergeron attributes the heavy use of religious terms as vulgarisms to religious oppression.

A large number of English words have been assimilated by Joual. Bergeron estimates that 7 percent of the words in his dictionary are anglicisms.

The meanings of many of these words are obvious to an English speaker. Among them are le background, la blind-date, baille-baille (pronounced bye-bye), jumbo, le black-eye, les blue

Bergeron is not a native Quebecer. He was born in St. Boniface, a French-Canadian suburb of Winnipeg, in Manitoba. His father's family came from Quebec but his mother was of a family that emigrated from France to Manitoba in this century.

After receiving a doctorate in France, he came to Quebec in 1964 to teach French literature at what is now called Concordia University, an English-language university in Montreal. In 1975, Bergeron gave up his job at Concordia and settled on a small farm in the mining and timber areas of northwestern Quebec.

Source: The Hartford Courant (Hartford, Conn.) April 26, 1981, p. A16.

While Paulston has chosen to focus on L2 culture in her interpretation of the meaning of communicative competence for L2 teaching, other methodologists have put aside considerations of cultural specificity to focus, rather, on *spontaneity of expression*. Thus Rivers (1972) has divided language learning into "skill-getting" and "skill-using," adopting a terminology for which she acknowledges her indebtedness to Parker (1970). As the title of her paper, "From Linguistic Competence to Communicative Competence," implies, she views language acquisition as going *from* production "exercises," "drills," or "activities," where the learner concentrates on formal accuracy, *to* interaction for a communicative purpose. It is up to the teacher or teaching materials to structure this interaction so as to require the use of vocabulary and points of grammar that have been presented. In the words of Rivers, "For any aspect of language structure a game or simulated activity can be invented which *forces the students into autonomous activity* [emphasis added] in which they produce the same types of responses as in an artificial teacher-directed exercise" (1973:31).

This progression from controlled structure practice to creative use of language for communication is similar to one she had advocated in an earlier discussion of L2 methodology. The difference lies in the amount of time spent in rule formation and structure drills of various kinds before these skills are applied in spontaneous interaction. Her earlier position was a reflection of audiolingual thought in its explicit directions to limit interaction with unfamiliar material to the advanced stages of learning.

> It is *only at an advanced stage*, where so many more features of the language are familiar, *that the teacher may begin to allow the student to listen to material unrelated to what he has been studying* [emphasis added], in which he must deduce meanings from context in a very rapid mental process of association. This process is possible only when the effort involved in retention has been considerably reduced by almost automatic recognition of language patterns. [1968:147]

Valette expresses a similar view of communicative competence and its acquisition. She provides a list of L2 program goals that "organizes objectives from the simplest behaviors (Stage 1) to the most complex (Stage 5)." In its descriptive categories and the progression they imply, the list is reminiscent of the audiolingual model of language learning:

1. Mechanical Skills: The student performs via rote memory rather than by understanding.
2. Knowledge: The student demonstrates knowledge of facts, rules, and data related to foreign-language learning.
3. Transfer: The student uses his knowledge in new situations.
4. Communication: The student uses the foreign language and culture as natural vehicles for communication.
5. Criticism: The student analyses or evaluates the foreign language or carries out original research. [1977:19–20]

Communicative competence fits in at Stage 4 of her description. "Listening comprehension as a communication skill falls into stage four of the taxonomy. Communication tests at this level evaluate the student's communicative competence, that is, the student's ability to understand what is being said by native speakers of the target language when they are using the language in a natural manner" (1977:102).

The association of communicative competence with the use of the language *in a natural manner* serves here to underscore the artificiality of the mechanical drills and rule generalizations included in the description of goals. Schulz and Bartz summarize this view that communicative language teaching implies a *progression* from rote structure drill to meaningful language use: "In summary, the classroom teacher needs to institute a progression from artificial exercises to real language use, from discrete linguistic objectives to communicative objectives, and from discrete-point tests to tests of communicative competence" (1975:67).

CONTROL AND CREATIVITY

The following statement represents the view that communicative competence is attained by careful sequencing of structure followed by communication activities. It is from the preface of a teaching methods book entitled *Creativity in the Language Classroom*. The association of "habit-formation structure drilling" and "transformations and variety" with structuralist and transformationalist schools of linguistic description, respectively, is in this instance a misleading attempt to provide theoretical justification for the teaching activities being presented.

We are convinced that habit-formation structure drilling is essential to effective foreign-language teaching. We hope, however, to bridge the gap between the two camps (structuralists and transformational grammarians) by showing that teachers must work continually toward transformations and variety to make learning permanent.

The authors go on to endorse the 1968 Northeast Conference Working Committee Report, which took a similar view of language acquisition:

Liberation . . . is, then, the gradual replacement, day by day, of rigid controls, which the teacher deliberately imposes on the student's behavior in the foreign language classroom, by more flexible controls until, finally, that behavior no longer corresponds simply to the controls imposed by the teacher, but rather, primarily to those which make up the foreign culture and its language. [Bird 1968:79]

> Source: I. Stanislawcxyk and S. Yavener, *Creativity in the Language Classroom* (Newbury House, 1976), pp. vi, 3–4.

For some, then, classroom goals of communicative competence are considered met when learners are provided with systematic practice in the use of structures and vocabulary that have been previously introduced and drilled. This sequential view of language learning, proceeding from habit-formation structure drilling to the communicative use of language or, to use terms that have gained some currency in discussions of L2 teaching, the *separation* of language learning into activities of *skill-getting* and *skill-using*, is, however, at odds with an understanding of language skills such as, above all else, the *interpretation, expression,* and *negotiation of meaning*.

From Meaning to Surface Structure

A very different perspective of communicative competence is that of the British applied linguist H.G. Widdowson. Noting wryly that "The term 'communicative competence' is now very much in fashion and for this reason alone it is well to be wary of it" (1978:163), he nonetheless makes regular use of the term in his own discussion of communicative approaches to the teaching of language. For Widdowson the initial focus of L2 study must be the interpretation of discourse: "The learner's task [is] one which involves acquiring a *communicative competence* in the language, that is to say, *an ability to interpret discourse* [emphasis added in both places] whether the emphasis is on productive or receptive behavior" (1978:144). He is careful to make a distinction between *linguistic skills* and *communicative abilities*. Although the acknowledged aim of all language instruction is the acquisition of communicative competence, the traditional focus has been on linguistic skills, which do not in and of themselves ensure the acquisition of communicative abilities. "On the contrary, it would seem to be the case that an overemphasis on drills and exercises for the production and reception of sentences tends to inhibit the development of communicative abilities" (1978:67).

The interpretation of discourse, where it is the starting point for L2 study, should relate directly to the needs and *present knowledge* of the learners. L2 acquisition will be most efficient where the learners may rely on their existing knowledge of the world, that is, on previously acquired aspects of communicative competence, to interpret meaning within a *new* linguistic code. Linguistic skills and communicative abilities, or *usage* and *use*, should never be treated in isolation from each other. As Widdowson puts it, "What the learner needs to know how to do is to compose in the act of writing, comprehend in the act of reading, and to learn techniques of reading by writing and techniques of writing by reading" (1978:144). Allright (1976:3) sums up this perspective quite nicely: "Are we teaching language (for communication)? Or are we teaching communication (via language)?"

There is a French proverb that says the same thing: *C'est en forgeant que l'on devient forgeron.* Just as one learns to be a blacksmith by being a blacksmith, one learns to communicate by communicating. Or, to put it differently, one develops skills by *using* skills. It is only when we have an incentive to communicate and the *experience* of communication that structures are acquired. In this sense, then, one might speak of going *from communicative competence to linguistic competence*.

LISTENING FOR MEANING

The following directions accompany teaching materials designed to develop oral communication abilities. The emphasis here is on general meaning and *coping with the unfamiliar* rather than on structural analysis and understanding every word.

This is an exercise in extended listening to unscripted, authentic English. The characters involved are real people talking about their real jobs and interests. Obviously dealing with such language will present formidable problems for many overseas students, but we believe it is a vital part of learning to communicate in English. Clearly an important problem is confidence. Most students will be quite unable to understand every word of what they hear. A major point of doing exercises like this is to give them the confidence not to panic as soon as they realize they have missed a word or a phrase, and to show them how *much* they can get out of a passage of this sort. . . . A major objective of this exercise is dealing with the unexpected and the unknown. So *don't* teach the students unfamiliar vocabulary, etc., before they hear it. And don't let them read the transcript on the first or second listening.

Source: K. Morrow and K. Johnson, *Communicate 1*, Teacher's Manual (Cambridge: Cambridge University Press, 1979), p. 38.

Where the focus is on meaning, on getting one's message across, it is impossible to remain within the structures that have been presented. Learners will initially acquire vocabulary and then use it creatively to convey their meaning. The vocabulary and structures they use will come from experiences in *interpreting* meaning in both spoken and written discourse. That is not to say that linguistic or formal exercises are not useful. They are. But they are of most use when they *accompany or follow rather than precede* communicative experiences, and they should be based on the needs generated by those experiences. These exercises will serve, in turn, to increase communicative competence so that it and linguistic competence become *mutually reinforcing*. Central, then, to a meaning-to-surface-structure approach to language teaching is the rejection of an atomistic or sequential view of language learning. The use of contrastive terms like *code-getting* and *code-using* or *skill-getting* and *skill-using* is seen as a distortion of the learning process. In the words of Kenneth Goodman, a psycholinguist well known for his research in L1 reading, "The reading process cannot be fractioned into sub-skills to be taught or subdivided into code-breaking and comprehension without qualitatively changing it" (1971:141).

Speech Act Theory and Literary Criticism. The concern in language learning with the relation of surface structure to meaning is part of a more general discussion of text interpretation, a discussion that has grown with the continued exploration of theoretical issues related to speech act theory. Whereas linguists have described the formal components of a text, literary scholars have traditionally focused on the *value* and *purpose* of these components. In literary criticism there has always been a concern with *how* and *why* written texts have different meanings for different readers. A brief look at the implications of speech act theory for literary criticism is therefore useful in understanding the issues involved in language learning.

Stanley Fish, an eminent contemporary critic, makes no distinction between literary language and "ordinary" or "real-world" language. He says that "the very act of distinguishing between ordinary and literary language . . . leads to an inadequate account of both" (1980:101). For him meaning develops in a *dynamic* relationship with the reader's or listener's experiences and expectations. Values, intentions, and purposes are at the heart of everyday language; they are not the exclusive property of literature. Interpretation of *all* texts begins, therefore, not with discrete linguistic forms but with the purposes and concerns of those who interpret them.

As we have seen in Section 1.1 of this chapter, speech act theory proposes as a unit of analysis not the freestanding sentence but an utterance produced in a situation *by* and *for* persons with *intentions* and *purposes*. For Fish the theory "poses a direct challenge to the autonomy of the text and to the formalistic assumptions of stylistics" (1980:69). *Stylistics*, born of a reaction to the subjectivity and imprecision of literary studies, attempts to go from a formal description of styles to an interpretation of an author's personality, of his or her way of organizing experience. The focus of stylistics within literary criticism is not unlike the focus of structuralism within linguistic studies. Fish sees this attempt to go from surface structures to meaning as misguided.

> The stylisticians proceed as if there were observable facts that could be first described and then interpreted. What I am suggesting is that an interpreting entity, endowed with purposes and concerns, is, by virtue of its very operation, determining what counts as the facts to be observed. . . . The difference in the two views is enormous, for it amounts to no less than the difference between regarding human beings as passive and disinterested comprehenders of a knowledge external to them (that is, of an *objective* knowledge) and regarding human beings as at every moment *creating the experiential spaces* [emphasis added] into which a personal knowledge flows. [1980:94]

Language teachers who view communication as beginning with the use of meaningful language are similarly concerned with personal knowledge and the creation of the experiential spaces that this knowledge requires. For them the development of communicative abilities begins with the interpretation of texts.

FORMS AND FUNCTIONS IN LANGUAGE LEARNING

In attempting to describe the distinction between structure and meaning, language form and language function, methodologists have found various pairs of contrastive terms. Although the pairs are by no means synonymous, and perhaps no one pair is satisfactory in itself, together they do give a sense of the range of concerns raised in discussions of communicative competence and L2 teaching.

Language Form	Language Function
linguistic competence	communicative competence
grammatical competence	communicative competence
language usage	language use
structure	creativity
linguistic skills	communicative abilities
knowledge	ability for use
skill-getting	skill-using
mechanical skills	communication
accuracy	fluency
language practice	language use
how something is said	what is said

Specification of Context

The third general perspective in communicative language teaching has to do not with the learning process itself but with the *selection* of the language to which the learner is exposed. Most language textbooks are, in fact, grammar books. They select and sequence language according to formal or structural criteria, which may, for instance, be imbedded in a passage or a dialogue. But these are not *texts*; they are, after all, *pretexts* for displaying grammar.

The grammar demonstration dialogue (Rivers 1975:22) goes something like this:

Paule: Où vas-tu ce soir?
(Where are you going tonight?)

Madeleine: Je vais en ville avec ma famille. Nous allons au cinéma.
(I'm going downtown with my family. We're going to the movies.)

Paule: Qu'est-ce que vous allez voir?
(What are you going to see?)

Madeleine: *Zazie dans le Métro*. Mes cousins vont voir le même film demain.
(*Zazie dans le Métro*. My cousins are going to see the same film tomorrow.)

This short exchange manages to include all but the third person singular of the present tense conjugation of the verb *aller: je vais, tu vas, nous allons, vous allez, ils vont*. Valdman cites it as "A poor example of an authentic speech transaction." What is *Paule's* intention? There is insufficient context for us to know. Is she looking for something to do? If so, a more likely query might have been

"Qu'est-ce que tu fais, toi, ce soir?" (What are you doing tonight?) Or is she responding to an earlier statement by *Madeleine*, who says she is going out in the evening? If so, a likely query might have been *"Où ça?"* (Where?) As Valdman wryly notes, "Surely the purpose of her question is not to provide *Madeleine* with the opportunity to rehearse the present indicative of *aller*" (1980:87). The more one tries to interpret the transaction, the clearer it becomes that it is, in fact, not discourse at all but an illustration of the present indicative paradigm of the verb *aller*. That is to say, an attempt has been made to put a verb conjugation in a "meaningful context"; of course the only conceivable context in which it becomes at all "meaningful" is a French textbook.

In addition to providing lots of examples of silly or meaningless discourse, grammar-based textbooks often pursue a paradigm for the sake of completeness, regardless of its usefulness for the communicative needs of the learner. As Wilkins has pointed out, "One danger in basing a course on a systematic presentation of the elements of linguistic structure is that forms will tend to be taught because they are there, rather than for the value which they have for the learner" (1976:8). He was not the first to signal the potential absurdity of syntactic paradigms presented for the sake of completeness. Jesperson (1904) notes the questionable practice of conjugating verbs in the classroom, including the irregular French verb *mourir* (to die). To make his point, he recounts the story of a Swedish dialectologist who was on a tour to investigate how extensively the strong form *dog* (died) was in use. The linguist asked a peasant if the people he knew said *jag dog* or *jag döde*. The peasant, who was not a linguist, replied, "Well, when we are dead we generally do not say anything" (1904:112).

Among those who have worked to produce an *alternative* to the grammatical syllabus are the preparers of the Council of Europe guidelines for the development of language teaching materials (Van Ek 1975). These guidelines for syllabus design are based on *notions* associated with various language *functions*. The term *notional* means *semantic* and is borrowed from linguistics, where it denotes grammars based on semantic, or meaning, criteria rather than on structural, or formal, criteria. Wilkins defines a notional syllabus as *"any strategy of language teaching* [emphasis added] that derives the context of learning from an initial analysis of the learners need to express such meanings"* (1976:23). He refers to this approach to the specification of the language to be taught as a *communicative approach*. *Communicative function*, or *social purpose*, determines the notional, or semantic, features of an utterance. The Council of Europe definition of a "threshold level" of language proficiency for adults with identified L2 needs specifies the following components:

1. the situation in which the L2 will be used, including the topics which will be dealt with;
2. the language activities in which the learner will engage;

3. the language functions which the learner will fulfill;
4. what the learner will be able to do with respect to each topic;
5. the general notions which the learner will be able to handle;
6. the specific (topic-related) notions which the learner will be able to handle;
7. the language forms which the learner will be able to use;
8. the degree of skill with which the learner will be able to perform.
   [Van Ek 1975:5]

The preceding framework makes no explicit reference to the *development* of communicative competence. Its focus is the identification of the contexts and topics of communication as a basis for syllabus design. It provides a taxonomy of functions and notions, a list of program objectives, but does not provide the communicative teaching strategies to go with them. Chapter 4 will look more closely at notional-functional approaches to syllabus design, including their strengths and limitations.

1.3 TOWARD A CLASSROOM MODEL OF COMMUNICATIVE COMPETENCE

A great deal of work with teaching and testing for communicative competence has been done in Canada, where there is widespread public support and even *demand* for the development of functional L2 skills. The promotion of bilingualism at both federal and provincial levels has resulted in a variety of experimental language teaching programs for learners of all ages and educational backgrounds. One of these programs includes an evaluation of communicative competence in French as a second language for schoolchildren in the province of Ontario. As a preliminary step in this evaluation, Canale and Swain (1980) conducted an extensive survey of communicative approaches to language teaching. Their purpose was to develop a theoretical framework for subsequent curriculum design and evaluation in L2 programs. The framework they have proposed and subsequently refined (Canale, forthcoming) merits attention because it brings together the various views of communicative competence we have considered and places linguistic competence, or sentence-level grammatical competence, into a proper perspective within the larger construct of communicative competence. The four components of communicative competence that this framework identifies are *grammatical competence, sociolinguistic competence, discourse competence,* and *strategic competence.* The remainder of this section elaborates on the nature of each of these components with examples from language learning and teaching. Together these four components suggest a model of communicative competence as a basis for curriculum design and classroom practice.

Grammatical Competence

Grammatical competence is *linguistic competence* in the restricted sense of the term as it has been used by Chomsky (see page 11) and most other linguists. It is that part of language performance with which we are most familiar, that is, the grammatical well-formedness that has provided the focus of L2 study for centuries. The descriptions of grammar we have followed have been different. *Traditional grammars*, which provide rules of usage that are proper for written language, have their foundation in the word classes or categories of meaning established for classical Greek and Latin. *Structural grammar* has focused on *spoken* language and provides an analysis of observable surface forms and their patterns of distribution. *Transformational generative grammar* is concerned with the relation between the grammatical interpretation of sentences and surface structure as a means of discovering *universal categories of grammar* and the *nature of human cognitive processes in general.* Though definitions differ, the goal in each case is an adequate description of the sentence-level formal features of language. A particular grammar represents an attempt to describe how the elements of language systematically combine. Deciding whether or not a particular structure exists or is possible is based on the frequency of occurrence of these structures in the speech and writing of native speakers, as it is on the intuitions of native speakers with long practice in the use of the language. These data and judgments then provide the linguist with a basis for stating a rule. No existing grammar is complete, of course, because language behavior is complex and to date has eluded satisfactory systematization.

The relationship between any one descriptive sentence grammar and language learning is yet another matter. Experienced language users can provide linguists with the data they need to formulate linguistic rules. Yet these same native speakers would in most instances be unable to formulate the rules themselves. *None of them learned to use the language by first learning the rules.* In fact, the rules are so complex that not even the linguist who formulated them could remember them all. Linguists themselves have been among the more outspoken critics of attempts to apply linguistic description to second language teaching. The remarks made by Chomsky at the 1966 Northeast Conference on the Teaching of Foreign Languages are now legendary.

> I should like to make it clear from the outset that I am participating in this conference not as an expert on any aspect of the teaching of languages, but rather as someone whose primary concern is with the structures of language and, more generally, the nature of cognitive processes. Furthermore I am frankly rather skeptical about the significance for the teaching of languages of such insights and understanding as have been obtained in linguistics and psychology. Surely the teacher of language would do well to keep informed of progress and discussion in these fields and the efforts of linguists and psychologists to approach the problems of language teaching from a principled point of view are extremely worthwhile from an intellectual as well as a social point of view. Still it is difficult to believe that

either linguistics or psychology has achieved a level of theoretical under-standing that might enable it to support a "technology" of language teaching. [Chomsky 1966:43]

Grammatical competence is mastery of the linguistic code, the ability to recognize the *lexical, morphological, syntactic,* and *phonological* features of a language and to manipulate these features to form words and sentences. Grammatical competence is not linked to any single theory of grammar, nor does it assume the ability to make *explicit* the rules of usage. A person demon-strates grammatical competence by using a rule, not by stating a rule.

Sociolinguistic Competence

Grammatical competence has been the domain of linguistic studies proper, but *sociolinguistic competence* is an *interdisciplinary* field of inquiry having to do with the social rules of language use. Sociolinguistic competence requires an under-standing of the social context in which language is used: the roles of the participants, the information they share, and the function of the interaction. Only in a full context of this kind can judgments be made on the *appropriateness* of a particular utterance in the terms elaborated by Hymes. Although we have yet to formulate a satisfactory description of the language code, we are even further from an adequate description of sociocultural rules of appropriateness. Yet native speakers know these rules and use them to communicate success-fully in different situations. One of the goals of intercultural analysis is to make *explicit* the rules of a culture and thereby help nonnatives to understand and adapt more easily to patterns with which they are unfamiliar.

Judgments of appropriateness involve more than knowing *what* to say in a situation and *how* to say it. They also involve knowing when to remain silent. Or, in fact, when to appear *incompetent.* Women of my generation may remem-ber being cautioned by their mothers not to talk up too much in class, not to "show-up" the boys, and counseled to "act dumb" on occasion so as to give the men in their lives a feeling of superiority. The *appearance of incompetence* in this instance was considered *appropriate,* that is, a sign of *sociolinguistic competence.* Similarly, Saville-Troike (1982) cites examples from several language communi-ties where speaking in a bumbling and hesitating manner is appropriate when one is speaking with those of perceived higher rank. She goes on to suggest that a speaker of a second language may be well-advised in some instances not to try to sound *too much like a native speaker* for fear of appearing *intrusive* or, conversely, *disloyal* from the perspective of the speaker's own L1 community. Paradoxically, then, there is a certain sociocultural competence evidenced by those L2 speakers who *deliberately* maintain a formal register or an academic style of speech in some situations where a familiar or informal register might be appropriate for native speakers. These L2 speakers are aware that such "prop-er" or "schoolbook" language is in keeping with the role of "stranger" or "foreigner" that has been assigned to them by native speakers and is thus more likely to promote successful communication.

A similar observation can be made for differences in *dialect*. A school playground incident recounted by my ten-year-old daughter, Julie, is a case in point. Her class had been studying a language arts text that described the use of slang expressions and offered examples of popular American slang—*groovy, flick, shades, hep-cat, blow my mind, cool man*. Julie is an adept mimic and loves to act. During recess she was regaling her friends with her "jivin'," making use of the words she had learned with all the appropriate gestures and body movements. A black classmate reacted assertively: *"Y'all don't talk like that. Us people talk like that. Y'all come to our neighborhood talkin' like that, y'all get yo ass kicked in!"*

Among adults the message may be a good deal more subtle. The *overstepping of social or linguistic boundaries* may meet with anything from a smile to subsequent avoidance. Successful L2 users have a sense, however, of the proper distance to be maintained and of the ways in which that distance is signaled. This understanding is very important to a theory of sociolinguistic competence.

Discourse Competence

Discourse competence is concerned not with the interpretation of isolated sentences but with the *connection* of a series of sentences or utterances to form a meaningful whole. Like sociolinguistic competence it is the subject of interdisciplinary inquiry. The theory and analysis of discourse bring together many disciplines—for example, linguistics, literary criticism, psychology, sociology, philosophy, anthropology, print and broadcast media.

Recognition of the theme or topic of a paragraph, chapter, or book, getting the gist of a telephone conversation, poem, television commercial, office memo, recipe, or legal document requires discourse competence. It is apparent from the preceding examples that the organizational patterns of discourse differ, depending on the nature of the text and the context in which it appears. Patterns do exist, however, and they play an important role in the interpretation and expression of meaning, a global meaning that is always *greater* than the sum of the individual sentences or utterances that make up a text. A description of the various structures underlying discourse is sometimes referred to as *discourse grammar* (Morgan 1981).

The connections that exist between sentences are often not explicit. That is to say, there may be no *overt* expression of a link between one proposition and another. Based on general knowledge of the real world, as well as familiarity with a particular context, a reader/listener *infers* meaning. The meaning of a text, then, to return to the premises of speech act theory explored in Sections 1.1 and 1.2, depends on the *values, intentions*, and *purposes* of the reader/hearer, as well as on those of the writer/speaker.

The following examples illustrate the role of *inference* in the interpretation of discourse:

1. Chico suddenly turned and ran because he saw a policeman coming down the street.
2. Chico saw a policeman coming down the street. Suddenly he turned and ran.

In the *sentence* example (1), the relation between the two propositions, *Chico suddenly turned and ran* and *he saw a policeman*, is explicit. Our knowledge of grammar and of the conventional meaning of the word *because* lets us relate the two parts of the sentence. In the *discourse* example (2), grammatical competence alone will not provide meaning. Interpretation requires an ability to make *a common-sense inference of the situation*. We might well interpret the discourse to mean *Chico turned and ran because he saw the policeman coming down the street*. But to do so requires us to make certain *assumptions* about *Chico, a policeman, the street*, etc. That is, we *create* a scenario in our head. Our interpretation could easily be invalidated, moreover, by contextual factors of which we are not aware. To illustrate, the incident involving Chico and the policeman might conclude as follows:

> Chico saw a policeman coming down the street. Suddenly he turned and ran. The 5th Street bus had just passed him by and he was going to be late for school again! There was no time to ask about Pedro. Maybe tomorrow.

Text *coherence* is the relation of all sentences or utterances in a text to a single global proposition. The establishment of a *global meaning* or topic for a whole passage, conversation, book, etc. is an integral part of both expression and interpretation and makes possible the understanding of the individual sentences or utterances included in a text. *Local* connections or structural links between individual sentences provide what is sometimes referred to as *cohesion*, a particular kind of coherence. Some examples of the formal cohesive devices that are used to connect language with itself are pronouns, conjunctions, synonyms, ellipses, comparisons, and parallel structures. The identification by Halliday and Hasan (1976) of various cohesive devices used in English is well known, and it has begun to have an influence on text analysis as well as on teaching and testing materials for English as a second language (ESL).

Kaplan's (1966) study of contrastive rhetoric is an example of discourse analysis applied to paragraph organization in the ESL context. His familiar diagrams illustrate what he considers to be dominant patterns of formal written discourse in major language groups. These diagrams attempt to describe how thought patterns are structured in formal written style. Their intent is to signal differences in organizational style and to aid learners in the interpretation and construction of L2 texts. To be sure, the proposed models may themselves reflect a cultural bias inasmuch as paragraph construction in English is represented as a straight line from which the other patterns appear to digress. Nevertheless, these diagrams are an important attempt to deal with meaning beyond sentence-level structure.

DOMINANT PATTERNS OF FORMAL WRITTEN DISCOURSE IN MAJOR LANGUAGE GROUPS

ENGLISH   SEMITIC   ORIENTAL   ROMANCE   RUSSIAN

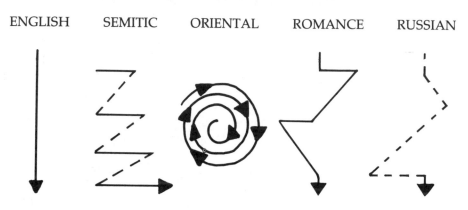

To summarize, discourse competence is the ability to interpret a series of sentences or utterances in order to form a meaningful whole and to achieve coherent texts that are relevant to a given context. Success in both cases is dependent on the *knowledge shared* by the writer/speaker and the reader/hearer—knowledge of the real world, knowledge of the linguistic code, knowledge of the discourse structure, and knowledge of the social setting.

Strategic Competence

There is no such person as an ideal speaker/hearer of a language, one who knows the language perfectly and uses it appropriately in all social interactions. None of us knows all there is to know of French or Japanese or Spanish or English. We make the best use of what we *do* know, of the contexts we have experienced, to get our message across. Communicative competence, whether in our native language or a second language, is *relative*. The strategies that one uses to compensate for imperfect knowledge of rules—or limiting factors in their application such as fatigue, distraction, and inattention—may be characterized as *strategic competence*, the fourth component of communicative competence in the Canale (forthcoming) framework. It is analogous to the need for *coping* or *survival strategies* identified in Savignon (1972b). What do you do when you cannot think of a word? What are the ways of keeping the channels of communication open while you pause to collect your thoughts? How do you let your interlocutor know you did not understand a particular word? or that he or she was speaking too fast? How do you, in turn, adapt when your message is misunderstood? Adult native speakers routinely cope with a variety of factors that, if not taken into account, can result in communication failure. The strategies we use to sustain communication include paraphrase, circumlocution, repetition, hesitation, avoidance, and guessing, as well as shifts in register and style. The dialogues below illustrate the importance of strategic competence. Examples (1), (2), and (3) are dialogues in which I was an indirect participant. Examples (4a) and (4b) are excerpted from transcripts of a test of oral language proficiency, the Foreign Service Institute (FSI) Oral Interview (Hinofotis, Lowe, and Clifford 1981).

1. Telephone operator: I have a collect call from Sandra. Will you accept the charges?

   Catherine: I'm sorry. She's not here right now.

   Telephone operator: (Adapting to the child's voice on the line.) It's *from* Sandra. Will you accept it?

   Catherine: Oh. . . . Yes.

2. A husband and wife were returning home from a shopping trip, and as they pulled into the garage they passed a group of neighborhood children playing on the lawn. Noting one child with whom she had not spoken for a while, the wife casually asked her husband, "I wonder how old Davie is now?" To which the husband replied, "I don't know. I'll ask him."

   Husband: (Shouting from the garage.) How old are you, Davie?

   Davie: Fine.

   Husband: Five?

   Davie: *Fine.*

   Husband: How *old* are you?

   Davie: Six.

3. The scene is a crowded New York delicatessen. A visiting Frenchman has just ordered a Swiss cheese sandwich.

   Waitress: What kind of bread do you want for your sandwich, white, whole wheat, or rye?

   Frenchman: (Wh)ye.

   Waitress: White?

   Frenchman: *(Wh)ye.*

   Waitress: *White?*

   Frenchman: Whole wheat.

4. The following excerpts (a) and (b) are from FSI interviews.

   a)   Native Speaker
          Examiner 1: What's a redneck?

      Nonnative Subject: Um hm.

NSE 1: What would you say? Have you heard this expression?

NNS: No.

NSE 1: Okay.

NNS: Um hum.

NSE 1: How 'bout, um . . . Let me try another one.

Native Speaker
Examiner 2: What's a, what's a . . .

NNS: Well! I would like to know what is a. (General laughter.)

NSE 1: Oh, (laughs) okay.

NSE 2: Oh, (laughs) well, ah . . .

NNS: Will you explain it to me?

NSE 2: A redneck is a . . . conservative, ah usually you find . . . ah, person living in the South very frequently.

NNS: Um hm.

NSE 2: Um, from rural areas of ah . . .

NSE 1: typically intolerant of different ideas . . .

NNS: Mm, mhm.

NSE 1: So you refer to a person as being a redneck, and it's ah slightly derogatory. It's a derogatory term.

NNS: Um hm. Ah, has it, has it anything to do with red tape?

NSE 1: No.

NNS: No.

NSE 1: That's interesting.

NNS: Mhm.

NSE 1: Ah.

NNS: Oh, oh. It's all red. (General laughter.)

b)   Native Speaker
Examiner: What's a redneck?

Native Speaker
Subject: A redneck. Oh gosh, I've heard that word a lot. (Laughter.) Um, um, I don't know what it means. It's a person who is not . . . How could you describe it? . . . a person who is not a deceiver, somehow it has a negative connotation. I've never used the word.

In the above examples native and nonnative speakers alike use strategies for coping with limitations in their knowledge or restrictions in the use of that knowledge in a particular setting. This ability to communicate within restrictions thus includes an ability to adapt one's communicative strategies to a variety of changing and often unexpected interpersonal conditions. Rephrasing, repetition, emphasis, seeking clarification, circumlocution, avoidance (of words, structures, topics), and even message modification (for example, the Frenchman's decision to have a Swiss cheese sandwich on whole wheat rather than on rye!) are among the strategies that we all use to meet the demands of ongoing communication.

In both L1 and L2 use this adaptation requires one to take the perspective of the other participants in a transaction, to *empathize* with the perspective of others. *Chambers Twentieth Century Dictionary* defines *empathy* as the "power of entering into another's personality and *imaginatively experiencing* [emphasis added] his experiences." Horwitz and Horwitz (1977:110) have described the relevance of this kind of imagination for language learning: "Empathy is necessary for communicative competence. . . . Given a 'complete' repertoire of all the appropriate linguistic and sociolinguistic skills, a person without empathy would still be unable to define from a mutual perspective (that of the other person as well as his own) what the particular interpersonal context was and what kind of language it required." In sum, the effective use of coping strategies is important for communicative competence in all contexts and distinguishes highly competent communicators from those who are less so. Strategic competence is thus an essential component in a descriptive framework for communicative competence. (For further discussion of this component refer to Schegloff, Jefferson, and Sacks 1977; Schwartz 1980; and Tarone 1981.)

One Hypothetical Model

The foregoing discussion of the components of communicative competence has said little about how these components interact to determine communicative competence in a particular context. What, for example, is the ratio of grammatical competence to sociolinguistic competence at the beginning stages of language acquisition? How far will self-assuredness or sportsmanship go in overcoming structural and/or sociolinguistic ineptitude? How do gestures and other paralinguistic features of communication fit into the framework?

To answer the last question first, gestures, distance, posture, and facial expressions communicate meaning along with the words we speak. Our use of these paralinguistic features may be conscious or unconscious. There is a gesture code just as there is a linguistic code; decisions to use a particular gesture along with or in place of words are made by each of us. There are sociolinguistic rules governing gestures, and there are sociolinguistic rules governing speech. A particular gesture may be appropriate in only the most informal settings. Their use by nonnatives may or may not enhance communication with native speakers. A gesture may serve as a coping strategy by either filling in for a word or expression or sustaining rapport throughout a momentary silence. Paralinguistic features, then, have many of the same attributes as linguistic features in the preceding theoretical framework of communicative competence.

SIGN LANGUAGE: THE POETRY OF MOTION

The illustrations below are from *Sign Language Among North American Indians* (Mallery 1881). They appear with the accompanying text by linguist W. Chafe in *The World of the American Indian*, Washington, D.C.: National Geographic, 1974, p. 152.

Drooping digits betoken rainfall in Shoshone; placed near the eyes, they signal weeping.

Forefingers placed like horns signify the second name of the Dakota chief Eagle Bull.

"Head of tribe," gestures a Paiute.

An Apache says "cold" or "winter." With querying signs it becomes "How many winters?" or "How old are you?"

A Hidatsa says "log house" with fingers set like logs.

Roaming the plains, buffalo hunters of many tribes could trade, make treaties, tell hunting tales and legends—without uttering a word. Sign language, derived from pantomime, gave them a medium of fluency and grace—"the very poetry of motion," as one admiring ethnologist put it. But theirs was a flexible art, and they could experiment—as charade players do today—until mutually intelligible gestures evolved. Plains Indians, visiting the East in historic times, loved to discourse with the deaf. In no time they chatted easily, without an interpreter cramping their style.

The manner in which the various components of communicative competence interact is open to speculation. The nature of this interaction would seem to depend, at least, on the nature and extent of the learner's language experience in both L1 and L2. Those who have learned a second language in a traditional, formal classroom environment would presumably present a profile different from those who have learned the language in a natural or immersion setting. The acquisition of L2 communicative competence poses the further problem of *transfer* from L1 competence. Can coping strategies developed in L1 be used in L2 communication? Are there universal sociolinguistic rules that provide a communicative base in L2 before the acquisition of a single linguistic structure? These questions may well arouse the same speculation as questions bearing on the transfer of the linguistic code. How helpful are cognates, for example? Do they *mis*lead—the false cognate problem—as much as they lead? Are similar structures a more likely source of continued error than clearly dissimilar structures? (Corder 1981).

The relation of self-assuredness to communicative competence is of particular interest. For Canale and Swain (1980:38), "exposure to realistic situations is crucial if communicative competence is to lead to *communicative confidence*" [emphasis added]. However, the relationship of communicative confidence to communicative competence is perhaps just the reverse; it may be that *communicative confidence leads to communicative competence.* To use the swimming analogy of which methodologists are so fond, communicative confidence in language learning may be like learning how to relax with your face under water, to let the water support you. Having once known the sensation of remaining afloat, it is but a matter of time until you learn the strokes that will take you where you want to go.

The diagram on the next page, representing an inverted pyramid, suggests a possible relationship between grammatical competence, sociolinguistic competence, discourse competence, and strategic competence as overall communicative competence increases. The proportions drawn have no empirical basis and are intended only to serve heuristically for other integrative descriptions. They serve, minimally, to illustrate that communicative competence is greater than linguistic or grammatical competence and that one does not go from one to the other as one strings pearls on a necklace. Rather, an increase in one component *interacts* with the other components to produce a corresponding increase in overall communicative competence.

The diagram shows how a measure of sociolinguistic competence and strategic competence allows a measure of communicative competence even before the acquisition of any grammatical competence. Universal rules of social interaction and a willingness or need to communicate through gestures, facial expressions, and any other available means may serve to get a message across without the use of language, provided there is a willing partner. (For a description of this process in native language acquisition, see Bruner's (1975a) article, "From Communication to Language—A Psychological

THE COMPONENTS OF COMMUNICATIVE COMPETENCE

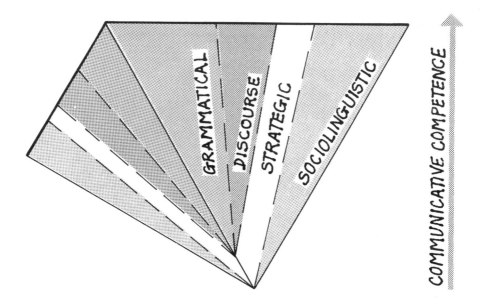

Perspective.'') Beginning with the inverted tip of the pyramid and moving upward, grammatical, sociolinguistic, and discourse competence increase along with a corresponding overall increase in communicative competence.

Strategic competence is present at all levels of proficiency although its importance in relation to the other components diminishes as knowledge of grammatical, sociolinguistic, and discourse rules increases. The inclusion of strategic competence as a component of communicative competence at all levels is important because it demonstrates that regardless of experience and level of proficiency one never knows *all* a language. The ability to cope within limitations is an ever present component of communicative competence. Whatever the relative importance of the various components at any given level of overall proficiency, it is important to keep in mind the *interactive* nature of their relationships. The whole of communicative competence is always something other than the simple sum of its parts.

1.4 A FINAL WORD ON DEFINITIONS

Lest we leave this discussion of definitions with the impression that communicative competence is a twentieth-century invention, we should include a few definitions from earlier times. Communicative competence may be new as a term, but it is not entirely new as a concept. Communication has been a goal of L2 teaching in many other times and places. That L2 programs have often fallen short of attaining their professed goal is due to a myriad of circumstances, many of which have nothing at all to do with the method of teaching. Lack of interest, lack of time, lack of funds for materials and qualified teachers are among the more obvious reasons why a well-conceived program may not produce the results hoped for. There are also instances where the goal of communication has been reached *in spite of* a particular method. In these instances it has often been teachers who have intuitively supplemented a method with activities designed to encourage language use "outside" the program. What's more, highly motivated learners have just as often stuck with a task—analysis of syntax or memorization of isolated vocabulary items, for example—and waited for the opportunity to use their newly learned information in a communicative setting.

That one learns to communicate by communicating, then, is not a new idea. It has been around as long as there have been language learners. The most celebrated early instance of an L2 learner proclaiming the virtues of language acquisition through language use is Montaigne's commenting in his *Essays* on having learned Latin. The sixteenth-century French philosopher learned to speak Latin by conversing with his tutor, as well as with his parents. "Without method, without a book, without grammar or rules, without a whip and without tears, I had learned a Latin as proper as that of my schoolmaster" (1580:I,26; my translation). One of the most important reasons for the widespread competence in Latin at the time was its use as the language of scholarship and communication in the church.

Comenius (1592–1670) is well known in the history of language teaching methodologies for his objection to the method of L2 teaching that had resulted from the teaching of skills of grammatical analysis in the Middle Ages. The preoccupation with grammatical analysis had grown so that by the Renaissance it was viewed as a method for actually teaching the language. In the words of Comenius, "Right from the very beginning of the course, youngsters are driven to the thorny complexities of language; I mean the entanglements of grammar. It is now the accepted method of the schools to begin from the form instead of the matter, from grammar, rather than from authors . . ." (1648, cited in Kelly 1969:227).

In the nineteenth century, proponents of the Natural Method—language learning through language use—spurned both phonetic and grammatical analysis. They rejected translation, which by the end of the eighteenth century had become the basis of L2 teaching. Denying that explanation was a necessary part of teaching, they claimed that learners should be allowed to discover for themselves how to function in their new language. "With respect to method, the artificial one must be given up and a more natural one must take its place. According to the artificial method, the first thing done is to hand the boy a grammar and cram it into him piece by piece, for everything is in pieces; he is filled with paradigms which have no connection with each other or with anything else in the world. . . . On the other hand, the natural method of learning languages is by practice. That is the way one's native language is acquired" (Petersen 1870:297–298).

Thirty-four years later, in his familiar treatise *How to Teach a Foreign Language*, the Danish methodologist and linguist Otto Jespersen would cite these words and conclude: "It is now half a century ago since N.M. Petersen uttered these golden words, and still the old grammar-instruction lives and flourishes with its rigmaroles and rules and exceptions" (1904:111). And again, "Language is not an end in itself . . . it is a way of connection between souls, a means of communication" (1904:4).

No, the course of language teaching methodology never has run smooth. And before we take too much pride in recent innovations we would do well to consider the long history of language teaching that has preceded us. The goal of *connection between souls* is one that many have held before us. It is a goal we would do well to keep in sight as we pursue the methods and means of communicative competence.

SUGGESTED READINGS

J.L. Austin. 1962. *How to Do Things with Words*. An influential collection of lectures delivered at Harvard in 1955 that traces the development of the author's theory of speech acts and classification of language functions. This work is the result of his reaction to the then widely held assumption that form equals function.

N. Brooks. 1964. *Language and Language Learning: Theory and Practice*. This guide to audiolingual methodology was widely referred to by foreign-language teachers in the United States during the 1960s, when audiolingualism was at its peak of influence.

N. Chomsky. 1972. *Language and Mind*. A collection of essays concerned with the interrelatedness of linguistics, philosophy, and psychology, as well as ways in which the study of language structure can contribute to an understanding of human intelligence. A good introduction to the volume is Chapter 4, "Form and Meaning in Natural Languages," the text of an informal lecture to an audience of teachers and students from secondary schools and colleges.

M. Coulthard. 1977. *Introduction to Discourse Analysis*. Summarizes the contributions of numerous linguists, philosophers, anthropologists, and others to the study of conversation. It concludes with a brief discussion of language teaching and learning.

K. Diller. 1978. *The Language Teaching Controversy*. An accurate summary of various schools of linguistic thought and their relationship to language teaching methods past and present.

J. R. Firth. 1930 and 1937. *Speech* and *Tongues of Men*. Firth's first use of the term *context of situation* is in *Speech*, but it is more fully developed and related to his overall view of language in *Tongues of Men*. Both offer enjoyable reading.

S. Fish. 1980. *Is There a Text in This Class?* Speech act theory applied to literary criticism. Challenges the distinction between ordinary language and literary language and demonstrates the role of the reader in giving meaning and value to a text. Includes an essay with the engaging title, "How to do Things with Austin and Searle."

G. Green and J. Morgan. 1981. "Pragmatics, Grammar and Discourse." The authors, both theoretical linguists, describe "a variety of kinds of knowledge and abilities" (that is, *pragmatics*) that interact to facilitate discourse production and interpretation. They conclude that "the role of linguistic competence is smaller than one might suppose." Green and Morgan are critical of Halliday and others who attempt to search for formal linguistic properties that constitute or contribute to coherence or text structure. Fish (1980) includes a similar criticism of Halliday. The explanation of meaning, in his words, "is not the capacity of a syntax to express it, but the ability of a reader to confer it."

A. Gregory and W. Shawn. 1981. *My Dinner with André*. For the philosophically inclined, an enjoyable feature-length film about language, communication, and performance in life and on the stage. Directed by Louis Malle. Also available as a paperback book.

E. Hall. 1959 and 1966. *The Silent Language* and *The Hidden Dimension*. Each explores the impact of nonverbal features of communication through the use of examples from a variety of cultures.

M. Halliday. 1978. *Language as a Social Semiotic: The Social Interpretation of Language and Meaning*. A collection of articles written between 1972 and 1976. Difficult reading but the repetition of themes from one chapter to the next affords a better understanding of Halliday's views than can be gained from any one chapter. A good companion volume is a collection of earlier papers (1956–1970) edited by G. Kress (1976), *Halliday: System and Function in Language.*

N. Holland. 1975. *5 Readers Reading.* Considers *who* reads *what* and *how* in a psycho-analytic perspective stressing the subjectivity of five readers (Sam, Saul, Shep, Sebastian, and Sandra) as each responds in an interview with the author (a literary critic and scholar) to the reading of William Faulkner's story, "A Rose for Emily."

D. Hymes. 1967. "Why Linguistics Needs the Sociologist." A very readable discussion of structural linguistics' concern with formal analysis; the interdisciplinary nature of *socio*linguistics; and the need for making reference to a *speech community, social positions,* and *styles of speech* in describing language use.

M. Joos. 1967. *The Five Clocks.* A readable classic that deals with the uses of styles and registers in human communication.

B. Kachru. 1981. "American English and Other Englishes." Varieties of English and the development of English as a universal or international language. One in a rich collection of articles related to linguistic diversity in the United States; see C. Ferguson and S. Heath (eds.), *Language in the U.S.A.*

J. Searle. 1970. *Speech Acts.* The classic summary of speech act theory as it is being used in discourse analysis. Encompasses many of Austin's ideas in a somewhat more rigorous theoretical framework.

RESEARCH AND DISCUSSION

1. Write your own definition of communicative competence.

2. How widespread is the impression among learners and teachers you know that communicative competence is limited to spoken language? What might be some of the reasons for this misunderstanding?

3. Can one distinguish between *receptive competence* and *productive competence*? Is it possible to understand what one cannot produce? Cite examples.

4. Roger Brown (1973:6), a Harvard psychologist well known for his research on first language acquisition, has described his experience with a two-week intensive Berlitz course in Japanese:

> On the day I finished my course . . . I was met outside the Berlitz door by a Japanese friend. He, thinking to give me an easy start, asked in Japanese: "Where is your car?" I was completely floored and could make nothing of the sentence except that it called for a reply. I realized then that my peak accomplishments had been narrowly adapted to a drill procedure in which almost all of a sentence was so well practiced as not to need to be processed deeply at all, leaving all my attention free to focus on some single new element and get that right. A sentence, however simple, drawn from the total construction potential of a language is a very different thing from the same sentence well prepared for by a pyramid of practice.

What similarities do you see between the Berlitz course described above and the *A-LM* methodology portrayed in Section 1.2? How do both fail to take into account the nature of communicative competence?

5. Look at some recently published language textbooks. Which of the three interpretations of communicative competence outlined in Section 1.2 do they appear to follow? Choose one of them for closer analysis of the means by which they propose to achieve communicative competence.

6. Identify a context in which you have heard the comment, "He speaks fluently, but he doesn't know his grammar." How is the word *grammar* being used? Is it judgmental? What are the implications of the comment?

7. The distinction between form and function in language may be summarized as follows: Functions may take many forms; a single form may have many functions. Illustrate with examples from both your native language and a second language. (Examples: (a) How many different ways can you think of to express an apology? Think in terms of gestures or body language as well as words; (b) Give as many different interpretations as you can of the utterance *"What did you expect?"*)

8. Come up with your own examples of instances where an imperative, declarative, and interrogative are not used for making a command, a statement, or for posing a question. What features can determine the function of the form in each case?

9. Advertisers, whose very livelihood depends on their communication skills, would find curiously naive the assertion that a message is contained within the confines of grammatical structure. Find examples of effective advertising. How do they get their message across? For example, what is behind the particular strategy employed by newspaper advertisements that imitate a *news item* format? Can you cite similar strategies on radio? on TV?

10. Think of contexts of situation for the following exchanges. Define *who, where, when,* and *what.* How many different contexts can you come up with?

    a) A: What year is it?
       B: 67.

    b) A: Hello.
       B: What are you doing here?

11. An amusing example of text coherence in the absence of any overt local connections (that is, cohesive devices) is offered by Widdowson (1978:29):

    A: That's the telephone.

    B: I'm in the bath.

    A: O.K.

    What situation can you create in your mind to interpret the above sequence? What words or utterances would you need to fill in for each speaker to make the connections between the utterances *explicit*? Make up your own example of a coherent dialogue that contains no local structural links.

12. The following passage has been scrambled from its original form. Use your knowledge of rules of cohesion to reconstruct it.

    1. But I don't know the first thing about it.
    2. If not, get a list of Illinois downhill ski areas from any local outdoor outfitters.
    3. If you're already into downhill, you probably have money.
    4. If so, go to Vail.

5. And some decent slopes reputedly are available in Wisconsin and to her neighboring northern states.

6. Several other areas are listed in *The Weekend Book*, available from the Illinois Office of Tourism in Springfield.

7. Downhill skiing: Yes, we have it in Illinois.

13. Look at the lists of tenets of language learning on pages 20 and 23. When put side by side, what strikes you about the two lists? Which one is more representative of your own language learning/teaching experience?

14. Recall a situation in your second-language learning experience when all of your "book learning" seemed to fail you, and you were simply left with your ability to cope, to make use of what can be called *strategic competence*.

15. James (1980) has used the term *microlinguistics* to refer to the formal system or code of a language and *macrolinguistics* to refer to linguistics in human interaction, the process of communication. Are these terms helpful in understanding what has happened to the scope of linguistic inquiry?

16. Choose a proverb or familiar quotation (for example, *An ounce of prevention is worth a pound of cure; Seeing is believing; Birds of a feather flock together*), and compare it with a scholarly statement of the same idea. Consider such things as length, syntactic complexity, range of vocabulary, appropriateness, and effectiveness. What does the comparison reveal about the nature of communicative competence?

17. What kind of *speech act* is a poem? Consider some poems as examples of texts. What are their *contexts*? How many levels of meaning do you find? Describe the role of the reader in the interpretation of meaning. Do you feel poetry has a place in L2 learning? in L2 teaching?

18. The focus of this chapter has been on language as a means of communication with others. There are, of course, other reasons for speaking. For example, have you ever talked to an animal? a doll or stuffed toy? a plant? Why? In terms of the three general categories identified by Halliday (see pages 14–15), what needs are met by this kind of talk? Does the talking we do in the presence of other people sometimes meet the *same* need as the talk we address to animals, plants, and even inanimate objects?

19. In *Linguistics Across Cultures*, Robert Lado (1957) observes that the potential for misunderstanding is often greatest between members of cultures that *appear* to have the most in common. As an example he cites the conflicts between British and American soldiers during World War II. How does his observation relate to the components of communicative competence?

20. Can you cite examples of persons who appear to have deliberately retained a nonnative accent? Is this a reflection of communicative competence? If so, how?

21. a) In your opinion what are the relative proportions of the four components of communicative competence outlined by Canale and Swain?

    b) Compare Margaret Mead's statement at the beginning of this chapter with the hypothetical model on page 46. How do her comments relate to the four components shown? Are the explanations of how communicative competence develops similar? Explain.

Chapter 2

L2 Acquisition Research

Language teaching has had an unfortunate history of failure to learn from its own experience.

—H. H. Stern

2.1 RESEARCH DESIGNS

Native Speaker Proficiency

The apparent ease with which children communicate in their mother tongue is an ever present source of frustration for adult L2 learners who after years of classroom study still struggle to put together a simple declarative sentence. In a curious example of role reversal, children who use a language with fluency may appear to the adult learner not only confident but arrogant or even rude. Adults, who are supposed to *know* and set examples, find the comparison of their language proficiency with that of children unsettling. Indeed, the predicament of the modern language teaching profession is that academic credit is earned and diplomas are awarded for the acquisition of skills that, in many cases, are not so well developed as those of a ten-year-old child.

Learning a first language, then, poses no problem. *Or does it?* The competence of native speakers, well developed though it may be, is *relative*. Mother-tongue proficiency varies widely from child to child and from adult to adult. Vocabulary range, articulation, critical thinking, persuasiveness, and penmanship are but a few of the many, many facets of competence wherein native speakers differ. Although schools do provide an opportunity to develop speaking abilities of various kinds—discussion, debate, drama, recitation, etc.—reading and writing abilities are clearly the more talked about concerns in our time (Education in the classical tradition was, of course, education for *oral* performance in public affairs. Literacy was thought of as serving the needs of *rhetoric*, which, in classical Greek, meant the *art of oratory*.) Here, as in other discussions of language competence, the distinction between form and function, between mechanical skills and conveyance of meaning, looms large.

A recent report by the National Assessment of Educational Progress, a U.S. federally sponsored project for monitoring the nation's elementary and secondary schools, distinguishes between "general reading skills" and inferential comprehension. The results of the assessment, which examined and compared reading achievement in 1970–1971, 1974–1975, and 1979–1980, indicate a good deal of progress in teaching children in the lower elementary grades to sound out words and phrases, but they also indicate a *decline* in reading comprehension at the secondary school level. The implication, then, is that what is defined as reading in the early years is not the same as the complex reasoning and *inferential abilities* that constitute reading in literature, social studies, science, and so on. The *New York Times* (Maeroff 1981) summarizes the findings: *"Learning to read is very different from reading to learn."* The *Times* goes on to quote Dorothy Strickland, former president of the International Reading Association: "As impressive as the steady growth of 9-year-olds has been, one must wonder if there is something that is or is not being done that militates against more enduring gains. We need to ask ourselves what can be done at the early stages of reading development to help produce more thoughtful, critical readers who are better prepared to shift to the more complex reading tasks of the middle grades."

If "native proficiency" is a somewhat nebulous entity, the relationship between first language learning and second language learning is even more unclear and has long been a subject of fascinating speculation. Throughout the years, various theories of L1 acquisition have been invoked by L2 teachers to support one view or another of L2 acquisition. Methods have been called "natural" or "direct" to suggest a desirable parallel with L1 acquisition. For example, the audiolingual method claimed it was following a "natural" sequence of acquisition by beginning with listening and speaking, followed by reading and writing. *Systematic inquiry* into the process of both L1 acquisition and L2 acquisition is a relatively new development. As such, it suggests some interesting and fruitful avenues of interdisciplinary research into the nature of communication and the acquisition of communicative competence.

Toward an Experimental Pedagogy

L2 acquisition research is such a rapidly expanding field that a summary of current trends as well as the implications for L2 teaching is beyond the scope of this book. Discussions of research findings, moreover, lead quickly to the details of a particular study or group of studies. There one runs the risk of following a single trail so far that one loses an overall perspective of the purpose of the research and how it fits with other data to contribute to our understanding of language acquisition.

The most significant feature of current L2 research is its focus on what actually happens in L2 learning, on *analysis of data* in place of extrapolation of theory from more general theories of language and human learning. Current research reflects concern for the *contexts* of language learning. One of the lessons we have learned from past reforms is that instructional programs should not be left to theorists but should rely ultimately on the experience of learners and classroom teachers. Rather than looking to linguistic and psychological theories alone to provide insights into the L2 acquisition process, methodologists are beginning to seek answers to specific classroom needs in research designed to explore a particular facet of the acquisition process. What will emerge from this research will undoubtedly be *options* in language learning and a greater appreciation of the complexity of the acquisition process.

It is the responsibility of both researchers and teachers to ensure that the research conducted addresses *classroom* needs and that the findings are responsibly interpreted and made available (and accessible) to the profession at large. Where there is no empirical basis for making a particular recommendation, it is important that researchers say so (Tarone, Swain, and Fathman 1976; Hatch 1979). Teachers, on the other hand, need to become familiar with the language of research so that communication is possible. They need to be comfortable with the theoretical and statistical terms used in reporting research in order to assess the significance of the questions being asked. Above all, it should not be assumed that research and teaching is an either/or proposition. Some of the best inquiries into the nature of L2 acquisition may well be made by those who are *both researcher and teacher*. The result will be what Piaget has called an *experimental pedagogy*.

> Experimental pedagogy is not a branch of psychology. . . . Experimental pedagogy is concerned, in practice, solely with the development and the results of pedagogic processes proper. . . . It is, for example, a question for experimental pedagogy to decide whether the best way of learning to read consists in beginning with the letter then graduating to words and finally to sentences, in accordance with the classical or "analytical" method, or whether it is better to work through these stages in reverse order. . . . Only a patient, methodical research program, using comparable groups of subjects for equally comparable periods of time . . . can permit a solution of the question; and there can be no question of seeking for a solution by means of deductive considerations based upon knowledge of psychology, however experimental in origin itself, about the role of "gestalts" in our perception. [Piaget 1970:21]

Research Questions

What are the questions that researchers and teachers are asking? They are asking some of the same questions that lay persons ask casually over tea or cocktails and perhaps heatedly at school policy meetings: Is it better to learn a second language while still a child? Will children whose home language is other than the school language encounter significant problems? Is L2 study best reserved for the academically talented? Can adults learn to speak an L2 with a native accent? Is the only way of learning a language to live in a community where it is spoken? Is it better to study a language for short periods of time throughout elementary school or wait until secondary school or even adulthood for more intensive study? How much does it help to learn grammar rules or do pattern drills? Why do classroom programs fail to teach you how to really speak a second language?

For research purposes, the preceding questions, as well as others of interest to teachers and educational policymakers, can be organized to permit systematic exploration of the variables involved. Many experienced researchers have sought to provide frameworks for variables in an attempt to chart a course, to describe from where we have come and to where we should go (for example, Jakobovits 1970, Schumann 1976, Swain 1977, Naiman et al. 1978, Anderson 1981). In L2 acquisition studies, as in any new research field, there are the inevitable problems of duplication of effort or, what is worse, *isolation* of effort, through lack of communication and consensus on research design and direction. Continued assessment of the goals and modes of inquiry in L2 acquisition research will encourage the use of data from one study to another and will perhaps serve to establish *networks of inquiry* or *paradigms* so that the field may continue to expand in an orderly and progressive way.

Most L1 acquisition studies look, perforce, at the language acquisition of children in their native environment. Data collection and interpretation is exceedingly complex. It becomes still more complex as the field of inquiry expands to look beyond the acquisition of sounds and syntactic structures to the acquisition of discourse strategies. How do children make conversation? How do they get their meaning across? L2 acquisition studies have the same focus as L1 studies but, in addition, must take into account the many variables informing the questions with which we began this discussion of L2 research goals. The learner may or may not be a child. He has already learned or is now learning his mother tongue. He may or may not have an immediate need to communicate in the L2. His contact with the L2 may be anything from 20 minutes of daily classroom exercises to total immersion in an L2 environment.

The WHO of Acquisition Research

Variables in L2 acquisition, not unlike the variables in communicative contexts themselves, may be grouped into four categories: WHO, WHAT, WHERE, and HOW. WHO has to do with the learners. How old are they? Is their mother tongue similar to the L2 they are learning? What needs and interests do the learners bring to the L2 learning context? The list of learner attributes is long and reflects a focus of attention on this particular collection of variables. Verbal intelligence, field dependence/independence, phonetic coding ability, tolerance of ambiguity, conceptual level, instrumental and integrative orientation, and ego permeability, are but a few of the personality traits, cognitive styles, aptitudes, and motivational measures that are included in this list of learner attributes.

VARIABLES IN L2 ACQUISITION: A KALEIDOSCOPIC VIEW

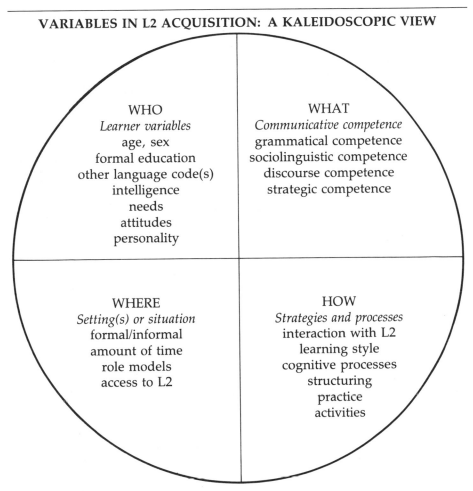

WHO
Learner variables
age, sex
formal education
other language code(s)
intelligence
needs
attitudes
personality

WHAT
Communicative competence
grammatical competence
sociolinguistic competence
discourse competence
strategic competence

WHERE
Setting(s) or situation
formal/informal
amount of time
role models
access to L2

HOW
Strategies and processes
interaction with L2
learning style
cognitive processes
structuring
practice
activities

L2 acquisition variables may be thought of as the brightly colored pieces of glass that reflect in the mirrored surfaces of a kaleidoscope. Our fascination with this optical instrument is rather like our fascination with language learning. Looking through the cylinder we see numerous reflections that appear as brilliant symmetrical configurations; these configurations may be constantly altered by a slight rotation of the instrument.

The WHAT of Acquisition Research

In most studies of L2 acquisition, acquisition has been defined in terms of phonological and syntactic features. The WHAT of L2 learning, following the model of L1 studies, has been for the most part *grammatical competence*. Thus the well-known studies by Dulay and Burt (1972, 1974) of Spanish L1 children learning English as a second language look at L2 development in terms of particular morphological and syntactic features, comparing them with features that exist in the L1. The grammatical features that they have traced are some of the same features included in language textbooks: negation, verb inflection, position and use of indirect objects, etc.

L1/L2 contrastive studies in general have been the subject of an extensive collection of research, and they continue to provide a basis for speculating on the *source* of learner errors. The grammatical system that a learner uses at any particular stage of L2 development is sometimes referred to as the learner's *interlanguage*. Interlanguage has been described as the learner's evolving system of language, *intermediate* between the L1 and the L2 (Selinker 1972). In this definition the L1 is seen as the starting point in a series of *approximative systems* (Nemser 1971) that increasingly come to resemble the forms used by native speakers of the L2. In a somewhat different view (Corder 1975, 1981), the starting point is not the L1 at all but rather a *simplified code*, a basic and perhaps universal grammar common to all language development, L1 as well as L2, with rules that are definitely not those of the mother tongue. Both views are useful in analyzing the nature of learner errors and establishing criteria for evaluating learner proficiency. In Section 2.3 of this chapter we shall explore further this important aspect of L2 acquisition.

RULES, RULES, AND RULES

As any language teacher or language learner knows, it is difficult to focus on learned rules of grammar when one has a message to get across. What is perhaps less obvious is *the difficulty of applying descriptive rules of grammar even when the focus is precisely those rules of usage*. The dialogue below between student and computer is recreated from data in a study by Garrett (1981) on learner *interlanguage* in which there is maximum opportunity for conscious monitoring of L2 forms: translation of sentences from English to German with access to a reference grammar and a dictionary. The data illustrate the often wide discrepancies between

1. The textbook or teacher *explanation* of a descriptive rule;
2. The learner's restatement or *conscious version* of that rule;
3. The learner's *application* of the "same" rule, that is, the description of learner performance.

(For further illustration of the discrepancy between verbalized language rules and actual language performance see Seliger 1979.)

Computer: TRANSLATE THE FOLLOWING SENTENCE INTO GERMAN. MAKE AS MUCH USE AS YOU LIKE OF THE REFERENCE GRAMMAR AND VOCABULARY PROVIDED IN THE STUDY HELPS.

The light couldn't show them who lay on the bed.

Student: Das Licht konnte ihr nicht zeigen . . .

Computer: Das Licht konnte *ihr* nicht zeigen . . . WRONG

Student: Das Licht konnte ihrem nicht zeigen . . .

Computer: Das Licht konnte *ihrem* nicht zeigen . . . WRONG

Student: Das Licht konnte sie nicht zeigen . . .

Computer:　Das Licht konnte *sie* nicht zeigen . . . WRONG

　Student:　I GIVE UP. HELP.

Computer:　Das Licht konnte ihnen nicht zeigen . . .

Recently there has been an attempt to gather information in terms of language *functions*. For example, how does an L1 Spanish child make requests in English? Does the form of the request reflect the context; does, for instance, the request, when addressed to an adult, take a form different from that addressed to a child? (Fraser, Rintell, and Walters 1980). An analysis of the functional use of language is a step toward the assessment of communicative competence. Such assessment requires, as we have seen, the understanding of a text, oral or written, in the communicative context in which it occurs. It must take into account the *roles* of the participants in a particular *setting* as well as the *function* of the *text* (see Chapter 1, page 15). Discourse analysis must consider the totality of how learners interpret and respond within a new linguistic code.

L1 acquisition studies have begun to focus on the development of discourse—what Bruner (1975b) calls the *ontogenesis of speech acts*—and L2 studies are not far behind. The problems are admittedly complex, but they need to be addressed if we are to strengthen communicative competence as a goal of instructional programs. *Conversations of Miguel and Maria* (Ventriglia 1982), for example, illustrates the strategies of L2 dialogue to serve communicative functions in a social context. "Language learning is viewed as drama, with children assuming roles of actors in social situations as they adopt strategies to practice language and to communicate in conversational settings." These strategies provide practice in the L2 and thus greatly influence communicative competence. The following conversation, which Ventriglia entitles "Give me the Sweetie," illustrates the selection of request forms to match the social context in which they are used. The scene is a *Cinco de Mayo* celebration at an elementary school for students in a bilingual Spanish/English program. One group is seated at a small table enjoying refreshments in a boisterous manner.

SELECTING REQUEST FORMS TO MATCH SOCIAL CONTEXT

Miguel: Hey, man! How you doing?

Carlos: Cool, man!

Maria: Gimme the sweetie! (Miguel grabs sugar from the bowl and flips it in the air.)

Rosa: Stop it! Look out! Don't, silly! I'm gonna tell!

Miguel: Hey, Carlos! Wanna play?

Carlos: Lemme have the sweetie!

Miguel: (Flipping the sugar.) There you go—right there! (Points under the table.)

Carlos: (Goes under the table.)

Miguel: How you doing?

Carlos: Gonna get some more.

Miguel: (Throwing the sugar.) Over there—You gotta hurry up!

Teacher: (Joins group.) I'm going to sit here and have a cup of coffee with you. Maria, please pass the sugar. Thank you.

Carlos: May I have some soda?

Maria: Please pass the sugar.

Teacher: Say thank you.

Maria: Thank you.

Teacher: Good afternoon, Miguel. How are you?

Miguel: (Turns away from the table, looking bored.)

Teacher: Good afternoon, Miguel. How are you?

Miguel: Good afternoon, Mrs. Baca. How are you?

Teacher: Have you enjoyed the party?

Miguel: Can I please go out to play?

Contrast the meaning and vivacity of the preceding dialogue with the strain and consciousness of form that are evident in the following example of classroom discourse. The dialogue below between Sue and her teacher was recorded in a first-year college French class. It is included in a study by Leemann (1980) on the relation of teacher/learner discourse patterns to the development of communicative competence. The students are in class, their books are open before them, and they are doing an exercise on question formation using *qui*, *que*, and *quoi*.

Teacher: Je pense à mes amis de Paris. Sue?
          (I'm thinking about my friends in Paris. Sue?)

Sue: Um . . . à quoi pensez-vous?
          (Um . . . what are you thinking about?)

Teacher: (Laughs.) Ça dépend si vous voulez offenser vos amis.
          (Pause.) Si vous voulez insulter vos amis. (Pause.)
          Qu'est-ce que vous avez dit? Répétez.
          (That depends if you want to offend your friends. If you want
          to insult your friends. What did you say? Repeat.)

Sue: Uh . . .

Teacher: Vous comprenez? Si vous considérez vos amis comme des
          objets . . . (laughs) vous dites "quoi."
          (Do you understand? If you consider your friends as
          objects . . . you say "what.")

Sue: Oh. A quoi pensez vous.
          (Oh. What are you thinking about.)

Teacher: Non, pas à quoi. (Pause.) Ce sont des personnes, n'est-ce pas?
          Ça (points to the word *quoi* on the blackboard), c'est pour les
          choses. Ça, c'est pour les choses, et ça (points to the word
          qui on the board), c'est pour les personnes.
          (No, not what. They are people, aren't they? That is for things.
          That is for things, and that is for people.)

Sue: Numéro huit, n'est-ce pas?
          (Number eight, isn't it?)

Teacher: Non. Numéro sept . . . excusez-moi.
          (No. Number seven . . . excuse me.)

Sue: Oh. A qui pensez-vous.
          (Oh. Whom are you thinking about.)

The teacher's attempt to engage Sue in conversation—by joking that *quoi* means *what* and may thus be perceived as an insult by her friends—fails because both teacher and student are intent on the formal grammar exercise at hand. The teacher's initial "statement," *Je pense à mes amis de Paris*, is meant to be responded to not with a meaningful comment but with the substitution of the corresponding interrogative pronoun.

The WHERE of Acquisition Research

The setting or situation of L2 use is the WHERE of acquisition research. If her exposure to the L2 consists primarily of "conversations" about the use of interrogative pronouns and other structural features in answer to textbook questions, Sue, in the classroom setting depicted above, may be expected to have a competence quite different from that of Maria and Miguel who, in the earlier example, use the L2 to meet a variety of social needs. Both the *amount of time* spent in practice and the *variety* of that practice in terms of the use of the L2 for problem solving and exchange of meaning *interact* with other situational and learner variables to determine communicative competence.

Moreover, the setting in which a language is learned is intimately related to language *retention*. A realistic discussion of language *learning* should reflect an awareness of the reverse phenomenon, language *forgetting*. Forgetting a language, or *language loss*, is an all too familiar experience. How many times have you heard someone say: *I've forgotten all the Spanish (English, French, etc.) I ever knew.* Only a summer away from study can, in some instances, give learners the impression that they have "forgotten everything." Similarly, learners who find themselves in a natural or an immersion setting may sense that their L1 competence is slipping away as their adeptness in a second language improves. The following note, written to a friend back home by an eleven-year-old American girl in the sixth month of a prolonged visit to Paris, echoes the feelings of many learners as they become increasingly immersed in a second language and culture.

LANGUAGE LOSS

Are things ~~your~~ going better for you? I hope so, it sounded as if you ~~weren'~~ ~~weren't~~ were not (what is that ~~a~~ contraction?) very happy.

What's happend to your old friends ~~Cynthy~~ Cynthia and Candy? How about Andy?

I set off well here, I'm very popular, I have lots of friends.

God save my English! It's going ↓.

I hope I didn't make too many mistakes in this letter!

Just how much of her mother tongue the youngster had "lost" in six months is a matter for speculation. Her feelings are nonetheless real and are familiar not only to *individual* language learners but, in those situations where their survival is threatened by competing linguistic systems, to *entire speech communities*. (In the introduction to *Language Death*, a study of the gradual displacement of Gaelic in the Scottish Highlands, Dorian (1981) provides an overview of the linguistic extinction currently underway "in virtually every part of the world.") The youngster's feelings illustrate the need for an understanding of language loss. For example, what features of language are most resistant to attrition? Does the age of the learner interact with the setting in which the language is learned to influence the rate and nature of attrition? What are the best ways to revive communicative abilities that have gone unused for a period of time? Clearly, research into language acquisition is incomplete without a study of language attrition. (For further discussion of the issues related to the loss of L2 skills, see Lambert and Freed 1982.)

The HOW of Acquisition Research: Strategies and Processes

Ultimately, we would like to know HOW second languages are learned and maintained. "Street learners," or those who are exposed to language in natural settings, may use strategies different from those who study in a classroom. Learners themselves often seek one or the other context, *structuring* their own practice according to their needs and style of learning. Those with one learning style may, on the other hand, learn and profit from a different style; that is, they may *learn how to learn*.

One important avenue of research is *foreigner talk* (Freed 1981), the study of interactions between native and nonnative speakers, to which we may compare the discourse between native speakers. For example, many of us have heard natives speak louder and even shout at nonnatives. This may help if one's hearing is impaired but not necessarily if one is foreign. Other strategies, however, such as *code simplification*, may facilitate acquisition and may even resemble strategies used by parents and others in talking with young children—the kinds of discourse strategies referred to as "baby talk," "motherese," or "caretaker speech."

Up to this point in the discussion the terms *learning* and *acquisition* have been used interchangeably. There is a professional self-consciousness about these terms at present, with some using one or the other term simply as a matter of style and others taking care to use both, for example, second language learning/acquisition. Some like the term "acquisition" because they feel it sounds more sophisticated and research-oriented than "learning." Krashen (1977) however, has used the two terms to make a careful distinction between what he considers two quite different processes. He distinguishes between *conscious* or *monitored processes*, which he calls *learning*, and *unconscious processes* ("picking up a language"), which he calls *acquisition*. Exercises that focus on structure and give the learner time to consult reference books or rehearse paradigms are examples of learning practice. Spontaneous or unrehearsed interaction, on the other hand, promotes acquisition. In the elaboration of his "monitor model" of language acquisition Krashen has attempted to clarify the role of learning exercises in making possible communicative use of the language. In successive statements based on data from L2 studies about the relationship between learning and acquisition, the role that Krashen attributes to learning, or conscious focus on forms, has become increasingly smaller. In his words, "Conscious learning makes only a small contribution to communicative ability" (1981:5). What Krashen is saying is that communicative competence is acquired through communication, not through conscious structure practice; or, to return to our French proverb, *C'est en forgeant que l'on devient forgeron* (One becomes a blacksmith by being a blacksmith). Central to acquisition success in Krashen's model is what he calls the "affective filter," which includes the attitude of the learner as well as other affective variables.

PRONUNCIATION ACCURACY

This model of the predictors of pronunciation accuracy illustrates the findings of studies by Purcell and Suter (1980) and Purcell (1981) in terms of Krashen's distinction between learning and acquisition. Affective factors ultimately determine the *extent* and *nature* of interaction with the L2 and the *learner's attention* to pronunciation accuracy. Pronunciation drills and exercises (that is, formal learning) were found to be of no significant influence. In the words of Purcell and Suter, "Teachers and classrooms seem to have had remarkably little to do with how well our students pronounce English" (1980:285).

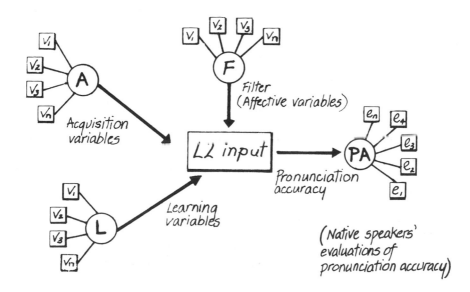

Krashen is not the first to be concerned with conscious and unconscious processes in language acquisition. There was a flurry of discussion in the late 1960s and early 1970s opposing the *habit formation* view of L2 acquisition to what came to be called *cognitive code-learning* theory. The former referred to the unconscious rote memorization and repetition associated with audiolingual methodology, whereas the latter was the conscious attention to rules of structure. The cognitive code-learning theory served to validate the already widespread practice of "modifying" audiolingual curricula by including explanations of the rules of grammar and phonology and introducing written materials along with dialogues and oral drills. The discussion began with Carroll's (1965) identification of these theories as the "two major theories of foreign language learning" that are reflected in current teaching practice, with habit-formation theory by far the more dominant. For Carroll the cognitive code-learning theory is "a modified, up-to-date grammar-translation theory." In this theory language learning is seen as "a process of acquiring conscious control of the phonological, grammatical and lexical patterns of a language, largely through study and analysis of these patterns . . . the theory attaches more importance to the learner's understanding of the structure of the foreign language than to his facility in using that structure." The assumption is that with an understanding or "cognitive control" over the structures, "facility will develop automatically with use of the language in meaningful situations" (1965:278). Carroll concludes with the suggestion that the audiolingual-habit theory be joined with some of the "better elements" of cognitive code-learning theory to yield a "revised theory" as a basis for a "dramatic change in [teaching] effectiveness" (1965:281).

The search for the "better elements" continues. The role of cognitive processes in the development of communicative competence remains undefined. The description of competence (WHAT), as we have noted, is intimately related to discussions of HOW language is acquired. A habit may be defined in terms of the repetition of sounds and structure with nativelike accuracy, *or* it may be the ability to make requests appropriate to a situation *or*, to extend the concept even further, the ability to deliver a persuasive presidential address. Although the last two tasks would not normally be considered "habits," success in all three activities does require *practice* with attention to the outcome. Discussions of the relationship of analysis to practice, of conscious to unconscious processes in the development of communicative abilities, rest on a *definition of terms*. What appear to be conflicting views may, in fact, be similar ideas expressed in different terms. Or, conversely, the use of similar terms to describe essentially different phenomena may conceal real conflicts in theories or research data.

The relation of theory to practice and the importance of learner attitudes are the subject of the three texts that follow. They are called *texts* because each is a self-contained illustration of L2 acquisition within a specific *context*. Each text looks, in its own way, at the WHO, WHAT, WHERE, and HOW of second language learning as outlined in Section 2.1. The first text, Section 2.2, is an example of what Piaget would call a *pedagogic experiment*, in this instance an attempt to promote the development of communicative competence as part of beginning-level L2 programs. It summarizes the research project that the author conducted in 1970 and that has been reported more fully elsewhere (Savignon 1971, 1972a, 1972b). The two remaining texts, Sections 2.3 and 2.4, span a seven-year period and illustrate a case-study approach to the acquisition of communicative competence in a *natural* environment. The first reports on a conversation with the author's son, Daniel, a seven-year-old at the time who was learning French as a second language. The second text is a follow-up study of Daniel and his two sisters seven years later. In all three texts the author has assumed the role of teacher/researcher.

2.2 TEACHING FOR COMMUNICATIVE COMPETENCE: A CLASSROOM STUDY*

Teachers of foreign languages have long known that mastery of the mechanics of a language does not ensure the ability to use the language for communication. Yet current teaching practice delays experience in authentic communication until the student has acquired a basic set of grammatically correct utterances.

Proponents of the audiolingual method or structural approach have cautioned teachers against moving too fast from controlled drills to free expression at the beginning levels. The assumption is that *allowing* learners to say something before they are first taught *how* to say it not only results in ungrammatical utterances, which are later difficult to eradicate, but also serves to *discourage* beginning learners. This position has meant devoting early lessons largely to dialogue memorization and structural drilling. When so-called directed communication is introduced, it is not communication at all because the structural frame, if not the lexical content, remains in the control of the instructor.

There are some teachers, comfortably fluent in the language themselves, who provide *informally* the opportunity for spontaneous self-expression on the elementary level. They are the exception, however. There is no acknowledged training in real trial-and-error communication until the intermediate or even advanced levels of instruction. Not until they reach these levels are learners encouraged to be innovative in the use of language as they interact with native or near-native speakers. After having insisted on accuracy and rapidity of response in the beginning stages, the teacher is now confronted with the delicate task of guiding, without discouraging, the learners' first attempts at saying what they really want to say in the foreign language.

---

* This text has appeared in a somewhat different form in the *Audio-Visual Language Journal* (1972a) and is included here with permission.

Even at these more advanced levels, what often passes for an evaluation of communicative competence is, in fact, an inaccurate reflection of a learner's ability to function in an authentic communicative context. In many high school and college classrooms these evaluations are based on prepared talks and/or oral interviews in which the instructor asks questions of the student, carefully limiting lexical and syntactical items to those with which the learner already has some familiarity. Though a global mark may be given for performance in the integrated skill, the trend in recent years has been to rely heavily on evaluations of the elements of language—pronunciation, syntax, and lexicon— made *apart from an act of communication*. The assumption underlying this discrete-point approach to testing language proficiency is that breaking down a skill into the elements of language and testing these elements separately affords greater objectivity and is, therefore, a more reliable evaluation of a student's proficiency than is a subjective evaluation of performance in the integrated skill.

Many language teachers share the impression, however, that students who do well on discrete-point tests of language proficiency are not always able to carry on a conversation in the foreign language. Other students enter willingly and effectively into a variety of communicative activities and yet perform poorly on traditional tests of proficiency. If this is true, discrete-point tests are testing something other than the skill required for effective communication. The language proficiency test may be said to measure *linguistic competence*, but actual use of the language for communication requires *communicative competence*.

With the distinction between linguistic and communicative competence in mind, the language teacher needs to take yet another look at current audio-lingual practice and ask to what extent methods of instruction and teaching reflect the professed but seldom realized goal: communication with native speakers of the language. Should practice in actual communication be postponed until the intermediate or even advanced levels of instruction—levels that the majority of our students never reach? Do hours spent drilling the mechanics of a language need to precede the learners' first attempts at encoding their own thoughts into that language? What is the effect on learner motivation of the failure to teach and to test from the beginning those skills that the student understands to be the end goal of language study, namely, communication? These were among the questions that led to a research project designed to assess the effectiveness of training in communicative skills as part of a beginning-level college French course.

Design of the Study

Three groups of beginning college French students, two experimental and one control, participated in the study, which ran for an eighteen-week period (one semester) and included a total of 42 students. Each group corresponded to a class section in the multisection beginning French program at the University of Illinois at Urbana-Champaign. This program used what may be described as a modified audiolingual approach to teaching French. The emphasis was on dialogue memorization and oral drilling of linguistic patterns, particularly in the beginning stages. More written work was included as the semester progressed, but there was no outside reader. Harris and Lévêque (1968), *Basic Conversational French* (fourth edition), was the textbook used by all sections. Of the three class sections randomly selected for inclusion in this study, the two experimental groups E_1 and E_2 were taught by the same instructor. The instructor assigned to the control group C was similar in terms of experience and language proficiency to the instructor for groups E_1 and E_2. Both instructors participated in the teacher orientation and training program and were under the supervision of the course chairman.

All three groups met for four 50-minute periods a week for *the same basic course of instruction in French*. In addition, each group spent one 50-minute period a week in a *different*, French-related activity. The control group spent this fifth period in the language laboratory, where they practiced the basic material presented in the course. This language laboratory program was a closely coordinated part of the elementary French program, and participation in it was required of all students enrolled in the regular class sections. The two experimental groups however did not attend the language laboratory. They were each subdivided into smaller groups of six or seven students for participation in two *separate* programs developed and conducted by the experimenter. For subgroups of E_2 the experimental program consisted of a series of cultural orientation sessions conducted in English. The program for subgroups of group E_1 consisted of training in performing specific communicative acts. Both experimental programs will be described more fully below.

A test of foreign language aptitude (Modern Language Aptitude Test, short form) was administered to all students at the beginning of the semester. High-school percentile rank was recorded as a measure of past academic achievement. Verbal intelligence scores (School-College Ability Test, verbal) were also recorded when they were available. All students who indicated that they had had previous experience with French, however brief, were excluded from this study, leaving a total of 42 students with no prior knowledge of French. All but one of these 42 students had studied a modern language other than French, usually at the secondary school level.

Assessment of achievement was expanded to include measures of communicative competence in addition to the more traditional measures of linguistic knowledge. The following test scores and grades were recorded for each student at the *conclusion* of the eighteen-week semester:

College Entrance Examination Board (CEEB) Reading Test in French

This test was administered as part of the final examination for all students enrolled in elementary French.

College Entrance Examination Board (CEEB) Listening Test in French

This test was administered as part of the final examination for all students enrolled in elementary French.

Instructor's Evaluation of Speaking Skill

Instructors were asked to evaluate the speaking skill of each of their students in terms of pronunciation, grammar, vocabulary, and fluency. A student's performance in the classroom was compared with that of students with similar training and ratings given along a six-point scale.

Final Grade in Course

Three one-hour examinations were given during the semester. These examinations were all departmental, and a grading curve was derived from the scores of students in all course sections. The final examination consisted of the CEEB tests of reading and listening comprehension and a departmental test of writing. Course grades were based on the final examination (30%), quizzes and *dictées* (20%), hour examinations (30%), pronunciation (10%), and daily preparation (10%).

Tests of Communicative Competence

A series of tests of communicative competence was administered at the conclusion of the semester. Each student was tested individually in a variety of communicative settings. These included discussions with native speakers, interviews, reports, and descriptions. The total testing time for each student was 30 minutes. The students were told that these "speaking tests" were a part of their final examination. A sign-up sheet was passed around with alternative slots assigned to each course section. In this way the students included in any one testing period were drawn equally from the three groups. The testing periods lasted from three to four hours each and were spread over three days.

The native speakers and other persons involved in administering and evaluating the tests of communicative competence were unaware of the nature of the experimental program. Orientation sessions were held for all testing personnel to establish uniform procedures. A total of 13 separate evaluations were made for each student by three different evaluators. These included objective measures of the *amount of information* conveyed or received in different communicative settings as well as more subjective evaluations of *comprehensibility, fluency, poise, effort,* and the *ability to initiate and to conclude an interview.* The tests of communicative competence and the evaluation criteria used are described in more detail below.

Cultural Orientation

The cultural orientation program for subgroups of E_2 consisted of a series of discussions and experiences directed toward creating an interest in French people and culture. The activities were planned to be the kinds of things an American teacher of French might do to interest his or her students in French culture, hoping thereby to increase their interest and achievement in the

French language. All activities were conducted in English, and no attention was given to any questions of a linguistic nature.

The sessions were led by the experimenter with the occasional participation of native French students studying in the United States, American students recently returned from a year in France, and a professor of French civilization. An informal atmosphere was maintained throughout the program. Most sessions were held in the classroom, but there were also three films and two evening gatherings at the home of the experimenter. The activities and the approximate number of class hours devoted to each of them are summarized in Table 2.1.

TABLE 2.1 CULTURAL ORIENTATION PROGRAM FOR SUBGROUP E$_2$

Number of class periods	Type of activity
3	French films. Philippe de Broca—*Le Roi de Coeur* (1966). Alain Resnais—*La Guerre est Finie* (1966). René Clément—*Jeux Interdits* (1952). Written reaction by the students followed by group discussion.
4	Discussion of the students' impressions of France and the French followed by an exploration of their basis in fact. Presentation of French views of Americans, stressing those criticisms that reveal cultural diversity.
2–2	Discussion of the current political, social, and economic situation in France.
3	Slides on French Impressionism, Versailles, modern art and architecture.
1	Introduction to French cuisine—wine tasting, *escargots*, *quiche*, *crêpes*, and *pâtisseries*.
1	Discussion of language learning problems, motivation for learning French, travel and work opportunities in French-speaking parts of the world.
2	Informal gatherings with French students studying in the United States and with American students recently returned from France.

Training in Communication

The aim of the training sessions in communication for subgroups E$_1$ was twofold: (1) to give learners the opportunity to use French in practical communicative settings beginning with the very first week of study and (2) to free learners of the impression that communication is measured solely in terms of linguistic accuracy. Innovation was not only encouraged, it was necessary in the communicative contexts defined.

The first meeting was devoted to a discussion of what it means to communicate. What are some nonverbal forms of communication? How do you evaluate a person's ability to communicate in a foreign language? How important are word order, pronunciation, and grammar in understanding a non-native speaker of English? One student finally said, *It's how well he gets his meaning across*. It was then explained that these sessions would be concerned with precisely that—getting meaning across in a variety of simulated as well as real situations.

At the second meeting the students enacted several different communicative situations *in English* and then watched as these same situations were enacted in French by a group of American students recently returned from a year of study in France. These situations included: (1) two new students meeting in the university residence, (2) two students and longtime friends meeting after summer vacation, (3) a student arriving home for lunch with his family, and (4) a student meeting her professor after class. All the dialogues, both English and French versions, were spontaneous and amusing; in no way did they resemble the dry-as-dust, if linguistically accurate, exchanges to which language teachers have become accustomed. The students enjoyed being themselves in a language with which they were comfortable. It seems worthwhile to note at this point that the intermittent use of English, not only initially but throughout the eighteen-week period, appeared to contribute significantly to a relaxed, informal relationship among the participants. This kind of group rapport was essential if meaningful communication was to take place in French.

We discussed the differences observed by the students in the French and American patterns of communication. The students said that the French appeared much friendlier. They were much amused by the handshaking and kissing and asked about it. They noted more use of gestures in the French exchanges. There were many interesting cultural contrasts in the linguistic content of these dialogues as well, but these, of course, were not apparent to the American students who were just beginning their study of French.

The students were then encouraged to "act French" in their own exchanges by adopting the nonverbal aspects of French communication that they had observed. As a start, during this second meeting we tried just saying hello in French. The first volunteer began confidently, walked up to the female experimenter, extended her hand and said, "Bonjour, Monsieur". . . and then blushed! Everyone laughed at this point, realizing how much they needed practice in linking expressions to actual meaning.

A variety of communicative tasks were defined for practice in subsequent sessions, with the focus not *French* but *how to do things in French*. Some examples are listed below.

1. Greetings
   a) Greet a new student.
   b) Meet a former professor.
   c) Meet a fellow student you have not seen all summer.
   d) Greet your mother.

2. Leave-taking
   (a), (b), (c), and (d) as above

3. Information-getting
   a) An American family in Chantilly wants directions to the museum.
   b) Ask for help in posting a letter.
   c) Inquire about the best way to go from Lyon to Paris.
   d) Find out all you can about a new French student.

4. Information-giving
   a) A new French student needs directions to the library.
   b) The same student wants to know when meals are served.
   c) The French student asks you what there is to do in Chicago.
   d) Tell the French student about yourself.

The exchanges were short (one to three minutes in length) and included one or two students and a fluent speaker. Subsequent situations included making introductions, extending invitations, ordering meals, paying compliments, and other specific communicative acts suited to this type of dialogue technique.

The other main areas of training were in description and reporting. Practice in describing an ongoing activity was provided through the use of pictures as well as classroom activities. Reporting skills were developed by group discussion on topics chosen by the students and by short individual reports on things such as family, studies, leisure activities, impressions of a film or other event.

The size of the group practicing these various skills at any one time was important in determining the success of the session. Ten appeared to be the optimum group size for the dialogues. In observing the group while one or two students acted out a situation with a fluent speaker of French, one was impressed by a sense of "community." All watched, listened, and enjoyed the presentation, trying to think what they would say in a similar situation. This active listening is in sharp contrast to most individual class recitations, which are easily reduced to a dialogue between the individual learner and the instructor while the others "tune out." The same presentations in smaller groups of four or five were not so much fun simply because the situation was in itself false. We were playacting but without an audience. These smaller groups lent themselves well, on the other hand, to discussion on topics of interest to the participants and to various descriptive exercises. It was important to the learners that they have an opportunity to say things they really wanted to say, in the dialogues as well as in the group discussions, *even if the expression of their thoughts did not fit the confines of the sample phrases in their textbook.*

Students were free at all times to ask how to say things in French, or simply to insert the English word, rather than stumble or stop talking. The fluent speakers working with the students responded by supplying the French equivalent or, when they did not understand what the student was trying to say, by asking for more information. Students felt a need for and asked for expressions like "How do you say in French . . . ?" "You mean . . . ," "I don't understand . . . ," "Please repeat . . . ." They were eager to learn and use expressions that could fill in while they paused to think—*voyons, alors, eh bien, d'accord, je veux dire que, truc, machin* (let's see, then, well, O.K., I mean, thing, watchamacallit), and so forth. With this kind of basic vocabulary and the feeling that *what* they said was more important than *how* they said it, the learners were relatively at ease in the communicative setting. In addition, they had the assurance and composure they needed to be able to make the best use of the French they knew.

The sessions were for the most part relaxed and fun—"entertaining," one student said. The majority of the students enjoyed using their knowledge of French in real situations. Many expressed the desire for more frequent meetings and even smaller groups, giving everyone more time to speak. There were some learners who expressed feelings of anxiety in the dialogue situations where they were on their own and performing for the group. These students all said they preferred the group discussions where no one felt any particular pressure to speak at any one moment. Group discussions were also popular because the participants were expressing their own ideas rather than performing in a hypothetical situation. Reality and novelty of expression were crucial to sustaining interest. Students resented being asked to repeat an idea just for the sake of practice.

Tests of Communicative Competence

Tests were developed to measure the learners' ability to communicate in four different communicative contexts: *discussion, information-getting, reporting,* and *description*. Students were told that these were tests of how well they could communicate in French in a variety of situations and that evaluation of their performance would be based on how well they got their meaning across. They were to concentrate, therefore, not so much on speaking perfect French as on using every means at their disposal to express their ideas and to make themselves understood.

Most of the testing situations were sufficiently flexible so that no specific lexical or syntactical knowledge was required. Care was taken to avoid discussion of or reporting on topics that had been presented in the training sessions in communicative skills. For that part of the test that asked for a description of an ongoing activity, vocabulary and even syntax were of course controlled by the objects and actions that the students were asked to describe. In this case, the objects and actions included were suggested by instructors of first-semester French who were in no way involved in the experimental program. The selection of these objects and actions was based on the vocabulary introduced in the textbook that was used by all course sections.

PART I: DISCUSSION

This first task was designed to be an informal interaction between the student and a native speaker of French who also knew English. The object of the exercise was to see how much information the student and the native speaker could exchange on an assigned topic in the four minutes allotted. The administrator began the discussion by introducing the student to the native speaker and giving them the subject of their discussion. Three topics were randomly assigned: (1) the advantages of a large university versus a small college, (2) the validity of a foreign language requirement in a liberal arts education, and (3) the role of students in university administration.

The native speaker was friendly toward the student, assuming the role of an interested teacher or friend. He helped the student to express himself by supplying French vocabulary when asked and by repeating or translating where needed. The atmosphere was not one of "testing" the student but rather of teamwork between the student and the native speaker.

A training session was held for the native speakers involved in Parts I and II of the test. The purpose of the session was to give the native speakers practice in conducting the discussions, as well as to establish criteria for evaluating a student's ability to communicate. The students who participated in this training session were first-semester French students who were not involved otherwise in the research program. Following some trial runs and discussions among the native speakers involved, none of whom had ever experienced *teaching* a second language, two criteria were set for Part I: (1) *effort to communicate* and (2) *amount of communication*. Effort to communicate was defined as a learner's willingness to express himself. Does he attempt an answer? How well does he sustain contact with the native speaker? Does he use gestures to help express himself? To assess the amount of communication that had taken place the native speaker asked himself how well he had understood the student's views on the topic of discussion. A six-point scale was used in rating both the effort and the amount of communication.

PART II: INFORMATION-GETTING

This task represented a formalized interaction with what many would consider a more typical Frenchman. The native speaker responded only to what he understood and made no attempt to help the student. The student was asked to interview the person with whom he had just been conversing in order to find out as much as he could about him in the four minutes allotted. The student was to take notes as they talked and then to write up the interview in English. It was explained to the student that the native speaker would not understand any English and would be unable to help him formulate his questions. Upon conclusion of the interview, sufficient time was allowed (two minutes was usually ample) for the student to write down in English what he had learned.

Five criteria were established for evaluating communicative skills in Part II: (1) *comprehensibility and suitability of the introduction;* (2) *naturalness and poise*, or the ability of the student to keep the interview in hand; (3) *comprehension* by the native speaker, the degree of hesitation in interpreting the student's questions, the number of repetitions; (4) the *comprehensibility and suitability of the conclusion*; and (5) *amount of communication,* how many accurate statements about the native speaker was the student able to make at the conclusion of the interview. The native speaker, again using a six-point scale, evaluated student performance on the first four criteria. The amount of communication that had taken place was obtained by counting the number of correct statements written in English by the student. The native speaker first checked these statements for accuracy. The scoring was then done by an evaluator who did not know the students and had not been present at the interview. One point was given for each item of information that had been correctly recorded.

PART III: REPORTING

After completing Parts I and II, students went to another room for the remainder of the test. In Part III students were instructed to talk first in English and then in French on an assigned topic. These reports were recorded directly on tape with no one present other than the administrator and the student. The English practice session was used so that students could organize their ideas on the topic before talking about it in French. It was stressed, however, that they did not need to say the same things in French that they had said in English. Three discussion topics were randomly assigned: (1) your family, (2) your life on campus this semester, and (3) your winter vacation. The students were first given one minute to talk in English and then three minutes to talk in French.

PART IV: DESCRIPTION

This was a test of the student's ability to describe an ongoing activity. It was explained to the student that an actor would enter the room and perform a variety of actions. The student was to describe first the actor himself and then his activities. As a warm-up for this exercise, the student was first given the opportunity to describe the actor and his activities in English.

The actor selected a series of specific activities to be carried out upon his entering the room. The warm-up sequence to be described in English was the same for all students and lasted 45 seconds. Immediately following the warm-up, the actor reentered the room carrying and wearing a variety of objects. He waited one minute to allow the student to describe him and then began to perform slowly and deliberately the actions that he had selected. The actor remained in the room for a total of two and a half minutes. The nature and sequence of the activities were different for each student, but the same number of actions were performed at the same pace.

Parts III and IV were evaluated from the tape recordings. A native speaker used a six-point scale to rate performance on each of Parts III and IV in terms of (1) *fluency* and (2) *comprehensibility*. Fluency was defined as the effort made by the student to speak. How much did he try to say? Comprehensibility was defined as the extent to which the native speaker felt he understood what was said. In addition to giving the above ratings, the native speaker wrote down in French what he understood from the recordings. *This was not a transcription of what the student said but rather an account of the ideas expressed, as understood by the native speaker.* Another evaluator then scored these accounts. For Part III *one point was given for each complete idea* understood by the native speaker. The definition of a "complete idea" was, of course, arbitrary, but guidelines that were easy to follow were quickly established. In general, isolated vocabulary items were ignored and credit given only for meaningful combinations of words. More important, since the basis of evaluation was the report in French written by the native speaker, the criterion for evaluation was clearly the amount of information conveyed by the student. There was no penalty for linguistic errors that did not affect meaning.

The native speakers' interpretation of what had taken place in Part IV was compared with the actor's account of what he had done. This provided a basis for measuring the accuracy of the student's description. *One point was given for each item of information* correctly conveyed. This meant that in the description of the actor *chemise* received one point, whereas *chemise rouge* received two points. In the description of the actor's activities later on, one point was given for each activity correctly described; *écoute la radio* received one point, whereas no credit was given for *radio* alone.

Findings and Interpretation

An analysis of variance indicated no significant differences among the three groups for the following independent variables, which are known to be related to achievement in second language study in a school setting: foreign language aptitude (MLAT), general academic achievement (high school percentile rank), and verbal intelligence (SCAT verbal). Table 2.2 gives a summary of this data.

TABLE 2.2 ANALYSIS OF VARIANCE, MLAT, SCAT VERBAL, AND HSPR*

			Group means	
Strategy	N	MLAT	SCAT verbal	HSPR
E_1	12	85.50	32.67	89.00
E_2	15	80.53	33.21	89.36
C	15	76.80	33.31	83.85
F-ratio		0.94	0.01	0.92

* High school percentile rank

There are no significant differences among groups.

The highly significant superiority ($p < 0.001$) of group E_1 (the group that received training in communication throughout the eighteen-week period) on tests of communicative competence supports the hypothesis that communicative competence can be taught and measured from the very beginning of a college French program. It is apparent, furthermore, that *without* such training beginning students in an audiolingual program similar to the one referred to in this study function relatively poorly in a truly communicative setting.

In spite of consistently significant differences in tests of communicative competence and in the instructor's evaluation of oral skill, there were no significant differences among the groups in standardized (CEEB) tests of listening and reading, nor were there any significant differences in final grades. This suggests that there is indeed a distinction between communicative competence and linguistic competence, and that, in this case, course grades and scores on standardized tests of second language skills reflect primarily the latter.

There was no indication that the elimination of the language laboratory and the substitution of practice in free expression in any way decreased linguistic accuracy. The communicative skills group (E₁) actually had higher mean scores than either of the other groups on the CEEB tests of listening and reading, on the instructor's evaluation of speaking skill, and on the final grade. Although the differences are not statistically significant in the case of the CEEB tests and final grades, further investigation is needed to show if significant differences would appear with continued French study. These findings point further to the *ineffectiveness* of the language laboratory, as used in this program, in reinforcing either linguistic or communicative competence. Table 2.3 summarizes the differences among the groups on measures of achievement.

TABLE 2.3 ANALYSIS OF VARIANCE, ACHIEVEMENT CRITERIA

Strategy	N	Group means				
		CEEB listening	CEEB reading	Instructor's evaluation of oral skill	Communicative competence	Final grade
E₁	12	9.00	8.08	19.92	66.00	4.33
E₂	15	6.20	6.67	15.87	44.27	3.67
C	15	6.67	6.00	14.80	34.27	3.80
F-ratio		1.11	0.56	3.98*	8.54**	2.06

* $p < 0.05$
** $p < 0.001$

The difference among group means on instructor's evaluation of oral skill is significant at the 0.05 level. The difference among group means on tests of communicative competence is significant at the 0.001 level. The Newman–Keuls technique was used to make multiple comparisons of the three strategy means for oral skill and for communicative competence. Applied to the group means for oral skill, this test showed the differences between E₁ (communicative skills) and E₂ (culture) and between E₁ and C (language laboratory) to be significant at the 0.05 level. There was no significant difference between E₂ and C. Applied to the group means for the communicative skills total, the Newman–Keuls test showed the differences between E₁ and E₂ and between E₁ and C to be significant at the 0.01 level. There was no significant difference between E₂ and C.

To summarize, all students received similar instruction in linguistic skills, and there was no evidence that one group knew more French than the other in terms of the level of linguistic competence attained. However, those students who had been given the opportunity to use their linguistic knowledge for real communication were able to speak French. The others were not.

To the extent that the basic audiolingual course in this study resembles current second language programs at both high school and college levels, the findings indicate that there is a need to distinguish between linguistic competence on the one hand and communicative competence on the other. In spite of the proclaimed goals of audiolingual methods, it would appear that the former and not the latter is typically rewarded in the classroom. A survey by Kalivoda (1970) of methods of testing speaking skill at the high school level supports this assertion. Ninety-three percent of the foreign language classrooms surveyed reported basing such evaluations primarily on the *recitation of memorized dialogues*. This is not the complete picture, of course. There are teachers who seek to go beyond the dialogues and drills and who are willing, from the beginning, to sacrifice linguistic accuracy for the sake of real self-expression. Too often, however, this freedom is discouraged by pressure to "cover" a prescribed number of dialogues or units and/or to prepare learners for standardized tests of achievement. The findings reported here suggest any teaching practices that promote communicative competence need, on the contrary, to be recognized and encouraged. The first step would be the adoption of testing methods that reward both learner and teacher efforts in this direction.

Experimentation is now needed to assess the effectiveness of a variety of techniques for providing training in communicative skills. Future studies should include different *proportions*, as well as different *kinds*, of formal training and practice in trial-and-error communication. In this connection, the role of the native language should be reconsidered: It can serve not only to translate meaning to or from the second language but also to create a predisposition for communication in the second language.

The teacher component also deserves special attention. Smith and Berger (1968) have suggested the relation of student-teacher interaction to achievement in terms of linguistic competence. There is reason to believe that this interaction is even more important in training for communicative competence. Practice in communication, by definition, forces learners to come out from behind memorized dialogues and ready-made phrases, leaving them in a particularly vulnerable position. The rapport they feel with the teacher as well as with classmates may be crucial in determining the success or failure of the venture.

Finally, the concept of communicative competence itself needs to be explored in more detail. What are the skills involved? How are they taught? Can they be measured discretely? The evaluation criteria used in this study were derived intuitively by a group of native speakers who were not teachers of French by profession. The use of larger groups representing a cross section of native speakers of French (in terms of age, geographical location, social position, etc.) might yield additional or different criteria.

While awaiting the results of these and other queries, the training and testing procedures outlined in this report should be of use to teachers in their own informal efforts toward making communication not only a professed but also a real goal of their second language classes. Their experiences and the reactions of their students will, in turn, raise new questions for the researcher.

2.3 TALKING WITH MY SON:
A LOOK AT NATURAL
L2 ACQUISITION*

As a teacher of French and, what is more, the wife of a native Frenchman, I am frequently asked if my children speak French. "Uh . . . well," I find myself replying to these understandable queries, "not the girls, but Daniel gets along pretty well even though we very seldom speak French with him at home." The girls (Catherine and Julie, ages 4 and 3), I explain, have not as yet had the opportunity for sustained French listening and speaking. Daniel (age 9), however, began speaking French two years ago when we spent the summer in Dauphiné.

My husband and I decided early in our parenthood not to insist that our children speak French with either one or both of us. Aware of the many ramifications of the bilingual question, we were concerned that the efforts we might make to encourage the use of French might adversely affect the development of English language skills and, subsequently, general academic progress. Even more important, to be honest, was the rebellion we had seen in the children of some of our bilingual-bicultural acquaintances. The attempt to enforce the use of a second language *in almost complete isolation of a peer group for whom the language is natural* can result in frustration and resentment. Much better, we decided, to have the children love Daddy and take pride in his ethnic distinction, than to impress our friends with the linguistic dexterity of progeny who, underneath, resent everything and everyone French. So, it was not until the occasion of his first sustained residence in France in the summer of 1972 that Daniel, then age 7, began speaking French.

My concern here is not, however, to discuss the pros and cons of bilingual education, a subject charged with political overtones that is the object of a good deal of controversy in communities around the world. My comments thus far have served, rather, to provide an introduction to a conversation that I have chosen to illustrate the concept of communicative competence and its implications for second language teaching and testing.

The analysis of children's speech in recent years offers important new perspectives in first language acquisition, showing among other things, the

* This text has appeared in somewhat different form in the selected papers of the Central States Conference on the Teaching of Foreign Languages (1974). Permission to include it here is gratefully acknowledged.

embryonic nature of language development. What to an adult appear as errors in a child's speech are, in fact, evidence of the child's insight into how the language works. A nine-year-old who says "He winded my watch" is demonstrating his grasp of a general rule of past-tense formation (sand, sanded; bat, batted; etc.). He has not yet discovered that wind, like find (but unlike mind), corresponds to wound. A three-year-old who, in response to the comment, "I was waiting for you," says "You was?" shows an understanding of the I-you relationship with verb form constant (I walk, you walk; I saw, you saw; etc.). In both cases there is an overgeneralization of a rule, which eventually will be refined. Parents attest, and research has shown, that such refinement will occur only when the child is good and ready. Repetition of the correct form (pattern practice, if you will) is of little avail in advancing the schedule of development (Ervin-Tripp 1971; Braine 1971).

The analysis of children's errors to discover more about second language learning strategies is even more recent. Data are as yet limited, but there is evidence to suggest that many of the productive syntactical errors made by children who are learning a second language are not due to interference from their first language. Rather, they are indications of the same kinds of generalizations made by children learning the language as their mother tongue (Dulay and Burt 1972). In L2 learning, as in L1 learning, errors are an indication not so much of learning failures as they are of learning strategies. As such, errors are not only inevitable, they are desirable. They offer evidence of language growth through language use, that is, the exchange of meaning rather than the parroting of memorized phrases.

This comparison of L1 and L2 learner errors offers further support for providing children in second language programs with the same kinds of multifarious opportunities for self-expression that are available to them in their first language. Whatever their provenance, be it first language interference or generalizations common to learning the language as a first language, we must learn to accept errors in second language use as a function of second language acquisition. Not until then shall we be ready to evaluate the progress of our students toward the goals both they and we presumably have in mind, namely, the ability to exchange ideas with native speakers. Increased familiarity with the errors or learning strategies of children engaged in spontaneous self-expression in a second language should give us a valuable perspective from which to make these evaluations of communicative rather than linguistic competence.

The conversation transcribed below, rudimentary though it may be, is of interest as an example of just such communicative competence as well as of the contrast it provides to the types of exchanges most often provided as models for beginning second language learners. It was the first conversation in French I had ever had with my son, and it came about because I was curious when I heard shopkeepers and relatives comment on how well Daniel spoke French. We had been in France for about two months. During that time neither my husband nor I had made any special effort to speak or otherwise teach French to our children. Our foremost concern was that they enjoy their visit. Rightly or not, with so many readjustments in our living patterns and relationships outside the family, we felt it important to maintain at home the English language to which they were accustomed. Daniel did have numerous contacts with French-speaking persons outside our immediate family, however, as is apparent from the content of our conversation. I should add that he agreed to speak French with me on this occasion because he was both intrigued by the idea of talking into a microphone and happy to have a few minutes reprieve from his nine o'clock bedtime.

Sandra	Daniel
(1) Alors, Daniel, on va discuter un peu, si tu veux. Dis-moi comment tu t'appelles.	Daniel.
(2) Et quel âge as-tu, Daniel?	Sept.
(3) Oui, et est-ce que tu aimes la France?	Oui.
(4) Et qu'est-ce que tu fais en France?	Fais mon bicyclette.
(5) Ah . . . tu fais du . . . tu fais de la bicyclette?	Oui.
(6) Est-ce que tu vas très vite?	Oui.
(7) Tu vas trop vite peut-être?	Non, non.
(8) C'est . . . c'est dangereux?	Um . . . fais le bicyclette?
(9) Oui.	Un tout petit peu.
(10) Un tout petit peu?	Oui.
(11) Tu n'as jamais eu d'accident? Tu es tombé une fois de ta bicyclette?	Non.
(12) Tu n'es jamais tombé?	Non.
(13) Non? Est-ce que tu fais bien attention aux voitures?	Uh . . . tout petit peu.
(14) Tu . . . tu vas doucement quand tu arrives au stop? Tu . . . tu vas doucement? Tu ne vas pas trop vite?	Non.
(15) Bon. Et qu'est-ce que tu fais à bicyclette?	Fais les commissions.
(16) Fais les commissions. Où est-ce que tu vas pour faire les commissions?	Viriville.

(17) A Viriville.

Oui.

(18) Oui. Et qu'est-ce que tu achètes? . . . Qu'est-ce que tu achètes? . . . Tu com-comprends?

Non.

(19) Bon. Uh . . . qu'est-ce que tu prends?

Uh . . . le pain, des pains chocolat, des . . . um . . . des . . . confiture.

(20) De la confiture, oui, et quoi d'autre?

Et la bifteck haché . . .

(21) Bifteck haché, oui.

Et c'est tout.

(22) C'est tout? Et . . . tu ne prends pas de pain?

Oui (with insistence).

(23) Oui, du pain. Combien coûte le pain?

Un franc, un franc et ten centimes.

(24) Ah bon. Un franc *dix* centimes.

Dix centimes.

(25) Oui, c'est ça. Est-ce que tu passes voir mémé et tatie quand tu vas à Viriville?

Oui, et prends des salades . . .

(26) Ah, tu prends de . . .

Et les lettres aussi.

(27) Et les lettres?

Oui.

(28) Oui. Est-ce que tu es content à Viriville?

Oui.

(29) Qu'est-ce que tu aimes à Viriville surtout?

Um . . . sais pas.

(30) Qu'est-ce que tu aimes? Il doit y avoir des choses que tu aimes particulièrement. Tu as des copains?

Oui.

(31) Qui sont tes copains?

Christian Christian.

(32) Christian et Christian, oui. Il y a deux Christian.

Oui.

(33) Oui. Qui sont ces deux Christian?

Le pain Christian . . .

(34) Ah, le . . . le pain Christian. Tu veux dire c'est le fils du . . . du boulanger.

Oui.

(35) Oui.

Et . . . Christian la . . . fait la bicyclette (a)vec moi.

(36) Ah oui, l'autre Christian qui fait de la bicyclette avec toi. Oui. Il a une soeur je crois, non?

Oui.

(37) Comment s'appelle sa soeur?

Uh . . . Chantal.

(38) Chantal, oui.

Et le l'autre Christian aussi . . . elle s'appelle Chantal.

(39) L'autre Christian a une soeur qui s'appelle Chantal, oui. Et dis-moi un peu, qu'est-ce que tu as fait aujourd'hui.

. . . eh . . . sais pas.

(40) Tu (ne) sais pas?

Non.

(41) Qu'est-ce que tu as fait? Quelqu'un est venu manger.

Denise elle vient manger . . . manger lapin. Moi pas aime le lapin.

(42) Toi tu aimes le lapin?

Pas aime le lapin.

(43) Eh, pardon?

Pas aime lapin.

(44) Tu n'aimes pas le lapin?

Non.

(45) Ah bon. Et qu'est-ce qu'on a mangé d'autre?

. . . des melons des pâté des olives noires des saucissons des . . . uh . . . fromages . . . et des . . . Qu'est-ce qu'il y a pour dessert /dizer/?

(46) Un dessert? Qu'est-ce qu'il y avait comme dessert?

Sais pas.

(47) Tu ne sais pas?

Qué s'appelle?

(48) Ça s'appelle un gâteau.

Gâteau quoi?

(49) Mais c'était un . . . un diplomate.

Diplomate . . . manger des diplomate . . .

(50) Oui.

Et c'est tout!

(51) C'est tout? Qu'est-ce qu'il . . .

Et le café et le vin.

(52) Le vin et le café, puis, à la fin du repas, qu'est-ce qu'il y avait à boire?

Vin (with irritation).

(53) Vin, et puis?

De l'eau.

(54) De l'eau, et puis autre chose, à la fin. Avec le dessert, qu/est-ce qu'on a bu?

Ah, champ . . . champagne.

(55) Champagne, très bien. Et maintenant je vois que tu es

Non.

en pyjama. Tu vas te coucher
maintenant?

(56)	Pourquoi?	Fais encore de ça.
(57)	Comment?	Fais encore des ça.
(58)	Tu veux faire encore de ça? Tu veux continuer à parler au micro?	Oui.
(59)	Oui. Mais il se fait tard je crois. Il est neuf heures et demie.	Bon.
(60)	Bon. Alors, tu vas te coucher?	Oui.
(61)	Avec qui (est-ce) que tu couches?	Julie.
(62)	Qui est Julie?	Julie . . .
(63)	Qui est-ce?	Savignon.
(64)	Julie Savignon. C'est ta soeur alors?	Oui.
(65)	Quel âge a-t-elle?	Deux ans.
(66)	Deux ans. Et tu as une autre soeur aussi?	Oui. Catie . . .
(67)	Catie.	Trois ans.
(68)	Très bien. Et est-ce que tes soeurs sont heureuses en France aussi?	Oui.
(69)	Oui. Très bien. Alors, au revoir Daniel. Merci de cet interview.	Au revoir.

One's first impression upon listening to or reading the above exchange
might be either "What a remarkably flowing, relaxed conversation for a little
boy who is just beginning to learn French!" or "What ungrammatical French!"
Both are true. Using the most common measures of linguistic competence,
Daniel's French would not score very high. Let us suppose for a moment that
this is a testing interview situation and compare Daniel's first few remarks with
what might be considered "acceptable" responses:

(1) *Daniel.*
Je m'appelle Daniel.

(2) *Sept.*
J'ai sept ans.

(3) *Oui.*
Oui, j'aime la France.

(4) *Fais mon bicyclette.*
Je fais de la bicyclette.

(5) *Oui.*
Oui, je vais (très) vite.

(6) *Non, non.*
Non, je ne vais pas trop vite.

(7) *Fais le bicyclette.*
Est-ce que c'est dangereux de faire de la bicyclette? (*Note:* This is a question asked of the interviewer to clarify a preceding question. As such, it would probably not be scorable or even allowable on most tests.)

(8) *Un tout petit peu.*
Oui, c'est un peu dangereux.

(9) *Non.*
Non, je n'ai jamais eu d'accident.

Clearly not a very high score unless you are generous and give credit for comprehension. Most replies are simply *oui, non,* or another single word. Verbs are without a subject, genders are wrong, etc. Nonetheless, the conversation is surprising in its relaxed, spontaneous nature (so different from the typical teacher-student interview). It is entertaining in its imaginative use of the French language and the insights it offers into a young American's first experiences with life in France. Judged by measures of *communicative competence* such as *effort* to communicate and *amount* of communication, our impression is somewhat different. Not bad at all, we might even concede, considering the range and rapidity of the questions in relation to the age and language experience of the child. (Rapidity as well as phonological features like pronunciation and intonation unfortunately cannot be judged from the written transcription provided here.) It is apparent, furthermore, that it was Daniel's *communicative* rather than linguistic competence that prompted the remark I heard frequently from neighbors and shopkeepers, *"Qu'est-ce qu'il parle bien français, Daniel!"* (Daniel speaks French so well!)

It is not my intention to provide an exhaustive analysis of the kind of errors or strategies evidenced in this dialogue. To do so would require far more extensive data than are currently available on children's speech in French as both a first and second language. It is of interest, however, to attempt some tentative descriptions of the kinds of errors noted. The categories I have used below are those defined by Dulay and Burt (1972). However, unlike these authors' careful adherence to the data of first language acquisition in making observations about English as a second language, my assigning an error to a particular category is, of necessity, extrapolative. My assignments of error are based, in part, on the observations of the acquisition of French as a first language by Guillaume (1927a, 1927b). Offered in a spirit of "consciousness raising," they have the virtue of compelling us to look at the "unlookable" and therein, perhaps, helping us to understand the learning and creativity they signal.

Interferencelike errors (French reflects an English usage)

> *oui* (l. 22)—stress for emphasis rather than French *mais oui* or, more appropriate in this instance, *si*; similarly, *vin* (l. 52)

> *un franc et ten centimes* (l. 23)—influence of English pronunciation of *franc* apparent; substitution of English *ten* for French *dix*; use of *et* corresponds to English *one franc and ten centimes*, not allowable in French

> *pour dessert* /dizer/ (l. 45)—influence of English pronunciation apparent: use of *pour* as in English *for dessert* rather than French *comme*

> *des olives noires* (l. 45)—influence of English pronunciation apparent

L1 Developmental errors (Do not reflect English usage but are likely to be made by children learning French as a first language)

> *fais mon bicyclette* (l. 4)—omission of pronoun subject; cf. also *prends les salades* (l. 25), *fais les commissions* (l. 15), *manger lapin* (l. 41)

> *fais encore de ça* (l. 56)—telescopic form of *Je veux faire . . .* ; use of *encore* with a verb to indicate *more* or *again*

> *elle vient manger* (l. 41)—lack of tense inflection; cf. also *manger lapin* (l. 41), *manger des diplomate* (l. 49), *qu'est-ce qu'il y a pour dessert?* (l. 45)

> *moi pas aime le lapin* (l. 41)—accusative for nominative pronoun (or emphatic nominative and omission of pronoun subject?); omission of *ne*

> *gâteau quoi?* (l. 48)—use of interrogative pronoun for interrogative adjective

> *sais pas* (l. 29; l. 46)—omission of *ne*; missing subject

> *Christian Christian* (l.31)—missing conjunction

> *Christian la . . . fait la bicyclette (a)vec moi* (l. 35) missing relative pronoun; similarly, *le l'autre Christian aussi . . . elle s'appelle Chantal* (l. 38)

> *le l'autre Christian* (l. 38)—redundant addition of nonelided form of article

Ambiguous errors (Can be categorized as either interferencelike errors or L1 developmental errors)

> *vin* (l. 52)—missing determiner; cf. also *champagne* (l. 54), *lapin* (l. 41)

> *mon bicyclette* (l. 4)—inappropriate gender of determiner; similarly, *la biftek haché* (l. 20)

> *des confitures* (l. 19)—use of plural for singular partitive form; cf. also *des pâté* (l. 45), *des diplomate* (l. 49)

> *sept* (l. 2)—omission of *ans*

Unique errors (Do not reflect English usage and are not found in acquisition data of French as a first language)

> *le pain Christian* (l. 33)—juxtaposition of nouns to show relationship

> *qué s'appelle?* (l. 47)—for *comment s'appelle?*

Aside from the insights it offers into the provenance of errors, the dialogue also leads us to make other, more general speculations on the strategies of second language learning. To the extent that the foregoing exchange can be considered an authentic example of a beginning stage of second language acquisition in a natural setting, it suggests strategies we might do well to not only *expect* but also *reward* in our classrooms. I have little doubt that with continued opportunity for self-expression, Daniel will develop his *linguistic* competence to the point where he could, if he desired, approximate the "acceptable" responses mentioned on pages 85–86. This seems a reasonable enough assumption, given the widespread observation of the ease with which children acquire a second language. His errors at this beginning stage provide us, therefore, with some interesting clues about the strategies of English-speaking children who are learning French as a second language. Rather than penalizing a student for similarly using these strategies, we should regard them as a necessary phase of second language acquisition and turn our attention, instead, to developing better measures of communicative competence.

One cannot help noting the *wide range of comprehension as compared to the level of production*. There was no concerted attempt on the part of the interviewer/ mother to structure the exchange according to what the child might be able to say. Although she had some awareness of the kinds of experiences he had had, the interviewer could not know what linguistic expression these experiences would assume. The child nonetheless followed the conversation with relative ease. The exchange was for him no mere formalistic exercise; he was understanding, feeling, and reacting (sometimes with discernible emotion) to what was being said. Note his irritation when asked if he didn't buy bread, to which he responds with emphasis *oui* (for example, "Haven't you been paying attention? I just said so!" [l. 22]). Or, his careful insistence that he did *not* like rabbit, "Pas *aime le lapin*" (l. 42). Further evidence of the child's level of comprehension and participation is his spontaneous contribution of additional information. When asked if he stopped by to see his grandmother and aunt after running the errands, he answers, "Yes . . . and I picked up lettuce . . . and mail, too" (ll. 25–26). Similarly, when asked who came to dinner, he replies, "Denise came to dinner. We had rabbit. I don't like rabbit" (l. 41). (These English equivalents are, of course, my interpretation of meaning based on the context; they are not an attempt at verbatim translation.) Even when the responses are a short "yes," "no," or "I don't know," they are without exception appropriate to the context and indicate a comprehension that far exceeds the ability to respond fully. This is similar to an observation that has been made in first language acquisition. Ervin-Tripp has reported that "typically, recognition precedes production. We know that people can understand many more words than they ever use. The number of cues for recognition is less than the information needed for accurate production, and in recognition we can often profit from redundancy" (1964:164).

Is it not a mistake, then, to look for complete sentences in the speech of beginning second language learners? Would it not be preferable to encourage participation in a wide range of contexts and let fullness of response develop with increased experience? Insistence upon complete sentences may, in fact, be so unnatural as to actually discourage language development. It is interesting to note, further, that *the length and intricacy of the responses increase as the conversation continues.* Much more information is being volunteered by the time we reach the topic of Daniel's friends and the dinner party than in our earlier discussion of his activities in France. Short as this model is, we can nevertheless speculate that responses become more elaborate as the learner's experience increases, as he becomes more at ease in expressing himself within linguistic restrictions. It is noteworthy, for example, that in response to the question, "How old are you?" in the very beginning of the exchange, Daniel answers *"sept"* (l. 2), whereas much later, and without any intervening model, he answers *"deux ans"* (l. 65) when asked how old Julie is and *"trois ans"* (l. 67) when asked about Catie.

Another salient feature of the exchange is *the semantic richness of Daniel's French as contrasted with its structural simplicity.* There are, as we have noted, few examples of structurally "acceptable" phrases in terms of standard adult French—pronoun subjects are absent, verbs lack inflection, *ne . . . pas* negation is represented as a simple *pas* before the verb, noun determiners are frequently absent or in the wrong gender or number. In short, there is an apparent inattention to those features we teachers of French usually emphasize in beginning lessons. There is, on the other hand, evidence of a rather wide range of vocabulary. Names for "things," in particular, seem to have caught his attention, as, for example, in the long string of substantives he supplies in response to questions about the kinds of errands he runs or what he had for dinner. He uses nouns creatively, moreover, to express relationships for which his French is not sufficiently sophisticated: *"Le pain Christian"* (literally, the bread Christian) means *"Christian, le fils du boulanger"* (Christian, the baker's son); in *"Christian Christian"* two proper nouns are juxtaposed to indicate *"Il y a deux Christian"* (There are two Christians); *"vin,"* with emphasis, means *"Je l'ai deja dit, du vin!"* (I already told you, wine!) In other words, just as has been observed in first language acquisition, a single substantive is frequently much more than just a name for something—it may express a fully developed idea. This suggests that in our classrooms we should pay much more attention than has hitherto been our habit to providing a semantically rich environment. We should give students what they ask for, words that have meaning for them.

In all these observations there remains, of course, the question of the extent to which child acquisition of a second language can be compared to adult acquisition of a second language. There are differences surely, just as there are differences in the acquisition patterns of children themselves; these, of course, will depend on the stage of cognitive development and first language acquisition (not to mention socioeconomic environment) of the child. Ervin-Tripp has suggested, however, that in spite of the many obvious sources of difference "the components may be similar in gross outline" (1964:349). But the point is, as she goes on to say, to study what these components consist of. The sample of second language competence that I have provided here will perhaps serve heuristically to encourage observation of beginning classroom French or Spanish or German, etc. for what it is, not for what we would like it to be. Increased observation and analysis will provide us with a surer sense of the strategies and stages that are involved in both child and adult second language acquisition.

In the meantime, however, it is not outlandish to propose that the observations offered here on the French competence of a young American boy, observations that in many instances are paralleled in studies of first language acquisition, suggest ways in which we as teachers of second languages can increase the learning that goes on in our classrooms. To summarize, these are as follows:

1. We should provide for semantic richness in early stages by letting our students learn the labels for all the things they want to know rather than put them off with talk of the importance of learning structures first, vocabulary later.

2. We should expect grammatical errors as the natural consequence of learning and exploring. Indeed, let us remember that *error* comes from the Latin *errāre, to wander, to explore*, from which we have the modern French verb *errer*.

3. We should provide for lots and lots of listening experiences, not that we may expect the learners to be able to reproduce everything they understand but that we may let them respond as they are able.

4. Whatever we do, we must do it in a meaningful context that involves the feelings and concerns of our students.

2.4 THREE AMERICANS IN PARIS: AN ETHNOGRAPHIC STUDY*

A persistent concern of second language researchers has been the documentation of L2 acquisition in natural environments, the study of "street learning" as it has been called to distinguish it from classroom learning. Documentation of L2 development, much of it on the model, if not of the scope, of Roger Brown's (1973) landmark study of L1 development, has been concerned primarily with the sequence of acquisition in terms of particular grammatical features. In tracing, so to speak, the *interlanguage* of the learner, L2 acquisition studies look for patterns of grammatical development. Is there a universal sequence? Does it resemble patterns of L1 acquisition? What is the relationship of rate of acquisition for different learners to learner error? What are the sources of errors—L1 interference, simplification or overgeneralization of L2 rules? Some of these studies have been longitudinal (on the Brown model) following one or

---

* This text first appeared in the *Modern Language Journal* (1981) and is reprinted with permission.

several learners over a period of time. Far more have been cross-sectional, contrasting data from different groups of learners at a particular point in time.

As promising and useful as these studies are, they do not afford a full view of the L2 acquisition process. Language *teachers* are perhaps the first to recognize that learner attitudes play the preeminent role in the development of competence in a second or foreign language. Important as it is to trace the acquisition of structure, attention must also be focused on the opportunities for interaction in the second language and on the use made of these opportunities by the learner. An analysis of the *occasions* for L2 use and the *attitudes* of the learner is of particular interest where the emphasis is on providing as "natural" a language learning environment as possible. In an environment where learners are expected to interact meaningfully in the language they are learning it is important to look at the *way* in which the learners interact.

The present study takes such an *ethnographic* approach to an analysis of the acquisition of French by three American children spending a year in Paris. In a sense it is an update of my 1974 report on a conversation with my seven-year-old son, Daniel, who at the time was just beginning to use French (see Section 2.3). The purpose of the earlier report was to contrast the skills Daniel had acquired in what could be called a "natural" L2 learning environment with the kind of skills typically emphasized in beginning language courses.

Much has happened since 1974. Almost all new textbooks now talk about communicative goals, communicative competence, "real" language use. Language teachers have begun to expand the curriculum to include the opportunity for meaningful, spontaneous expression at beginning levels. And there seems to be a concern for creating the kind of a "natural" language learning environment described above. Daniel has also grown up. From his modest beginnings he is now a fluent speaker of French, and, perhaps more important to his father and me, he is as proud of his French heritage as he is of his American heritage.

It is Daniel's *pattern* of L2 use, in conjunction with the patterns of his two sisters, that is proposed as a useful perspective from which to look at classroom models in L2 programs. The "natural" setting of three L2 learners in Paris is of interest inasmuch as it represents what most language teachers concerned with communicative competence would view as an ideal language learning situation. In an immersion setting such as this one there is a *maximum amount of context*—that is, the learner is surrounded by the second language and uses it to convey meaning—and a *minimum amount of grammar explanation*. In sum, it is a 24-hour communicative classroom.* A better understanding of that environ-

---

* For some methodologists the situation described here would be more appropriately defined as *submersion*, the term *immersion* having come to mean the use of the L2 as a medium of instruction in an otherwise L1 environment. I am nonetheless uncomfortable talking about *submersion* in this instance because the expression lacks, for me, the suggestion of support and sustenance for learners as they begin to cope in a new environment.

ment can only lead to a better evaluation of what the classroom *can* and *should* provide. A comparison with the classroom seems even more compelling in light of the dilemma we currently face in setting goals for classroom foreign language programs. Considering all that we have yet to learn about the development of communicative competence—in school *or* in the street—a better understanding of what happens in an immersion situation of this kind should be of help in setting realistic goals for learner achievement and in evaluating classroom methods or materials that purport to be "communicative" or "natural."

In looking at the acquisition of French by my three children I decided early in the year not to attempt to trace the development of grammatical features. I made this decision for several reasons. First, I was well aware that the process of data collection is not only tedious but the variables are so numerous—age, native language, contact with the L2, to name just a few—as to make interpretation of findings at best speculative. Second, I was frankly afraid of interfering with the acquisition process. My primary concern was that my children enjoy their French experience, make friends, have fun. For this to happen it was important that I do nothing that might be interpreted as a preoccupation with language development. I was specifically concerned lest the weekly or so recording sessions required for the documentation of syntactic features reveal how involved I was with language, and that this might make the process much more self-conscious and perhaps even lead to competitiveness among the children. Third, and at the same time, I was aware of something much more important happening. The result is the present report.

Our Paris experience came about as a result of my husband's decision to direct our University of Illinois Study Abroad Program. We set out not without apprehension. Could we get used to big city apartment living? How would the children fare in school? We were particularly concerned about Daniel who was to be a high school freshman. The school where he had been accepted made it clear that he would have to take all classes at his grade level. There was no provision for regrouping for special subjects such as French where he would have more difficulty. We had made our decision, however, to seek regular French classroom environments for all three children rather than to take advantage of either the many private bilingual schools in Paris or the public schools with special classes for recent immigrants. In addition to Daniel, age 14, there was Catherine, age 9, and Julie, age 8. Their formal learning in French at the time of our departure consisted of a summer of twice weekly private tutoring in grammar and reading for the girls and the equivalent of two semesters of beginning college French for Daniel. He completed the second semester with a grade of B the summer before we left.

As I look back at our adaptation I am aware of how well it fits the classical sociological model of cultural adaptation described by H. Douglas Brown (1980b). Following an initial period of euphoria—isn't it great to be in France, great food, great scenery, lots of new things to explore—there was the sudden realization that we were not at home, and that we, not the French, were the ones who were going to have to adapt. A couple of anecdotes will serve, I think, to illustrate the impact of this realization.

The first day of school Daniel met in the school courtyard with the one hundred or so other students at his grade level. The school director called out names, and students stood and indicated which class they were in. Things were going smoothly until "Savignon" was called. Daniel stood up, announced his class, and was immediately and smartly reprimanded for daring to address the director with his hands in his pants pockets! We learned of the incident later in the day when Daniel came home and announced that that did it! He wasn't setting foot back in school! Meanwhile, in another school courtyard, his sister Catherine, whose name had inadvertently been omitted from the class roster, was standing in tears, unable to explain to a concerned teacher why she hadn't gone with her class.

These incidents are cited to show that all did not go smoothly and that there was plenty of opportunity for *anomie*, a feeling of alienation, to arise as the children pursued their acquisition of French. According to Lambert's (1963) theory of L2 acquisition, it is precisely at the moment of greatest alienation that success in the experience is determined. Either learners retreat to their native culture and, consequently, fail to acquire the L2, or they resolve their feelings of anomie and go on to become bilingual.

Not only were there many sources of frustration, anxiety, and anger for the children, who faced linguistic as well as cultural barriers, there were such sources for their parents as well. There were also the good times when we were given preferential treatment as Americans. Our response to all this was to band together as a family and to provide an emotional security at home that would help us to cope with the newness of the world around us. Although we were eager that our children learn French, my husband and I made no demands or even suggestions that they use French with us at home. To do so, we sensed, would have created a source of tension between us and the children and rendered impossible the very family closeness we needed to create. On the other hand, once in a francophone environment my husband and I began to use French increasingly between ourselves. These patterns were to change, however, as the year progressed.

The patterns of French-language use that ultimately emerged during the year can be described as four distinct stages.

In Stage I (August–December) the parents spoke a combination of French and English to each other, but they spoke English to the children. The children spoke English to each other. English was maintained by the parents at home to provide security at the time of immersion in the francophone environment.

Stage II (December–April) was brought about by a further immersion. This time we traveled to a family vacation camp in Senegal with a number of other families, all of whom were French speaking. As we began eating meals and mingling on a daily basis with many other French speakers, the family nucleus broke up. When we came together again at the end of the two-week period, French had become the natural channel of communication between parents

THE EMERGENCE OF L2 COMMUNICATION

English - - - - - -
French ————

Stage I

Mom
Dad
Julie
Daniel
Catherine

Stage II

Mom
Dad
Julie
Daniel
Catherine

Stage III

Mom
Dad
Julie
Daniel
Catherine

Stage IV

Mom
Dad
Julie
Daniel
Catherine

and children. By this time, also, the communicative strategies of the children were sufficiently developed to allow this communication.

Stage III (April–August) emerged somewhat more gradually. It began in certain limited contexts and spread until by mid-April the children were using French exclusively with each other. Their use of French among themselves began with discussions at the dinner table and came to include not only their private discussions but their games and all the taunts and squabbles typical of a growing family. This third stage lasted until we left France in August 1979.

Stage IV (August 1979–Present) represents the continuation of Stage III channels of communication in an anglophone environment. Although the children now speak English in the outside world, their most intimate transactions take place in French.

The following summary statements can be made about L2 input and output for the children during the year:

Exposure to natural language

1. Input is not all "meaningful." However, there are numerous contextual cues to meaning.
2. There is a gradual increase in output.
3. There is a maximum use of coping strategies to survive in the outside world. (Catherine's response, for example, when asked on the first day of school who she was and why she hadn't gone to class, was: *"Je ne sais pas, je ne sais pas, je ne sais pas. . . ."*)

Language learning activities

1. Reading and writing tasks are everyday class activities. It would be wrong to say there is no formal language instruction in a natural environment of this kind.
2. There is no systematic speaking or listening practice. The L2 is simply the medium of interactions of all kinds.
3. There are no contrastive studies, such as translation or grammar explanations, that take into account the L1.

The most noteworthy feature in these patterns is, of course, the gradual adoption of French until it becomes the language of the most intimate interpersonal relations with parents and siblings.

As language teachers, the question we now have to ask is "How successful was the experience?" The fact of the children's now daily use of French for communication stands out as the most obvious mark of success. The children have very positive feelings about French and France. They write letters to French friends. They seek out other French speakers in the community. Maintenance of L2 use, then, stands out as the first criterion of success.

A second criterion of success is functional language skills. What can the learners *do* in French? The best measure here is the children's academic success. All three completed the year's work and were promoted to the next grade or level. They also made friends in French and demonstrated an ability to function in a variety of social settings. They could answer the telephone, run errands, make polite conversation. The above measures are valid indicators of communicative competence and ones that we should set for L2 programs of all kinds.

The third criterion is the linguistic competence of the children. How is their syntax, spelling, pronunciation, vocabulary? Is it distinguishable from a native speaker's? The conversation transcribed as follows lets the children speak for themselves.

Maman: Bonsoir, Daniel.

Daniel: Bonsoir, Maman.

Maman: Je crois que la dernière fois que j'ai eu une conversation en-
           registrée avec toi tu avais sept ans.

Daniel: Ah oui, cela est vrai.

Maman: Est-ce que tu te rappelles de ça?

Daniel: Oui.

Maman: Nous étions à Viriville cet été là et tu venais à peine d'apprendre
           le français et commençais à parler un petit peu. Tu as bien
           accepté de parler avec moi.

Daniel: Oui, je parlais très peu mais je parlais quand-même.

Maman: Oui. Est-ce que tu peux nous dire un peu ce que tu fais. Enfin je
           sais que nous venons de fêter tes seize ans.

Daniel: Oui.

Maman: Est-ce que tu peux nous dire ce que tu fais cette année comme
           programme d'études et . . . comment va ta vie?

Daniel: Ah, ben, je fais beaucoup de science et de math et j'étudie pas
           mal la grammaire anglaise aussi et l'histoire du monde vers le
           commencement, uh . . . des âges classiques et . . . ma vie va
           très bien à vrai dire.

Maman: Tu peux parler un peu de tes soeurs?

Daniel: Ben, j'ai deux soeurs, la plus vieille qui s'appelle Catherine qui a
           douze ans et la deuxième qui s'appelle Julie qui a onze ans
           et . . . elle sont très gentilles.

Maman: Est-ce qu'elles parlent français aussi?

Daniel: Oh oui très bien. D'ailleurs, uh . . . elles parlent mieux que
           moi.

Maman: Tu crois qu'elles parlent mieux que toi?

Daniel: Ah oui, je pense.

Maman: Pourquoi cela? Qu'est-ce qui te fait dire cela?

Daniel: Ben, elles ont eu peut-être plus de pratique pendant l'année
           qu'on a passée en France . . . et je pense que dans le cas de
           Catherine elle a beaucoup lu . . .

Maman: Oui

Daniel: . . . plus que moi aussi . . .

Maman: Oui.

Daniel: . . . alors je crois qu'au moins Catherine s'est entraînée un peu
           plus dans la langue française que moi et puis leur accent est
           mieux aussi.

Maman: Tu crois?

Daniel: Je pense oui.

Maman: Est-ce que ça te gêne?

Daniel: Non, pas du tout. Je m'accepte comme je suis.

Maman: Est-ce que tu aimes parler français?

Daniel: Oui, beaucoup. C'est un plaisir de parler ce soir d'ailleurs, comme ça.

Maman: Et est-ce que tu peux m'expliquer comment tu te sens maintenant que tu parles français avec tes deux soeurs parce que avant de partir en France nous parlions à la maison toujours anglais et maintenant que nous sommes de retour vous continuez à parler non seulement français avec vos parents mais aussi avec . . . entre vous les enfants?

Daniel: Oui, ça est devenu un rite disons uh . . . je sens bizarre si je parle anglais à Catherine ou à Julie . . . ça s'est développé comme ça. Puis il y a une genre de fierté dedans aussi . . . une puissance qui vient avec . . . que je peux parler avec Catherine ou Julie dans la rue et puis personne ne comprenne quoi c'est . . . ça donne un peu de super, quoi . . . on sent bien quoi.

Maman: Tu te sens un peu supérieur?

Daniel: C'est ça. Plus spécial quoi. On sent bien.

Maman: Oui. Est-ce tu crois que . . . quelle est la réaction de tes camarades de classe quand ils savent que tu parles français ou qu'ils t'entendent parler français?

Daniel: Ben je crois que ça les impressionne . . . dès qu'on leur dise que je sais bien parler français couramment ils veulent toujours que je leur dise quelque chose en français . . . Comment est-ce qu'on dit cela . . . ou juste simplement "Dis quelque chose en français!" Alors là c'est toujours dur. On ne sait pas quoi dire quoi. C'est . . . c'est un peu gênant.

Maman: Oui. Tu penses faire quelque chose avec le français dans ta vie?

Daniel: Ben, j'aimerais peut-être m'installer quelque part en Europe oui. Si ça aiderait ou non je ne sais pas . . . peut-être en Canada aussi, je ne sais pas. On ne sait jamais . . . oui je pense que ça aurait un effet.

Maman: Uh . . . ta petite soeur Julie est là avec nous ce soir. Je ne sais pas si elle aimerait peut-être parler un peu au micro.

Julie: Oui.

Maman: Tu aimerais dire quelque chose, Julie?

Julie: Ah oui . . . je voulais dire que moi aussi je suis un peu fière de parler français dans la rue quand personne ne te comprenne

mais alors comme ici on habite à l'Université où il y a beaucoup
de gens qui parlent français il y a des fois qu'on parle français
avec toi . . . uh ma mère . . . ou bien Daniel . . . um il y a
quelqu'un à côté de nous qui comprend le français . . . ben
. . . ben ça gêne un peu qu'il comprend.

Maman: C'est vrai? Tu t'es trouvée gênée des fois parce que tu m'as dit
des choses que tu voulais que personne n'entende et puis tu t'es
rendue compte que quelqu'un t'avait comprise?

Julie: Oui.

Maman: Tu peux nous dire un peu ce que tu fais?

Julie: Ben . . . à l'école?

Maman: Oui . . . ou . . . à l'extérieur . . . avec des amis, ce qui t'in-
téresse dans la vie.

Julie: Ben . . . à l'école j'aime beaucoup les math . . . je travaille surtout là-dessus et . . . uh . . . ben . . . à la maison quand je
rentre je travaille mon violon . . . je fais plutôt . . . c'est surtout
ça que je fais, mon violon.

Maman: Tu aimes ton violon?

Julie: Oui.

Maman: Tu travailles beaucoup ton violon?

Julie: Oui.

Maman: Combien est-ce que tu travailles?

Julie: Ben . . . j'essaie de faire deux heures, des fois même trois
heures, ça depend.

Maman: C'est beau. C'est beaucoup.

Julie: Oui, je sais.

Maman: Oui. Et qu'est-ce que tu penses faire quand tu seras grande,
dans la vie?

Julie: Uh . . . je ne sais pas . . . je veux peut-être être violoniste
. . . peut-être uh . . . docteur, je ne sais pas.

Maman: Eh bien, tu as le temps de décider en tout cas.

Julie: Oui.

Maman: Est-ce que tu aimerais poser des questions à Daniel?

Julie: Ah . . . je ne sais pas quoi lui poser.

Maman: Est-ce que tu es contente de parler français avec lui ou est-ce
que tu trouves ça un peu bizarre maintenant que tu habites
aux Etats-Unis et . . . ?

Julie: Non, moi j'aime bien. J'aime bien habiter ici mais toujours
parler français, parce que . . . ça fait comme si on était en

France mais . . . mais comme on est toujours en Amérique.

Maman: Oui.

Julie: On fait des choses ici . . . comme Papa est français on fait des choses ici un peu au . . . à la française quoi.

Maman: Tu aimes ça?

Julie: Oui.

Maman: Bon. Alors on n'a pas eu une discussion avec Catherine parce qu'elle n'est pas là ce soir. Où est-ce qu'elle est?

Julie: A la bibliothèque, je pense.

Maman: Bon alors, merci beaucoup de cette entrevue. Vous êtres très gentils. Je crois que c'est l'heure d'aller vous coucher bientôt maintenant, n'est-ce pas?

Julie: Ben oui.

Maman: Quelle heure est-il?

Daniel: Ben il est neuf heures cinq.

Maman: Oui ben alors effectivement il est l'heure d'aller se coucher. Allez. Bonne nuit tout le monde. Au revoir.

Daniel: Bonne nuit.

Julie: Bonne nuit.

The salient features of this conversation are its comprehension, fluency, ease, and nativelike pronunciation. The accent is of course an important concern and, like fluency and ease, cannot be evaluated from a transcription of this kind. The reaction of the French linguist Albert Valdman on hearing the tape recording is therefore pertinent. He characterized Julie's accent as "decidedly Parisian," whereas Daniel's was French with no particular regional quality. The children's positive feelings come through, however, even in the written version. All are happy to use French and use it with varying degrees of skill.

If we wanted to look for grammar errors there are lots to find. *Commencement des âges classiques, la plus vieille (= l'aînée), une genre, et puis personne ne comprenne, dès qu'on leur dise, en Canada,* and *je sens bizarre* are among the more obvious. Daniel is aware that his accent and grammar are perhaps not so good as Catherine's, in particular, who is a bookworm and keen grammarian. Furthermore, Julie and Catherine both have their own distinguishable style of speech. Julie, for example, was characterized by her violin teacher in Paris as affecting the elitist, sophisticated style associated with the "Madeleine" quarter of Paris, whereas Catherine had the forthright down-to-earth manner of the popular district around the Gare de Lyon.

Without going into an analysis of the children's written communicative competence, the following note provides just one example of the kinds of messages I find on my kitchen table when I return from work.

GETTING A MESSAGE ACROSS

> Chère Maman,
>
> Je suis chez Cynthia, J'ai
> bien travaillé et je
> pense que sa vas allér.
> (sa aller très & dois j'ai
> regardé dans ton miroir!)
> Je t'aime,
> Julie.

The message may not be clear out of context. It has to do with violin practicing and efforts to keep a straight bow. What is important to me is that Julie takes advantage of one of the few opportunities she has to write in French. She takes risks and never sticks to what is sure.

How can we summarize from this brief report of the experiences of three Americans in Paris? The lesson for those of us who would like to prepare our students to communicate in a second language appears to be threefold. First, we have to recognize the differences in environment. There is no way we can duplicate the L2 community in our classroom. In the "street" the opportunity for language experience is infinite, unlimited by the textbook, the knowledge of the teacher, or the time of day. We have to face this fact in reaching a decision on how best to spend the time and expertise we *do* have available to us. Perhaps more important, we need to view the L2 acquisition process as one that takes students from classroom to street and back again to classroom. Levels of competence wax and wane with changes in exposure and emphasis. We need to analyze the occasions for L2 use in the learners' environment, and we need to help them successfully integrate those occasions into their language program. The role of the teacher as well as the role of the classroom depends on this analysis.

Second, we must acknowledge that the classroom has traditionally focused on linguistic competence. It may even be true, as Valdman and Moody (1979) have suggested, that native speakers *expect* classroom learners to speak with linguistic precision. Yet intelligent and successful L2 users give other accounts of how they learned to communicate. I am grateful to Ruth Crymes (1980) for sharing this verbatim report of a famous L2 learner, Margaret Mead:

> I am not a good mimic and I have worked now in many different cultures. I am a very poor speaker of any language, but I always know whose pig is dead, and when I work in a native society, I know what people are talking about and I treat it seriously and I respect them and this in itself establishes a great deal more rapport, very often, than the correct accent. I have worked with other field workers who were far, far better linguists than I, and the natives kept on saying they couldn't speak the language, although they said I could! Now, if you had a recording it would be proof positive I couldn't, but nobody knew it! You see, we don't need to teach people to speak like natives, you need to make the other people believe they can, so they can talk to them, and then they learn.

It is interesting to me to note the number of times that both French and Americans have commented on how nice it is that our children are "bilingual." The phrase *perfectly bilingual* has been used several times, perhaps to underscore what "bilingual" continues to mean in the minds of laymen: a parallel or identical competence in two languages. And yet the brief oral and written samples I have given are ample evidence of linguistic imperfections. The dilemma we face in the evaluation of student performance is clearly far from resolved.

Third, we do not know enough about L2 development at this point to advocate either a "communicative syllabus" or a "natural method." Any deliberate reduction of materials, that is, of language input, or stylization of the teacher's role—particularly if that role is unnatural to the teacher—may not be in the best interest of the learner. Perhaps our best strategy is to *prepare learners for street learning and encourage them in it*. We can do this best by not getting in the way of acquisition, by not deliberately limiting learner contact with the L2, while at the same time providing learners with a systematic presentation of the linguistic structure of the language. More important than the analysis of linguistic structure, however, is the presence of *role models*, people who use the language to communicate. A teaching staff that routinely use the L2 in exchanges among themselves is ideal. Native-speaker visitors, exchange students, shortwave or even local radio stations all provide further access to language. They serve not only to show the range of the L2 in actual use, they provide the learner with the opportunity to do lots and lots of listening.

Finally, we should encourage the development of both linguistic competence and communicative competence, recognize the difference between the two, and be flexible enough in our evaluations to provide for a variety of learner strategies. Some measure of communicative competence is attainable by all who seek it. It is up to us to encourage them along the way.

2.5. A FINAL WORD ON
L2 ACQUISITION

This chapter has approached L2 acquisition studies from the broad or wide-angle interactional perspective provided by the observation of human communication in a variety of contexts. These contexts may include any number of the many variables that combine in kaleidoscopic fashion to reflect patterns of language acquisition. Contexts may occur naturally, as in examples of street learning, or they may be manipulated as part of an experimental design. Time of observation is an additional variable. Studies of language learning, like studies of language, may be either cross-sectional (or *synchronic*), that is, concerned with events existing at a particular point in time, or they may be longitudinal (or *diachronic*), concerned with selected phenomena as they change over time. Methods of research also vary. They include case studies of individual learning strategies as well as large group studies where individual patterns of acquisition are undiscernible in statistical reports of group averages.

Throughout all discussions of contexts and research methods, the emphasis has been on the need for an analysis of communicative intent, of language function in addition to language form, as a way to improve our understanding of the acquisition process. *The interpretation of meaning in a context that includes the shared experiences and activities of the participants is, as we have seen, an important part of this analysis.*

A discussion of L2 research would be incomplete, however, without at least briefly mentioning a quite different avenue of inquiry: the clinical examination of brain activity. *Neurolinguistic research* is concerned with the relationships between human language and neural, or nerve, systems. It may be thought of as representing the extreme opposite end of the broad, wide-angle view of language acquisition on which we have been focusing. Neurolinguists look at language function through a microscope, so to speak. Thus Selinker and Lamendella (1981) have used the term *microbehavioral* to describe this neurofunctional approach to the study of language acquisition. Subjects with speech disorders resulting from brain damage of various kinds have provided a major source of data in the exploration of the language functions of the brain. Patterns of recovery from *aphasia*, or loss of speech, in bilingual or multilingual patients in particular, have been observed by neurolinguists to test hypotheses regarding the existence of different kinds of bilingualism (Paradis 1977; Whitaker et al. 1981).

Although opinions differ about the potential value of neurolinguistic research for language teaching programs, language teachers and researchers should nonetheless be aware of the directions this research is taking. Here, no less than in other avenues of research, the need for responsible interpretation of findings cannot be overemphasized. Where claims for one or another approach to L2 teaching are based on biological evidence, it is important that this evidence be confirmed and its relevance demonstrated. Failure to do so may lead to the perpetuation of "scientific" views regarding L2 acquisition that have little basis in fact.

A not so distant case in point is the attention that was given the views of a well-known Canadian neurophysiologist, Wilder Penfield. In a 1953 address to the American Academy of Arts and Sciences, Penfield advocated early teaching of second language, basing his views in part on neurophysiological evidence of loss of brain plasticity at adolescence. Maturational changes in the brain, he reasoned, suggested a biological timetable for L2 learning, which should be taken into account in planning school curricula. Proponents of L2 instruction in the primary grades (FLES, as it was known in the United States) were delighted to hear these views from so eminent a scientist. In their enthusiasm some extended Penfield's propositions in such a way as to imply that L2 acquisition was physiologically impossible after the onset of puberty. Penfield's remarks were reprinted and widely distributed by the Modern Language Association of America (MLA).

Penfield's point, however, was *not* that adults cannot learn or acquire a second language; children simply have an easier time of it for both physiological and psychological reasons. In subsequent discussion he took care to note that what he termed the "direct" method of learning language can succeed even with adults. As evidence he cited the example of Joseph Conrad, the celebrated Polish-born author who learned English on a British ship as a young adult and went on to become one of the English language's most skillful stylists. (Were he writing today, Penfield might give the example of novelist Jerzy Kosinski, who learned English as an adult immigrant to the United States.) For Penfield, the "direct" or "mother's" method was "far more successful than the school-time learning of secondary language in the second decade of life (language education)" (1959:240). In his view the impetus for language learning in both children *and adults* should be "not to collect words nor to acquire language. It should be *to achieve success in games and problems and success in learning about life and delightful things*" (emphasis added) (1959:241).

Discussion of the relationship between brain maturation and language acquisition, both first and second, continues. Following Penfield, Lenneberg (1967) supported the view of a biologically *critical period* for L2 acquisition prior to the onset of puberty. There now seems to be general agreement, however, that whatever the role of *cerebral lateralization*—that is, the establishment of most language functions in the left hemisphere of the brain—this process has been completed by the age of about five (Krashen 1975). After this age the plasticity of the nervous system, its ability to compensate for left-hemisphere brain damage by shifting language functions to the right hemisphere, declines noticeably.

BRAIN HEMISPHERES

The sketch below shows some of the functions typically located in the right and left hemispheres of the adult brain, along with a popular test for hemispheric dominance.

Test Yourself

Here's how to tell which side of your brain is dominant: Determine which way your eyes turn while you are thinking. (A co-worker or friend can tell you.) If they swing right, chances are you're left-brained; if left, your right brain is probably dominant.

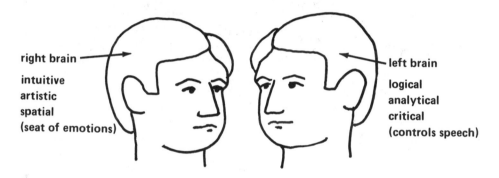

right brain
intuitive
artistic
spatial
(seat of emotions)

left brain
logical
analytical
critical
(controls speech)

The implications for language acquisition research are clear. Beyond the age of five the reasons for success or failure in L2 learning or acquisition must be sought not in terms of maturational factors alone but within a larger framework that includes *social*, *cognitive*, and *affective* factors as well. Continued advances in our understanding of the human brain, along with more comprehensive descriptions of the WHAT of language use, will no doubt continue to provide clues about the HOW of L2 acquisition.

SUGGESTED READINGS

D. Ausubel. 1964. "Adults vs. Children in Second Language Learning: Psychological Considerations." An influential article by a cognitive psychologist who criticizes certain features of the audiolingual approach for their incompatibility with effective learning processes in adults. Does not propose the elimination of pattern drills but recommends making them "meaningful."

J. Bruner. 1975b. "The Ontogenesis of Speech Acts." Emphasizes the importance of *joint experience* and *joint action* in the development of linguistic communication. Reports briefly on a pilot study that used videotape to record the interactions between a mother and her child for subsequent analysis in terms of language functions.

C. Burstall et al. 1974. *Primary French in the Balance.* A large-scale longitudinal study of French L2 achievement in British schools. Findings were interpreted as supporting the postponement of L2 study until late primary or secondary level. Burstall's 1975 paper, "French in the primary school: The British experiment," summarizes the earlier report.

J. Carroll. 1981. "Conscious and Automatic Process in Language Learning." Offers a unified theory of language learning. A restatement of the role of cognitive processes in habit formation with a good review of Skinnerian operant conditioning.

J. Chun. 1980. "A Survey of Research in Second Language Acquisition." A good introductory overview of recent research.

B. Edwards. 1979. *Drawing on the Right Side of the Brain.* A most enjoyable introduction to neurolinguistic investigations into cerebral lateralization and the functions of the right and left hemispheres of the brain. The author is an art teacher who has been able to improve her students' drawing ability dramatically through the use of exercises that encourage mental shifts from verbal, logical (left brain) thinking to a more global, intuitive (right brain) mode. Richly illustrated.

S. Felix. 1981. "The Effect of Formal Instruction on Second Language Acquisition." A comparison of the strategies of German high school students learning English as a second language in the classroom with the strategies of naturalistic learners. Marked differences in linguistic output are seen to result from classroom demands to use structures with which the learner is not yet comfortable. One result is the random selection of a structure from a given repertoire. (This study nicely complements the Garrett (1981) study cited in this chapter.)

N. Flanders. 1970. *Analyzing Teaching Behavior.* This book has provided a model for countless research projects having to do with classroom interaction analysis. Includes guides to coding verbal communication, which are of particular help to language teachers seeking to improve their classroom interaction.

E. Hatch (ed.). 1978. *Second Language Acquisition: A Book of Readings.* A representative collection of papers on L2 research including the editor's own paper, "Discourse Analysis and Second Language Acquisition." The volume concludes with a useful summary of additional studies, all based on empirical data, and with an extensive bibliography.

E. Hatch. 1980. "Conversational analysis: An Alternative Methodology for Second Language Acquisition Research." Uses conversational analysis to explain differences in learner success in children and adults. Offers some illustrations of discourse between native and nonnative speakers.

S. Krashen, M. Long, and R. Scarcella. 1979. "Age, Rate and Eventual Achievement in Second Language Acquisition." A comparison of the findings of numerous studies. Distinguishes between *rate* and *achievement* in accounting for apparent differences in adult and child acquisition in both *formal* and *informal* environments.

D. Larsen-Freeman (ed.). 1980. *Discourse Analysis in Second Language Research*. A collection of papers relating conversational analysis to learning and teaching a second language. Provides an excellent introduction to research-oriented attempts to document the nature of talk and relations between utterance form and discourse environment. Specific references are to ESL.

D. Larsen-Freeman. 1982. "The WHAT of Second Language Acquisition." Comprehensive overview of research directions from a discourse perspective. Extensive bibliography.

N. Naiman, M. Frolich, H. Stern, and A. Todesco. 1978. *The Good Language Learner*. An attempt to identify some of the important learner variables in L2 acquisition. Interesting collection of case studies that reveal a variety of learning strategies. Complements the empirical investigation of the relationship between learner characteristics and learning outcomes in a classroom environment.

C. Paulston. 1980. *Bilingual Education: Theories and Issues*. A useful exposition of the broad social issues underlying research in bilingual education. Helps to explain the apparent contradictions in findings and the limitations of comparisons of bilingual programs in different sociopolitical contexts.

S. Savignon. 1972. *Communicative Competence: An Experiment in Foreign Language Teaching*. A small-scale comparative study that succeeded in demonstrating the importance of communicative practice in the development of functional skills. Describes teaching strategies and tests for a communicative approach.

G. Scherer and M. Wertheimer. 1964. *A Psycholinguistic Experiment in Foreign Language Teaching*. An early attempt to demonstrate that audiolingual methods are superior to grammar-translation methods. The results were disappointing for proponents of audiolingualism.

D. Slobin. 1971. *Psycholinguistics*. Good introduction to the methods and implications of the psychological study of language and speech. Includes discussions of grammar theories, child language development, and language and cognition.

P. Smith. 1970. *A Comparison of the Cognitive and Audiolingual Approaches to Foreign Language Instruction: The Pennsylvania Foreign Language Project*. A controversial, large-scale study comparing teaching methods in Pennsylvania secondary schools. A confounding of variables contributed to the failure of one approach to appear superior. For a series of critiques of the research design and the conclusions drawn from the data, see the October 1969 issue of the *Modern Language Journal*; see also J. Carroll (1969).

H. Stern. 1976. "Optimal Age: Myth or Reality?" A very readable and intelligent discussion of the maturational issue in curriculum planning. Contrasts the Burstall et al. findings (1974, cited above) with Penfield's thesis of a biological timetable for language learning.

RESEARCH AND DISCUSSION

1. Compare Penfield's views concerning the "direct method" of language learning with those of Montaigne cited in Chapter 1. What are the implications of their views for school programs?

2. Make arrangements to observe an L2 classroom. Note the language interaction (1) between learners and (2) between learners and teacher in terms of the following: language *code* (L1 or L2), *teacher talk* vs. *learner talk, correction of structural errors, authenticity* of language in terms of its use to convey meaning. Better yet, arrange with a classmate or colleague to visit a class *together*. Compare notes. (If facilities permit, videotape a class for subsequent analysis.)

3. Look at a recent issue of *Language Learning, TESOL Quarterly, The Modern Language Journal,* or another L2 professional journal. How many articles are reports of research? What questions do they ask? What research methodologies do they use? Do they include a statement of implications for classroom teaching?

4. Think of a particular language learning environment, perhaps a classroom in which you are a teacher or student. How many variables can you list that affect the progress or success of individual learners? What is the *relative* importance of the textbook? the teacher?

5. Can you think of a situation where street learners—those who had "picked up" the L2 in an informal setting—found themselves in a class with those who had studied the L2 exclusively in a formal or classroom setting? Did the difference in learners' previous experience emerge in class activities? What were the reactions of the two groups of learners?

6. Language learning has frequently been compared to learning how to swim or play a musical instrument. What parallels do you see? If you are a musician, you might like to study the writings of Shinichi Suzuki (1969), the revered Japanese violin teacher, and compare the issues he raises with those in language learning.

7. Look at one or more comparative studies of L2 achievement. What were the criteria of evaluation; that is, how was "success" in language study defined?

8. Summarize the findings of the classroom study described in Section 2.2 in terms of (1) the proportion of time allotted to communicative activities for each group and (2) the relative achievement of each group by assessing *both* communicative competence and grammatical (linguistic) competence. What support do these findings give to the view that the encouragement of learner self-expression at beginning levels of instruction does not hinder and may actually encourage the development of grammatical accuracy?

9. How do acts of *writing* differ from most acts of *speaking* in terms of the opportunity for conscious attention to form? What are the implications of this difference for language teaching?

10. Consider the observation that in the beginning stages Daniel's French was marked by a "wide range of comprehension as compared to the level of production." What are the implications of this observation for classroom teaching? What is the inevitable consequence of forcing learners to speak before they are ready?

11. How would you characterize the differences in L2 acquisition between Daniel, Catherine, and Julie ("Three Americans in Paris")? What does the fact that all three children stayed at grade level tell you about their *relative* gains in French?

12. Compare the generalizations on age, rate, and eventual attainment in Krashen, Long, and Scarcella (1979) with the observations of the children's L2 attainment in "Three Americans in Paris." Are they consistent?

13. Assuming a *natural* L2 learning environment, that is, a community where the L2 is the language of communication, what are some of the obvious differences between children and adults in terms of the nature of their interaction with native speakers? Cite specific examples if you can. How are these differences likely to affect the rate of acquisition?

14. Describe your own L2 learning experience(s) with reference to the variables listed on page 57. Can you recall contexts in which you were particularly *happy* as a language learner? particularly *unhappy*?

15. Have you ever "lost" a language you once "knew"? Explain. If a learner's proficiency is evaluated at the end of a course of study, what does this evaluation tell us about the proficiency of the same learner three months later? three years later? Discuss with respect to the issue of language attrition raised in this chapter.

16. Write your own definition of *interlanguage* based on the discussion of the concept in Section 2.1 and on the examples in Section 2.3, "Talking With My Son."

Chapter 3

Learner Attitudes
and Interests

"Why, Huck, doan' de French people talk de same way we does?"
"No, Jim; you couldn't understand a word they said—not a single word."
"Well, now, I be ding-busted! How do dat comes?"
"I don't know; but it's so. I got some of their jabber out of a book. S'pose a man was to come to you and say Polly-voo-franzy—what would you think?"
"I wouldn't think nuffin; I'd take en bust him over de head . . ."
"Shucks, it ain't calling you anything. It's only saying, do you know how to talk French?"
"Well, den, why couldn't he say it?"
"Why, he is a-saying it. That's a Frenchman's way of saying it."
"Well, it's a blame ridicklous way, en I doan' want to hear no mo' about it . . ."
—Mark Twain, *The Adventures of Huckleberry Finn*

Huck Finn's beloved companion, Jim, would not make a very good language learner. His mind has been made up. Any way of talking other than his own is just plain "ridicklous." Jim's words may make us smile, but the attitudes they reveal are ones many of us have no doubt heard expressed before, perhaps in a not so amusing fashion. In this chapter we shall take a look at issues of learner, teacher, and community attitudes as they relate to L2 acquisition. Section 3.1 defines the term *attitude* and explores the interrelation of learner attitudes and L2 achievement. Section 3.2 looks in particular at teacher attitudes and their effect on program development. Section 3.3 describes the Language for Specific Purposes trend in curriculum development and gives examples of surveys used to determine learner needs and interests.

3.1. ATTITUDES
AND ACHIEVEMENT

Of the many variables in language acquisition considered in the preceding chapter, learner attitude is the most pervasive. If all the variables in L2 acquisition could be identified and the many intricate patterns of interaction between learner and learning context described, ultimate success in learning to use a second language would most likely be seen to depend on the attitude of the learner. We are a long way from such a complete description of L2 acquisition processes, however, so the above assertion can be neither proved nor disproved. Yet acquisition studies to date (for example, Gardner et al. 1976; Krashen 1981), as well as the experiences and intuitions of countless learners and teachers, point to the importance of attitude—or affective variables—over and above considerations of intelligence, aptitude, method, and time spent on learning. We learn what we want to learn. In L2 learning, as in any other kind of learning, there is a good deal of difference between what is available to be learned and what is learned.

Learners and Learning

Only the learner can do the learning. This is commonly observed in the classroom. A language teacher with more than 40 years of classroom experience told of his efforts to teach French prepositions with place names to an advanced grammar class. His exasperation was not unlike that of a novice teacher. It seems they had reviewed the rules with numerous examples: *au Mexique, au Canada, au Brézil,* but *à Chicago, à Montréal, à Londres.* Shortly thereafter, one class member announced that she was going to spend the weekend with her family *au Détroit.* "I finally told them," the teacher concluded with a sigh, "that there was no point in my telling them over and over. They weren't going to learn it until they decided they *wanted* to learn it."

Street learners are no different. Some quickly integrate the L2 environment and go on to develop the communicative skills they need to participate even more fully. Others may live in an L2 environment for years with no appreciable increase in L2 use. At a TESOL (Teachers of English to Speakers of Other Languages) international conference, an American teacher of English who had lived in Tokyo for the past seven years was having lunch with some former colleagues. He noted the din in the conference center. He was tired, he said, to be in the presence of so much talk, so many meanings converging on him at once—waitress's requests, loudspeaker announcements, conversation with companions, greetings from passersby, snatches of dialogue from adjoining tables. He explained that in Japan his daily existence was undisturbed by such intrusions. He neither spoke nor understood Japanese. He lived *submerged,* quite literally, *within* Japanese culture. Like a *submarine* he had a support system all his own. He and a handful of English-speaking acquaintances lived inside their own miniculture, closed to the L2 culture around them.

Measurement of Learner Attitudes

Webster's Third International Dictionary defines *attitude* as a physical, mental, or emotional *position*. The word derives, as does *aptitude*, from the Latin root *aptus*, meaning *suited* or *fitted*. In discussions of L2 learning, attitude has come to include *conscious mental position*, as well as a full range of often subconscious *feelings or emotions* (for example, security, self-esteem, self-identity, motivation). Together they are sometimes referred to as *affective variables*. (The issue of learner aptitude will be addressed more fully in Chapter 6.)

Affective variables play an important role not only in L2 acquisition but in L1 acquisition as well. The role of noncognitive factors, such as motivation and self-identity, in mother-tongue acquisition has been well documented through the research of sociolinguist William Labov (1965) and others, and is summarized by Hymes (1971:17) as follows:

> Sociolinguistic work recurrently finds that self-identity is crucial to differential competence and to heterogeneity of speech communities. . . . Failure to consider this goes together with the simplistic assumption that sheer quantity of exposure should shape children's speech. . . . Nonstandard speaking children in fact hear as much television and radio as other children and of course, hear their teachers all day. These facts puzzle some teachers; the point is that identification and motivation are what count, not exposure.

Hymes goes on to illustrate with the following anecdote: "At Columbia Point school in Boston in July 1968, after a discussion sparked off by these questions concerning exposure, the one black mother present later volunteered: 'You know, I've noticed that when the children play "school" outside, they talk like they're supposed to in school; and when they stop playing school, they stop.' "

A pioneer in the exploration of learner attitudes in relation to second language achievement is the Canadian psychologist Wallace Lambert. His identification of two types of *orientation—integrative* and *instrumental—*is well known and has led to some thought-provoking discussions of the contribution of these and other learner attitudes to achievement in various contexts (Gardner and Lambert 1972). To review, an *instrumental* orientation to learning stresses the *utilitarian* value of L2 proficiency, of which getting a pay raise or a better job or a good grade in school are examples. In contrast, an orientation is said to be *integrative* if it reflects an openness toward another culture group, an openness that may include *a desire to be accepted* as a member of that group. Related to this desire for acceptance is the notion of anomie, or a feeling of cultural alienation. The theory is that the more proficient one becomes in an L2, the more precarious one's place becomes in one's native culture. Drawing nearer to another culture through the acquisition of its language is accompanied by a sense of forsaking the familiar for the unknown. Successful bilingualism depends on the *resolution* of these feelings of social uncertainty and the *acceptance* of both cultures, not as conflicting but as parallel systems of values.

(See Section 2.4 for a discussion of this phenomenon with reference to a particular L2 learning situation.)

One problem in documenting the role of attitude in L2 learning is the difficulty in measuring the attitudes themselves. The development of attitude questionnaires, or scales, is by no means a simple task. Even those accepted as valid by experienced researchers are open to criticism. Are the learners expressing their *honest* feelings or merely ones they think are *acceptable*? Can one be sure the learner has interpreted the question as it was intended? Oller (1979), for example, has criticized attitude research on both counts, thus questioning the findings that have resulted. In response, Gardner (1980) has affirmed his confidence in the empirical validity of the scales on which his data are based. The debate among researchers is likely to continue.

An alternative approach to attitude measurement is of course to look not only at what people *say* but at what people *do*. Attitudes toward other culture groups are no doubt best reflected in the social contacts we make, the journals we read, the programs we support. It is one thing to *express* a value, another to *act* on that value. It is one thing to ask a group of learners to attend a social function hosted by members of a minority culture, and something else again to see how many actually show up. It is one thing for parents to endorse L2 programs in the schools, but it is quite another to vote the tax dollars needed to support them.

Attitudes: Cause and Effect

A further difficulty in attributing achievement to attitudes is the complexity of the cause and effect relationship. Do positive attitudes toward an L2 culture lead to L2 proficiency? Or does success in L2 acquisition, for whatever reason, lead in turn to positive feelings toward L2 acquisition, resulting eventually in positive feelings toward L2 culture? There is some evidence that initial success in L2 learning, at least in classroom settings *outside* the L2 culture, leads to positive attitudes and further success. In the classroom study summarized in Chapter 2 (Savignon 1972b), for example, it was found that among learners who initially had expressed no particular desire to learn French those who earned a grade of A or B were more likely to express a desire to continue their study. Similarly, a large-scale longitudinal study of French in British schools showed that "achievement variables have a more powerfully determining effect on later behavior than attitudinal variables. . . . This would suggest that the acquisition of foreign language skills and the development of attitudes toward foreign language learning during later years may be powerfully influenced by the learner's initial and formative experience of success or failure in the language learning situation" (Burstall 1975:399). In other words, nothing succeeds like success!

To judge from still other studies, increased L2 proficiency does not *necessarily* lead to more positive attitudes toward L2 culture. Learners residing in an L2 culture may find that, as they are able to participate more fully in the culture, they discover more things they dislike about it. Familiarity, as the saying goes, may breed contempt—or a *renewed sense of self*. Witness the following poignant journal entry:

> I just don't know what to do right now. I might have been *wrong* since I began to learn English, I always tried to be better and wanted to be a good speaker. But it was *wrong, absolutely wrong!* When I got to California, I started imitating Americans and picked up the words that I heard. So, my English became just like Americans. I couldn't help it. I must have been funny to them, because I am a Japanese and have my own culture and background. I think I almost lost the most important thing I should not have. I got California English including intonation, pronunciation, the way they act, which *are not* mine. I have to have *my own* English, be myself when I speak English. [Preston 1981:113]

Of course not all L2 learners share the feelings expressed above. Many take pride in passing unnoticed in the L2 culture, in being taken for a native speaker. The difference in attitude is a matter of context, perceived status of the L2 in relation to the L1, level of proficiency, and individual experience.

Although there is clearly disagreement on how best to measure attitudes and the cause and effect relationship between attitudes and achievement, there is unanimity on one point: *The teacher can teach but only the learner can learn.* The teacher can encourage the learner and provide *occasions* for acquisition, but it is up to the learner to make the most of these occasions.

Insights into the importance of attitudinal variables have understandably led teachers to look for ways of promoting positive feelings toward L2 culture. Many curricula now give attention to *small-c culture* (that is, day-to-day living patterns) as opposed to *capital-C culture* (usually the literary and artistic masterpieces of a civilization). In addition, field trips and exchange programs provide learners with cross-cultural experiences, which, it is hoped, will decrease their native ethnocentrism and increase their desire to learn the new language.

Such efforts have met with some success. However, the age of the learners, their past experiences, their home and community environment are among the important out-of-classroom variables that need to be taken into account in any attempt to influence attitudes toward another culture group. This is not to say that school programs that combine language teaching with cross-cultural experiences are not of value. To the contrary, these experiences are in many instances an integral part of language learning itself. Courses in culture alone, moreover, may provide a reasonable alternative to language study for some students. But the inclusion of culture should always be valued in its own right. It should never be viewed as a way to "motivate" learners, that is, to coax or prod them into acceptance of linguistic goals. This is all the more true where linguistic goals have been set by teachers or administrators without regard for the needs and interests of the learners themselves.

On the Other Side of the Desk:
Teacher Attitudes

Although it is helpful that we understand the learner from a psychosociological perspective, it is equally important that we attend to the *other side of the desk*, to the attitudes that teachers bring with them into the classroom. Curricular innovations may be prompted by learner interest or even demands, but they ultimately depend on teachers for their implementation. The perception teachers have of their role, their own L2 experiences and proficiency, and the self-selection process at work in academia that has put them in the position they occupy all influence the views teachers have of their goals. Not until we have taken a critical look at teachers' attitudes, both individual and professional, will we be ready to determine what obstacles still lie in the way of creating the kinds of learning environments that will be most helpful to our students.

Our problem in this connection is not only intramural. An article in *Flight Time* (April 1981), the magazine of Ozark airlines, spoke of the importance, for professional and leisure-time travelers, of learning to speak another language and stressed the need for American business to adapt to overseas demands in today's competitive market. A timely boost, or so it seemed, for the language teaching profession. The article went on to give some practical tips on how to go about choosing a program of study. College courses should be avoided, it cautioned, because they are *"slow and cumbersome, with unnecessary emphasis on grammar."* This criticism, which is heard all too often, represents a clear challenge to academic L2 programs.

ATTITUDES SOMETIMES DIFFER

Source: C. Hancock, "Student Aptitude, Attitude and Motivation," in D. Lange and C. James (eds.) *Foreign Language Education: A Reappraisal* (Skokie, Ill.: National Textbook Co., 1972), p. 144.

The teacher can teach, but the learners can walk away. And they often do. In the United States fewer than 18 percent of all public school students in grades 7–12 are studying a second language. Fewer than 2 percent ever reach the third-year level. These figures were reported by S. Frederick Starr in a background paper for the President's Commission on Foreign Language and Area Studies. "For the vast majority who quit after a year or two," says Starr, "the most enduring legacy of the experience is bitterness and frustration. Later, when such students find themselves on local school boards, they recall their unsuccessful learning experience, often to the detriment of language programs" (1979:39). Upon attending the annual meeting of the Modern Language Association, Fred Hechinger of the *New York Times* had his own observations to add (1979):

> The topics discussed by the language association illustrate much of what is wrong with modern-language scholarship: The field is concerned with practically everything except language—literature, sociology, psychology and a smattering of economics.
>
> Examples from the program: "The Development of Literary Consciousness in the 16th Century French Literature," "Cognitive Psychology and the Teaching of Literature," and, under the Foreign Language listing, a panel on "Historical Germanic Syntax: Methods and Results."
>
> Good scholarly topics all, but in the view of some foreign language experts, not the kind of academic model that encourages college-bound high school students to choose a foreign language. University faculty members engrossed in such scholarship are not likely to take much interest in teaching foreign languages to undergraduates or preparing foreign-language teachers.

But the times are changing, some will protest. College curricula now recognize goals other than literary criticism. Language courses are being redesigned to respond to a wider range of learner needs. Teachers no longer insist on beginning with structure drills ("I ate breakfast yesterday. I will eat breakfast tomorrow.") Communicative language teaching seems to have won the day. True. There are some promising initiatives and a new interest in L2 acquisition research on all levels. Yet recent reports on L2 teaching and research in university language departments in Canada (Stern 1981) and the United States (Schulz 1980) indicate that we have only just begun. Where changes have occurred they are minimal. And there are still many teachers—at the elementary, secondary, and college levels—who share the views on language teaching expressed by a prospective student teacher, a native speaker of Spanish. When asked what he hoped to gain from his teaching-methods course, he wrote the following: "I would like to learn the methods of teaching foreign languages, i.e., how to teach verbs, pronouns, articles, etc. because I will be doing my student teaching next semester and have had no previous methods course."

"Verbs, pronouns, articles, etc." were the structures he had come to equate with language. He had yet to understand that language is communication, and that the role of the language teacher is to help learners to get along in real-life situations, to find satisfaction in the discovery of other ideas and new ways to self-expression.

Community Values

Teachers are by no means solely to blame, of course, when L2 programs fail to find support. The perceived value of L2 study and support for programs reflects broad-based community and, ultimately, political and economic values. The school administrator who tells a language teacher that her fourth-year course will be combined with a study hall the following year "since it is mostly a reading and independent study program anyway" is reflecting those values.

Lack of support in one context may simply be a reflection of indifference. Elsewhere, a community may *deliberately limit* L2 acquisition to protect themselves against the perceived incursions of a rival language group. It is not uncommon for schools to teach languages while parents and peers actively *discourage* their use outside class. Listening to L2 radio broadcasts, for example, may be forbidden in the home.

On the other hand, a community may regard L2 acquisition as common-place and expect a functional use of two or more languages of *all* learners. The following dinner table conversation serves nicely to illustrate the importance of community support. A new mother was asking for advice on bilingual child-rearing. As an American who was planning to return with her husband to his native Iran, she wanted her daughter to grow up using both English and Farsi. The other guests, many of them graduate students from various countries in the world, discussed the pros and cons of one parent consistently using one language, the importance of role models, and the need at some point for peer support. They talked thus for some time, sharing experiences and insights, before an African teacher quietly intervened: "I believe you are making too much of a rather simple situation. My compatriot here," indicating the Senegalese gentleman on his left, "spoke both my language and his own by the age of five and was able to switch easily from one to the other as the situation required. When he went to school, he learned to use French in his studies. Later he learned Spanish and today he is a teacher of English."

In Senegal, as in many countries of the world, bilingualism is the norm and enjoys widespread support. Not everyone goes on to become a teacher of languages, of course, and the proficiency of the Senegalese gentleman was certainly exceptional and rightly admired. Yet some measure of communicative competence in more than one language is in many communities considered in no way unusual or difficult to attain.

In the absence of such widespread support, L2 teaching is more challenging to be sure. Yet there is evidence that when an effort is made to develop programs that respond to the interests and communicative needs of learners,

U.S. ATTITUDES TOWARD OTHER LANGUAGES

Community values in regard to second language learning and some problems with classroom programs are the subject of the following article by *New York Times* foreign correspondent Flora Lewis.

FOREIGN AFFAIRS

Speaking In Tongues

By Flora Lewis

There are countries in the world where language is the most divisive political issue. Belgium and Canada are racked by the argument, which reflects real rivalry for economic and social benefits.

In parts of the U.S. the problem is reaching similar proportions. Some demographers predict it won't be long before it's nationwide. The time for a sensible approach is before it starts tearing at the country's unity.

There seems to be a good deal more public awareness of most Americans' poverty in the resource of foreign language, and sometimes even their own, than appears on the surface. In November 1979, when the President's Commission on Foreign Language and International Studies presented its findings, it concluded that "Nothing less is at issue than the nation's security." It bemoaned "the complacent and defeatist attitude" of officialdom toward the nation's linguistic shortcomings: "Americans' incompetence in foreign languages is nothing short of scandalous, and it is becoming worse," the commission said. Then one more report was shelved.

It isn't surprising that at a time of sharp budget cuts that are going to affect many aspects of education and culture, support for language study is languishing. But the problem isn't just money, it's attitudes.

That shows in the conflict over "bilingualism" in areas with large Spanish-speaking populations. The term is turned on its head. Instead of the real meaning of fluency in two languages, it has come to be used as a euphemism for sticking to one's mother tongue.

It should be obvious nonsense to imagine that anybody gains when people can't understand each other. Babel didn't collapse because the workers couldn't communicate but because they didn't try to learn.

Gregory Jaynes once reported in The New York Times with delicious satiric insight about the quarrels of Western intelligence agents dumped in a delapidated town in Cameroon, ostensibly to watch the fighting across the river in Chad when Libyan troops took over. The Americans, he said, went about proclaiming that anybody in the world could understand English if it was shouted loudly enough.

The syndrome is widespread, and unattractive. English is the dominant and official language of the U.S., and of course every American needs to know it. Lack of ease in using it not only condemns people to second-class citizenship, with all that implies in terms of jobs, standing, access to the culture. It also weakens the sense of national identity and the sharing of values to which the country is dedicated.

But there is no reason why requiring that basic education be in English should exclude English-speaking Americans from other languages. Where a second language is widely used, as Spanish is in Florida and the Southwest, the shattered feeling of community would be immensely improved if all the other pupils were required to study Spanish. That would be more like bilingualism.

The emphasis of those who do urge the value of breaking out of the single-language mind-box is mostly on utility. The commission report stressed the need for language ability in defense, business abroad, foreign relations and research. True, these things are important. But it's a mistake to think languages are only good for certain careers and travel.

They are tools for enriching everyday life, as music, hobbies, sports add zest to humdrum existence. They open the door to enjoyment of humor, legend, drama, food, the wisdom of tradition, from another point of view, and therefore help broaden and brighten the mind.

Refusal to accept anybody else's language as worth knowing reflects the same narrow-gauge kind of head, the same stubborn ignorance, as that of the fundamentalist I heard about who denounced people speaking in other tongues, saying, "If English was good enough for Jesus Christ, it's good enough for them." The story is apocryphal in both senses.

Certainly, nobody can ever learn all the languages of the world. There are thousands. This argument for trying a few stems from considering only the immediate professional utility of multilingualism. It leaves out the fun and fantasy of having more than one track to think along.

And that is mainly what is wrong with the way Americans are taught foreign languages, as though they were computer programs. Along with the infinitives and subjunctives, maybe even before, should come the attractions. Perhaps a better way to start learning French is with a menu and recipes, German with an account of a soccer game, anything with news about familiar subjects.

Americans need to talk with the rest of the world and with each other. When we come to think of it as not just a chore and a conflict but as an adventure, like space with everybody going into orbit, we'll be safely launched.

Source: New York Times, February 4, 1982.

classrooms are filled and programs thrive. Faced with plummeting enrollments and the threat of extinction, some U.S. college programs have discovered a new clientele when courses were redesigned to emphasize practical professional and social L2 use. Indicative, for example, is a commercial option introduced in the Department of French at the University of Illinois (Urbana-Champaign) in 1978 that now attracts more than 50 percent of all undergraduate French majors. Other students combine business and conversational French with majors in commerce or engineering. Sims and Hammond (1981), in *Award Winning Foreign Language Programs*, offer an inspiring account of 50 programs on the secondary level that have flourished in spite of the discouraging national trend. The reason for the success of these programs is no secret. It lies in the attitudes of those who design and staff them. As teachers, we have an immediate stake in the future of our programs. Not only must we understand the societal values at large that influence learner attitudes, we must also take account of our own values and attitudes to see where they may be standing in the way of the curricular innovations that are needed.

3.2 ATTITUDE SURVEYS FOR TEACHERS

Foreign Language Attitude Survey for Teachers (FLAST)

The Foreign Language Attitude Survey for Teachers (FLAST) has been developed to help teachers discover their own attitudes and assumptions regarding L2 learning and teaching. It has been used in methods classes and in-service workshops to help participants focus on the way their values are reflected in teaching practices. This focus, in turn, provides a basis for the discussion of alternative views of language learning and the implications for language pedagogy. Though the survey was designed for use with foreign-language teachers in American schools (de Garcia, Reynolds, and Savignon 1976), the items are readily adapted for use in other contexts.

FOREIGN LANGUAGE ATTITUDE SURVEY FOR TEACHERS (FLAST)

DIRECTIONS: For each of the following questions decide whether you strongly agree, agree, have no opinion, disagree, or strongly disagree and check the appropriate box.

1. The grammar-translation approach to second language learning is not effective in developing oral communication skills.   strongly 0 0 0 0 0 strongly
agree   disagree

2. Mastering the grammar of a second language is a prerequisite to developing oral communication skills.   strongly agree   0 0 0 0 0   strongly disagree

3. When a foreign language structure differs from a native language, sometimes extensive repetitions, simple and varied, are needed to form the new habit.   strongly agree   0 0 0 0 0   strongly disagree

4. Generally the student's motivation to continue language study is directly related to his or her success in actually learning to speak the language.   strongly agree   0 0 0 0 0   strongly disagree

5. Gestures and other kinesics should be taught and evaluated as an integral part of language acquisition.   strongly agree   0 0 0 0 0   strongly disagree

6. A good foreign-language teacher does not need audiovisuals to build an effective program.   strongly agree   0 0 0 0 0   strongly disagree

7. Individualizing instruction is really not feasible in foreign language classes.   strongly agree   0 0 0 0 0   strongly disagree

8. It is important for students to learn rules of grammar.   strongly agree   0 0 0 0 0   strongly disagree

9. German and French are harder to learn than Spanish.   strongly agree   0 0 0 0 0   strongly disagree

10. Most proficiency goals set for high school students are unrealistic.   strongly agree   0 0 0 0 0   strongly disagree

11. Second language acquisition is most successful when based on an oral approach.   strongly agree   0 0 0 0 0   strongly disagree

12. It is of primary importance that student responses in the target language be linguistically accurate.   strongly agree   0 0 0 0 0   strongly disagree

13. Upper-level sequences of secondary school language instruction should concentrate on the study of literature and the refinement of written grammar and translation skills.   strongly agree   0 0 0 0 0   strongly disagree

14. The sound system of the foreign language should be taught separately and at the beginning of the first sequence of instruction.   strongly agree   0 0 0 0 0   strongly disagree

15. Taped lessons generally lose student interest.   strongly agree   0 0 0 0 0   strongly disagree

16. Ideally, the study of Latin should precede the study of a modern foreign language.   strongly agree   0 0 0 0 0   strongly disagree

17. Dialogue memorization is an effective technique in the process of learning a second language.   strongly agree   0 0 0 0 0   strongly disagree

18. One problem with emphasizing oral competence is that there is no objective means of testing such competence.   strongly agree   0 0 0 0 0   strongly disagree

19. One cannot teach language without teaching the culture.   strongly agree   0 0 0 0 0   strongly disagree

20. The teaching of cultural material in a second language course does not necessarily increase student motivation to learn to speak the language.   strongly agree   0 0 0 0 0   strongly disagree

21. An effective technique for teaching sound discrimination of a second language is to contrast minimal pairs.   strongly agree   0 0 0 0 0   strongly disagree

22. The language lab is most effective if used every day.   strongly agree   0 0 0 0 0   strongly disagree

23. Learning a second language requires much self-discipline.   strongly agree   0 0 0 0 0   strongly disagree

24. The teaching of listening and speaking skills should precede reading and writing.   strongly agree   0 0 0 0 0   strongly disagree

25. Pattern practice can provide meaningful context for learning to use the target language.   strongly agree   0 0 0 0 0   strongly disagree

26. The culture content of a language course should be geared to contrasting contemporary lifestyles and ways of doing things.   strongly agree   0 0 0 0 0   strongly disagree

27. The language lab is more beneficial for beginning language students than for students at advanced levels.   strongly agree   0 0 0 0 0   strongly disagree

28. Today's students won't take foreign languages because they don't want to work.   strongly agree   0 0 0 0 0   strongly disagree

29. Cultural contrasts and language skills are best taught and tested separately. strongly agree 0 0 0 0 0 strongly disagree

30. The ability to speak a language is innate; therefore, everyone capable of speaking a first language should be capable of learning to speak a second. strongly agree 0 0 0 0 0 strongly disagree

31. Students should master dialogues orally before reading them. strongly agree 0 0 0 0 0 strongly disagree

32. Cultural information should be given in the target language as much as possible. strongly agree 0 0 0 0 0 strongly disagree

33. The language laboratory is an invaluable aid for teaching and learning a second language. strongly agree 0 0 0 0 0 strongly disagree

34. Second language acquisition is not and probably never will be relevant to the average American student. strongly agree 0 0 0 0 0 strongly disagree

35. Students who do not read well can still be successful in learning to communicate in a second language. strongly agree 0 0 0 0 0 strongly disagree

36. Simulated real-life situations should be used to teach conversation skills. strongly agree 0 0 0 0 0 strongly disagree

37. To learn a second language, one must begin the study at an early age. strongly agree 0 0 0 0 0 strongly disagree

38. If language teachers used all the audiovisual equipment, materials, and techniques the experts say they should, there would be no time for eating and sleeping, much less teaching. strongly agree 0 0 0 0 0 strongly disagree

39. All students, regardless of previous academic success and preparation, should be encouraged, and given the opportunity, to study a foreign language. strongly agree 0 0 0 0 0 strongly disagree

40. Foreign-language teachers need not be fluent themselves to begin to teach effectively for communication. strongly agree 0 0 0 0 0 strongly disagree

41. One of our problems in teaching a second language is that we try to make learning "fun" and "a game." strongly agree 0 0 0 0 0 strongly disagree

42. Students should answer a question posed in the foreign language with a complete sentence.   strongly agree   0 0 0 0 0   strongly disagree

43. Pattern practice is an effective learning technique.   strongly agree   0 0 0 0 0   strongly disagree

44. Students who have problems with English should not take foreign language classes.   strongly agree   0 0 0 0 0   strongly disagree

45. The establishment of new language habits requires extensive, well-planned practice on a limited body of vocabulary and sentence patterns.   strongly agree   0 0 0 0 0   strongly disagree

46. When a student makes syntactical errors, this should be accepted by the teacher as a natural and inevitable part of language acquisition.   strongly agree   0 0 0 0 0   strongly disagree

47. If L1 teachers taught grammar as they should, it would be easier for us to teach a second language.   strongly agree   0 0 0 0 0   strongly disagree

48. Language learning should be fun.   strongly agree   0 0 0 0 0   strongly disagree

49. One can exchange ideas spontaneously in a foreign language without having linguistic accuracy.   strongly agree   0 0 0 0 0   strongly disagree

50. Most language classes do not provide enough opportunity for the development of conversation skills.   strongly agree   0 0 0 0 0   strongly disagree

The responses are not meant to be scored in any way. The answers teachers give will depend on their interpretation of the questions as well as on their second language learning and teaching experiences. A *comparison* of responses, however, will reveal the *differences* in attitude among teachers working together, presumably toward similar goals. An exploration of these differences is the first step toward clarification of program goals and the ways in which they can best be met.

Building a Climate of Trust

Communicative language teaching requires a sense of *community*—an environment of trust and mutual confidence wherein learners may interact without fear or threat of failure. Good teachers have long recognized the value of community in all learning environments and have found ways to encourage group cohesiveness and responsibility. Communicative language teaching depends on these traits. Without community there can be no communication.

Community Language Learning (CLL), a teaching strategy in the humanistic tradition of psychologist Carl Rogers (1951, 1967) and described by priest/psychologist Charles Curran (1972, 1976, 1978), offers a useful example of the concern for community. In what he has called a *counseling-learning* approach to teaching, Curran emphasizes the *affective* needs of the learner. His model involves the teacher as a person, an interested person who has the resources to help class members say whatever it is they want to say. He contrasts this supportive model with the role of the teacher/knower in a conventional classroom:

> Creative communication involves not an expression of the segmented self but a total openness of the self. Such communication would have to be present in an authentic community. Community also suggests the genuine engagement of the knower-teacher in the classroom as a part of the learning community. Our present intellectualized model of learning has removed the teacher from any relationship with the learner, other than an abstractive intellectualized one. A nonincarnate god-figure seems to be the dominant image by which the teacher presently relates to the group. [1972:30–31]

Students involved in Community Language Learning cite a freedom from tension, a freedom to communicate similar to that which emerged in the Savignon (1972b) research on teaching for communicative competence. Crucial to these feelings, in both instances, is the absence of the teacher as judge and the replacement of an emphasis on grammatical forms with a concern for helping students to express their own thoughts.

As we seek ways to build community, to create a climate of trust favorable to learning, and to strike a delicate balance between leadership and permissiveness, the following questions may help. They are taken from a guide to values clarification in the classroom (Simon and Clark 1975:56). (The meaning of the term *values clarification* and the influence it has had on L2 teaching techniques will be discussed in Chapter 5.)

BUILDING A CLIMATE OF TRUST

1. Am I worthy of trust?
2. Do I keep youthful confidences as a sacred trust?
3. Do I really *like* these kids with whom I work?
4. Am I a real person? Am I trying to be self-actualized?
5. Do I share my own dreams, or do I sit on a high and distant plane looking down from experience, ego or authority?
6. Do I have something real to contribute?
7. Do I direct imperiously or do I lead democratically?

8. Am I obsessed as a teacher with subject matter, rather than with the individual?

9. Do I *expect* my students to get into trouble or do the wrong thing?

10. Can I feel comfortable in making a mistake?

11. Can I find something to like in each individual with whom I work?

12. Can I truly trust both youth and adults?

13. How far do I go in setting a personal example?

14. Am I consistent in living what I teach?

As the authors point out, a perfect score on all 14 questions might mean that a person is no fun to live with! Yet positive answers to most are needed for trust to be present.

3.3 IDENTIFICATION OF LEARNER NEEDS AND INTERESTS

Communicative language teaching begins with an identification of the needs and interests of the learners. Learner needs may be *immediate* and *specific*, as in the case of university students enrolled in a specialized course of studies, adult immigrants, guest workers, or technicians being sent to train personnel in another culture; or they may be *nonimmediate* and *varied*, as in the case of learners in traditional school programs. Many learners, in fact, come to school programs not with any communicative needs at all but rather out of curiosity and an interest in discovering more about the world about them. In all cases the needs and interests of the learners can be defined and programs designed to meet them. Curriculum design, in whatever context, begins with needs assessment.

Language for Specific Purposes

Language for Specific Purposes is the name generally given to programs developed in response to specific adult occupational or social needs. The range of programs is wide indeed according to the contexts in which the learner will be required to use the L2. The emphasis may be on oral communication for basic survival, it may be on business correspondence, or it may be on the interpretation of technical writing in a specialized field. There is no limit to the specificity of the task so long as it responds to the L2 goals of the learner.

English for Specific Purposes (ESP), in particular, has become a strong trend in L2 teaching today. English for airplane pilots, nurses, economists, lawyers, restaurant managers, automobile mechanics, and tourists are all examples of ESP. A large subgroup within these specialized programs has to do with the communicative uses of English in the fields of science and technology. This study of scientific English has become known as EST (English for Science and Technology). Another, somewhat overlapping, subgroup is English for Academic Purposes (EAP). ESL programs to meet specific *vocational* needs (for example, airplane pilots, police, bank clerks) are sometimes referred to as VESL.

The proliferation of acronyms to refer to L2 programs of all kinds reflects the significant effort being devoted worldwide to the development of materials and the creation of courses to meet an array of specialized goals. Some of this effort occurs within academic settings. Much does not. With what is perhaps increasing frequency, business and government groups are turning to private language schools or to their own teams of specialists to provide the materials and the on-the-job practical L2 training they require.

Goals for General L2 Programs

There remain many second language learning contexts, of course, where learner needs are neither immediate nor apparent. Secondary school and even college or university students often have no immediate use for L2 skills. Their career goals may be as yet undetermined, and there may be no way of anticipating the eventual use to which they will put their knowledge of another language. Some learners may enroll in L2 courses for the purely *instrumental* purpose of meeting university entrance or graduation requirements. For learners on the secondary and elementary school levels, L2 study may simply be a required component of the general curriculum.

Where L2 study is required, learners' success will depend on the extent to which they share the values and goals of the community that is prescribing their studies. Where learners have a *choice*, their progress will depend on the ability of the program to respond to the interests they bring with them to the program. Although learners may be initially attracted to L2 study because they consider it to be challenging, elitist, or even exotic, chances are that if they do not subsequently experience *success in terms of their own interests*, they will not pursue their study for long.

Understandably, teachers and program directors may *assume* they know what interests learners. Or they may feel they know what is "in the best interests" of learners. There have always been those who applaud L2 study for its purported value in developing critical thinking. It is no coincidence that as the communicative value of Greek and Latin began to wane after the Renaissance, supporters of these languages heralded them as the best subject matter for mental discipline. Today there are those who seek to preserve L2 programs with a similar appeal. They promote L2 study as an exercise in linguistic analysis. The very fact that L2 acquisition by way of this route is arduous and requires long years of persistent application, they reason, makes it valuable for the development not only of the *mind* but of the *character* as well. For those who hold this view, the answer to lagging enrollments is obvious: Make L2 study mandatory; maintain or, as necessary, reinstate foreign language requirements. It matters not, say the votaries of this view, that the majority of learners fail to develop functional skills in languages they have little interest in learning in the first place; what counts is the exercise itself. But need we settle for so little?

A more promising view of school programs is that they can provide learners with communicative experiences on which to *build* as their needs are progressively defined. Beginning courses can be general in nature, introducing learners to a wide range of communicative language use, both oral and written. They should be flexible enough to permit learners to pursue and experience success in those aspects of L2 use that appeal to them most. So far as possible, special tracks or interest groups should be created at more advanced levels of study. On the secondary level this may take the form of minicourses of from two to four weeks on topics of specific interest. On the university level, a second language major can consist of several options—for example, literature, linguistics, civilization, commercial studies. Whatever the pattern, it is *L2 study for a purpose*. Programs should be developed and receive their continued support in response to the attitudes and interests of the learners themselves.

Needs-Assessment Surveys for Learners

Needs-assessment surveys have been used successfully as a first step in the revision of existing programs. In some cases they serve to *confirm* impressions of learner interests. In others they *dispel myths* about learner attitudes. In all cases they point to ways in which school programs can be made more responsive to learner needs.

This chapter on attitudes and interests concludes with four practical illustrations of needs-assessment surveys that are used in quite different contexts. The first is the translation into English of a survey used to discover the communicative needs in English of French-speaking elementary school children in Quebec (Malenfant-Loiselle and Jones 1978). The second is an attitude survey adapted and much abbreviated from the motivational and interest scales used by Gardner and Lambert (1972). This particular version was used by a secondary school teacher to aid her in the redirection of her foreign language program (Harbour 1982). The third illustration is a survey of interests among L2 students at the University of Delaware. The outcome, along with an appeal for a new curriculum, is reported in Gilgenast and Binkley (1981). The fourth is a questionnaire designed to yield information about learner attitudes regarding a specific L2 course and its components (Boylan, cited in Lett 1977). All four approaches are encouraging in their focus on the learner. They may be easily adapted for use in other L2 teaching contexts.

QUEBEC MINISTRY
OF EDUCATION
STUDENT QUESTIONNAIRE

School: _____

Directions: Mark an X in the box that says what you want to say.
When there is no box, write in your own answer.

1. Sex? .... Boy   ☐

                                               Girl   ☐

2. What grade are you in? .... 4th grade   ☐

                                               5th grade   ☐

                                               6th grade   ☐

3. How old are you?............................... 9   ☐

                                               10   ☐

                                               11   ☐

                                               12   ☐

4. What is your father's profession? _____

5. What is your mother's profession? _____

6. Does your father work? .... Yes   ☐

                                               No   ☐

7. Does your mother work outside your home? .... Yes   ☐

                                               No   ☐

8. What is your father's native language? .... French   ☐

                                               English   ☐

                                               Other (Write in)

                                               _____

9. What is your mother's native language?................. French   ☐

                                               English   ☐

                                               Other (Write in)

                                               _____

10. What language do you speak at home?.................... French ☐

    English ☐

    French/
    English ☐

    Other ☐

11. Are you studying English in school this year?.......... Yes ☐

    No ☐

12. In your opinion, how well are you doing in

    English? (If you are studying English) .... Well ☐

    Fair ☐

    Not very
    well ☐

13. Do you have English-speaking friends?.................... Often ☐

    Sometimes ☐

    Never ☐

14. Do you watch T.V. programs in English?................ Yes ☐

    Which ones:

    _____

    No ☐

15. Do you listen to English radio programs?................ Yes ☐

    Which ones:

    _____

    No ☐

16. Do you speak English? .... Often   With whom?... Mother ☐

    Sometimes   Father ☐

    Never   Visitors ☐

    Relatives ☐

    Brother/Sister ☐

    Teacher ☐

    Friends ☐

17. Do you read in English? .. Often   What?............ Magazines ☐

                           Sometimes   Books ☐

                           Never   Comics ☐

                                                     Other ☐

18. Do you write in English? Often   To whom? ...... Friend ☐

                           Sometimes   Relative ☐

                           Never   Others ☐

19. Do you have friends who speak English at home?.... Yes ☐

                                                           No ☐

20. Do your parents invite English-speaking friends
to your home? .... Often ☐

                                                          Sometimes ☐

                                                           Never ☐

21. Would you like to be able to speak English?............ Yes ☐

                                                           No ☐

Why? _____

_____

_____

22. What would you like to be able to say in English? _____

_____

_____

23. Describe the last time you needed to speak English outside class. (Where
and when?) _____

_____

_____

24. What are your favorite hobbies? (Name at least three.) _____

_____

_____

Thanks for your help.

ATTITUDE QUESTIONNAIRE FOR
FOREIGN-LANGUAGE STUDENTS

(Adapted from Gardner and Lambert 1972)

1. Level in foreign language study:	2. Class:	3. Expected Grade:	4. Sex:
0 1st year	0 Fresh	0 A	0 Male
0 2nd year	0 Soph	0 B	0 Female
0 3rd year	0 Junior	0 C	
0 4th year	0 Senior	0 D	
		0 F	

DIRECTIONS: For each of the following questions decide whether you strongly agree, agree, have no opinion, disagree, or strongly disagree and check the appropriate box. Read each item carefully.

1. Through my experience in foreign language study I have discovered that some aspects of American culture are not as good as I had previously thought.
   strongly agree   0 0 0 0 0   strongly disagree

2. I wish I could speak another language perfectly.
   strongly agree   0 0 0 0 0   strongly disagree

3. Our lack of knowledge of foreign language accounts for many of our political difficulties abroad.
   strongly agree   0 0 0 0 0   strongly disagree

4. I want to read the literature of a foreign language in the original.
   strongly agree   0 0 0 0 0   strongly disagree

5. Knowledge of a foreign language is not really necessary for travel or business abroad because most well-educated foreigners speak English.
   strongly agree   0 0 0 0 0   strongly disagree

6. If I planned to stay in another country, I would make a great effort to learn the language even though I could get along in English.
   strongly agree   0 0 0 0 0   strongly disagree

7. The study of a foreign language is mostly a waste of time.
   strongly agree   0 0 0 0 0   strongly disagree

8. I think that a stay abroad for a year or more would be one of the most valuable experiences of my life.
   strongly agree   0 0 0 0 0   strongly disagree

9. Foreign travel is high on my list of things I want to do. — strongly agree 0 0 0 0 0 strongly disagree

10. On the whole, I feel I am doing well in French/Spanish. — strongly agree 0 0 0 0 0 strongly disagree

11. I enjoy studying French/Spanish. — strongly agree 0 0 0 0 0 strongly disagree

12. I wish there were less emphasis on speaking and understanding French/Spanish in this course. — strongly agree 0 0 0 0 0 strongly disagree

13. French/Spanish is my least preferred course. — strongly agree 0 0 0 0 0 strongly disagree

14. In my French/Spanish class, I am generally not prepared unless I know the instructor will ask for the assignment. — strongly agree 0 0 0 0 0 strongly disagree

15. I resent having to spend so much time on French/Spanish at the expense of my other studies. — strongly agree 0 0 0 0 0 strongly disagree

16. I have found the laboratory sessions to be a worthwhile part of my overall experience in French/Spanish this year. — strongly agree 0 0 0 0 0 strongly disagree

Below are six reasons students frequently give for studying French/Spanish. Please read each reason carefully and rate it, indicating the extent to which it is descriptive of your own case.

1. I think it will some day be useful in getting a good job. — strongly agree 0 0 0 0 0 strongly disagree

2. It will help me better understand the French/Spanish people and their way of life. — strongly agree 0 0 0 0 0 strongly disagree

3. One needs a good knowledge of at least one foreign language to merit social recognition. — strongly agree 0 0 0 0 0 strongly disagree

4. It will allow me to meet and converse with more and varied people. — strongly agree 0 0 0 0 0 strongly disagree

5. I need it in order to meet college requirements. — strongly agree 0 0 0 0 0 strongly disagree

6. It should enable me to think and behave as do the French/Spanish people. — strongly agree 0 0 0 0 0 strongly disagree

UNIVERSITY OF DELAWARE QUESTIONNAIRE FOR LANGUAGE STUDENTS

1. What is your major? _____

2. What languages have you studied? _____
   _____ No. of years _____
   _____

3. What language course are you currently enrolled in? _____
   _____

4. Does your major department allow you elective hours that you could use
   for further language courses? _____

5. Would you be interested in going further with a language if the right
   course were offered dealing with your area of interest? _____
   Suggestions: _____
   _____

   _____

6. Which of the following would interest you as future courses?

Culture and civilization of the foreign country	much	OK	little
Ethnic language studies	much	OK	little
Conversation	much	OK	little
Short stories and fiction	much	OK	little
Business German/Spanish/French, etc.	much	OK	little
Scientific writing	much	OK	little
Grammar review	much	OK	little
Interpretation and translation	much	OK	little
Nonfiction readings	much	OK	little
(any preferred subject? _____)			
Writing and composition	much	OK	little
Plays	much	OK	little
Poetry	much	OK	little
Contemporary issues (readings and discussions relevant to today's culture and problems)	much	OK	little
A survey of literary history	much	OK	little

Minicourses: seven weeks of two courses
chosen from:

a) Letter writing (business and informal)	much	OK	little
b) Culinary arts	much	OK	little
c) Creative writing	much	OK	little
d) Travel (skills for survival)	much	OK	little

e) Other suggestions: _____

_____

_____

LEARNER ATTITUDE TOWARD SELECTED COURSE COMPONENTS

This questionnaire asks you to indicate the extent to which you *react positively* or *negatively* to specific aspects of your language course.

Please read each statement carefully, and then circle the number that best describes how you feel. (An explanation of the numbers is right above the items.)

(CIRCLE ONE NUMBER ON EACH LINE.)

strongly positive	moderately positive	slightly positive	slightly negative	moderately negative	strongly negative
+3	+2	+1	−1	−2	−3

1. Communicating in small groups. +3 +2 +1 −1 −2 −3

2. Being able to rewrite compositions. +3 +2 +1 −1 −2 −3

3. The extent to which my instructor encourages me to think for myself. +3 +2 +1 −1 −2 −3

4. Listening to each other's oral presentations. +3 +2 +1 −1 −2 −3

5. The total classroom atmosphere. +3 +2 +1 1 −2 −3

Each of the preceding questionnaires was developed by teachers or program administrators interested in knowing more about the learners they serve. Learner responses in each case have provided a basis for program development or reform. An initial survey of learner interests and needs, along with regular and systematic learner evaluations of the effectiveness of programs in meeting those needs, provides a valuable perspective for the *selection of materials* and the *shaping of a curriculum*—topics that we shall now discuss in Chapters 4 and 5.

SUGGESTED READINGS

H. Brown. 1980. *Principles of Language Learning and Teaching*. Includes a good discussion of Carl Rogers's contribution to learning theory as it relates to behaviorist and cognitive theories of psychology.

R. Gardner and W. Lambert. 1972. *Attitudes and Motivation in Second-Language Learning*. A collection of studies by two influential researchers in the relationship of attitude to L2 acquisition. Includes scales used to measure attitudes as well as extensive reports of empirical findings.

R. Gardner and P. Smythe. 1981. "On the Development of the Attitude/Motivation Test Battery." Summarizes the technique applied in the development of the attitude/motivation test battery used by Gardner and others with particular reference to the reliability and validity of the measures.

J. Lett. 1977. "Assessing Attitudinal Outcomes." A readable overview of various approaches to attitude measurement in foreign language education.

R. Mackay and J. Palmer. 1981. *Languages for Specific Purposes*. A collection of papers addressing LSP program design and evaluation, including needs assessment.

T. Mollica (ed.). 1976. Special issue of the *Canadian Modern Language Review* devoted to attitudes and motivation. Includes papers by Cziko and Lambert, Gardner et al., Savignon, Stern, Tucker et al., Yalden, and others.

J. Oller, Jr. 1979. *Language Tests at School*. See Chapter 5 for a discussion of the need to validate measures of affective variables.

P. Simon, 1980. *The Tongue-Tied American*. Written by a U.S. congressman, not for language experts but for the general public, this book dramatically documents the second language inadequacies of most Americans. Among the problems cited is the overemphasis on literature and the publication records of teachers in college-level L2 programs.

B. Spolsky. 1981. "Bilingualism and Biliteracy." Discusses the relevance of sociolinguistic concepts such as *speech community*, *status*, *values*, and *social group* to language acquisition. Describes *code-switching* (switching from one language to another) as "a method of dealing with the tensions created by uncertainty between two statuses or the desire to maintain both."

G.R. Tucker. 1977. "Can a Second Language Be Taught?" A discussion of L2 learning worldwide within a broad framework of political, economic, and social realities. Makes the point that "despite research, experimentation or innovation second language teaching programs or bilingual education programs will *not* succeed or thrive unless they are consistent with government policy."

F. Williams. 1976. *Explorations of the Linguistic Attitudes of Teachers*. A collection of reports on teachers' reactions to children based on children's use of language. The focus is the social significance of language features, stereotyping, and cross-cultural judgments in multiethnic American society. Attitude measurement in these studies makes extensive use of the *semantic differential* scale (Osgood, Suci, and Tannenbaum 1957). (See the Glossary for an illustration of this technique.)

RESEARCH AND DISCUSSION

1. What were your own reasons for studying a second language? Why did you continue your study? Compare your reasons with those of classmates or colleagues. To what extent do you think your reasons for L2 study are likely to be shared by your students?

2. Do you consider yourself bilingual? Why or why not? What influence is your answer likely to have on your attitude toward teaching or on your actual teaching performance?

3. Anomie is not unique to second language learners. Anyone who has left a familiar culture to join another is likely to experience feelings of alienation. Anthony Bailey was seven in 1940 when he was evacuated from wartime England to spend four years with an American family in Dayton, Ohio. He expresses his sense of divided loyalty (or double identity) as a "self-consciousness or an awareness of distance from those who are simply one thing or the other, British or American. It means that people are occasionally unsure of me, and of my background; a man in a Hampshire shop the other day, hearing me ask for something, said, 'You must be from Canada.' It gives one a frequent fit of melancholy or nostalgia—when in Britain missing America, when in America missing Britain" (1980:151). Have you ever experienced similar feelings? Discuss both the advantages and disadvantages of biculturalism.

4. Analyze your present L2 learning or teaching situation in terms of national political and economic support, community support, and school administration support. Where you can, cite specific incidents or data to support your view. What is the impact of these factors on learners? On teachers?

5. Trace L2 enrollment patterns in U.S. public schools prior to World War I, between World War I and World War II, and from 1945 to the present. What national attitudes do these patterns reflect? (For help in gathering data, see Starr 1979, Brod 1976, and Watts 1963.)

6. With your classmates, try role playing a discussion between persons who hold different views on the value of L2 study in schools. The characters you choose to play will depend on your own community. They might include, for example, a college-bound learner, a vocationally oriented learner, a taxpayer, a school counselor, a member of a minority language group. (To fairly represent a particular constituency you may need to interview one or more of its members.)

7. Wilkins has made the following assertion:

> A characteristic of the general language courses is that the learner commonly does not claim the return on his investment in learning until that learning has been proceeding for some years. He does not expect to be able to use the language communicatively as soon as the learning effort has begun, and since he or she is often in a situation where the occasion to use the language rarely arises, it does not really matter if the development of communicative ability is deferred. [1974:121]

Do you agree? If you or someone you know teaches a general language course on the secondary or university level, poll the learners for their views.

8. The question posed by Allright and cited in Chapter 1 is intended to be rhetorical: Are we teaching language (for communication)? *or* are we teaching communication (via language)? Yet not everyone would agree that communication *is* the goal of L2 study. What are your own views? Compare them with those of your colleagues or classmates. Compare them with those of Wilkins cited above.

9. Can you cite an example of an L2 program that you consider to be particularly successful in attracting and retaining students? To what do you attribute its success?

10. Parkway School District in Chesterfield, Missouri, whose foreign language program was one of 50 award-winning programs cited by the American Council of Teachers of Foreign Languages (Sims and Hammond 1981), has the following placement policy: *Students may repeat any language level without penalty up to grade ten.* What do you think is the effect on learner attitudes? What underlying teacher attitudes does the policy reflect?

11. Go through the Foreign Language Attitude Survey for Teachers (FLAST) with classmates or colleagues, adapting it as necessary to fit your situation. On which responses do you show the sharpest differences of opinion? Why? What are the implications of these differences for program development and implementation?

12. Adapt one of the four needs-assessment surveys included in Section 3.3 for use in your own teaching context. If possible, administer it to a group of students or prospective students. Do the results correspond to your expectations?

13. Summarize the views expressed by Flora Lewis in her *New York Times* article, "Speaking in Tongues." Do you agree with them?

14. As a teacher have you provided learners with opportunities to express their attitudes or interests with regard to a program of studies or a particular class or classroom activity? If so, what have you found to be the value of these surveys? the limitations?

Chapter 4

Selection of Materials

The great danger today is of slogans, collective opinions, ready-made trends of thought. We have to be able to resist individually, to criticize, to distinguish between what is proven and what is not, so we need pupils who are active, who learn early to find out by themselves, partly by their own spontaneous activity and partly through material we set up for them; who learn early to tell what is verifiable and what is simply the first idea to come to them.

—Jean Piaget

A Teacher's Dream

Teachers dream of finding the ideal materials: materials that are at once accurate and imaginative, that offer both sequence and flexibility, and that provide variety yet respond to well-defined instructional goals. For some, the dream of ideal materials is frustrated by the lack of any real choice. Budget restrictions, state or regional selection criteria, or the need to comply with the wishes of a course chairperson or curriculum supervisor may leave individual teachers with little voice in the selection of the materials they use. Once adopted, moreover, materials often remain in the curriculum for a number of years. Funds spent to purchase or develop ancillary materials, such as visual aids, tape recordings, and computer programmed activities, as well as the time invested by the teacher in course development, add to the cost of change.

For others, teachers with considerable if not complete freedom in the selection of the materials they use, the dream of the *ideal* is no less elusive. New textbooks on the market make promises, look attractive, and are written by responsible professionals. Yet they often fail to withstand the classroom test. The language samples they provide may seem contrived, limited in scope, or irrelevant to learner interests. Explanations and activities may be mechanical, repetitive, vague, or simply too infrequent. The pitfalls of materials preparation are many, as most authors and publishers will readily agree. Perhaps more to the point, however, is that no single book, regardless of the care with which it has been written, can ever meet universal standards of excellence, or even adequacy, inasmuch as such standards are scarcely definable in the first place.

Textbooks are written for general audiences and thus cannot, in themselves, meet the needs of a particular L2 class. The authors of these textbooks cannot foresee all the needs of individual teachers and learners. The search for materials leads, ultimately, to the realization that *there is no such thing as an ideal textbook*. Materials are but a starting point. Teachers are the ones who make materials work; they make them work for their students and for themselves in the context in which they teach.

Teaching materials need not be textbooks (that is, a collection of written or oral texts selected and sequenced for the learner with accompanying explanations and activities). But they most often are. New teachers are particularly dependent on a textbook. With little experience to rely on, they understandably look to a textbook to tell them what to teach and how to teach it. To the novice, a special annotated teacher's edition with supplementary explanations and suggestions for class activities is particularly welcome.

It is often said, on the other hand, that an experienced teacher can teach with any text, even the telephone book! Though there is as yet no report of someone's actually having tried this, the exaggeration does serve to underscore the liberation from the textbook that comes with experience. By relying less on the prescribed program of a textbook and more on strategies and activities that have proved successful in the past, the experienced teacher is better able to share with learners the responsibility for structuring the class. Materials then become a *resource* in pursuing the language activities at hand. In some instances these materials are even collected or created by the learners themselves who, thus, compose their own textbook.

This chapter looks at these issues of materials selection. Section 4.1 will first consider the range of options available in materials—from a complete textbook package at one extreme to no textbook at all at the other. It will then look at selected commercial materials in terms of the language samples and learning activities they provide. Section 4.2 includes a summary of guidelines for textbook evaluation along with a checklist to be used in comparing materials. Section 4.3 offers an example of how *authentic* L2 materials, radio newscasts in this instance, can be used to provide structure and sequence for an entire course. The perspective throughout this chapter remains that of preceding chapters: In a communicative classroom the L2 is never viewed as static, as a list of features to be transmitted to the learner. It is seen, rather, as a *dynamic means of self-expression* created by the learners with the help of their teachers.

4.1. THE OPTIONS

Textbook or No Textbook?

In deciding on which materials to select, it is important to keep in mind the range of options. Most common in classroom materials is the textbook that combines language samples, explanations, and activities into a single volume. When intended to promote skills in oral as well as written language, a textbook is often accompanied by both sound recordings and visual aids. From early audiolingual days to the present the textbook package has proved a popular concept and is probably most typical of beginning-level general language materials that are now on the market. Some of the more elaborate packages include not only sound recordings and visual aids but student workbooks, unit tests, games, and other activities.

At the opposite extreme from the textbook package is the absence of prepared materials. Community Language Learning is one example of a "no textbook" approach (see Chapter 3). With the help of the teacher/counselor who serves as an interpreter, beginning learners themselves provide the L2 data (that is, the *text*) based on their own communication interests. Working in small groups of four to seven, learners initiate conversations in their native language. With the teacher providing a model, the learners translate their utterances into the second language. These L2 conversations are recorded and may be played back later for reflection on grammar and vocabulary. The conversations may also be put in writing. This learner-initiated approach to materials development requires, of course, that the learners have an L1 in common and that the teacher is fluently bilingual.

Another "no textbook" approach to course development is that of teachers who draw on their knowledge of the L2, as well as of learner interests, to provide a corpus of language activities that is unique to a particular context. The early FLES (Foreign Languages in Elementary School) programs in the United States, for example, often relied of necessity on this kind of approach. L2 teachers in the elementary schools began with children's games, songs, and stories, calling on their previous experience with children or on recollections of their own childhood to guide them in their choice of activities.

With advanced learners the "no textbook" option is more widespread. Some years ago, a colleague and I were persuaded by students in our advanced French conversation class that we were better off without a ready-made collection of readings designed to stimulate discussion. Considering that these students were from diverse professional curricula, that there was ready access to French feature films at local cinemas, and that the library was well supplied with current francophone newspapers and magazines, we agreed to let the learners themselves determine the topics and activities for the semester. Class organization (including the exchange of names and addresses and the selection of teams responsible for weekly programs) was the focus of our initial meetings. These organizational needs offered a natural opportunity to use French communicatively and, in so doing, to create our own *community*. Of course, the experience and achievement of the individual learners were different and depended on the knowledge they brought with them, their various roles in the group, and the topics they selected. Each class member had a dictionary and a reference grammar and kept a personal notebook of relevant vocabulary, points of grammar, and bothersome phonological features.

In another example of the "no textbook" option, Hinofotis, Bailey, and Stern (1981) describe a university course in English communication skills for nonnative graduate teaching assistants. It relies not on a book of pronunciation exercises—a practice common in this kind of course—but on videotapes of individual learners teaching in their own classrooms. These tapes are the basis for a discussion of classroom communication, as they are for a diagnosis of individual difficulties.

Between the extremes of a self-contained textbook package or program on the one hand, and no textbook at all on the other, there lies a full range of options. Readers, recordings, films, games, and grammar reviews prepared especially for L2 learners abound. In addition, there is the full range of materials, both oral and written, intended for native speakers. Graded readers, textbooks of style and structure, crossword puzzles, and similar word games may give special attention to matters of language per se. Other materials, such as newspapers, cartoons, novels, radio and television shows, advertisements, and the like may simply provide *occasions* for language use. All should be considered for what they have to offer an L2 program.

The WHAT of Teaching Materials:
Structural, Notional-Functional,
and Situational Syllabuses

When materials are prepared especially for learners, a decision has to be made on the kinds of L2 samples or texts to include. Will they be primarily didactic in nature, that is, illustrative of forms or functions? Or will they also engage the learner in communication? Will they be new materials written for the textbook itself? Or will they be collected and perhaps edited from existing written and/or oral materials? How will they be sequenced? The answers to these questions help to establish the criteria for selecting and sequencing the content of teaching materials.

The first thing to look for, then, in evaluating a textbook is *organizational framework*. Most L2 textbooks on the market today follow one of three basic patterns: structural, notional-functional, or situational. Many, however, reflect a *combination* of two or even all three of these paradigms. That is, a syllabus may best be described as situational/structural, situational/notional-functional, notional-functional/structural, or even structural/situational/notional-functional. In such cases, one paradigm typically provides an overall focus, which the others then enhance or enrich. Some examples will illustrate how this works.

The *structural syllabus* is the framework with which teachers are most familiar. It introduces points of grammar in terms used by linguists to describe discrete structural or formal features of language. It begins, therefore, not with the immediate communicative needs of the learner but with the categories of a descriptive grammar: definite and indefinite articles, present tense conjugation of regular and irregular verbs, adjective formation and position, adverbs, prepositions, past tense conjugation of regular and irregular verbs, and so on. Considerations of complexity, difficulty for the learner, and frequency of occurrence may all provide guidelines in the selection and sequencing of the formal features to be included in a structural syllabus.

A *notional-functional syllabus*, on the other hand, organizes language content by functional categories; it provides a means of developing structural categories within a general consideration of the communicative functions of language. Setting up a notional-functional syllabus begins with the specification of the communicative needs of the learner: a description of (1) the situations (roles, setting, and topics) in which the learner will use the L2 and (2) the activities in which the learner will engage. This specification provides the basis for establishing categories of communicative function, or *functions*, for which the learner should be prepared: to advise, to express uncertainty, to report factual information, to greet, etc. These functions are then considered in terms of the semantic concepts, or *notions*, related to their performance. Notions are general concepts of meaning such as time, frequency, duration, dimension, location, relationship, etc. A consideration of notions in relation to various functions of language leads in turn to an identification of necessary or useful L2 *forms*, that is, grammar and vocabulary.

In the final analysis, then, the result of a notional-functional syllabus is a list of language forms. What distinguishes a notional-functional syllabus from a structural syllabus, however, is the way in which these forms are selected. By focusing on the communicative needs of the learner, the notional-functional approach to syllabus development has the virtue of highlighting the uses to which language is put rather than the grammatical categories that are used to describe it. To illustrate, a communicative function of identifying or reporting (including describing and narrating) may be related to the general spatial notion of location. For English, this notion leads to the identification of lexical items such as *here, there, inside, outside, behind, in, on, at, near*, etc.

Although the combined term *notional-functional* is most often used to refer to a semantic, or meaning-based, syllabus, the term *notional* may be used alone. Wilkins (1976), in fact, refers simply to *notional syllabuses*, using *notional* as an umbrella term to include both general concepts *and* functions of language. General concepts are concerned with semantic and grammatical categories, and functions with speaker's intent. The following items give a sense of the scope of a notional-functional approach to the specification of items to be included in a syllabus. They appear under "A" in the index of notional categories that Wilkins proposes for a notional framework for the teaching of English.

Abandon	Acquiesce	Affirm
Abjure	Acquit	Agent
Absolve	Admiration	Agree
Abuse	Admit	Agree to
Accuse	Advise	Allege
Acknowledgement	Advocate	Allow (Concede)

Allow (Permit)	Applaud	Assert
Amazement	Approbation	Assertion
Anaphora	Approval (Approbation)	Assess
Anger	Approve (Endorse)	Astonishment
Annoyance	Argue	Attitude
Anteriority	Argument	Attribution
Anxiety	Ask	Authorize
Apology	Assent	Award

Where language functions provide the framework of a syllabus, language structures will appear and reappear as they are related to specific notions. The sequence of the functions themselves depends on the textbook writer's view of their immediate usefulness to the learner, their role in the functions to be subsequently introduced, or some other criteria. Functions and forms may reappear as learners increase in L2 competence and are ready to expand their repertoire. Thus beginners may know one appropriate way to apologize for bumping into a peer or coworker, but more advanced learners may be able to apologize in a variety of ways depending on the nature of the offense, the social status of their interlocutor, and the degree of sincerity they wish to convey.

A *situational syllabus* is one that presents language samples in a situation or setting. The familiar phrase book for travelers is an example of materials in which situations provide the main organizational paradigm. Vocabulary and expressions are grouped into situations—at the airport, at the bank, at the pharmacy, etc.—that will presumably be encountered or anticipated by the learner. More commonly, however, situations serve an ancillary role in a syllabus that has either structures or functions as its basic organizational paradigm. In this case, situations may provide the titles of units or chapters: First Day of School, At the Fair, Going Shopping, etc. They may reflect specific learner needs, or they may simply be of presumed general interest. Their *main purpose*, however, may be no more than to provide a *pretext*, a dialogue or reading selection illustrative of the grammar points or functions being introduced or reviewed in the unit.

A *theme* or topic may also provide an organizational framework. Like situations, themes define a context for the introduction of language samples and experiences. In the case of a theme, however, the context is expanded to give a continuity of topics or situations from one unit to the next. For example, the theme of a beginning Spanish textbook for American high school students might be the adventures of a teenage brother and sister on an exchange visit to Mexico City. Situations might then include arrival, greetings and getting acquainted, first day at school, a weekend excursion to the mountains, and so on. Language forms and functions would be related to each situation, and additional examples provided as desired. A theme or topic, then, quite readily combines with other organizational frameworks—structural, functional, or situational—to give a desirable overall unity. As was noted at the outset of this discussion of organizational frameworks, many textbooks tend to be hybrid in respect to organization, reflecting a combination of two or more paradigms.

Regardless of the organizational framework chosen, there must be a *selection* of items. Whether the choice is in terms of structures, functions, or situations, it is a matter of establishing a finite list from among infinite possibilities. We know the most about the structural features of language, and yet there is no such thing as a complete structural analysis of a language. Even if there were, the pages that would be required to set down all the rules would be many more than could be contained in a textbook for learners. As for the situations in which we use language, these are obviously unlimited although it is, of course, possible to select high-frequency situations for a particular group of learners. The selection of functions is no less problematic inasmuch as we have nothing even approaching a comprehensive list of the communicative or social purposes of language and how they are realized by native speakers, let alone how and when they are realized by learners. In spite of the difficulties their selection presents, however, textbook writers today are increasingly looking to functions to provide answers to the problems of syllabus design.

The HOW of Teaching Materials: Experiences and Activities

With the understanding that L2 acquisition is the result of language use, which, we must further understand, does not proceed in a lock-step, error-free fashion, comes the realization that the choice of an organizational framework is perhaps less important than the intrinsic interest and problem-solving opportunities of the materials themselves. When the attainment of some measure of communicative competence is seen to depend on the development of strategies for the negotiation of meaning, the communicative use of the L2 at the beginning as well as at advanced levels of instruction becomes a clear priority. As the organizational framework of materials is being determined, then, attention should also be given to the *process* implicit in their design. What are the learners expected to *do* with the language samples included? Are they expected to recite, recombine, or otherwise reproduce them? Or are the samples intended primarily to provide learners with the data they need to be able to use the language for their own communicative purposes? It is quite common, for example, to find textbooks that emphasize productive skills of writing and speaking at the expense of opportunities for simply listening to or reading a wide variety of written and spoken discourse. This emphasis limits the learners' exposure to L2 data and helps to create the mistaken impression that learners should be able to reproduce all that they understand.

Attention to interpretive strategies is crucial, as we have seen, for the development of communicative competence on all levels, and this should be recognized in materials design. As teachers look at the process or theory of L2 acquisition implicit in a textbook, they need to ask themselves what importance has been assigned to understanding and to conveying meaning. What opportunities are there for problem solving, negotiation, and self-expression? Are these activities at the core of the program? Or are they given a subordinate role that provides little more than a sugarcoating for a structural or functional pill? Opportunities for communicative L2 use go far beyond a textbook, of course, and should be a concern of the curriculum in a much broader sense—which is the topic that we will explore more fully in Chapter 5. Materials can and do make an important contribution to the shape of a curriculum, however. Their evaluation should include, therefore, consideration not only of the WHAT of L2 acquisition but of the HOW as well.

Textbooks and Breakfast Foods: The Bandwagon Phenomenon

The preface or table of contents is not always the best guide to either the content of a textbook or the author's view of language learning. Since labels can be misleading, it is important in evaluating materials to distinguish between what a textbook *says* it does and what it *does*. In L2 teaching materials, as in other marketing ventures, the bandwagon phenomenon is familiar. It leads to the promotion of a certain image as fashionable, an image that most materials, new or revised, then try to emulate. Such materials seek to reflect the new image yet not stray too far from the familiar, the tried and the true to which classroom teachers have become accustomed. In this respect, the promoters of teaching materials are no different from the makers of breakfast cereals: They need to entice consumers with claims for a new and improved product yet at the same time satisfy tastes for tradition and stability.

What "nutritious" and "natural" are today to breakfast foods, "communicative" and "functional" are to language texts. How much change has actually taken place is debatable. Just as cereals containing "all natural" honey are no less sweet, so "asking questions" may be no more than a new label for an old unit on the formation of the interrogative. That is, functional labels may be used to introduce the structural categories that continue to provide the basic framework. Or, to use a metaphor from another supermarket aisle, so-called functional approaches to syllabus design may be no more than "structural lamb served up as notional-functional mutton" (Campbell 1978:18).

From "The Basics" to Communicating by All Means: Examples

It is always easy to find fault with what others have tried, and, in their attempt to provide language activities for learners, language textbooks are particularly vulnerable to criticism. From old standbys—"La plume de ma tante"—to attempts at modernity—"The waterbed has sprung a leak"—language taken out of context in another time or place is an easy target for ridicule. Yet teachers continue to rely on prepared materials for day-to-day classroom activities. The pace in most instructional programs is so demanding that even experienced teachers look to materials to give them inspiration and, more than occasionally, an answer to the question, "What shall we do today?"

The examples that follow provide an overview of where we have been and where we seem to be going in materials development.

THE BASICS

These excerpts from a 1953 college French textbook are representative of the grammar-translation approach using a syllabus based on traditional grammatical categories, such as gender, plural of nouns, etc. Rules are stated at the beginning of each chapter, often with reference to L1 (English in this case) grammar. Of additional interest in these excerpts is their rather narrow view of "culture," a view typical of language textbooks up until the advent of audiolingualism in the early 1960s. Note in the introductory remarks the distinction that is made between *culture* and *everyday scenes*. Such everyday scenes are, of course, very much a part of culture in the anthropological sense of the term and are an integral part of modern materials.

A return to the emphasis on grammar rules in evidence here is sometimes endorsed by advocates of what has become known in American education as the "back-to-basics" movement. More *basic* to L2 use, however, than the ability to recite rules is, as we have seen, *experience* in communication.

From the Preface:

In this new edition, the authors have retained most of the basic characteristics of the original work, including its simplicity and conciseness and its aim of mastering first what is absolutely essential.

However, a certain number of features more in accordance with progressive methods used in the teaching of languages have been introduced in this alternate edition. . . . In accordance with current trends in beginning grammars, phonetic transcriptions, considered by many instructors to be of dubious value, have been omitted throughout. . . . The French reading passages are entirely new. As in the former edition, they are correlated with the grammar and illustrate primarily grammatical points. They deal with France and French life and, with the exception of two selections of a more cultural nature, present everyday scenes, placed for the first part of the book in the country, and for the second half in the city.

From the Table of Contents:

Lesson I
Gender—Plural of Nouns—Definite Article—Indefinite Article—Personal Pronoun Subjects—Present Indicative of *Etre*—Negation.

Lesson II
Possession—Possessive Adjectives—Present Indicative of *Avoir*—Interrogation.

Lesson III
Contractions—Partitive Construction—Regular Conjugations—Present Indicative of *Donner*—Use of *Est-ce que.*

From Lesson I:

1. *Gender.* All French nouns are either masculine or feminine. Nouns denoting males are masculine. Those denoting females are feminine. Learn the gender of other nouns as you meet them in the vocabularies.

2. *Plural of Nouns.* To form the plural of most French nouns add *s*, as in English, to the singular. This *s*, however, is not pronounced.

3. *Definite Article.* The French equivalent of English *the* is *le, la,* or *les*.

Use *le* before a masculine singular noun beginning with a consonant: *le jardin,* the garden.

Use *la* before a feminine singular noun beginning with a consonant: *la maison,* the house.

Use *l'* (contraction of *le* or *la*) before a singular noun of either gender beginning with a vowel or a mute *h*: *l'enfant,* the child, *l'homme,* the man.

Use *les* before all plural nouns: *les jardins,* the gardens; *les maisons,* the houses; *les enfants,* the children; *les hommes,* the men.

The following exercises relying on translation, question-and-answer drills of structure, and verb conjugations are typical of grammar-translation materials.

A. Read aloud and translate:
   Voici un village.
   Il est dans une vallée.
   Voilà la rue et les maisons.
   Où est l'église?
   Elle est sur la place.
   L'église et l'école sont sur la place.

B. Answer in French:
   (1) Où est le village? (2) Où est l'église? (3) Où sont l'église et l'école? (4) Où sont un homme et une femme? (5) Qui (Who) est avec Marie?

C. Conjugate the following sentences:
   (1) Je suis sur la place, tu es sur la place, etc.

Source: W. Micks and O. Longi, *The New Fundamental French.* (Oxford: Oxford University Press, 1953).

THE NEW KEY

Behaviorist psychology, structural linguistics, and American defense dollars combined, as we have seen in Chapter 1, to produce a direction in L2 teaching that became known as audiolingualism, or the "New Key." With beginnings in the 1940s, the influence of audio-lingual tenets on materials development reached a peak in the 1960s. The following excerpts show the basic organizational framework of a popular college French textbook written in 1965. The assertion of the primacy of oral skills, the emphasis on nativelike performance, and the concern with a careful sequence of discrete linguistic items are all typical of materials written in this period.

From the Preface:

This textbook considers listening comprehension and speaking proficiency to be the primary language skills. The other skills, reading comprehension and the ability to express one's thoughts in writing are *derived* from these two primary skills. Accordingly, the beginning of the course stresses the ability to perceive and reproduce accurately the sounds of French. . . . Each unit contains a short dialogue and vocabulary manipulation exercises designed to develop control of the sound system in meaningful sentences. Only a few new sounds are presented in each unit.

From Unit I:

A bord du France

I.   Dialogue and Substitution Drills

The following conversation takes place between two friends, Jacques and Guy, greeting each other on board the luxury liner, Le France, which is steaming toward Le Havre.

Jacques: Ça va, Guy?	Everything going all right, Guy?
Guy: Oui, pas mal. Et toi?	Yes, not badly. And (with) you?
Jacques: Ça va.	O.K.
Guy: Où va ta femme Alice?	Where is your wife Alice going?
Jacques: Elle va à Nice.	She's going to Nice.
Guy: Avec qui?	With whom?
Jacques: Avec sa cousine Annick.	With her cousin Annick.

The sentences of a language are composed of a small number of sound units, which are perceived as being distinct from each other. These units are called *phonemes*. The first step in learning to speak a foreign language is to identify the phonemes in different contexts and to produce them in the same way as native speakers do. The first six lessons of the text are designed to lead to this goal.

II.   The Phoneme / i /

III.   The Phoneme / u /

IV.   The Phoneme / a /

Source: S. Belasco and A. Valdman, *College French in the New Key* (Lexington, Mass.: D.C. Heath, 1965).

GRAMMAR IN CONTEXT

The following exercises are an example of an increasing trend in learner materials to provide a visual context for language structures being introduced. Although the focus in this particular written exercise is grammar—use of the present perfect with *since* or *for*—the intent is to make the practice more meaningful by using illustrations that provide a setting in which the structures are used. Contextualization of this kind is helpful not only for children but for learners of all ages.

EXERCISE C

Use the words in brackets to write a sentence that describes the events illustrated in the picture series. Use the Present Perfect + *since* or *for* . . .

3 years ago

2 years ago

now

Example: (have, our dog, Tiny)

We have had our dog, Tiny, for three years.

1.

10 years ago

6 years ago

now

(live, here)

19

Source: M. Sacco, *Has/Had* (Hull, Quebec: Canadian Government Publishing Center, 1979).

GETTING THINGS DONE

The functional approach to syllabus design is illustrated by these pages from an English program for German secondary school students. Note the focus here on context of situation and *doing things* in an L2. The restaurant menu is a familiar text for language teaching materials in both structural and functional approaches. What makes this instance different from the structural treatment of "In the Restaurant" are not so much the texts themselves but what the teacher and learners do with them. The texts are examples of what a native speaker might say in this context and are not to be memorized. There are no names assigned to the speakers; learners play themselves. The teacher is not supposed to divide the class into two groups—waiter or waitress and customer—for practice. Instead, the class is to think up additional ways of *ordering* in English using structures and vocabulary they already know. Then they practice in small groups using utterances from the example texts and their own contributions.

GETTING THINGS DONE; in a Restaurant

Examples
. . . . : Are you ready to order?

. . . . : Yes. I'd like a hamburger, french fries, and a cola, please.

. . . . : Bring me a bacon, lettuce, and tomato sandwich, please.

. . . . : And what would you like to drink?

. . . . : Milk, please.

* * *

. . . . : May I take your order?

. . . . : I'd like a small pizza with sausage, please.

. . . . : And you sir?

. . . . : I'd like a large pizza with mushrooms and ham.

. . . . : Would you like something to drink?

. . . . : Yes. Bring us two colas, please.

. . . . : Thank you.

* * *

. . . . : Would you like some dessert?

. . . . : I don't know. Could we look at the menu again, please?

. . . . : Of course.

Language material
Are you ready to order?

Bring me . . . please
        us

Task 1   Complete the language material.

Task 2   In small groups practise ordering a meal from the menu on the next page. Take turns being waiter or waitress.

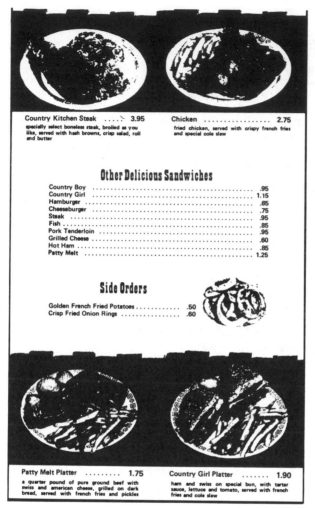

Source: H.E. Piepho et al. *Contacts, Grade 8* (Bochum, West Germany: Ferdinand Kamp, 1979).

CREATIVITY AND COPING

Though the preceding model of a restaurant menu is perhaps rather typical of American short-order fare, it is still but a sample and should be supplemented in the classroom by other examples. Practice in ordering from a menu or performing any other communicative function is incomplete if it does not include practice in coping with the unfamiliar, the unexpected. This admittedly unusual menu from a Detroit, Michigan, restaurant illustrates the creative use of language—the use of finite means to express infinite meanings. It is intended to surprise and amuse and calls for the use of coping strategies (strategic competence), which are an integral part of communicative competence. Its inclusion here among samples of textbook materials serves as a reminder that no matter how good they may be, prepackaged materials are simply a starting point. To be most effective they should be supplemented with real-world examples of what they present.

"CHATZ"

CONCOCTIONS, COOKERY, AND CONVERSATION

Strictly the Nibbles

CHILI con Queso Peso Hot, spiced cheese dip with tortilla chips. Olé!.. **1.95**

ITALIAN FRIES Seasoned, breaded and quick-fried zucchini sticks. Atsa nice!.. **1.95**

AMERICAN FRIES Fluffy and hot potatoes with the skin on. A star spangled delight..... **1.50**

ONE ALARM CHILI Ultra beefy and slightly spicy. No fire truck needed! **2.50**

The Lord of the Rings Regally batter-fried onion hoops, your majesty... **1.95**

CRUNCH! Basket of tortilla chips with salsa for dipping........ **1.50**

ON TRAYS

Gypsy Rose Beef Tender strips of beef sautéed with crispy vegetables..... **5.95**

MOO GOO FRY PAN Stir fry vegetables served over rice in the oriental tradition **4.50**

MY LITTLE CHICKADEE Moo Goo with tasty chicken added....... **5.50**

JACQUES CRUSTACEAN Shrimp and selected vegetables stir-fried and served with soy sauce.... **5.95**

FLOUNDER'S DAY SPECIAL I'm a sole fish Almondine, sautéed and topped with roasted almonds......... **6.50**

(ABOVE ENTREE'S INCLUDE ROLL AND BUTTER)

Au Jus Gonna Like This! Thinly sliced roast beef piled high on a French roll with a cup of hot, seasoned au jus for dipping... **4.50**

Spudley Do Right Potato skins overflowing with seasoned ground beef and melted cheese **4.95**

The Mucho Macho Nacho Tortilla chips crowned with beef and melted cheese.. **4.25**

CHATZZZ CHEEEEZ A cheese bored. (Or maybe interested, who knows?) **4.95**

Food for Thought
WE WOULDN'T STEER YOU WRONG

Bunch O' Burgers

OLE SMOKEY Smokey cheese and barbeque sauce......... **3.95**

YODEL Swiss cheese...... **3.95**

WIMPY'S Cheddar cheese... **3.95**

HOCKEY PUCK Boring by itself **3.50**

Bacon Your Pardon Bacon... **3.95**

Smothered Brothers Sautéed Onions **3.75**

Robin Hood Mushrooms from the forests **3.95**

ALL BURGERS SERVED WITH LETTUCE TOMATO, PICKLE, AND FRENCH FRIES EACH ADDITIONAL ITEM..... **.75**

the Garden of

CHATZ

ALL SALADS - 3.50

ZORBA the CRISP Mediterranean style salad of mixed greens, feta cheese, beets, black olives, and julienne of roast lamb served with an herbed cream dressing

ZELDA'S FOWL Sliced chicken on garden greens with tomatoes, southern pecans, citrus fruits and crowned with poppy seed dressing

Leave it to Cleaver Fresh mixed greens, julienne of ham, chicken, Swiss cheese with sliced tomato and olives, choice of dressing

SEA SEA RIDER Tasty shrimp, artichokes, olives, and egg nestled on a bed of shredded lettuce, your choice of dressing

ON THE HOUSE Very basic, very nice.............. **1.50**

MISS STEAKS
DINNER ONLY FROM 4 P.M.

ROAST PRIME RIB OF BEEF AU JUS............. 9.95

CHARBROILED NEW YORK SIRLOIN STRIP STEAK 9.95

Both dinners served with potato, roll, and butter

YOUR JUST DESSERTS

SAY CHEESECAKE!.....2.00 with strawberries........ **2.50**

"Bye Bye Miss American Pie"..1.75 à la mode............. **2.25**

BLACK FOREST CAKE... 2.00

I Scream, You Scream, We ALL Scream for ICE CREAM Vanilla, Chocolate, Rum Raisin, or Piña Colada Ice One Scoop **.95** Two Scoops **1.50**

to wash it down

COFFEE • TEA • MILK SANKA • ICED TEA • POP .95

WINE NOT

	BOTTLE	½ BOTTLE
WHITE		
SOAVE	9.50	5.00
CHABLIS	9.00	
CHENIN BLANC	11.50	
LIEBFRAUMILCH	11.50	6.50
SPARKLING		
KORBEL BRUT	14.50	7.50
ROSE		
Rose of CABERNET SAUVIGNON	8.50	4.50
RED		
VALPOLICELLA	9.50	5.50
GAMAY BEAUJOLAIS	10.00	

GAMBITS

The following presentation is from a series of innovative materials developed by the Public Service Commission of Canada. It illustrates an attempt to focus on a function of language, in this case the restatement or clarification of a position. The expressions provided in the right-hand margin are gambits or strategies frequently used by native speakers to introduce a restatement of their views, linking it to what has preceded. The provocative list of *A Few Extreme Positions* and the related activities give learners an opportunity to choose from among these gambits in the expression of their personal views. In so doing, they are given the chance to develop valuable interaction skills.

SUBJECT-EXPANSION LINKS — RESTATEMENT   **23**

CORRECTING ONESELF

Levels 2-4, class, speaking, 15 minutes

At times we have to clarify ourselves. Perhaps we said something we didn't really mean, and as a result we may have gotten ourselves so entangled in words that it is best to start the statement all over again.

> **What I mean is**
>
> **What I meant is**
>
> **Let me put it another way**

State one of the extreme positions from the list below to the class. Then extricate yourself, starting with one of the gambits to the right. After a while, make up your own extreme positions.

> **What I'm saying is**
>
> **What I'm trying to say is**

A FEW EXTREME POSITIONS

1. *Women are lousy drivers.*
2. *I can't stand teachers (kids, English Canadians, etc.).*
3. *I wouldn't live in Toronto, (Montreal, Newfoundland, Yellowknife, Ottawa, etc.) if you paid me to.*
4. *I never use slang (swear words, insults, etc.).*
5. *Smokers (politicians, academics, bureaucrats, etc.) drive me up the wall.*
6. *Artists (public servants, students, etc.) are a bunch of lazy bums.*
7. *I never lie (swear, drink, smoke etc.).*
8. *I never have to look up a word in the dictionary.*
9. *Your own extreme position*

> **Don't get me wrong**
>
> **Don't misunderstand me (on this point)**
>
> **Let me rephrase what I just said**
>
> **If I said that I didn't mean to**

FURTHER ACTIVITIES

1. Discuss in class why some of the above positions are extreme. Try to state your views as freely as you can, and if you find that you want to restate them, use the links of this section.

2. Do you have any prejudices of your own? Get together with someone you feel you can trust and ask yourselves (a) What is the basis of my prejudice? (b) What will happen to my human relationships if I hold on to my prejudice? Use gambits from this section to correct yourself if necessary.

Source: E. Keller and S. Warner, *Gambits: Links* (Hull, Quebec: Canadian Government Publishing Center, 1979).

TELEPHONE GAMBITS

The following materials focus on language functions in the specific context of telephone conversations. Examples are provided of ways in which participants indicate they are following the conversation with varying degrees of agreement, doubt, surprise, etc. The expressions listed in this case are all rather colloquial in nature and might not be considered appropriate by native speakers in formal exchanges between, for example, strangers or coworkers. The matter of *appropriateness* in the selection of forms to serve various functions presents problems not only for learners but for textbook writers as well.

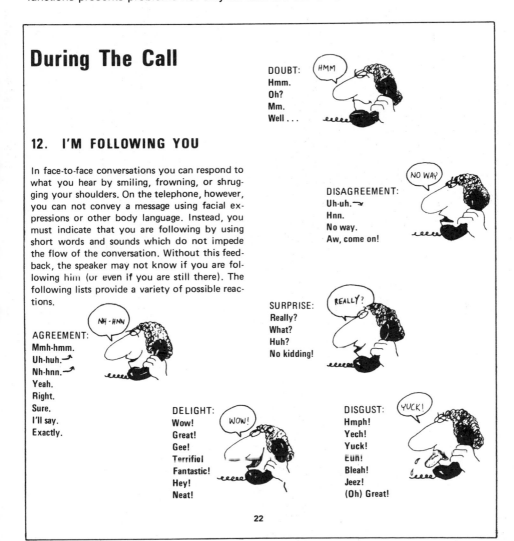

Source: J. Fox et al., *Telephone Gambits* (Hull, Quebec: Canadian Government Publishing Center, 1980).

COMBINING ORGANIZATIONAL FRAMEWORKS

This introduction to a unit in a secondary school French program illustrates the combination of several organizational frameworks in textbook development. In this case the content of the unit is stated in terms of structures (language), functions (communication), and situation.

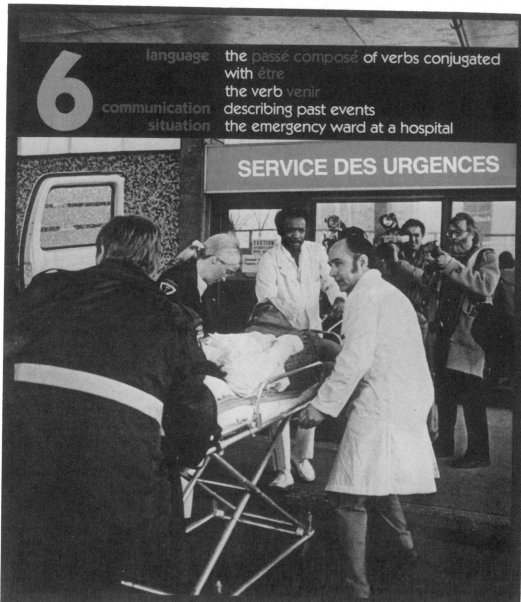

Source: G.R. McConnell et al., *Vive le français* (Don Mills, Ontario: Addison-Wesley, 1980).

NOTIONS AND FUNCTIONS

The language sample below appears in an introductory English textbook entitled *Notion by Notion*. The notion introduced here is "completed action." The function with which it is associated in this case is writing an informal (daughter to parents) account of something one has done. The facsimile of a handwritten postcard is intended to suggest authenticity. As an example of discourse, however, the postcard message is unconvincing. Its purpose is clearly not to convey meaning but to display a structural feature of English: past tense formation. In this case, then, we have an example of materials that are not really what they claim to be. Discrepancy between what a textbook *says* it does and what it in fact *does* is not uncommon, and noting this discrepancy is an important part of materials evaluation.

---

26 COMPLETED ACTION

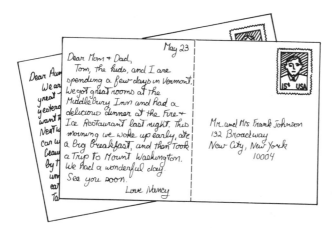

A
Use the cues below to write a postcard to a friend or a family member in your country. Tell about a recent trip. Practice the past tense (in parentheses).

find (found) a good hotel	meet (met) some interesting people
eat (ate) dinner	buy (bought) souvenirs
take (took) a train	spend (spent) a lot of money
see (saw) tourist attractions	speak (spoke) English
go (went) sightseeing	have (had) a great time

B
Use the cues to write sentences in the past tense. Change the underlined word(s) to pronouns. See the example.

1. When did <u>Bill</u> break in his new <u>shoes</u>? (a week ago)
   He broke them in a week ago.
2. When did <u>John</u> do over <u>the assignment</u>? (before class)
3. Where did <u>Barbara</u> write down <u>Bob's address</u>? (in her notebook)
4. When did <u>Susan and Carol</u> make up <u>the guest list for the party</u>? (last week)
5. Where did <u>Mrs. Miller</u> hang up <u>her coat</u>? (in the closet)
6. When did <u>Mr. Rogers</u> read over <u>the letters from his lawyers</u>? (this afternoon)
7. When did <u>Brenda</u> try on <u>her new dress</u>? (after lunch)
8. When did <u>Mr. Grayson</u> throw away <u>those old newspapers</u>? (this morning)
9. When did <u>Linda and Dan</u> give up <u>their apartment</u>? (last month)
10. Where did <u>Michael</u> put away <u>those old tests</u>? (in the top drawer of the desk)

52

Source: L. Ferreira, *Notion by Notion* (Rowley, Mass.: Newbury House, 1981).

INFERENCE

The exercise below calls for small groups to suggest a likely script for the missing half of a telephone conversation. Learners are asked to find different ways of saying something appropriate to the context. The emphasis here is clearly on meaning rather than structure, on inference of function rather than form.

Unit 9

Getting Information

~~~~~~

Listening In

This is the conversation that you have been completing orally. Practice it in small groups, and try to find different ways of saying the missing parts.

Kathy Riley: Oh, hi Beth. Why weren't you at school today?

Beth Miller:

    Kathy: So you caught it too. Seems like everybody's been getting the flu.

    Beth:

    Kathy: Well, you may not feel very sick now, but you'd better be careful. When my brother Jim caught it he didn't stay in bed and then he got awfully sick.

    Beth:

    Kathy: You've got to be kidding, Beth. Boy, if I were sick in bed I'd watch TV or something. How can you stand to be doing your school work?

    Beth:

    Kathy: You won't fall behind, Beth. We didn't do that much today   in algebra we didn't even have any homework.

    Beth:

    Kathy: Let me think. I'm pretty sure we don't have anything in history either. But of course we had an assignment in French.

Source: J. Boyd and M. Boyd, *Connections*(New York: Regents Publishing Co., 1981).

INFERENCE USING AUTHENTIC MATERIALS

Magazine and newspaper pictures and cartoons can serve the same pedagogical function as the illustration and incomplete dialogue in the preceding textbook example. In this case, learners use contextual cues and their knowledge of the world to infer a context of situation (roles of participants, setting, topic) and suggest the language forms that might be used to express that context. The cartoons reproduced below are from the classroom collection of Lucy Schmidt, French teacher in Calgary, Alberta, Canada.

Source: New Woman magazine, May 1982.

READING BY ALL MEANS

The following pages are from a textbook designed to improve reading skills in English. This somewhat lengthy excerpt is included to illustrate the attention given to contextual cues and coping strategies in the interpretation of a text and is an example of Goodman's advice to L2 teachers (1971:142): "As in learning to read a first language, reading should always involve natural, meaningful language and should avoid the trivial and keep the focus on comprehension strategies." This unit entitled "Remembering" is one of five units dealing with a variety of reading tasks, such as reading narratives, reading for general information, and reading for specialized information.

REMEMBERING

A Note About ...

Kamala Markandaya is from a Brahmin (high-caste) family from South India. For more than twenty-five years, she has had a distinguished career as a writer. When she was a young woman, she left her home in India, traveling to London where she supported herself by working in a law office. In London, she wrote her first novel, *Nectar In A Sieve*, about the life of an Indian woman. She took the title of the book from a line of poetry by a British poet, Samuel Coleridge:

Work without hope draws nectar[1] in a sieve[2]
And hope without an object cannot live.

---

[1]*nectar:* a sweet liquid; also the part of a plant that attracts bees.

[2]*sieve:* sounds like *live;* a utensil for separating liquid and solid parts. So, nectar runs out of a sieve.

Think about the meaning of these two lines of poetry while you read "Remembering," which is taken from *Nectar In A Sieve*.

Source: F. Dubin and E. Olshtain, *Reading By All Means* (Reading, Mass.: Addison-Wesley, 1981).

During the First Reading

Keep on reading even if you do not understand all the words. Ask yourself these questions:

- Who is telling the story?
- Is she telling about events that happened recently? Many years ago?
- Is the storyteller a young woman? A mature woman?

Remembering

KAMALA MARKANDAYA

These special Indian terms will help you better understand the story:

Bullock cart. A wagon drawn by large animals, bullocks.

Sari. The traditional dress of Indian women.

Dhal. Cooked, dried lentils, of the legume family of plants.

Curds. Typical Indian food, like yogurt.

Paddy. The place where rice is grown and rice in general.

1 A woman, they say, always remembers her wedding night. Well, maybe they do; but for me there are other nights I prefer to remember, sweeter, fuller, when I went to my husband matured in mind as well as in body, not as a pained and awkward child as I did on that first night. And when the religious ceremonies had been completed, we left, my husband and I. How well I remember the day, and the sudden sickness that overcame me when the moment for departure came! My mother was in the doorway, no tears in her eyes but her face bloated with their weight. My father standing a little in front of her, waiting to see us safely on our way. My husband, seated already on the bullock cart with the tin trunk full of cooking vessels and my saris next to him. Somehow I found myself also sitting in the cart, in finery, with downcast eyes.

2 Then the cart began to move. It lurched as the bullocks got awkwardly into rhythm, and I was sick. Such a disgrace for me . . . How shall I ever live it down? I remember thinking. I shall never forget . . . I haven't forgotten, but the memory is not sour. My husband soothed and calmed me.

3 "It's a thing that might happen to anybody," he said. "Do not fret. Come, dry your eyes and sit up here beside me." So I did, and after a while I felt better, the tears left my eyes and dried on my lashes.

4 20   For six hours we rode on and on along the dusty road, passing several villages on the way to ours, which was a good distance away. Halfway there we stopped and ate a meal: boiled rice, dhal, vegetables and curds. A whole coconut apiece, too, in which my husband nicked a hole with his scythe for me so that I might drink the clear milk. Then he unyoked the bullocks and led them
25 to the small pool of water near which we had stopped, giving them each a handful of hay. Poor beasts, they seemed glad of the water, for already their hides were dusty.

5   We rested a half-hour before resuming our journey. The animals, re-freshed, began stepping jauntily again, tossing their heads and jangling the
30 bells that hung from their red-painted horns. The air was full of the sound of bells, and of birds, sparrows and bulbuls mainly, and sometimes the cry of an eagle, but when we passed a grove, green and leafy, I could hear mynahs and parrots. It was very warm, and being unused to so long a jolting, I fell asleep.

6   It was my husband who woke me—my husband, whom I will call Nathan, for
35 that was his name, although in all the years of our marriage I never called him that, for it is not meant for a woman to address her husband except as "husband."

7   "We are home," he cried. "Wake up! Look!"

8   I woke; I looked. A mud hut, thatched, small, set near a paddy field, with
40 two or three similar huts nearby. Across the doorway a garland of mango leaves, symbol of happiness and good fortune, dry now and rattling in the breeze.

9   "This is our home," my husband said. "Come, I will show you."

10   I got out of the cart, stiff and with a cramp in one leg. We went in: two
45 rooms, one a sort of storehouse for grain, the other for everything else. A third had been begun but was unfinished, the mud walls were not more than half a foot high.

11   "It will be better when it is finished," he said. I nodded; I wanted to cry. This mud hut, nothing but mud and thatch, was my home. My knees gave, first the
50 cramped one, then the other, and I sank down. Nathan's face filled with concern as he came to hold me.

12   "It is nothing," I said. "I am tired—no more. I will be all right in a minute."

13   He said, "Perhaps you are frightened at living here alone—but in a few years we can move—maybe even buy a house such as your father's. You would
55 like that?"

14   There was something in his voice, a pleading, a look on his face such as a dog has when you are about to kick it.

15   "No," I said, "I am not frightened. It suits me quite well to live here."

16   He did not reply at once but went into the granary and came out with a
60 handful of paddy.

17   "Such harvests as this," he said, sliding the grains about in his hand, "and you shall not want for anything, beloved!" Then he went out to get the tin trunk and after a while I followed.

After the First Reading

1. Is the story told by

   - A young woman?
   - A mature woman?
   - The husband?

2. What do you think is the main theme of "Remembering"? Select *one* from the list below:

   - To tell why the woman was disappointed over her marriage
   - To tell about the woman's feelings—her fear, sickness, strangeness—on her wedding day
   - To tell about her husband's good qualities

(Check your own answers after the Second Reading)

During the Second Reading

Now read the story a second time. Look for the organization of the narrative.

   - What are the three scenes—the separate divisions in the story?
   - What is the sequence of events—the way in which one scene follows another?
   - What is the story line—what happens during each of the scenes?

APPLYING STRATEGIES

A. The Sequence of Events

1. The Wedding starts with: 1. _____
                                          _____
                                          _____

2. The Journey starts with: 2. _____
                                          _____
                                          _____

3. The Arrival Home starts with: 3. _____
                                          _____
                                          _____

B. The Story Line

What happened during each of the three scenes? Some information is given by the author; some is implied and must be supplied by the reader. Circle all the answers that are possible.

The Wedding

1. The ceremony was:
   - a) traditional
   - b) fancy
   - c) religious

2. The bride was:
   - a) very young
   - b) dressed in finery
   - c) looking at everyone

3. The bride and groom traveled:
   - a) in a bullock cart
   - b) on dusty roads
   - c) on foot

The Journey

4. While traveling:
   - a) the bride was sick
   - b) they stopped for food
   - c) the weather was hot and dry

5. The husband:
   - a) calmed his new wife
   - b) cared for the animals
   - c) slept during the journey

The Arrival Home

6. The mud hut:
   - a) had no neighbors nearby
   - b) had a garland of mango leaves over the doorway
   - c) had three rooms finished

7. The husband and wife:
   - a) liked each other
   - b) trusted each other
   - c) respected each other

C. Finding Context Clues

Use context clues to guess the meaning of the *italicized* words in the left-hand column.

New words and expressions

1. Line 8: My mother . . . no tears in her eyes but her face *bloated* with their weight.

2. Line 13: The cart began to move. It *lurched* . . . the bullocks got awkwardly into rhythm . . . and I was sick.

3. Line 16: My husband *soothed* and *calmed* me.

4. Line 17: "It's a thing that might happen to anyone. Do not *fret.*"

5. Line 29: The animals, refreshed, . . . stepping *jauntily* . . . tossing their heads and jangling their bells.

6. Line 31: The air was full of the sound of bells and birds, *sparrows* and *bulbuls* mainly.

7. Line 41: A garland of mango leaves . . . dry now and *rattling* in the breeze

Guess the meaning

1. The mother is sad because her daughter is leaving. There are no tears in her eyes, but she is ready to cry. Her face is filled with the weight of her tears.

   So, *bloated* = _____

   _____

2. The motion of the cart was not steady because the bullocks got awkwardly into rhythm.

   So, to *lurch* = _____

   _____

3. The memory is not sour because her husband soothed and calmed her.

   So, to *soothe* and to *calm* = _____

   _____

4. She felt disgraced. She said to herself, "How shall I ever live it down?"

   So, to *fret* = _____

   _____

5. After having food and water the animals moved in a lively way.

   So, *jauntily* = _____

   _____

6. Sparrows and bulbuls are not bells.

   So, *sparrows* and *bulbuls* = _____

   _____

7. The mango leaves were dry. When they moved in the breeze they made a noise.

   So, to *rattle* = _____

   _____

8. Line 44: I got out of the cart, stiff and with a *cramp* in my leg.

Line 50: My knees gave, first the *cramped* one . . .

8. She had been sitting many hours in the cart, asleep. Her legs were stiff when she tried to walk. She felt a pain in her leg.

So, a *cramp* = _____

D. Understanding the Characters

Now use clues to understand the people in the story. Circle all the correct answers. There may be more than one.

1. What was the woman's age at the time when she tells the story?

   clue: There are other nights I prefer to remember . . . when I went to my husband matured . . . not as a pained and awkward child.

   a) Less than 20 years
   b) 20-30 years
   c) Over 30

2. What were the mother's feelings about her daughter?

   clue: . . . no tears in her eyes but her face bloated with their weight.

   a) Sad to see her leave
   b) Remembering her own wedding day
   c) Unsure about her future life

3. What were the father's feelings about his daughter?

   clue: my father . . . waiting to see us safely on our way.

   a) Protectful of her
   b) Unsure about her future life
   c) Feeling pride that he had fulfilled his duty as a father

4. What was the woman's relationship with her husband during their lives?

   clue: . . . although in all the years of our marriage I never called him that . . .

   a) Traditional
   b) Formal
   c) Respectful

5. What were the husband's feelings towards his wife?

   clue: "It will be better when it is finished," he said.

   a) Ready to care for her
   b) Wanting to please her
   c) Hoping for a good life with her

E. Appealing to the Senses

Writers help the reader see places, experience tastes, and hear sounds through the words they use. Re-read paragraph five. Does it emphasize seeing, tasting, or hearing? What sentences helped you to decide? Write in the words used in those sentences:

1. _____ the bells. (line 29).

2. The air was _____ _____ _____ _____
   of bells and birds . . . (line 30)

3. the _____ of an eagle. (line 31)

4. I could _____ mynahs and parrots. (line 32)

5. Do the words you wrote in 1–4 emphasize:

   a) seeing?

   b) hearing?

   c) tasting?

Talking About . . .

With a partner, talk over your reactions to "Remembering."

1. How did the husband make his bride feel welcome and comfortable in her new home? What was across the doorway (paragraph eight)?

2. Notice that at the end (line 62) the husband promises his bride that "you shall not want for anything, beloved." Remembering the title of the novel from which this selection is taken, *Nectar In A Sieve*, ask each other:

   • What do you think happened to this husband and wife who lived in a mud hut with thatched roof in an Indian village?

   • In their life together, do you think they always had enough to eat?

3. Is there an incident in your own life that you will always remember? Talk about it, then listen to your partner's incident.

Summary / Reading Narratives

Here are the most important strategies you practiced in Chapter 1 for reading narratives:

   • You read the entire selection for the main point, without looking up unfamiliar words in the dictionary

   • You read the selection again; this time you looked for organization, key words, and details

34 SUMMARY

- You found the sequence of events that tied the story together
- You found the time signals that helped you understand the story
- You used context clues to guess the meanings of unfamiliar words and expressions
- You looked for the author's implications

A bullock cart.

COMICS

The final example in this collection of textbook illustrations is that of a comic book format, which has proved popular with school-age readers in many cultures. The page shown here is from an English reader for German learners entitled *Horror*. The familiar story line and illustrations provide a maximum of context for the interpretation of the dialogue. (Learners who find vampires unappealing might prefer comics like Charles Schulz's *Peanuts*, a series that has been translated into many languages!)

Source: R. Barret et al., *Horror Issues 2* (Munich, West Germany: Langenscheidt–Longman, 1978), p. 14.

The preceding samples of teaching materials have represented a variety of organizational features and exercises. Although by no means inclusive, they do provide an overview of both structural and functional considerations and of the trend in recent years toward more functional, communication-based activities. An appreciation of the differences these materials represent in terms of their underlying view of language and how it is learned is important in the systematic evaluation of their merit. This evaluation is the topic to which we now turn in the following section.

4.2. MEASURING UP: MATERIALS EVALUATION

Summary Guidelines

The major considerations that should go into the evaluation of teaching materials are summarized in the questions below. These are considerations central to the theory and practice of communicative language teaching that has been explored in this and preceding chapters. They have to do with (1) the assumptions that the materials make about the learner and the learning process, (2) the content of the materials, and (3) the implied role of the teacher. Because they are intended to apply to a broad range of teaching and learning contexts, these questions are of needs broad in scope and are best used for purposes of general discussion and interpretation. They may also serve as a basis for the development of a checklist of features suited to a specific context.

1. To what age level are the materials addressed? Are they consistent in this respect with regard to layout, design, illustrations, and choice of vocabulary, as well as with regard to activities involving learner attitudes and feelings?

2. What is the presumed L2 background of the learners for whom the materials are intended; that is, what, if any, prior experience with the langauge is assumed?

3. Is the learner treated as an intelligent human being whose capacity for partnership is taken seriously?

4. Are explanations clear and appropriate to the level of instruction and the age of the learners? Is there an avoidance of unnecessary *metalanguage* (professional jargon) in talking about language and communication?

5. What is the learner expected to do with the materials? Do all exercises and activities require answers in a complete sentence and/or the use of specific structures? Or do they give equal attention to the conveyance of meaning and the creative use of language?

6. What opportunity is there for learners to relate the materials to their personal interests and experiences?

7. Do the materials go beyond a "four skills" approach to L2 acquisition—that is, listening, speaking, reading, and writing—to reflect an understanding of the communicative abilities—interpretation, expression, and negotiation, for example—underlying *all* language use?

8. Is the L2 presented as a neutral means of communication, detached from its historical, cultural, and human values? Or is there an awareness that in acquiring a second language one is acquiring a new perspective on interpersonal relations?

9. Is there a clear rationale for exercise types and their relation to both the short-term and long-term goals of the learners?

10. Are the learners encouraged to use the L2 in the daily conduct of class activities? Are they shown ways of saying, *I'm sorry I don't understand, What do you mean? Let me explain, What's the word for* _____ *?* etc.

11. Are learners encouraged to look for language samples outside the textbook and outside the classroom?

12. What classroom arrangements do the materials suggest? Is there provision for working in pairs and small groups as well as for working with a whole class?

13. What provisions are made for evaluation of learner progress? Are testing guidelines consistent with the stated and implicit objectives of the program?

14. Are the materials attractive? Are there photographs, drawings, charts, colors, etc. that invite the learners to browse, ask questions, start a conversation?

15. What are the criteria for the selection and ordering of language samples? Is the basic organizational framework structural, functional, or situational?

16. How realistic are the language samples? Is the context sufficient to convey meaning?

17. If there is more than one L2 culture, is this made clear? Similarly, do the materials reflect an awareness of varieties within the L2?

18. What registers are used? Are they appropriate to the learners' intended use of the language? Is a distinction made between written and oral discourse?

19. What role is assigned to the teacher? What special skills does this role require?

20. What supplementary materials are available? Are there student workbooks? a teacher's guide? visual aids? To what extent do they enhance the major themes or content of the textbook?

A Checklist for Textbook Comparison

A ready-made checklist is useful to teachers who know what they are looking for in materials but need a way to organize their evaluations of several different textbooks or textbook programs for purposes of comparison. The following checklist is included as an example. It has been translated and adapted from one developed by Hans-Eberhard Piepho (1976), a leading European proponent of communicative language teaching. Comprehensive and easy to interpret, this particular model is suited to a wide range of teaching situations.

A CHECKLIST FOR TEXTBOOK COMPARISON

Organization

	Yes	No	Required	Optional
1. The materials include				
authentic prose texts.	☐	☐		
authentic dialogues (i.e., excerpts of conversations actually spoken by native speakers).	☐	☐		
texts written for the textbook.	☐	☐		
dialogues written for the textbook.	☐	☐		
vocabulary and grammar drills and exercises.	☐	☐		
activities for the application of grammar rules.	☐	☐		
activities for creative language use.	☐	☐		
activities for text interpretation.	☐	☐		
The materials also include				
workbooks and/or work sheets.	☐	☐		
learning objectives and content outline.	☐	☐		
teacher's guide.	☐	☐		
tests.	☐	☐	☐	☐
slides.	☐	☐	☐	☐
transparencies for an overhead projector.	☐	☐	☐	☐

	Yes	No	Required	Optional
pictures and/or wall charts.	☐	☐	☐	☐
tapes presenting texts from the book (e.g., dialogues, readings).	☐	☐	☐	☐
tapes presenting texts for listening practice.	☐	☐	☐	☐
tapes with grammar and pronunciation exercises and repetition drills.	☐	☐	☐	☐

	Yes	No
2. The sequence (of units, lessons, chapters) is divided into required and optional, basic and supplementary components.	☐	☐

3. Themes, situations, content, etc., are justified and explained to the learners

	Yes	No
through introductions and summaries.	☐	☐
in the native language.	☐	☐
in the second language.	☐	☐
through footnotes in each section.	☐	☐
through visual contextual clues.	☐	☐
not at all.	☐	☐

4. The learners' books are illustrated

	Yes	No
with original photographs.	☐	☐
with technical drawings (diagrams, charts, tables).	☐	☐
with symbols.	☐	☐
with cartoons or comics.	☐	☐
with collages.	☐	☐
with simple line drawings.	☐	☐

	Yes	No
5. The chapters, texts, exercises, and tasks are marked in such a way that the learners can recognize the nature of the task or learning activity by recurring symbols or titles.	☐	☐

Yes No

6. There are instructions in the textbook

   for individual work. ☐ ☐

   for group work. ☐ ☐

   for self-assessment. ☐ ☐

7. Vocabulary lists are

   second language → native
   language. ☐ ☐

   native language → second
   language. ☐ ☐

   second language → second
   language. ☐ ☐

   at the end of each section. ☐ ☐

   in subject groups. ☐ ☐

   alphabetical. ☐ ☐

   glossed in the margin. ☐ ☐

8. Grammar presentations are

   in both the second and native
   language. ☐ ☐

   in the second language only. ☐ ☐

   in the native language only. ☐ ☐

   inductive. ☐ ☐

   deductive. ☐ ☐

   both inductive and deductive. ☐ ☐

   interspersed throughout the units. ☐ ☐

   in a separate section within each
   unit. ☐ ☐

	Yes	No

Content

9. The themes for each chapter are

   historical, geographical, or political. ☐ ☐

   technical or scientific. ☐ ☐

   literary. ☐ ☐

   entertaining. ☐ ☐

   stimulating and provocative. ☐ ☐

   unrelated, selected to illustrate
   language functions, vocabulary, or
   points of grammar. ☐ ☐

10. The sequence of the themes reflects a
    definite scheme for the expansion of
    the learners' range of real-world
    experiences ☐ ☐

11. The structural patterns of the second
    language are taught by means of

    systematic tasks and exercises. ☐ ☐

    imitation and reproduction of
    dialogues. ☐ ☐

    oral expression of opinions and
    viewpoints about information in the
    texts. ☐ ☐

    pattern drills. ☐ ☐

12. Information (themes, topics,
    functions, and linguistic forms) is
    presented through (choose one)

    dialogues. ☐ ☐

    prose texts. ☐ ☐

    picture and dialogue combinations. ☐ ☐

    picture and text combinations. ☐ ☐

    picture and word and text collages. ☐ ☐

	Yes	No
14. Through systematic practice the learners learn how to express their own views on a topic.	☐	☐
15. The learners can check their own written work.	☐	☐
16. The materials on tape represent a normal speech rate.	☐	☐
17. The written exercises are for reinforcement purposes.	☐	☐
an expansion of the skills of written expression.	☐	☐
18. The learning objectives are		
explicit in the materials themselves.	☐	☐
revealed only on tests.	☐	☐

4.3 AN EXAMPLE OF THE "NO TEXTBOOK" OPTION: RADIO IN A STUDENT-CENTERED ORAL FRENCH CLASS*

Oral French, conversational French, *cours pratique*, whatever the rubric, the problem is the same: There has to be something to talk about. Learners need an incentive for spirited participation, and the teacher must provide for variety and interest without dominating class activities. In developing an intermediate or advanced course designed to allow practice in spontaneous self-expression, teachers of French have looked primarily to literary texts, cultural readers, and/or various French newspapers and magazines to provide the basis for short student presentations, which, ideally, will be followed by group discussion. Although many of these materials certainly are provocative and offer opportunities for oral practice, all too often the ensuing discussion is less than lively. The teacher ends up prodding and prompting a discussion for which the majority of the students are unprepared (both linguistically and culturally) or in which they are frankly uninterested. It is after repeated experiences of this kind that the teacher notes, and justly so, that leading a conversation class can be a good deal more taxing than preparing a lecture for a literature course.

---

* Originally published in a slightly different form as "A L'Ecoute de France-Inter: The Use of Radio in a Student-Centered Oral French Class" (Savignon 1972c).

The most important disadvantage shared by all kinds of readers, literary texts, and journals is that they offer examples of written French that are lexically and stylistically unsuited as models for oral practice. Through their exclusive use the learner is denied the opportunity for listening practice, which is crucial to the development and maintenance of speaking skills. Radio, on the other hand, offers a unique opportunity for developing the listening skills necessary for proficiency in speaking. *Live* material in particular, not canned broadcasts edited and preserved for later consumption, offers learners an exciting challenge while providing a variety of up-to-the-minute discussion topics rich in cross-cultural implications. What follows is a description of a student-centered oral French course that, as a starting point, received daily newscasts via shortwave from *France-Inter*.

Ici Paris, Office de Radiodiffusion-Télévision Française. Nous allons rejoindre France-Inter pour Inter-Actualités. (This is Paris, ORTF. Now we join France-Inter for Inter-News.)

Jean-Claude Bourret vous parle. (This is Jean-Claude Bourret.)

"Cassius Clay a trouvé son maître," titre *France-Soir sur cinq colonnes à la une.* . . . (Front page headlines in *France-Soir:* "Cassius Clay has met his match.")

Six gangsters, le visage caché par des cagoules, ont attaqué ce matin à 10h15 un camion. . . . (Six gangsters, their faces hidden by ski masks, attacked a truck at 10:15 this morning.)

Opération de la dernière chance en ce moment même au-dessus des Grandes Jorasses. . . . (A last ditch rescue attempt is taking place at this very moment in the Grandes Jorasses mountains.)

Vingt-quatre heures après la prise de contrôle des sociétés françaises par l'Algérie, . . . (Twenty-four hours after Algeria seized control of French-owned companies, . . .)

Une ménagère hollandaise a eu une très fâcheuse surprise en ouvrant la boîte de petits pois. . . . (A Dutch housewife had a nasty surprise when she opened a can of peas.)

French broadcasts were available for our use thanks to the efforts of a colleague (Nelson 1972) who was instrumental in obtaining a shortwave receiver for the Department of French (University of Illinois at Urbana-Champaign) and in training a graduate assistant to receive and tape-record a weekday news program of *France-Inter*. By means of a telephone hook-up, students, faculty, and even francophones outside the university community could then listen to these recordings any time of the day or night simply by dialing a telephone number. The popularity of the daily newscasts was reflected in the number of calls received. Although the newscasts constituted an assignment for only one intermediate-level conversation class with an enrollment of ten, the number of calls averaged 2000 a month! The recorded newscasts were approximately seven minutes in length. They often began with the musical coding or *indicatif*, which students came to identify with *France-Inter* news, and ended with the announcement of the horse-racing results. A typical program included brief reports on a variety of topics, which were local, national, and international in scope. To the American student, *France-Inter* offered action, drama, news, weather reports, and anecdotes in language that was both fresh and real.

The students with whom I worked had had no previous practice in listening to French radio. Although they were for the most part third-year and fourth-year college students with a major or a minor in French studies, they found the exercise difficult at first. By way of initiation I asked them to listen to the broadcasts daily for a week, gleaning whatever information they could. (Most students reported listening three or four times to each tape over the telephone.) At the end of this first week of listening the students brought into class their questions, partially understood phrases, and, often, total misconceptions. Because I had kept my own notes during the week, I was able to provide vocabulary items where these were the key to understanding a report. Most often, however, it was not a question of vocabulary but of format and cultural context.

I explained the *revue de presse*, a summary of headlines and editorials from national newspapers. A brief résumé of French-Algerian relations supplied sufficient background for understanding the current conflict over oil rights. Then, pulling down a map to locate the Grandes Joasses, we talked about *alpinisme* (mountain climbing). My role here was to situate an item in the appropriate cultural context by means of the kind of "culture capsule" described by Taylor and Sorenson (1961). Responding to learners' questions and misunderstandings was more satisfying to me personally and more efficient pedagogically than attempting to provide *a priori* insights into French culture. There was, after all, no way to predict the content of the next day's news. The learners, who attended class *after* their listening experience, asked for information that they knew they needed.

When the context was familiar, as in the accounts of American or of widely publicized international occurrences, comprehension increased. Knowing something already—for example, about recent developments in Vietnam or the Clay–Frazier fight—learners, freed of "cultural noise," could concentrate their attention on the French language itself. This redundancy of content, the repetition in French of something the learners already knew in English, permitted a rapid expansion of vocabulary and structure recognition, particularly in the early weeks of listening when students needed it most. The boost this achievement gave to class morale, moreover, was of no slight consideration. As students gained in both confidence and listening skills, they were ready to tackle the culturally more foreign items.

Students were exposed to many different styles of speech and regional accents through the interviews, eyewitness accounts, and public speeches that *France-Inter* incorporates into its newscasts. The breathless description by a helicopter pilot of an attempt to save two alpinists, an excerpt from an address by President Pompidou, an interview with a peasant who had found an enormous mushroom (later on display in Paris) all provided a variety of meaningful listening experiences not otherwise available in advanced language courses.

The most important and all-inclusive contribution of *France-Inter* to developing the communicative skills of my students is that it brought lively, up-to-date French language and culture into the classroom, to which the students responded with an enthusiasm akin to the enthusiasm of a Year Abroad student who steps off the plane at Charles de Gaulle airport. *This is for real.* No more book phrases to be drilled and then inserted in a simulated exchange. Once the student is put in contact with the real thing, the teacher can step back from center stage. The teacher is no longer master of ceremonies but coach, as the learners, individually and as a group, work toward understanding and responding to this new presence.

In the weeks that followed, students reported regularly in class on the preceding day's news. I encouraged them to say whatever they could about a particular item, even if it was no more than *"On a dit quelque chose à propos de l'Algérie"* (They said something about Algeria). This usually stimulated reactions from other students who could supply additional and even conflicting information to which others in turn responded, and so on. After reports and discussion, I distributed written texts of the preceding day's news. (It took a native French secretary 15 to 20 minutes to make a transcription from the tape recording.) Students used these texts as a further check on their comprehension.

Once goals and procedures had been established, my role for the remainder of the semester was to give the students the help they asked for in developing their communicative competence. My final evaluations of student achievement were based on reports of both familiar and unfamiliar news items. These reports included not only an account of the facts themselves but an interpretation reflecting the cross-cultural context. To this end the reports and discussions of current events continued at each class session. We frequently went to the language laboratory to listen to the tape for that day or a preceding day. We listened as often as we liked, stopping the tape whenever we wanted to share or test our understanding. (I can say *our* here because I too, being a nonnative speaker of French, increased my communication skills and cultural insights as a result of listening to *France-Inter* daily for 18 weeks.)

Other class activities included reports, discussions, debates, skits, impersonations, games, and informal conversation. The learners themselves were responsible for planning class sessions, even to the point of determining where we would meet. Class was scheduled twice weekly for two consecutive hours. We typically met for the first hour in the assigned classroom, or in the language laboratory, working with the news reports and other activities that seemed to suit the classroom setting. The second hour was often spent elsewhere, either in the apartment or residence hall of a class member or at a coffeehouse.

The impetus provided by the radio news was apparent in many of the activities. The concept of a *revue de presse*, for example, prompted a discussion of major French daily and weekly journals and their diversity of opinion, as it did of the newspaper as a political force and, ultimately, of why there is no practice in American broadcasting equivalent to a *revue de presse*. Students looked to French periodicals for more information on an event that either was mentioned briefly in the news or was followed for several days and required more background information. The drama of a French schoolboy who had been accused and taken to court for allegedly striking a professor is one example of a news story that held class interest for several weeks and prompted research into the judicial system and student activism in France.

Native speakers, especially exchange students from France, sometimes served as resource persons. The discussion of current events in France not only gave the American students practice in getting information from native speakers but also led in some cases to more fully developed personal relationships between Americans and visiting French students. Impromptu skits frequently simulated, or were a takeoff on, an incident reported on the news: Imagine a scene between a housewife who finds a dead mole in a can of peas and the storekeeper to whom she returns to complain; interview Joe Frazier after the Clay–Frazier fight; imagine a discussion between a gang of mobsters plotting a holdup. The subjects of serious discussions and debates—the war in Vietnam, student demonstrations, the position of the Catholic Church on contraception and abortion, the entrance of England into the Common Market, and so on—most often had been treated to some extent in the newscasts. Reports on an item of American origin were particularly useful in launching class discussion. The students already knew the subject and had opinions about it, and now they had the vocabulary necessary to talk about it in French.

At the beginning of the semester there were no more than two or three students who could report, in detail and with any degree of accuracy, on a single short news item. Initially, the amount of comprehension for some students was close to zero. As the semester progressed, more and more students were able to report with the others, correcting or adding details, until all items in any one newscast were included. After the first eight weeks every student could report fully on at least one item of news from each broadcast. This progress was not only encouraging to me but to the students themselves, who could measure it quantitatively. It offered them a feeling of achievement particularly needed in intermediate language courses, which often appear to stretch out as an interminable plateau. The range and depth of their understanding varied, but by the conclusion of the 18 weeks each student was comprehending sufficiently to make the experience self-sustaining beyond the end of the course itself. Students remaining in the community had continued access to the broadcasts by means of the telephone. One student felt confident enough to initiate the use of shortwave radio in the high school where she would be teaching. Another student later sent a postcard from Paris to say he had satisfied his desire to visit Longchamp, the racetrack he knew from listening to the racing report. The impact of the experience had been different for each student, but as they left the course, the last in a sequence of oral French courses, they did not leave spoken French behind them. They took *France-Inter* with them and thus much of France within them.

*

This chapter has presented an overview of recent initiatives in syllabus design and materials development along with guidelines for materials evaluation. The range of options is vast, offering choices suitable to all teaching contexts. Most difficult perhaps is the *selection* of materials from among the choices available. Although some textbooks may not be all they claim to be—and despite the bandwagon phenomenon that certainly exists—many textbooks on the market *do* provide excellent alternatives to established programs. In addition, teachers today have at their disposal an increasing number of authentic materials— radio and television programs, books, comics, games, puzzles, magazines— which can bring added interest and variety to any class.

With an understanding of the needs of a particular context in terms of such things as instructional goals, available class time, out-of-class learner contact with the L2, and the training and L2 proficiency of the teaching staff, the selection of appropriate materials can begin. Bearing these needs well in mind, materials can be evaluated and compared to reach the best decision for those concerned.

SUGGESTED READINGS

S. Ashton-Warner. 1963. *Teacher*. An inspirational account of learners' creation of materials congruent with their own life experiences. Their teacher, herself a novelist, tells how Maori children in New Zealand learned to read by writing their own stories.

B. Bettelheim and K. Zelan. 1982. *On Learning to Read: The Child's Fascination with Meaning*. A very readable yet knowledgeable discussion of the development of L1 literacy and of the problem with most primers: "empty texts–bored children." The issues raised are of equal interest to those concerned with beginning-level L2 reading materials.

C. Blatchford and J. Schachter (eds.). 1978. *On TESOL '78*. Includes a collection of plenary addresses by well-known methodologists (Campbell, Rutherford, Finocchiaro, and Widdowson) intended to familiarize an American audience with the notional-functional syllabus emanating from Europe. Includes criticisms of the limitations of the approach.

M. Breen and C. Candlin. 1980. "The Essentials of a Communicative Curriculum in Language Teaching." Discussion of interpretation, expression, and negotiation as the communicative abilities underlying competence. Emphasis should be less on selection and ordering of data and more on the way learners interact with the data, that is, the teaching-learning process.

C. Brumfit. 1980. "From Defining to Designing: Communicative Specifications versus Communicative Methodology in Foreign Language Teaching." Argues for the retention of grammar as the basis for syllabus design. Functions and situations may be thought of "as a spiral round a basically grammatical core."

N. Hart, R. Walker, and B. Gray. 1977. *The Language of Children: A Key to Literacy*. The report of the Mount Gravatt (Australia) research project on the words and expressions used by young children to communicate. A "core language" is provided here as a basis for the development of beginning reading materials.

C. Hosenfeld. 1979. "Cindy: A Learner in Today's Foreign Language Classroom." An account of the coping strategies of an American high school student learning to read French. This case study is of value because it helps teachers to remember how it feels to be a beginning reader, an inexperienced player in what Goodman (1976) has called a "psycholinguistic guessing game."

C. Johnson. 1979. "Choosing Materials That Do the Job." Looks at the realities of L2 textbook adoption in American schools. Extensive bibliography.

E. Joiner. 1974. "Evaluating the Cultural Content of Foreign Language Texts." A checklist to assess the portrayal of L2 culture in teaching materials.

R. Lafayette. 1978. "Coping with 'Innovative Overchoice': A Curriculum Model." Documents the increasing diversity of L2 curricula and advocates adoption of a "core plus open time" approach to curriculum development. Examples are drawn from American secondary school programs.

H. Madsen and J. Bowen. 1978. *Adaptation in Language Teaching*. A guide to achieving congruence between teaching materials, learners, and the teacher's background and personal style. ESL oriented.

J. Munby. 1978. *Communicative Syllabus Design*. Describes a procedure for carrying out a needs analysis with reference to such variables as the learner's identity as an individual, physical and psychological settings, interactional roles, etc. Worth reading if only for the stir it has created. For a sharp criticism of Munby's approach to needs analysis, read the review of his book by A. Davies (1981.)

D. Ross. 1981. "From Theory to Practice: Some Critical Comments on the Communicative Approach to Language Teaching." Criticizes equating communicative language teaching with notional-functional syllabus design, by British applied linguists and methodologists in particular.

F. Smith. 1971. *Understanding Reading*. Valuable reading for all language teachers. Although the topic is L1 reading, the discussion offers many insights useful for L2 teaching and testing. The role of *redundancy*, the availability of information from more than one source, is explained with numerous examples. Smith defines comprehension as "the reduction of uncertainty."

R. Stern. 1976. "Sexism in Foreign Language Textbooks." The issue taken here with the portrayal of women serves to call attention to a more general problem in materials development: the risk of cultural stereotype and the complexity of the responsible representation of a second culture in the midst of diverse and changing values.

E. Stevick. 1980. *Teaching Languages: A Way and Ways*. Highlights three nontraditional approaches to L2 teaching that have received increased attention in recent years: Silent Way (Gattegno 1972), Counseling-Learning Community Language Learning (Curran 1972), and Suggestopedia (Lozanov 1979). See, in particular, Chapter 16, "Materials for the Whole Learner."

T. Terrell. 1980. "A Natural Approach to the Teaching of Verb Forms and Function in Spanish." Illustrates the application of communicative, rather than formal, criteria to the selection of verb forms to be presented in an introductory Spanish course.

A. Valdman. 1978. "Communicative Use of Language and Syllabus Design." Proposes a revision of syllabus design to involve the learner in the largest number of communicative transactions in the shortest period of time.

A. Valdman and H. Warriner-Burke. 1980. "Major Surgery Due: Redesigning the Syllabus and Texts." Sees as ill-advised the replacement of traditional situational-structural syllabuses by notional syllabuses, advocating, rather, a modified situational-structural syllabus that gives semantic notions higher priority than surface features in selection and ordering. Notes, in addition, the need to abandon insistence on completeness and perfection of learner language: "Only if foreign language teachers abandon insistence on perfection and completeness . . . can acquisition of deep semantic notions and practice in the functional use of language be given priority."

J. Van Ek. 1975. *Systems Development in Adult Language Learning: The Threshold Level in a European Unit/Credit System for Modern Language Learning by Adults*. The result of a collaborative effort by J. Trim, R. Richterich, D. Wilkins, K. Bung, and others to provide a definition of L2 "threshold competence" in terms of notions and functions. The project was sponsored by the Council of Europe to promote the integration of different language groups within the Common Market and to adapt L2 teaching to adults with a wide range of professional and social needs. Specific examples here are for English, but similar threshold levels have been specified for French (Coste et al. 1979) and Spanish (Slagter 1980).

H. Widdowson. 1978. *Teaching Language as Communication*. Examines the distinction between language usage and language use with particular reference to ESL teaching materials and exercise types. Demonstrates not only the inadequacy but the inappropriateness of the term *four skills* (that is, listening, speaking, reading, and writing) to describe language use, or communicative abilities.

RESEARCH AND DISCUSSION

1. What does the term *syllabus* mean to you? Is it a day-to-day schedule of activities and pages in a textbook to be "covered"? Or is it a set of guidelines for the selection and sequencing of items to be taught? How does it differ from *curriculum*? (If you would like help in defining these terms, see the Glossary provided in the back of this book.)

2. Select a unit from an introductory L2 textbook. What attention is given, respectively, to the phonological, grammatical, and semantic systems of language? Share your analysis with classmates.

3. What advantages do you see for a functional syllabus? a structural syllabus? a situational syllabus?

4. In the selection of materials, what consideration must be given to the strengths and weaknesses of the teachers who will use them? Contrast, for example, the needs of a multisectional beginning Spanish college program, staffed primarily by inexperienced nonnative speakers, with the needs of a course taught by an experienced native speaker.

5. How does class size affect materials selection? For example, compare the Community Language Learning conversation group of four to seven learners with a typical public school classroom. What provisions can be made for small group work in the latter?

6. a) G. Gerngross, a teacher of English in an Austrian secondary school, writes the following:

   > As long as I follow the structure of a coursebook, work is usually rather dull and doesn't take very much account of the pupils' needs. But it is convenient and to some extent predictable. As soon as I really bother about the students' needs, teaching becomes largely unpredictable. [personal communication]

   Have you had a similar experience? Discuss in relation to materials selection.

   b) Lucy Schmidt, a secondary school French teacher in Calgary, Alberta, Canada, writes:

   > I like to stress learner participation in the choice and preparation of teaching materials. This personalization takes more preparation time and/or coordination effort but in the long run is *highly effective*. [personal communication]

   Discuss in relation to your own experience.

c) Sook-Hee Kim, a native of Korea who has just begun her L2 teaching career, has the following to say:

> I agree that materials are but a starting point and that teachers are the ones who make materials work for their students and for themselves, but I think it is difficult for beginning teachers to provide variety and interest without a textbook to provide a certain structure. [personal communication]

Comment in relation to (a) and (b) above.

7. Specialized L2 courses are often developed through the cooperation of language teachers and technical experts with a firsthand knowledge of the area of specialization. Such alliances are not without their problems, however, as a teacher in a private language school in Tokyo once noted: "Businesses send us people. We don't have the technical expertise but we teach them how to communicate at a very rudimentary level, to explain how to screw bolts, etc. While technical consultants know the subject area, they often require too much in terms of accuracy. They don't understand that a non-native can say in 10 words what a native speaker might say in 30!" Comment in relation to the coping strategies or *strategic competence* discussed in this and preceding chapters. Is there, in needs assessment, a danger of *overspecification* of structures and vocabulary?

8. In their study of the characteristics and behaviors of the successful foreign language teacher, Politzer and Weiss (1969:59) found that "better results were obtained by the pupils of those teachers who went beyond the procedures strictly prescribed by the curriculum—teachers who were concerned with supplementing the curriculum rather than merely implementing it. . . . It seems that the efficiency of the individual teacher increases with the amount of his *personal* stake and *personal* contribution to the instructional processes." What are the implications of this finding for materials selection?

9. If you teach an L2 other than English, prepare a list of telephone gambits on the model of those on page 153.

10. Use the checklist on pages 171 to 175 to compare (1) a pair of textbooks with similar stated *objectives*—for example, communicative competence—and (2) a pair whose stated *organizational frameworks* are similar—for example, notional-functional.

11. Do you remember a favorite language textbook? Why? What do you remember most about it?

12. Collect some vacation postcards you have received from family and friends. Would they be suitable as texts for L2 learners? Why or why not? Compare them both structurally and functionally with the sample postcard on page 155.

13. If you are a classroom teacher, make a list of the activities you use that emphasize listening or reading for general comprehension of the main ideas. Give specific examples of ways in which these activities both provide contextual cues and encourage learners to make use of them.

14. Arrange with a colleague or classmate to visit an L2 classroom. Keep a record of the time spent on L2 experience (L2 use for a communicative purpose) as opposed to L2 analysis (explanations, drills, or exercises designed to focus on specific structures or functions).

15. Goodman makes the following observation about the reading process (1971:138):

> In order to derive meaning from language the language user must be able to provide semantic input. This is not simply a question of meaning for words but the much larger question of the reader having sufficient experience and conceptual background to feed into the reading process so that he can make sense out of what he is reading. All readers are illiterate in some senses, since no one can read everything written in his native language.

Find a text in your native language you cannot read, that is, of which you can make no sense even though you are familiar with the graphic and syntactic systems being used. What is the advantage for learners of learning to read from materials on topics in which they are interested and have had prior experience? In what ways does familiarity with a topic, *redundancy of information*, compensate for a lack of syntactic knowledge?

16. Using as a model the radio course described in Section 4.3, explore the possibility of using magazine advertisements in a beginning reading course. Find examples of advertisements with numerous contextual cues to meaning. Products available in the L1 culture, and therefore familiar to the learners, would perhaps be a logical first step. What opportunities do advertisements provide for entry into L2 culture? What motivational advantages are there for the learners who thus begin to read from *authentic* materials? What might be criteria for sequencing examples of advertisements?

17. Provide beginning readers with a collection of L2 magazines and have them select the items, including advertisements, cartoons, pictures, etc. they find of interest. (These items may be cut out and mounted for classroom use.) Do their choices correspond to what you would have selected? What factors seem to have guided the learners' selection?

18. What possibilities exist in your community for receiving live L2 radio broadcasts via either standard or shortwave frequencies? Are there television programs or advertisements that could be recorded for classroom use? (Cable television provides access to an increasing variety of local and international broadcasts.)

19. If you had your choice, would you prefer to teach with a single, comprehensive textbook (containing, for example, language samples, linguistic and cultural explanations, and exercises) or with a collection of materials or modules with related yet different emphases (for example, reference grammar, authentic documents, projects or special topics, and problem-solving activities)?

20. How do the linguistic backgrounds of the learners affect materials selection? Contrast, for example, the needs of a group of learners with no L1 or lingua franca in common (for example, an ESL class at an American university) with those of a group of learners who share the same cultural and linguistic background (for example, a Spanish class in an American high school or an English class in a Japanese elementary school).

21. The following personal account of a language learning experience was written by an ESL teacher following her stay in Iran. What insights does it provide into the role of individual learning styles in determining the appropriateness of materials?

> In Tehran they sold books for children in Persian that had fantastic art work. It was this art work which greatly attracted me, and I decided I wanted to

learn to read using these children's books. My husband said I shouldn't waste money on them as they contained no vocabulary lists or transcriptions . . . and therefore, all my time would be spent looking up words in the dictionary and mispronouncing a good part of what I read. Finally at the end of the first month of our stay John agreed to try some.

To my delight we had enormous success with them. The stories were so entertaining that they led to a much greater effort learning to read than did the [L2] classroom readers. In fact, studying now became that part of the day that we looked forward to as a special treat. The illustrations greatly aided our understanding of much of the action. We underlined words which we were unsure of and later consulted an Iranian friend about their meanings. An added bonus was the insight these stories gave us into Iranian culture. [J. Schumann and F. Schumann 1977:245]

Chapter 5

Shaping the Curriculum

All this, of course, takes time and involves noise and movement and personal relations . . . and above all communication, one with another: the vital thing so often cut off in a schoolroom.

—Sylvia Ashton-Warner

These are challenging times to be a teacher of languages. As the world gets smaller and as nations and the diverse ethnic populations within them depend increasingly on one another for their well-being, the importance of cross-cultural communication continues to grow. Learning to speak another's language means taking one's place in the human community. It means reaching out to others across cultural and linguistic boundaries. Language is far more than a system to be explained. It is our most important link to the world around us. Language is culture in motion. It is people interacting with people.

Just as there is no one set of ideal teaching materials, so there is no universal teaching method suited to the many contexts of language learning. What language teachers today need, more than another ready-made method of teaching, is an appreciation both of language as an expression of self and of the ways in which meanings are created and exchanged. As they shape curricula for the language programs of tomorrow, teachers should see the learner as a physical, psychological, and intellectual being with needs and interests that extend far beyond those of the language classroom. The most effective programs will be those that involve the whole learner in the *experience* of language as a network of relations between people, things, and events. The balance of features in a curriculum will and should vary from one program to the next, depending on the particular learning context of which it is a part. Development of a curriculum should begin, however, with an awareness of the full range of potential options, and choices should be made consciously from among those possibilities.

Putting Some Order in
"Innovative Overchoice"

Many innovations in curriculum planning have been proposed in recent years that have offered both novice and veteran teachers a dizzying array of alternatives. Games, yoga, J.S. Bach, and silence have all been proposed as aids to L2 acquisition. Teacher talk, minicourses, drama, videotapes, and values clarification are among the many features that have been credited for program success. All proposals have something to offer, no doubt, if no more than the enthusiasm of those who make them. The interest sparked by a new and perhaps unconventional approach is undeniable and may contribute to the development of yet other methods that suit a particular context. Teaching, being as much art as science, thrives on innovation and reaction. As with all new methods, experience will be the final judge of their success.

In an attempt to put some order into what Lafayette (1978) has aptly called this "innovative overchoice," it is perhaps helpful to think of an L2 curriculum as having five potential components. These components may be looked upon as clusters of activities or experiences related to L2 use and usage—clusters that provide a useful way of categorizing teaching strategies designed to promote communicative L2 use. The use of the term *components* to categorize these activities or experiences seems particularly appropriate in that it avoids any suggestion of sequence or level. Experimentation with communicative teaching methods has shown rather that all five components can be profitably blended at all stages of instruction. This blending is not only desirable, it is inevitable inasmuch as the components clearly overlap. No L2 curriculum, any more than the L2 proficiency it promotes, should ever be thought of as atomistic, as neatly divisible into separate tasks. The organization of L2 learning activities into the following components or thematic clusters serves, then, not to sequence an L2 program but rather to *highlight the range of options* available in curriculum planning and to suggest ways in which their very interrelatedness may be maximized for the learner:

Language Arts

Language for a Purpose

My Language Is Me: Personal L2 Use

You Be, I'll Be: Theater Arts

Beyond the Classroom

These components differ markedly from those to which L2 methods courses and teacher-training manuals typically address themselves; they suggest, further, areas to which increased attention needs to be given in teacher preparation. Teachers trained to take an essentially audiolingual, "four-skills" view of language learning, (that is, listening, speaking, reading, and writing) are in many cases lacking the perspective needed to shape a communicative curriculum.

This chapter takes a look at each of the five components listed above, defines them, and offers examples of the kinds of activities or experiences they include. The examples provided are from actual practice. They are strategies used by classroom teachers to promote the communicative use of the languages they teach. These strategies, then, are the practice congruent with the theory of communicative competence that has been explored in preceding chapters.

5.1 LANGUAGE ARTS

Language Analysis

If Language Arts is the first component on the list, it is because it represents what language teachers have learned to do best—most often because it is all they have been taught to do. Language Arts focuses typically on rules of usage. It provides explanations of how language works. When L2 teachers observe that students do not know their grammar what they often mean is that the learners have not acquired a metalanguage for talking about syntax and morphology. That is, they cannot identify and name object pronouns, indirect objects, past tense markers, and the like. Their *language use* may be fine, but they lack experience in analyzing it. This, of course, poses a problem for L2 teachers who then need to provide learners with an explanation of the system being used. Learners with prior experience in linguistic analysis have a decided advantage. (Another cause of teacher complaints about students' lack of grammar is, of course, a discrepancy between the language forms used by students and those perceived by the teacher to be proper or correct. In most cases such discrepancies reflect not a lack of grammar on the part of the student but simply the use of a *different* grammar.)

Language analysis, like a language syllabus, may be structural or functional. Although the former is more familiar to teachers and learners, the latter has the virtue of including semantics and sociolinguistic rules of use. There is no reason why a Language Arts component should not include both kinds of analysis. Language Arts should include attention to rules of language and language behavior along with systematic practice in their application. The particular focus of this component is perhaps best summed up in an anecdote involving a twelve-year-old girl. She was responding to her mother's attempt to bring attention to the way in which she and her young friends were expressing themselves. The mother suggested that someone try to summarize in a sentence or two an argument that had just been presented. Her daughter's reaction was, "Ding-a-ling-a-ling, bell's just rung. Time for Language Arts!" Language Arts, then, involves stepping back momentarily from communication in order to look at the forms that that communication is taking.

Deductive and Inductive Approaches

Deductive and inductive approaches to language analysis are not only useful but can be used in combination to provide variety as well as to respond to different learning styles. In a deductive mode, rules are stated and examples then given, as in the following presentation of adjective agreement in Spanish:

> After the verb *ser* the predicate adjective agrees with the subject in number and gender.
>
> El es norteamericano.
>
> Ellos son norteamericanos.
>
> Ellas son norteamericanas.
>
> Ella es norteamericana.

In the inductive mode, on the other hand, language data are provided, and learners are encouraged to work out rules or generalizations for themselves. This process is sometimes referred to as *discovery learning*. An inductive approach to teaching the same rule of adjective agreement in Spanish would be to provide learners with the sample sentences above along with the following instructions.

> Working in small groups or pairs study the above sentences. What rule can you give to explain the different forms of the adjective *norteamericano*?

Discovery learning lends itself to functional as well as structural analyses of language. For example, the initial exchanges from a series of encounters might point to the conclusion that the following are all forms of greeting in English: *How are you? Hi, Hello, What's new? How's it goin'?* Similarly, learners can be given excerpts from a series of dialogues and asked to select the greeting appropriate to each from a choice provided. Following exercises of this kind, the explicit statement of a rule, when possible, often helps learners to organize the data they have observed and to confirm their understanding.

For adult learners with prior experience in linguistic analysis, a deductive statement of rules is efficient and provides a good introduction to structural or functional features, which can then be followed with examples and practice. Both adults and young children, on the other hand, are capable of learning through experience alone quite complex linguistic rules of grammar as well as sociolinguistic rules of appropriateness. (In a class of beginning learners who do not have an L1 in common, the teacher, of course, has no choice but to proceed through induction.) Regardless of the age and linguistic backgrounds of the learners, moreover, the inclusion of inductive or problem-solving approaches to rule generalizations is important for the help it gives learners in developing strategies for analyzing language data on their own. As they learn to analyze data for themselves they will become more efficient learners both inside and *outside* the classroom—a critical step on the way to becoming communicatively competent.

Spelling, Vocabulary Expansion, and Other Goals

Language Arts includes many of the exercises used in mother tongue (L1) programs to focus attention on formal accuracy. Spelling tests, for example, are important if writing is a goal. They may be written lists of words, crossword puzzles, dictation passages, or spelling bees. Among the many activities included in L2 Language Arts are such things as *vocabulary expansion* through definitions, descriptions, synonyms, antonyms, L1/L2 cognates and false cognates; *pronunciation exercises* and the contrast of L1/L2 sounds; *patterned repetition* of verb paradigms and other structural features; *contrast of L1/L2 grammars; substitution of one structure for another*, for example, affirmative for negative, future tense for present tense; *substitution of one register for another*, for example, informal for formal.

Analysis of the formal features of language should also include contexts that extend beyond sentence level. That is, it should consider the formal features of discourse that contribute to text *cohesion*. Text cohesion is achieved through the use of devices for connecting discourse and may be demonstrated to learners by the systematic deletion of these devices from a text, as in the following example:

Fill in the blanks:

Downhill skiing: Yes, we have _____ in Illinois. And some decent

slopes reputedly are available in Wisconsin and other neighboring north-

ern _____ . But I don't know the first thing about it. If you're already

into downhill, _____ probably have money. If so, go to Vail. If

_____ , get a list of Illinois _____ ski areas from any local

outdoor outfitters. Several other _____ are listed in *The Weekend*

Book, available from the _____ Office of Tourism in Springfield.

As we have seen in Chapter 1, formal cohesion is but one feature of a more general text *coherence*, the connectedness of discourse through its relation to a common topic or purpose. Both cohesion and coherence are familiar terms in the analysis of discourse, and attention to these features is of particular value in L2 language analysis because it requires going *beyond* structural cues to look at meaning and interpretation.

Language Arts Games

There are many Language Arts games that learners of all ages enjoy for the variety and group interaction they provide. As long as they are not overused and are not promoted as the solution to all manner of L2 learning problems, Language Arts games are a welcome part of a teacher's repertoire. The following examples are among the favorites of experienced teachers. Each provides an occasion to practice grammar, pronunciation, or vocabulary in a game format.

Memory test. This activity has been a popular party game for decades and is easily adapted to an L2 classroom. The association of vocabulary items with physical objects makes the words all the more real, which facilitates recall. Learners should be encouraged to contribute objects that have special meaning for them.

Place on a tray ten (10) familiar items—for example, scissors, fork, pencil, penny, button. Cover the tray with a towel so that nothing can be seen. Each player needs a pencil and a piece of paper. Uncover the tray and leave the objects exposed for three minutes. During that time players look at the items and try to memorize everything they see. No one may write anything during this period. When the three minutes are up, the tray is removed. Players now have three more minutes in which to write down the names of the items they remember. A player who succeeds in remembering the names of all the items should call out "Finished!" If all items are correct, that player wins the game; if not, the player who lists the most items within the three-minute writing period wins. There are two ways to score; the more lenient method is to disregard errors in spelling as long as the names of items have been recalled. As objects become more familiar and learners more proficient, exact spelling can be required.

Draw a word. Words are written on folded slips of paper and placed into a hat. Players in turn draw a word and must then use it in a complete sentence. To give added interest, establish two categories of words: "Easy Words for Novices" and "Hard Words for Scholars." Hard words used correctly are worth twice as much. Learners can help to create a more elaborate game by writing words on colored cards, using different colors for nouns, verbs, adjectives, and adverbs. These cards can be added to at any time and used in numerous adaptations of the above format.

Scrambled passages. One way to have learners focus on features of cohesion and coherence is to scramble the sentences of a text and ask the learners to put them back in order (see Chapter 1, Research and Discussion, no. 8). A game adaptation of this same exercise is the distribution of slips of paper, each bearing a chunk of connected discourse from a reading passage, dialogue, etc. Learners compare sentences or utterances and position themselves in a line to read off the reconstructed text. Limit the number of chunks per passage (and thus group size) to no more than seven or eight. A typical classroom will accommodate three or four groups working at once, on the same or different texts.

I'm going on a trip. This round-robin game encourages participants to listen to what others are saying and promotes pronunciation accuracy as they repeat what classmates have said. One player begins, "I'm going on a trip and am taking ＿＿＿＿＿＿ " (a suitcase, an umbrella, a tennis racket, my sister, or any other single item or person). The next player repeats "I'm going on a trip and am taking _____ ," repeating the item supplied by the first player and adding a second. As the game continues, the list of items gets longer and longer and may be as realistic or as nonsensical as the players wish to make it. For a team competition, award one point for each item correctly remembered and pronounced. Many adaptations of this format are possible—for example, "We went on a picnic and took . . . ," "Happiness is . . . ," "If I had a million dollars I would . . . ," "To succeed in life one must . . . ."

Group amnesia. This is another favorite party game, one that is especially useful in promoting learner interaction. Adaptations of this format are used in L2 classrooms to provide practice in the use of particular structures and vocabulary—for example, interrogative verb forms and high-frequency adjectives. For added interest, give learners an opportunity to contribute ideas for identities and prepare the cards themselves.

Cards are prepared with the names on them of famous persons like Napoleon, John Lennon, Princess Diana, etc. Pin a name on the back of each player who then proceeds to learn his or her identity. Players move about the room asking questions of classmates—for example, "Am I alive?" "Am I an American?" "Am I a woman?" "Am I an actor?" Questions may be answered with *only* "Yes" or "No." Players may not ask the same person more than one question at a time. They may come back and ask a second question of the same person only after they have asked someone else a question. When players think they have discovered who they are, they go to the person directing the game to check their guess. A correct guess wins. A wrong guess sends the player back to ask more questions. Two wrong guesses and a player is eliminated. The first five players to correctly guess their identities win the game.

GROUP AMNESIA

Hangman. (A lugubrious title but all in fun!) One team thinks of a word and draws a number of blanks to represent the letters in the word. The other team tries to guess the letters in the word. "Is there an O?" "Is there a T?" etc. For each wrong guess, a section is added to a dangling stick figure. The object is to guess the word before the figure is completed.

HANGMAN

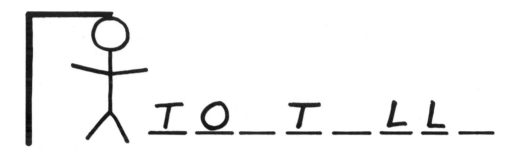

Odd man out. This word game is adapted from a collection of games prepared specifically for learners of English as a second language (A. Wright et al. 1979) and resembles the concept generalization task frequently included in tests of general language proficiency. Like most other games, this one works best when learners are encouraged to contribute items that reflect their special interests. Although the focus is on word usage, interaction among participants is inevitable. Groups of words are prepared, each containing an "odd man out," for example:

a) horse, cow, mouse, *knife*, fish

b) *bicycle*, bus, car, motorcycle, truck

c) green, *big*, orange, brown, red

d) Ford, Cadillac, *Honda*, Plymouth

(Note: The focus in each set should be *semantic* rather than structural!) Players write down the word from the first group that they think is the "odd man out" and then compare responses. As individual players announce their choices, the other players are asked if they agree. If they disagree, they should be given the opportunity to say why.

Drawings. This timeless vocabulary expansion activity is cited in Jesperson (1904) and is a good example of meaning preceding form. Learners are each assigned a subject to illustrate by a drawing on the chalkboard. Although the learners are told to draw only those features they can explain to their classmates in the L2, they most often find themselves drawing much more. "The result is that [their] interest is aroused for what all the things are called, and [they] pay close attention to the words when the teacher says them!" A variation is to have one learner describe an object (house, animal, city street, etc.) to another or several other learners who attempt to draw it on the board or at their desks.

L1 and L2 textbooks abound in ideas for additional Language Arts activities appropriate for different ages and levels of cognitive development. These activities may not play a central role in the development of communicative abilities, but they are nonetheless a worthwhile component of a program that sets communicative competence as its goal. Many learners, moreover, come to a language classroom *expecting* a systematic presentation and drill of L2 structures, pronunciation, and vocabulary. This expectation alone does not justify an emphasis on analysis and drill at the expense of opportunities for language use. It does, however, illustrate the value of language analysis as a reassuring frame of reference for many learners as they develop their ability to use the L2 for communication.

This analysis and practice should include, as we have seen, the functional as well as the structural features of language. A Language Arts component provides an opportunity to bring explicit attention not only to grammatical forms and rules of language usage but to the ways in which the functions of language are met in different settings—to the use of language to inquire, to describe, to invite, to suggest, to require, etc. What's more, analysis of communication should include not only structures and functions but *all* the features elaborated in Chapter 1—grammatical competence, sociolinguistic competence, discourse competence, and strategic competence.

To illustrate the contribution of strategic competence, for example, a teacher could ask learners to consider the characteristics of nonnative speech. They might begin by noting the features of communication that signal the nonnativeness of persons with whom they (1) interact personally or (2) have occasion to observe on television. In the case of public figures such as government leaders, entertainers, and athletes, learners should ask themselves in what ways their nonnative speech contributes to the image they project. In the case of nonnatives they know personally, they should consider how natives in turn *respond*. That is, in what ways do native speakers adapt their own manner of speaking in response to a nonnative interlocutor, an example of the *foreigner talk* or code simplification discussed in Chapter 2. What should emerge from such observation and discussion is an awareness of communication as a process of negotiation, with success dependent on the cooperation of all involved.

Any and all analyses are useful provided they are related to experience in L2 use. The important thing to remember about Language Arts is that it is a component that must be integrated with other components of the curriculum. It should never, as is too often the case, become the sole focus of the course. Teachers and learners who understand this will always want to relate their understanding of how language works to the use of language for a purpose.

METALANGUAGE

The cartoon below is a playful reminder of the risk of talking so much about rules and abstract theories that we lose sight of our reason for talking about them in the first place. *Metalanguage*—whether structural terms like *phoneme*, *morpheme*, *object*, and *determiner*, or discourse terms like *speech act*, *cohesion*, *coherence*, and *notion*—is no replacement for language.

shoe

Source: Daily Illini, September 23, 1981.

Reprinted by permission of Tribune Company Syndicate, Inc.

5.2 LANGUAGE FOR A PURPOSE

Language analysis contrasts with language experience: the use of language for real and immediate communicative goals. The recent attention to language courses for specific purposes (see Chapter 3) has served to underscore the fact that not everyone is learning an L2 for the same reasons and that attention to the specific communicative needs of the learners is important in the selection and sequencing of relevant materials. *Every* program with a goal of communicative competence, however (regardless of how seemingly distant or unspecific the communicative needs of the learners), should give attention to opportunities for meaningful L2 use, opportunities to focus on message rather than on form.

Immersion

In some contexts the major focus of an entire L2 program may not be on language *instruction* at all but on providing *occasions for language use* through the establishment of the L2 as a medium of instruction in the general curriculum. *Immersion programs*, for example, use an L2 to teach history, mathematics, science, and other school subjects. These programs may be whole or partial; that is, the entire curriculum may be taught in the L2 or only one or a few courses may be selected for inclusion. The rationale for immersion is that it provides maximum opportunity for language use with a clearly defined purpose: to learn history, mathematics, science, etc. The emphasis in these programs, to use Krashen's terms (see Chapter 2), is on acquisition rather than on conscious learning.

Immersion programs are well known in Canada, where they have received support, in particular, from anglophone parents who want their children to develop communicative abilities in French. The instructional program adopted by the Ontario Ministry of Education (1977), for example, offers immersion classes as an option at all levels of instruction, elementary through secondary school. Immersion is common, of course, for all learners, in Canada and elsewhere, whose L1 is not the language of public instruction in their community. These learners include Southeast Asian immigrants in Britain, Spanish-speaking Americans, nonfrancophone residents of Quebec, and Senegalese who speak Wolof or one of the other native Senegalese languages at home and French in school. The learning contexts in these examples differ, however, in an important way. It makes a difference if (1) all learners share an L1 and are acquiring an L2 with the teacher as primary model or if (2) the L2 is in fact an L1 for many or even the majority of a learner's classmates. The term *immersion program* is used to refer specifically to the first example, but immersion in an L2 community—be it a classroom, place of work, or neighborhood—is a context of language acquisition for many. In the case of school immersion, the social status of the school language in relation to the home language, the perceived rewards for learning the L2, and parental as well as peer support for immersion are all important factors in determining program success.

There are a number of immersion programs for L2 learners in American public schools. Milwaukee, for example, now has immersion programs in German, Spanish, and French; and Cincinnati and San Diego boast partial immersion programs in Spanish and French. These and similar initiatives in the United States are receiving increased attention as functional L2 competence becomes a more widespread goal (Rhodes 1981). A recent national seminar on the implementation of the international school concept in American secondary education has emphasized the importance of using the L2 as a medium of instruction in at least a portion of the curriculum (Purves 1981).

Short of total immersion, there is an opportunity within whatever time is allotted the language program to *use* the L2 in the study of some related topic. In secondary school programs, minicourses on diverse topics such as cooking, art, women, cinema, and drivers' training have served to spark learner interest while providing a natural occasion for L2 use. Similarly, an intermediate-level English reading and composition course for nonnative university students may be built around a theme, such as American music, current events, etc. The fourth semester of a college requirement may be successfully turned into a civilization course taught in the L2. Lafayette (1980) reports on the outcome of one such experiment in French. Though no special attention was given to grammar per se, students in the civilization course performed as well on tests of grammatical competence as their counterparts in a regular fourth-semester grammar course. They also learned a good deal about French civilization.

Opportunities for Purposeful L2 Use in Every Classroom

Language for a Purpose is by no means limited to immersion contexts. Every L2 class is an opportunity for purposeful L2 use. It suffices for learners and their teachers to realize the importance of making the most of this opportunity. Where the learners come from a variety of L1 backgrounds, as in an English course for foreign students at an American or British university, the L2 constitutes the lingua franca of the classroom. This provides a learning context wherein day-to-day classroom assignments, announcements, etc. must be conveyed using the L2 plus whatever gestures and other available visual cues are appropriate. What clearly counts in this instance is getting the message across.

Where learners and teachers have an L1 in common, the situation is of course somewhat different. L2 use seems less natural to these learners in that they already share a means of communication. In this case, it is up to the teacher to progressively establish the L2 as the language of routine class activities. When this happens, the L2 needs of the learners then become quite immediate and specific. Assignments with page and exercise numbers, date due, and special instructions provide practice in listening for meaning. Simple requests such as *Please close the door, Open your books, Pick a partner* are useful expressions for beginners to understand. *They need not be able to produce them.* On the other hand, learners do need to know how to ask a classmate to repeat something, to let others know they have not been understood, to request explanations. Teachers should provide learners with the means to meet these rudimentary classroom needs from the very beginning of instruction and respond in kind. As they progress, more and more of the activities in the Language Arts and other components of the curriculum can take place in the L2, thus providing a maximum amount of classroom discourse.

Crafts and motor activities of various kinds are another fruitful source of opportunities for L2 use. Recipes can be prepared for a holiday or international fair. Learners can be coached in soccer, chess, or gymnastics. Model airplanes can be constructed, fabric can be tie-dyed, papier-mâché masks can be designed, all following directions in the L2. The possibilities are virtually limitless once purposeful language use is seen as an important component of the curriculum.

Comparisons With the Direct Method
and the Natural Method

The purposeful uses of the L2 described in the above examples bear some resemblance to both the Direct Method and the Natural Method—teaching methods that from the time of their initial elaboration in the nineteenth century have continued to evoke controversy. Language for a Purpose differs, however, from these methods (at least as they came to be practiced in some settings) in important ways. Four of these differences deserve emphasis.

1. The focus of the activity is content, not language learning.

2. Recourse to the learner's native language is seen as natural and desirable; such *code-mixing* and even *code-switching* is a feature of natural L2 use.

3. Learners are not expected to give error-free, nativelike responses to teacher questions; learners should respond as they are ready and able.

4. The goal is the *gradual* adoption of the L2 as a community language while support and encouragement are provided for the learners.

However, Language for a Purpose is similar to the Direct and Natural Methods in its reflection of the view that learners learn best by doing. Use of the L2 for real communication—in classroom management, in lessons in culture and grammar, in crafts and games, or even in a full program of academic study—allows the learners to experience the language, to use it as their own.

5.3 MY LANGUAGE IS ME:
PERSONAL L2 USE

Much has been written about personalized L2 use. In *Caring and Sharing in the Foreign Language Classroom*, Moscowitz (1978) has collected ideas for involving learners' personal values and reactions in language learning. Along similar lines, Wattenmaker and Wilson (1980) have described activities for encouraging self-expression, many of which involve the opinions and attitudes of classmates on a variety of topics guaranteed to evoke controversy. Galyean (1977) has emphasized the need in language education for an accepting relationship between learners and teachers. All these methodologists have been concerned with the *affective* as well as the cognitive aspects of language acquisition. They seek to involve the learner psychologically as well as intellectually.

Discovery of Values

A source of inspiration for many of the personalized activities now being recommended for L2 classrooms is the exercises in values clarification designed for school curricula in general. These exercises are used to help learners both get acquainted with their classmates and use the class to explore their own attitudes and values. Simon, Howe, and Kirschenbaum (1972), the authors of one well-known collection of values-clarification exercises, are careful to emphasize that their goal is *not* to teach a particular set of values nor to evaluate the values held by individual learners. Values clarification is concerned not with the content of people's values but with the *process* of valuing, that is to say, with the *discovery* of values. The self-awareness that results leads, in turn, to greater self-acceptance and a better understanding of interpersonal relations.

Talking About L2 Learning and Other Things

An important contribution to an understanding of My Language is Me is the work of Curran (1972), cited in Chapters 3 and 4. Curran observes the sense of inadequacy he personally felt when he was called on as a respected psychologist to make a professional presentation in a language he spoke nonnatively. Although he was a distinguished professor, he felt foolish for mispronouncing French before the native-speaker audience. Many of the learner dialogues recorded in accounts of Community Language Learning have to do with the feelings of inadequacy and apprehension that participants experience as they use the L2 to communicate. In providing an opportunity to share these feelings, the discussion contributes to the creation of a community of learners, who are better able to work together toward common goals.

My Language is Me implies, above all, *respect* for learners as they use the L2 for self-expression. Inherent in all language teaching there is the risk of either conscious or subconscious domination of learners by those who seek to impose their personal criteria for competence. Patterns of language dominance found in society at large appear in the classroom as well. They may even be exaggerated by the special nature of the relationship between teacher and learner. Although Language Arts activities provide an appropriate context for attention to formal accuracy, Personal Language Use does not. A learner's description of his or her anxiety in the L2 classroom should be met with understanding and reassurance, not with the overt correction of pronunciation or verb tenses. Most teachers know this and will intuitively focus on meaning rather than on form as learners express their personal opinions or experiences. Yet textbooks or tests that repeatedly emphasize structural accuracy may cause teachers to feel guilty about their inattention to learner errors on these occasions. An understanding of the importance of opportunities for self-expression and of the ways in which a distinction can be made in a curriculum between Language Arts and My Language is Me should help to assuage that guilt.

The Learner's L2 Personality

Respect for learners as they use the L2 for self-expression requires more than simply restraint in the correction of nonnative features. It requires an acceptance of the possibility that nativelike performance may not, in fact, even be a goal of the learner. Since a personality inevitably takes on a new dimension through its expression in another language, it needs to discover that dimension on its own terms. Learners should not only be given the opportunity to say what they want to say in the L2, they should be encouraged to develop an L2 personality with which they are comfortable. Some students of English, for example, might not want to sound like native Americans. They might well prefer to speak English with a trace of their native accent. The poignant diary entry of the Japanese student cited in Chapter 3 is a case in point. Sociolinguistic rules of appropriateness may also differ for those learners. They may feel more comfortable maintaining a degree of formality that would be unaccustomed in the interpersonal transactions of natives. *It is one thing to analyze and appreciate native language behavior, quite another to adopt that behavior for one's own.* My Language is Me calls for a recognition of the individual personality of the learner.

Some Ways to Begin

There are many ways to incorporate Personal Language Use into the curriculum. The following examples are but a small sample that are intended to serve as a starting point for learners and their teachers while they discover those that will work best for them.

Getting acquainted. Initial class sessions should be spent getting acquainted. In more advanced classes, learners can introduce themselves briefly and talk about their L2 backgrounds and goals and any special interests they may have. It helps to put everyone at ease if classmates, following the teacher's example, feel free to ask questions or otherwise express their interest in what others are saying. An exchange of addresses and telephone numbers may also be appropriate. One class member can write the information on the board for the others to copy. In beginning-level classes, let learners select an L2 name, if they wish, from a list you provide. It may or may not resemble their L1 name. Names can be written on cards, placed on desks, or pinned to clothing.

Names and adjectives. Have each learner think of a self-descriptive adjective, perhaps one that begins with the same letter as his or her name. (Provide beginners with a list of choices.) Each then learns the names and adjectives of two classmates and introduces them to the others. (A background of music as learners move about exchanging names and adjectives can help to create a more relaxed atmosphere.)

Students are people too! It will help you to get to know your students as individuals if early in each term you have them fill out five-by-seven-inch cards with their name, address, special interests, and what they hope to learn from the course. Do wait until a week or so has passed, however, to request this information. Learners will volunteer more information if they have first had a chance to get acquainted with you and their classmates.

Scavenger hunt. This familiar party game can be used to help learners and teachers get better acquainted. Everyone receives a card on which are the following instructions:

Find someone who:

1. had eggs for breakfast   _____

2. collects stamps   _____

3. plays a musical instrument   _____

4. is a newcomer to town   _____

The list of characteristics may be as long as you like and may be the same or different for each participant. The game continues until all players have filled in the name of a classmate for each characteristic.

Journal. Have learners keep a weekly journal. Initial entries for beginners will be only one sentence; advanced learners may want to write a paragraph or even a page. Allow class time for consultation with the teacher or a native-speaker aide on the choice of words and structures. *Journals should not be evaluated for grammar or style but should be responded to with comments and queries about the content.*

Personal vocabulary. Learners keep a list of vocabulary words that have special meaning for them. Include contributions from these lists in regularly scheduled spelling tests or spelling bees.

That's incredible! Each learner recounts to the class a personal experience. Stories can be prepared ahead with the help of the teacher. Class members vote on the authenticity of the anecdote. The object is to fool the class, and often the most incredible stories are, in fact, true! This activity can be made into a team contest by dividing the class into two groups. Each team member who fools the majority of the opposite team earns a point for his or her team.

Family tree. Learners bring in pictures of family members to introduce to classmates. Or they may prefer to bring in a picture of themselves when they were younger. In one variation, a special bulletin board is created for a *Celebrity of the Week.* A baby picture is posted with the question "Who is it?" At the end of the week the "celebrity" is introduced and interviewed by classmates. (In this and other activities involving self-revelation, always take care to respect the wishes of the learner. Those who do not wish to share information about their family or their childhood should never be forced to do so. The more you get to know your students, the better you will be able to judge the appropriateness of a particular activity for them.)

Grouping. Use a variety of personal characteristics such as hair color, first letter of given name, height, color of socks, etc. to divide learners into groups for classroom activities of the kind described in these pages. Take care, however, to avoid racial, social, national, and other distinctions that might make some learners uncomfortable.

The art of storytelling. Learners sit in a circle and someone begins a story. To help provide focus, a theme can be set in advance—for example, "The funniest sight I've ever seen," "My earliest memory," "A true-life adventure." The next person adds a sentence and the story continues around the circle. When it is completed, the group may wish to put the story in writing. A teacher or an advanced learner can help with the editing.

Rank order. Learners rank order a list of recording stars, leisure activities, vacation spots, world leaders, etc. They then divide into small groups to compare and discuss their preferences. Let learners themselves make up the lists for subsequent rank-order activities.

Brainstorming. One member of the group volunteers an abstract or concrete noun—for example, love, work, mother, bread, television. All then contribute words or expressions suggested to them by the first word. They continue to build on one another's contributions until they have a constellation of associated words written on a chalkboard or overhead transparency. As a follow-up activity, advanced learners can look for relationships between the words evoked and discuss possible differences in the concepts that underlie them. This activity is related to the semantic differential approach to attitude measurement (see Chapter 3) and is of particular interest when participants come from different linguistic and cultural backgrounds. As a variation, participants can brainstorm alone or in pairs and then compare their lists with classmates.

THE SEMANTIC NETWORK

Unlike a computer, which retrieves data according to a fixed program, the mind—as this diagram illustrates—can creatively summon up words, images or memories by proceeding along one or several interlacing networks of association.

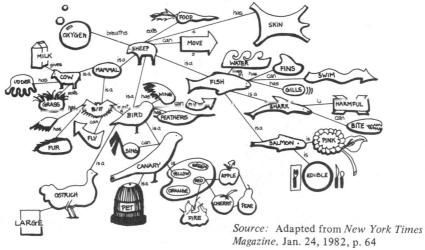

Source: Adapted from *New York Times Magazine*, Jan. 24, 1982, p. 64

Survey. A team of researchers interviews class members to learn their views on some issue, major or minor—for example, ideal family size, the best pizza in town, their most admired public figure. Researchers record answers and report to the class. Surveys may be of the *yes/no/no opinion* format or open-ended. They may be conducted by several teams of two learners who do their interviewing simultaneously or by a single team during individual study or lab work. Written surveys and reports are also possible. Learners should pick issues that interest them. Use public opinion polls and attitude surveys in L2 magazines and newspapers as models.

Famous authors. Personal Language Use may take many forms. The pages reproduced below are from books prepared by students in a secondary school French class. Each class member was given the opportunity either to write a simple story with illustrations or to translate into French a favorite childhood storybook. A native-speaker aide was available as a resource. The books chosen for translation were in many cases treasured possessions that the learners wanted to bring with them into their new language. The eagerness with which classmates read one another's books was an unanticipated bonus. This, then, is an example of how learners may become involved in reading and writing through the use of materials they themselves have created.

FAMOUS AUTHORS

Source: French IV Class, Urbana High School, Urbana, Illinois. Diane Andrews, teacher.

Personal reading. Give advanced learners an opportunity to read in depth on a particular topic or the works of a single author. The redundancy of information and writing style will facilitate comprehension as well as promote reading for personal enjoyment and the satisfaction of improving reading ability.

5.4 YOU BE, I'LL BE: THEATER ARTS

Theater as Reality

"All the world is a stage," as Shakespeare has reminded us (*As You Like It*, II, 7). On this stage we play many roles in our daily lives, roles for which we improvise scripts from the models we observe around us. Parent, child, sister, brother, teacher, student, employer, employee, friend, and foe—all are roles that imply certain prescribed ways of behaving and speaking. Sociolinguistic rules of appropriateness have to do with these expected behaviors. Familiar roles may be played with little conscious attention to style. New and unfamiliar roles, on the other hand, require practice with an awareness of how the meanings we intend are being interpreted by others.

If the world may be thought of as a stage, with actors and actresses who play their parts as best they can, theater, on the other hand, may be seen as an opportunity to know reality, a reality that may go unnoticed by players caught up in the familiar roles of their daily lives. In providing an occasion to focus on feelings and relations, theater serves for both actors and audience as an avenue to the discovery of truths. Any sense of a distinction between role and reality fades, then, if we consider life and stage as intimately entwined in human relations.

Fantasy and playacting are a natural and important part of growing up. Make-believe and the familiar "you be, I'll be" improvisations of which children are so fond are routes to self-discovery and growth. They allow young learners to experiment, to try things out—like hats and wigs, moods and postures, gestures and words. As occasions for language use, role playing and the many related activities that constitute Theater Arts are likewise a natural component of L2 learning. They allow learners to experiment with the roles they play or will play in real life.

Theater, then, is real and provides an opportunity for real language use. Role playing allows learners to explore situations that would otherwise never come up in a classroom. Fantasy, moreover, is welcomed by learners who do not want to spend all of their time in class talking about grammar, themselves, or the opinions of their classmates. The acceptance of play as a component of a curriculum has an additional virtue: It increases the possibilities for a variety of ensemble or group-building strategies that are well known in the theater and have much to contribute to the creation of community within an L2 classroom. Like a rehearsal, the language class must be open and conducive to the sharing of ideas and experiences. Participants should be comfortable with one another if they are to feel free to experiment. They should not be afraid to be wrong in front of their classmates because this exploration is what rehearsals are for.

Setting Up the Situation

Stephen Smith, a professionally trained actor and a teacher of English as a second language, stresses that when teachers do role playing, dialogue work, improvisation, scene study, or play production in language classes, they need first to set up the situation. They cannot just ask the learners to stand up and *act*. Teachers must prepare learners by providing them with the necessary tools. Experience with what is known in theater training as *method acting* is a part of this preparation. "Method acting involves establishing the true emotions and motivations of a character, then producing those emotions truthfully. . . . The method actor, like the language learner, is not as concerned with the words that come out of the mouth as with what those words mean to the speaker, why he chose those words, and what the words mean to all who hear them" (forthcoming).

Theater Arts can provide learners with the tools they need to *act*, that is, to observe, to relate, to experiment, and to create in a second language. The Theater Arts component of an L2 curriculum includes the following activities:

1. Ensemble-building activities involving listening, observation, movement, and games;

2. Pantomime, the use of gestures and facial expression to convey meaning;

3. Unscripted role playing—for example, *commedia dell'arte* improvisations where a situation is described to the actors who then create their own lines as they go along;

4. Simulations, a more open-ended form of unscripted role playing;

5. Scripted role playing—that is, the use of a prepared script to interpret characters in a dialogue, skit, or play.

We will consider each of these activities with examples.

Ensemble Building and Pantomime

One of the best introductions to Theater Arts is pantomime. Pantomime helps learners to become comfortable with the idea of performing in front of their peers without concern for language. The first activity described below is an ensemble-building technique that provides an introduction to pantomime. It is followed by examples of pantomime and related introductions to Theater Arts.

Living sculpture. This activity can take place in either the L1 or the L2, depending on the proficiency of the learners. It works best in a carpeted room where participants can wear slippers or socks. Participants divide into an even number of small groups (four to six members each), which are then paired. One group in each pair is the "sculptor," and the other is the "clay." Sculptors then decide how to fashion their clay to represent a familiar object or scene. When decisions have been reached, members of the clay groups stand limp, close their eyes, and allow themselves to be positioned according to the wishes of the sculptors. When the sculptors are satisfied with their design, members of the clay groups open their eyes and try to guess what they represent. Once they have guessed, the group roles are reversed, and a new set of sculptures is created.

Line-up. Another good ensemble-building activity related to pantomime is one that helps newcomers to an L2 classroom adapt to the linguistic disadvantage at which they suddenly find themselves. Slips of paper are numbered consecutively, one for each member of the group. Numbers are then distributed randomly with care taken to see that each number is seen *only by the person to whom it is assigned.* Then, in total silence and with no written communication of any kind, group members line up in numerical order. This takes very little time and leaves learners with marvelous confidence in their communicative resourcefulness.

What is it? This activity shows learners how important gestures can be in communication. Pantomime imaginary situations for the others to guess— for example, washing down an elephant, changing a tire, playing basketball, making and eating a sandwich. The teacher may want to begin, followed by class members who can present their pantomimes individually, in pairs, or in small groups.

L1 Transactions without words. Learners enact familiar scenes, perhaps a series of greetings between persons of various social relationships—for example, mother and son, teacher and student, best friends. Ask the class to consider any differences they observe. What do gestures and facial expressions tell them about the possible relationship between the participants?

L2 Transactions without words. Introduce scenes from an L2 culture similar to those that have been presented for the L1. These may be enacted by teachers or native-speaker recruits. Videotapes of native-speaker enactments played without sound are marvelous for this purpose and may be used again and again. Direct learners' attention to proxemics, kinesics, and other relevant visual cues. Optional follow-up: Ask for volunteers to perform the same transactions they have just observed to see if they can *act* like an Italian, a German, a Japanese, etc.

L1 Transactions with words. Pantomimed transactions are repeated, this time with words. Ask learners to comment on the choice of words. What cues do they provide to the relationship of the characters? Script writing for short scenes illustrating different forms for the same function in the learners' L1 is a good follow-up activity.

L2 Transactions with words. Pantomimed transactions are repeated, this time with words. If videotapes were used, simply turn on the sound for this second viewing. Encourage beginners to comment on their observations and impressions. What does the L2 sound like to them? Do their impressions conform to those they held previously? Advanced learners can comment on word choice, intonation, role relationships, and underlying functions.

A stranger to these parts. This exercise focuses on coping and negotiation and is related in this respect to *Line-up* described above. Set up a scene like a small shop or restaurant. Four or five people are going about their shopping or dining when a stranger enters who does not speak the language of the others. As the stranger tries to make his or her wishes known to the shopkeeper, waiter, etc., the others gather around to try and help. The stranger should use a make-believe (or real!) foreign language and attempt to communicate.

Simon says. This is another good ensemble-building exercise that gets learners to move about. A group leader gives directions to be followed by the others—for example, "Stand up," "Take three steps to the left," "Turn around," etc. Directions can become very detailed and are then best directed at individuals—for example, "Take Paul's notebook and put it on Mary's head." In this case, it becomes a game of *Robot.* Asher (1969, 1977), has made extensive use of this type of activity in the elaboration of a well-known structurally based L2 teaching method called, appropriately, the Total Physical Response. With beginners the emphasis should be on *understanding* only; as learners advance they will want, in turn, to give commands to their classmates and even the teacher. Teachers might want to be careful to give only commands that they themselves will be willing and able to carry out!

Unscripted Role Playing

Once learners have an understanding of the relation of Theater Arts to language learning and feel comfortable interacting with their teachers and classmates, they are ready for unscripted role playing or improvisation. The opportunities for improvisation are endless and should be provided at all levels of instruction. The following examples illustrate the range of possibilities. A collection of role playing situations can be kept in a file box of five-by-seven-inch cards. Organized by topic, function, or degree of role complexity, these cards can be ready for class use at any time.

a) Define a situation and have two or three learners ad lib an exchange. The teacher or an advanced learner can play the role of a native speaker, and learners play themselves. Examples: (1) You are in the post office to mail a letter and are unsure of postal rates (asking for information); (2) you have just bumped into a passerby and knocked her packages to the ground (making an apology); (3) you would like to invite a foreign visitor to your home for dinner (extending an invitation). At the conclusion of each skit allow for class discussion of what took place, the misunderstandings that occurred, and the feelings of the participants. If desired, repeat the same scene with the same or other actors.

b) As learners progress, the improvisations can get longer and explore a variety of functions and registers. For example: (1) complain to your best friend about your raise, or (2) complain to your boss about your raise.

c) Advanced learners can be assigned more complex roles—for example, X is a waiter in an expensive restaurant, Y has invited Z to dinner and would like to impress him with a good meal yet must be careful not to exceed his budget.

d) An effective strategy is to assign roles individually so that they are unknown to the other members of the cast. For example, three strangers are sharing the same train compartment. X is told she is a gregarious middle-aged grandmother returning home from a visit with her family. Y is an outgoing ten-year-old with a passion for card games. Z is a meticulously dressed young woman on her way to an important job interview; she has a splitting headache. As the action unfolds, the audience tries to guess the context and roles from the words and actions of the players.

e) Give players the first line and the last line of a script. (Class members will be happy to volunteer suggestions.) It is up to the players to fill in the middle. S. Smith (forthcoming) describes the following variation to this activity. Each student writes one sentence on a piece of paper. Collect the papers and redistribute them to the class so that no student gets his or her own paper. Divide the class into groups of three to four students. Allow five to ten minutes for groups to meet and discuss or practice a scene. The scene can be about anything, but it must include the sentences written on the pieces of paper. The class reassembles and each group improvises its scene.

f) Imagine a scene between two characters in a novel or play studied in class. It is also fun to imagine a scene between two characters who are *not* in the novel, perhaps the neighbors or servants of a famous protagonist.

g) Create all the above scenarios using hand puppets in place of actors. This technique works especially well with children and helps involve those who might be shy about acting in person.

Simulations

Like role playing, simulations are a familiar technique in teacher training, management training, theater rehearsals, and other training programs. Simulations can be described as simplifications of real-world situations. They involve learners in activities that may range from surviving in the desert to organizing a citizens' campaign to block the construction of an airport. To the extent that they involve the discussion of alternatives and decision making, they are related to the values-clarification activities included in Personal Language Use. Simulations can be as straightforward as arranging a hotel accommodation, but most often they are more complex than the limited, closed exchange between the desk clerk and a hotel guest.

Among the better known simulations, or *simulation games* as they are sometimes called, are such commercial board games as *Monopoly, Clue, Risk,* and *Pay Day.* These games allow learners to take the role of a real estate developer, detective, military strategist, or a more mundane head of household trying to budget from one end of the month to the next. They are fun to play and have been used successfully in many L2 classrooms. Of even greater value for language learning, however, are games that provide a maximum amount of verbal interaction. The simulations that are most interesting and effective in the language classroom are those that require the participation of all members of the group to meet a stated goal. Group interaction is promoted by placing the learners in a fictitious situation or environment with the outcome dependent on their collective communicative competence.

Survival, for example, is a simulation game developed for native speakers that can be easily adapted for L2 classroom use (K. Jones 1974). Learners find themselves on a desert oasis as survivors of a plane crash. They must find a village within 30 days or they will die from lack of food. Before the game begins, each player is given information that is known to no one else in the group. This information is vital to the survival of the group. For example, one player is designated a mapmaker; another learns that he or she has a compass with which to guide the group in their searchings; another has a diary in which to log their progress and keep a record of when they find water, since they must have water every four days if they are to survive.

Given the description of the information or special talents that they possess, participants are free to be themselves, to contribute and to interact as they wish. In the example above, finding the village requires the cooperation of all. This cooperation begins with the pooling of resources. From there, group members decide on a direction to pursue, justify their choice, and persuade others if necessary. Ultimately, they all have to accept the consequences of their choices. In other words, because their very lives depend on the exchange of ideas and meaning, the learners must listen to everyone, negotiate, and use whatever resources they have at their disposal to get their meaning across to one another.

Simulations provide learners with an opportunity to develop social skills such as decision making, persuading, influencing, and so forth. What's more, it taps their creativity as they formulate the most efficient, logical, or practical way to achieve their goal. The degree to which they succeed ultimately determines the success of the activity.

Scripted Role Playing

Another activity in Theater Arts, quite different from the unscripted role playing and simulations illustrated in the preceding sections, is role playing *with* a script. Prepared scripts may be effectively used with learners of all levels of proficiency. Their use gives learners the opportunities to interpret, to focus on the meaning or intent of dialogue (including pronunciation, intonation, facial expression, gestures, and a host of other paralinguistic and nonverbal features of communication). In theater, all these features are carefully monitored for maximum effectiveness. The scripts used can be anything from poetry readings to three-act plays. They may be simply read through in class for practice, or they may be developed into a full stage production with costumes, props, and lights. As learners learn to interpret the dialogues written by others, some will want to write scripts of their own. They should be encouraged and given the help they need to express themselves in language appropriate to the roles they wish to create. Matters of style and register take on new significance for learners as they strive for authenticity in their portrayal of an irate parent, a contrite friend, an aggressive used-car salesman, etc.

Any dialogue qualifies as theater so long as it is *written to convey meaning*. Most dialogues are meaningful, of course, with the frequent exception, as we have seen, of those written expressly for L2 textbooks! Textbook dialogues are most often created not for the meaning they convey but for the grammatical forms or vocabulary they display (see Chapter 1). An attempt to interpret these dialogues leads one quickly to the realization that as characterizations they are no more real than the stick figures popular in audiolingual days. For there to be theater, language has to have function as well; unless, of course, it is the Theater of the Absurd!

"Why You Must Be My Wife!":
A Theater Game for
Language Learners*

Eugene Ionesco, author of *The Bald Soprano (La Cantatrice Chauve)* (1950) has credited his classroom L2 learning experience and L2 textbooks in particular with the inspiration for the absurd dialogue with which his play begins (and ends!).

> Scene: A middle-class English interior with English arm chairs. An English evening. Mrs. Smith, an Englishwoman is darning some English socks. Mr. Smith is seated beside her reading an English newspaper.

> Mrs. Smith: There, it's nine o'clock. We've drunk the soup, and eaten the fish and chips, and the English salad. The children have

---

* This section is based on an earlier report, *"Other Peoples Languages: A Game Everyone Can Play"* (Savignon 1973a).

drunk English water. We've eaten well this evening. That's because we live in the suburbs of London and because our name is Smith.

Mr. Smith: (Continues to read, clicks his tongue.)

Mrs. Smith: Potatoes are very good fried in fat; the salad oil was not rancid. The oil from the grocer at the corner is better quality than the oil from the grocer at the end of the street. However, I prefer not to tell them that their oil is bad. . . .

In the middle of this one-act drama there is a delightful scene where a married couple is reunited, after a presumed separation of but a few hours, only to discover they are not man and wife after all. In playful turnabout, a team of textbook writers (Coulombe, Barré, Fostle, Poulin, and Savignon 1974) turned the Ionesco scene into a game for language learners. It has since been enjoyed by learners and teachers of all ages and from diverse cultural backgrounds—an outcome with which Ionesco himself would no doubt be pleased.

Why you're my wife! (*Mais vous êtes ma femme!* in its original version) differs in important ways from the Language Arts games described in a preceding section—from, that is, crossword puzzles, spelling bees, and even *Who am I?* Though certainly fun and even instructive, these activities constitute, for the most part, playing with words and surface structures and, as such, are only a more palatable form of such things as vocabulary drills and grammar reviews. A more rewarding game in terms of the communicative goals of an L2 program is one that, like the simulations described in a preceding section, has the following attributes:

1. It provides the fullest amount of emotional involvement possible. Each player has something clearly at stake.

2. It offers a format that is simple enough to be understood by all players yet supple enough to allow for adaptations to suit the needs of the players in terms of their age, number, degree of communicative competence, and so forth.

3. Success in playing the game depends not on any arbitrary criteria of grammatical accuracy (spelling, pronunciation, verb placement, etc.) but on the ability to use the language to discuss, to explore, to deceive, to explain, to reveal, to conceal, to cajole, to describe, to enact, ... In sum, to engage in the whole range of interpersonal transactions in which we are all involved daily in our mother tongue. Herein lies the *authenticity* of the exchanges.

An additional advantage of *Why you're my wife!* is that it can involve the teacher not as a director or referee but as a player. Like ensemble-building games or games played to get people acquainted at social gatherings, games that involve teachers as players help teachers relate to their students not as students but as other players. This makes it easier for teachers both to subsequently relinquish the authoritarian role to which they are accustomed and to respond to *what* is said rather than to *how* it is said.

To play, each player is given a card showing his or her identity (age, nationality, profession, etc.) along with the identity of a family member for whom he or she is looking. Players move about the room asking questions of anyone they choose in the search for their missing relatives. They must also, of course, answer questions put to them. When the answers a player receives correspond to the identity of the person for whom he or she is searching, the player exclaims, "Why, you're my wife!" or father, or sister, or grandfather, as the case may be. These two players then team up to look for a third member of the family, a fourth member, and so on until the whole family is reunited.

There is much noise and moving about as players become alternately frustrated and encouraged in their searches. But it all happens in the L2 and without the slightest prodding from the teacher, who can either remain on the sidelines and serve as coach or take a card and join the melee. As a follow-up to the game itself, participants often enjoy getting acquainted with the other members of their family, improvising dialogue about their lives, what they have been doing since they were last together, etc., and then introducing their newly found families to the other members of the class. The game is played in a spirit of unabashed fun, and the results are often hilarious.

SAMPLE PLAYING CARDS AND FAMILY LISTS FOR "WHY YOU'RE MY WIFE!"

Once they understand the game, learners will want to make up their own variations. Cards can be laminated for durability. Kept in envelopes—one envelope per family with the number of members marked on the outside—they are ready to be shuffled and used at any time.

Distinguishing characteristics of each individual (The sequence of information is deliberately different for each person and corresponds to the sequence found on the playing card.)

FAMILY No. 1

Father: 50 years old, engineer, Italian, Toronto, apartment, 2 children

Mother: interior decorator, French, 45 years old, 2 children, apartment, Toronto

Son: Canadian, 25 years old, apartment, Ottawa, car, journalist

Daughter: teacher, Canadian, 22 years old, apartment, Toronto, no car

FAMILY No. 2

Father: restaurant manager, 2 children, house, Dallas, Mexican, 40 years old

Mother: waitress, 2 children, house, Dallas, Mexican, 33 years old

Daughter: Mexican-American, Dallas, house, bicycle, 4th grade student, 10 years old

Son: high school student, Dallas, house, 14 years old, motorcycle, Mexican-American

Grandmother: unemployed, 65 years old, Mexican, Dallas, apartment, 2 children

Grandfather: 65 years old, Mexican, Dallas, apartment, 2 children, restaurant owner

FAMILY No. 3 . . . etc.

Playing cards (Playing cards are provided for each family member. They include the identifying characteristics for that player along with the characteristics of the family member being sought. For example, playing cards for the *Father* and the *Mother* in Family No. 1 would look like this.)

ME	MY WIFE
50 years old	interior decorator
engineer	French
Italian	45 years old
Toronto	2 children
apartment	apartment
2 children	Toronto

ME	MY SON
interior decorator	Canadian
French	25 years old
45 years old	apartment
2 children	Ottawa
apartment	car
Toronto	journalist

Source: Adapted from the Games Packet for Coulombe, Barré, Fostle, Poulin, and Savignon, *Voix et Visages de la France, Level 1* (Chicago: Rand McNally, 1974).

The game generates emotional involvement from the beginning. Players have a clear-cut task and soon realize that the more they talk, the faster they will advance. The rules are quickly understood by all, and they may be adapted to fit the circumstances. Any number from 8 to 30 or more may play. The descriptions of the family members can remain within the vocabulary familiar to learners or they may include new items. In the latter case, the teacher may want to serve as a reference person. The descriptions might reflect the special interests of the local community (farming, mining, fishing, etc.) or those of a community where the L2 is used. Most important, players are free to interact away from the teacher's ears. The form their exchanges take will vary greatly according to the communicative competence of the players. Completion of the task, however, depends not on the absolute grammatical accuracy of the exchanges but on their outcome. If a query or a response is incomplete, inaudible, or incomprehensible, it is another player, not the teacher, who will express his or her dissatisfaction. And this is how it should be because this is the way life is.

Planning Time and Space
for Theater Arts

All the theater and other communication activities that have been described work best when they are well integrated into the curriculum. In the words of Sylvia Ashton-Warner (1963) cited at the beginning of this chapter, communication "takes time and involves noise and movement and personal relations."

For the L2 classroom this implies not disorder but the carefully planned use of time and space to maximize the incentive for productive interaction. Many efforts to include Theater Arts, games, and other interaction activities fail because teachers have not fully anticipated the possible outcomes—for example, not enough time, too much noise, confusion about procedure, too slow a pace to sustain learner (and teacher!) interest. A class cannot just "play a game." Nor should simulations, role playing and other opportunities for interaction be saved for parties, a rainy day, or the last few minutes of the class period. To be most effective, communicative activities must constitute an integral part of the classroom program.

Some experimentation is needed to determine which activities work best with a particular group. Chances for success are greater, however, if the teacher is enthusiastic and open to suggestions. Once they understand what is involved, learners themselves often prove the best source of creative ideas. The following guidelines will help to ensure a successful beginning.

1. Prepare learners for an activity by thoroughly explaining its nature, purpose, rules, etc. If either special props or supplies are needed, have them assembled well in advance.

2. Set a time limit and never let an activity drag on. For some activities the use of a sandglass or a kitchen timer may be appropriate to help maintain a lively pace.

3. If an activity is not working well for any reason, stop it and try something else.

4. Try using a game at the beginning of a class period as a focus for the activities to follow.

5. For future reference keep a notebook of activities tried and the outcome—degree of success, ideas for improvement, variations, etc.

6. Never overuse an activity, regardless of how popular it may be.

Classroom space should be planned as well as classroom time. Most of the Theater Arts and other activities require seating arrangements other than the traditional straight rows of chairs all facing the teacher. In the overwhelming majority of classrooms today, furniture may be moved about to suit the activities. In those rare instances where chairs are bolted to the floor and an alternative room assignment is impossible, the area around the chairs can be used for stand-up games, role playing, etc. The diagrams below suggest ways of arranging a communicative classroom. (If necessary, desks can always be returned to their original position at the end of the class period.)

WAYS OF ARRANGING A COMMUNICATIVE CLASSROOM

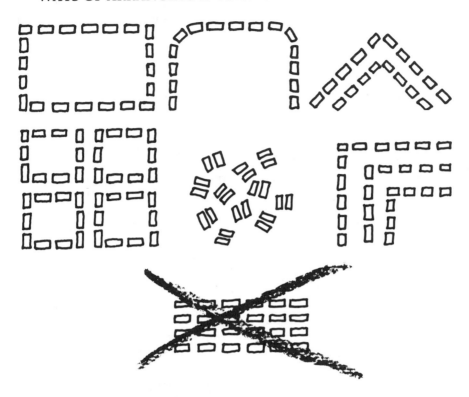

5.5 BEYOND THE CLASSROOM

Regardless of the variety of communicative activities in the classroom, their purpose remains to prepare learners for the L2 world beyond, a world on which learners will depend for the development and maintenance of their communicative competence once classes are over. The classroom is but a rehearsal. The strength of an L2 curriculum depends ultimately on the extent to which it reaches out to the world around it.

Exploration of an L2 Community

When learners live within or adjacent to an L2 community, systematic interaction with that culture should be an integral part of the curriculum. The interaction may take many forms, depending on learner interests and level of proficiency. For example, learners may bring in grocery or other ads from local newspapers to decide where certain products may be had at the most advantageous prices. They may be sent on shopping expeditions in teams of two or three to price and otherwise inquire about a major purchase—a used car, a watch, a camera—and report back to the class. Weekly calendars of community events can be compiled as a regular activity. Class visits to a courtroom trial, a public auction, or a church bazaar provide introductions to aspects of L2 culture that learners might not experience on their own. Local radio and television broadcasts are another source of topics and activities that take learners Beyond the Classroom.

Where an L2 community is not close enough for daily or weekly contact, a special field trip could be arranged. This requires a good deal of preparation on the part of everyone and can involve the community as well as students in planning and fundraising. The trip itself may be a one-day excursion to an L2 community in a major city, or it may be a tour or exchange visit abroad. Excursions of this kind are increasingly becoming a feature of American secondary school programs. And there is no reason that they need be confined to class members. Parents, grandparents, and other community members may also be given an opportunity to participate. For many, it may be the first opportunity to share in the discovery of a language community other than their own, and their enthusiasm may lead to increased support for L2 programs in general. One teacher who took her parents along on what was their first trip to Europe was overjoyed at their response. "Now," they said, "we understand your dedication to language teaching all these years!"

A full semester or year of study in an L2 community is offered by an increasing number of colleges and universities, and the study and work programs sponsored by public universities have made experience abroad available to students of limited financial means. In some cases, the increased participation in these programs by not only language majors but students in many different curricula is having a welcome influence on classroom instruction. Learners preparing to study abroad and those who have returned from such an experience are not content to learn *about* language. They are looking, rather, for classes that will help them to develop and maintain functional L2 skills.

TIPS FOR PICKING UP THE LOCAL LANGUAGE

The following strategies for language learners are adapted from *The Bridge* (Winter 1981:22) a magazine, which is unfortunately no longer published, for persons with cross-cultural business and professional interests. The suggestions offered will be helpful not only to exchange students and others who venture forth out of the classroom and into the L2 community but to teachers who want to give learners the kinds of classroom experiences that will enable them to cope in the L2 world beyond.

- LISTEN TO THE MELODY OF THE LANGUAGE
  Each language has its own intonation patterns—rises, falls, pauses—you can listen to without even trying to catch the accent. Or use a string of nonsense words and say it "like French" or whatever. Listen to the radio and watch TV. Can you catch the emotional tone even though you can't understand a word?

- THINK SOUNDS
  Think sounds, not the written word, since in many languages the way a word is pronounced may have little relation to its spelling.
  Work on those "strange"

sounds which don't exist in your native language. Practice short phrases containing these difficult sounds. Watch people's faces when they talk, for lip position on certain sounds.

- LEARN PHRASES, NOT WORDS
  Words seldom exist in isolation. You may not even be understood if you pronounce the language word by word, rather than running them together in appropriate breath groups.

  Use a tape recorder to get short conversations you can listen to and repeat. Concentrate on pronouncing clearly those words similar to your native language (the cognates) because you'll have a tendency to substitute the word you already know.

- PRACTICE ON SOMEONE
  Learned a new phrase? Find someone to try it out on. Embarrassed about starting a conversation? Try talking to the kids; it's easier.

  Practice asking people what time it is, how to get to a well-known local attraction, or when the next bus is due. Find excuses to start a conversation. Each time you're able to ask a question and understand the response, you'll gain a bit more confidence.

- TAKE SOME RISKS
  Risk making friends in the new culture rather than spending time with people from your own country.

  Ask questions; be curious.

  Be brave enough to ask for language corrections once you know a native speaker well. Most people won't be so impolite as to correct you unless you request it. Then repeat the correction, in context, to see if you've caught on.

- GO AHEAD! READ AND WRITE
  Read the billboards, signs, headlines, advertisements, labels on packages. Try to associate the written words with what you've heard.

  Carry a notebook to write down new phrases or expressions as soon as you hear them. Then *use* them to communicate an idea of your own.

  Make yourself a set of flashcards with words or phrases in the new language on one side and your native language on the other.

- OBSERVE THE NONVERBAL COMMUNICATION
  There's much more to communicating than learning sounds, words and the structures of the language; you need to know how to use them in culturally appropriate ways.

  Watch interaction patterns: How do people interrupt each other to take turns speaking? Who speaks first? How far apart do they stand? When do they touch? Who? How do they show respect? Authority? What gestures do they use and can you tell what they mean? When is eye contact made? What's the difference between man-to-man, woman-to-woman and man-to-woman speech?

  And after all this observation, go practice!

Stay "tuned in" to your new language as many hours a day as possible, alternating between observation/listening and active practice with anyone who will cooperate. You'll be surprised how quickly you can communicate.

Bringing the L2 Community
Into the Classroom

Representatives of the L2 community should be regular visitors to the classroom. They should be allowed to interact with learners in the L1 or the L2, as
appropriate, in discussions of contrastive culture as well as on specific language projects. Some years ago, a team of evaluators, of which the author was a
member, visited a large suburban American high school and found that the
native-speaker aid whom the foreign language department was fortunate to
have had been assigned to monitoring pattern practice drills in the language
lab. The explanation given for her assignment reflected the then accepted
audiolingual view of L2 acquisition: In the view of the language teachers, the
native speaker's Spanish was "too advanced for the students!" In fact, however, the learners were missing one of the few opportunities they had to try out
their Spanish in a communicative situation and to develop the strategies
needed to *interact with* and *learn from* a native speaker. How much better for
them if this valuable interaction had been made an integral part of their
classroom activities.

Magazines and newspapers are another means of bringing the L2 community into the classroom. Save back issues to cut up and use for displays and
illustrations. Good pictures are especially important and take time to collect.
Learners can help in the selection of large color pictures that can be laminated
and used as visual aids in all kinds of Language Arts and other activities. Every
classroom should have a good collection. Bookstores will sometimes donate
back issues of magazines.

Shortwave radio is another contact with a distant L2 world (see Chapter 4).
In addition to receiving commercial broadcasts, some teachers have involved
learners in ham radio operations in the L2. Similarly, cable television is bringing distant as well as locally produced programs into classrooms and homes.
Interested teachers will find a wealth of information regarding currently available programming from the cultural services of various nations as well as from
their area television stations.

Pen pals are an old-time favorite, and if international telephone rates
continue to decrease, phone pals may one day become a reasonable alternative.
Learners may correspond as individuals or as a class, perhaps teamed up or
"twinned" with a group of students of the same age in an L2 community. A
class newspaper is one way to exchange information on topics of interest in the
school or community. The preparation of a newspaper can involve everyone in
some capacity—as reporters (sports, food, fashion, etc.), feature writers, crossword puzzle and other word game experts, cartoonists, layout artists, and
editors. Items may be in either the L1 or the L2 or both.

Simply Getting Out

Any activity that provides an occasion for L2 use outside the regular classroom
makes the language seem that much more real. A teacher who uses the L2 to

greet learners in the corridor, cafeteria, or at a football game is helping to bridge the gap between classroom and reality. Francisco Oller, a teacher of English at Turabo University in Puerto Rico, has turned these casual encounters into an integral part of his course. Students who stop to chat with him in his office or in the corridor are awarded tokens. The longer they talk, the more tokens they receive. The tokens are then credited toward their course grade. On last report, Mr. Oller has been deluged with students and is delighted!

Make telephone use an integral part of a language program by providing learners with the opportunity to use the telephone for a variety of communicative purposes. Most telephone companies will loan telephone sets to schools for in-class rehearsal. Follow up by having learners (1) call willing L2 speakers in the community to obtain a prearranged piece of information and (2) call you at your home or office to get a special assignment or information about the next day's quiz. As possible, have learners call local or long distance toll free numbers to get information about store hours, movie schedules, airplane flight information, telephone numbers, and so on.

Immersion weekends are popular in some programs. Everyone goes off for a day or two of conversation, songs, good food, and fun—all in the L2. Such excursions need not be elaborate and seem to thrive where the cost of participation is kept to a minimum. They also offer a good way to involve native speakers of different ages, to welcome visitors, and to establish contact with permanent residents of the community. Ervin (1976) gives a description of one of these camps, a Russian language camp held in Ohio, with practical suggestions for others to follow. A word of caution is perhaps in order: Successful camps may grow! The International Language Village near Bemidji, Minnesota, with an annual summer enrollment of more than 2000 young people, began in 1961 when Concordia College sponsored a two-week summer camp in German for 75 students!

Music has long been recognized for the contribution it can make to language learning, and choral groups—organized perhaps to sing at school events and in community hospitals and nursing homes for Christmas and other holidays—provide a way to bring foreign languages out of the classroom and into the community. Play productions, bake sales featuring ethnic specialities, and international fairs are others. The latter two sometimes serve as fund raisers for class excursions or student exchange visits.

One of the most ambitious examples ever of going Beyond the Classroom has to be a secondary school group's reenactment of La Salle's journey in 1681 up the St. Lawrence Seaway and down the Mississippi River. The expedition required two years of preparation, including extensive research on, among other things, canoe building, period clothing, wilderness survival, and the famous "voyageur" songs that provided rhythm for the paddles as the explorers made their way (Lewis 1977). Such interdisciplinary focus is a prime example of how language study can and should be related to other subject areas in a school curriculum. Funds for the project were contributed from American, Canadian, and French governmental, business, and civic organizations of all kinds. The expedition itself, scheduled to coincide with the 1976 American Bicentennial, lasted eight months and was greeted by throngs of people at every port along the way from Montreal to the Gulf of Mexico. The organizer and leader of the expedition, French teacher Reid Lewis, continues to receive standing ovations from audiences, young and old, as he tells the story in song and pictures of this modern day adventure.

We need not be a Reid Lewis to take our learners Beyond the Classroom. Just a little dream will do. It begins with an awareness of the L2 world around us and of the importance of bringing it just that much closer.

5.6 PUTTING IT ALL TOGETHER

Integration of Components

How do we put it all together? Is there an optimum combination of Language Arts, Personal Language Use, Language for a Purpose, Theater Arts, and Beyond the Classroom? These questions must be answered by individual language teachers for their learners and the goals they have set for their programs. If the case studies and empirical investigations in L2 acquisition research have taught us anything, it is that each learner is unique. Learners come into our classrooms with many different experiences. Their cultures, families, styles of learning, temperaments, and goals all combine to make individual learners quite different from one another. To the complexity of the learner, of course, must be added the complexities of the teachers and of the learning environments in which they teach. Finally, the need for variety must be taken into account. Learners who are bored with rule recitation, sentence translation, or dialogue memorization may just as easily lose interest in games, role playing, or getting-acquainted activities if these are allowed to become routine. Difficult as it is, the teacher's task is to understand the many influencing factors involved and then respond to them creatively.

Teachers need help, of course. That help can come from administrators, from the community, and from the learners themselves. Methodologists and teacher training programs have a responsibility, too. It is their job to see that classroom teachers have the perspective and experience they need to respond to the realities of their world—a changing world where the old ways of language teaching may just not be the best ways.

If language analysis has remained the mainstay of the vast majority of school L2 programs, it is because that is the way it has always been. Notwithstanding John Dewey, the celebrated American proponent of experiential education, schools have continued to value analysis over experience. In L2 teaching this has been particularly true. In the United States, for example, it was not until the mid-nineteenth century that modern foreign languages were even considered worthy of inclusion in the curriculum. Up until that time, French and other modern languages, along with dancing and embroidery, were considered suitable diversions for young ladies while their brothers went off to school to study Latin and Greek. So it was that when modern languages were eventually introduced into the curriculum, they were taught, as befitted an "academic" subject, on the model of Latin and Greek.

The optimum combination of the analytical and the experiential is a focus of current research. There are those who would emphasize the need for language use, for language acquisition, to counterbalance the long tradition of language analysis, of concern for usage. Others feel that we are in danger of overemphasizing the experiential in a kind of "anything goes as long as you get your message across" approach to L2 teaching. In interpreting the findings of my 1972 study (summarized in Chapter 2), I was deliberately cautious in suggesting that communication activities should constitute at least 20 percent of available class time. Subsequent research suggests that the percentage is probably much higher. Central, of course, to a discussion of the optimum balance of activities in an instructional program is an understanding of communication and, thus, of communicative language use. The problem at present is that some of the activities being introduced as communicative are not communicative at all but structure drills in disguise. Grammar often remains the hidden agenda.

Treatment of Learner Errors: Summary Guidelines

A discussion of the integration of the components of a communicative curriculum would be incomplete if it did not provide summary guidelines for the treatment of learner errors. As was noted in preceding chapters, in the days of audiolingualism learner errors were not really a problem, at least not in theory. They were simply not allowed. Methodologists were explicit in their admonition to teachers not to tolerate errors lest they became a "habit," difficult if not impossible to "eradicate" at a later date. (*Fossilization* is the term sometimes used today to refer to the process of stabilization whereby nonnative forms become a permanent feature of an individual's L2 performance.) In practice, however, teachers were far from comfortable with the doctrinaire audiolingual view of errors. Confronted as they were with the inevitable nonnative structures employed by those learners who sought to go beyond textbook phrases to express their own meanings, it is little wonder that most teachers found it expedient to base their evaluations of speaking ability on the recitation of memorized dialogues (Kalivoda 1970).

Now that students have been "liberated" and are encouraged to develop a degree of communicative competence that more than likely will include other than native performance with respect to some features, teachers are quite legitimately concerned with error correction. When, how, and what features to correct are questions that deserve attention from those who advocate a communicative approach to L2 teaching. Based on the discussions of the L2 acquisition process and learner errors in preceding chapters, the following summary guidelines to error correction would seem to offer a reasonable response.

1. Pay strict attention to formal accuracy in all Language Arts activities. Expect and require similar attention from learners.

2. Never tell learners that grammar "isn't important." Explain rather that it is quite common for even advanced learners to understand a rule yet be unable to use it properly in spontaneous conversation.

3. Encourage learners to express themselves even when they are unsure of the appropriate forms for their message. With this practice, and your help, they will increase their L2 proficiency.

4. Never say to learners "You were supposed to have learned that last semester" or "You're too advanced to be making such errors!" Recognize that the acquisition of L2 structures has its own timetable and that your role is to support and to guide rather than to humiliate.

5. Do not expect learners to be able to use a structure just because it has been presented and drilled in class. The inclusion of too many points of grammar in most introductory textbooks gives a misleading impression of the L2 acquisition process. Many of these same features are not fully integrated into a learner's L2 competence until many months or years later.

6. a) As learners engage in conversation, unscripted role playing, and other communicative activities, make notes from time to time on persistent errors for later treatment in Language Arts activities.
   b) Just because you have reviewed them in Language Arts, do not expect that these errors will be eliminated in subsequent spontaneous L2 use.

7. When learners are expressing their own meaning (as in Language for a Purpose, Personal L2 Use, and Theater Arts), do not correct forms directly, but *do* ask for clarification of things you do not understand. That is, show a sincere interest in the *content* of the message.

8. When you *do* understand what a learner has said, whether or not the expression of the message was structurally native, convey your understanding by restating the learner's message in native form. You might say, for example, "Oh, you mean that . . . ," "Is that right that . . . ," or "I agree (don't agree) that . . . ." Your students will be grateful for this opportunity for confirmation or correction of the forms they have chosen.

9. As a matter of courtesy to the learners, always correct their errors in written expression—either directly or indirectly through the use of a code to indicate error types (for example, wrong verb form (vb), wrong gender (gen), misspelling (sp), etc.). They need and deserve your help in improving their writing competence. In other than Language Arts activities, however, your evaluation of their writing should be based on the *ideas expressed* rather than on linguistic form. (Structural and spelling errors might be corrected in pencil, and the red pen saved for reactions to content.)

10. If students ask for or otherwise express a willingness to have you correct

them while they are speaking extemporaneously, by all means do so. Learners differ greatly in this respect. An interruption welcomed by one student would send another into an embarrassed silence for the remainder of the class period. Learn to be sensitive to learners' needs and expectations.

More complete answers to questions regarding the treatment of learner errors and the optimum balance of curricular components in any context will be found in the experiences of classroom teachers, as well as in the findings of further empirical research. Those answers depend, in the final analysis, on the ways in which we measure learner achievement. What are the teacher's goals? What are the learner's goals? And by whose yardstick do we measure success? This is the subject of the next and concluding chapter.

SUGGESTED READINGS

E. Allen and R. Valette. 1977. *Classroom Techniques: Foreign Languages and English as a Second Language*. A good collection of tried and true techniques for presenting and drilling structural features of language.

J. Asher. 1977. *Learning Another Language Through Actions*. Many illustrations of ways to make physical activity an integral part of a communicative classroom.

R. di Pietro. 1982. "The Open-Ended Scenario: A New Approach to Conversation." Examples of classroom role playing that give attention to the *strategic* dimensions of natural discourse. Initial situations provide participants with information and experiences on which to base their responses in subsequent encounters.

A. Gradisnik. 1980. *Helping Parents Learn a Second Language With Their Children*. These materials were developed for the Multi-Language School, Milwaukee Public Schools, with the cooperation of its staff, parents, and pupils. They include valuable language learning hints along with sample dialogues and many useful, everyday expressions parents can begin to use at home with their children. The words to songs sung by children enrolled in the program and recorded on an accompanying tape cassette complete the package. Available in German, French, and Spanish.

C. Graham. 1978. *Jazz Chants*. A professional jazz entertainer and teacher of ESL has put together a collection of "chants" (conversational English set to a clear, steady beat) to heighten the learner's awareness of the natural rhythmic patterns of spoken American English. A form of Theater Arts that highlights the contribution music and rhythm can make to a communicative curriculum.

F. Grittner. 1974. "The Teacher as Co-Learner." A respected voice in American foreign language education speaks out against a technocratic "systems approach" to curriculum development in favor of interest-centered programs that involve learners in decisions concerning course content.

J. Hendrickson. 1978. "Error Correction in Foreign Language Teaching." Helpful overview of the treatment of learner errors from audiolingual classrooms to the present.

K. Johnson and K. Morrow (eds.). 1981. *Communication in the Classroom*. A collection of papers illustrating materials and techniques that have been used by textbook writers and classroom teachers to engage learners in communication.

K. Jones. 1982. *Simulations in Language Teaching*. An experienced author of simulations describes the benefits of using simulations for language learning purposes, including reality of function, realism of materials, involvement, motivation, and friendships.

A. Maley and A. Duff. 1978. *Drama Techniques in Language Learning*. An emphasis is placed on the expression of learners' individual personalities in large and small group activities involving movement, observation, interpretation, and interaction.

J. McConochie. 1981. "Shopping for Community Contacts." Describes "errand assignments" for language learners in an L2 community. Teams of two members each, an interviewer and a reporter, are sent on specific missions—for example, to seek information on stock market prices, to purchase iron-on seam binding, to interview a local barber about the trade of haircutting. Useful insights into the importance of *strategic competence* in real-life situations.

C. McGaw. 1980. *Acting is Believing*. This basic methods book for students of theater is a good source of activities and exercises for the language classroom as well. Teachers with little or no theater experience will discover ways of making drama rehearsal techniques an integral part of L2 learning.

G. Moscowitz. 1978. *Caring and Sharing in the Foreign Language Class*. Techniques for relating L2 learning activities to learner attitudes and interests.

R. Nelson and R. Wood. 1975. *Radio in Foreign Language Education*. Practical advice for teachers with no prior experience in the use of shortwave radio.

L. Newmark. 1971. "A Minimal Language-Teaching Program." An insightful account of the components of a college program that provides "structurally disorganized experience of language in use." Three hours per week are devoted to conversational encounters in which, at the request of both learners and their native-speaker models, discussion topics are "allowed more and more to follow the spontaneous interests of the participants."

C. Nine-Curt. 1976. *Non-Verbal Communication*. Many examples of nonverbal features of communication with particular reference to the differences between Puerto Rican and Anglo-American cultures.

A. Omaggio. 1979. *Games and Simulations in the Foreign Language Classroom*. Language games collected from textbooks and other sources, the majority of which are keyed to points of grammar or culture. Extensive bibliography.

C. Rogers. 1961. *On Becoming a Person*. Valuable background reading for an understanding of language as an expression of self. The author, a distinguished psychologist, begins his book, "I speak as a person, from a context of personal experience and personal learnings."

H. Seelye. 1974. *Teaching Culture: Strategies for Foreign Language Educators*. A readable and practical guide to an often neglected dimension of L2 learning.

S. Simon, L. Howe, and H. Kirschenbaum. 1972. *Values Clarification*. This handbook of strategies has been a source of inspiration for many L2 teachers and materials writers. The examples themselves are all in English and are intended for use with native speakers.

G. Stanford. 1977. *Developing Effective Classroom Groups*. Excellent background reading in group dynamics along with a valuable collection of structured experiences for promoting group responsibility and productive interaction. This is a book every classroom teacher should read.

H. Stern. 1980. "Language Learning on the Spot, Some Thoughts on the Language Aspect of Student Exchange Programs." Illustrates the importance of coping strategies in natural L2 acquisition.

H. Stern et al. 1980. *Module Making: A Study in the Development and Evaluation of Learning Materials for French as a Second Language*. A project to develop materials that emphasize not language but *content* and *activities* in order to engage learners in matters of real concern to them. The modules reflect, on a smaller scale, the Language for a Purpose philosophy of immersion programs.

J. Swaffer and M. Woodruff. 1978. "Language for Comprehension: Focus on Reading." Describes a university multisectional reading program that successfully combined simple physical responses to commands, gymnastics, and yoga breathing with reading for global meaning. Strategies of inference and reading for main ideas were actively encouraged.

B. Taylor. 1981. "Content and Written Form: A Two-Way Street." Excellent discussion of the dynamic interplay of content and language in the writing process. Examples of ways in which learners can be helped to learn the elements of written form and organization *experientially* through productive feedback on the expression of their own ideas.

H. Taylor. 1981. "Learning to Listen in English." Discusses the need for training learners to tolerate great quantities of unknown language while they identify the parts they *do* understand.

T. Terrell. 1977. "A Natural Approach to Second Language Acquisition and Learning." An update of the Natural Method with an important emphasis on the need for extensive listening practice at beginning levels.

R. Via. 1976. *English in Three Acts.* Exercises in relaxation, scene study, improvisation, and other drama study techniques related to conversation skills. Concludes with a collection of short plays for the ESL classroom.

B. Wattenmaker and V. Wilson. 1980. *A Guidebook for Teaching Foreign Language.* Values clarification and other exercises for French, German, and Spanish. Includes pages to be reproduced for classroom use.

A. Wright, D. Betteridge, and M. Buckby. 1979. *Games for Language Learning.* A collection of activities for ESL that are adaptable to most languages and learner age levels.

L. Wylie and R. Stafford. 1977. *Beaux Gestes: A Guide to French Body Talk.* An amusing resource book of French gestures. Photographs are captioned in both French and English.

RESEARCH AND DISCUSSION

1. Show how Language Arts, Language for a Purpose, Personal Language Use, Theater Arts, and Beyond the Classroom cut across traditional "skill" areas of listening, speaking, reading, and writing. Give examples of specific experiences and activities.

2. Of the five L2 curriculum components illustrated in this chapter, which ones received the most emphasis in your own L2 learning? in your L2 teaching? Are there components with which you feel *most* comfortable as a teacher? With which one do you feel *least* comfortable? Why?

3. Recent statistics show that fewer than 2 percent of American secondary school students study a foreign language for more than two years.
    a) Given this limited experience, what priorities would you set in terms of the curriculum components outlined in this chapter?
    b) Would these priorities change if you could be sure that learners would pursue their language study for four years or more?

4. In a description of an experimental L2 program at the University of California in San Diego, Newmark writes:

    Our experiments with various modifications of the basic minimal program suggest that the most dramatic improvement in students' ability to use the language come from increasing our sophistication about how to induce students to attend to instances of language use rather than from increasing our sophistication about how to order the student's experience according to the supposed dictates of one or another linguistic analysis. [1971:18]

   a) What are the implications of Newmark's observation for materials selection in terms of the distinction between *what* and *how* discussed in Chapter 4?
   b) Of the various activities or techniques described in this chapter, which in your opinion provide the most incentive for the learner *to attend to language in use*? Why?

5. Find an example of the deductive presentation of a grammar rule in the L2 you teach and share it with classmates. Then present the same rule *inductively*.

6. Divide a short, coherent text into chunks and have a group of classmates reassemble them as was described in the *Scrambled passage* activity on page 192. Can you identify features of cohesion and coherence that provided cues to the proper sequence of the chunks?

7. Share with classmates a language arts game you have enjoyed as a learner or used successfully as a teacher. (Or find a description of this kind of a game in a textbook or journal article.) On what particular forms or functions of language does it focus?

8. In the L2 you teach, make a list of the ten expressions you consider most immediately useful to a classroom learner in exchanges with the teacher. As a start, see the suggestions on page 198. (If you are presently teaching, ask your students to prepare a similar list and compare the results.)

9. Translate the word *bread* into a language, other than English, that you know well, and complete two lists of associations—one for English and the second for the other language. How do the lists differ? What cultural associations do they reflect? Compare your lists with those of a classmate.

10. Try the *Line up* activity described on page 208. Share your reactions with classmates.

11. Think for a moment of your own L2 classroom learning or teaching experiences. In retrospect what activities contributed most to ensemble-building or the creation of a community spirit? Think of extracurricular excursions or gatherings, as well as of classroom activities, that helped learners to feel more comfortable with one another.

12. Adapt the *Why you're my wife* game on pages 212–215 for use in your own teaching context. Prepare a list of identities for each of seven families (four to six members each) that reflect those of typical families in the L2 culture you teach. Be sure that the family composition, occupations, place of dwelling, and other features you choose to include are a true reflection of the culture you want to represent. To make the game sufficiently challenging, pick no more than three or four major cities as places of residences for the various family members and use the same age or identifying traits for more than one person.

13. Compile a list of the L2 radio or television programs that are available in your community. Do not overlook shortwave broadcasts and cable television.

14. Hold a half-day workshop to try out some of the games and activities described in this chapter along with those contributed by colleagues or classmates. Take turns assuming the responsibility of group leader. As a follow-up, set aside time to talk about your feelings and reactions to these activities.

15. See if you can find some information on an L2 immersion weekend that has taken

place recently in your own or a nearby community. Who participated? How did it get started? What were its special features?

16. Interview teachers who work in a context similar to your own to find out what extracurricular activities have been most successful for them. Prepare descriptions of these activities to share with classmates.

17. Find out what work, travel, and study-abroad programs exist at secondary schools and colleges in your area.

18. Contact government cultural services, educational exchange services, and professional language teachers organizations for information about travel possibilities for student groups.

19. Describe a small-scale interdisciplinary project that would require the participation of a teacher or other professional in a field *other* than language study—for example, physical education, law, history, home economics, health, drama.

20. In what ways do the activities described in this chapter provide opportunities for nonnative teachers to continue to develop their own communicative competence? How important do you feel this is to ultimate program success?

21. What have been your reactions to corrections by others of your L2 errors? In what contexts have you found corrections most helpful? least helpful? Compare your reactions with those of your classmates or colleagues.

Chapter 6

Testing

Normally, in out-of-school conversations, our focal attention as speakers and listeners is on the meaning, the intention, of what someone is trying to say. Language forms are themselves transparent; we hear through them to the meaning intended. But teachers, over the decades if not centuries, have somehow gotten into the habit of hearing with different ears once they go through the classroom doors. Language forms assume an opaque quality. We cannot hear through them; we hear only the errors to be corrected.

—Courtney Cazden

With this chapter we come full circle to where we began our exploration of communicative competence in Chapter 1, to a discussion of tests and what they measure. Tests are commonly used to measure the outcome of instructional programs and are therefore a fitting topic for the final chapter in a book on communicative language teaching. Just as important, tests may be used to guide the development of instructional programs. Large-scale standardized tests, in particular, have a way of shaping curricula. Even teachers sometimes ask of each other that eternal question posed by students, "Will it be on the test?" In other words, is a particular concept or activity worthy of our time and attention?

We may all at times bemoan the preoccupation with testing that seems to characterize much discussion of second language teaching. The concern of the L2 teaching profession with tests and testing theory began to grow in an unprecedented way during the 1950s and 1960s when audiolingual methods of teaching were at their peak of influence. This concern has continued through the 1970s and on into the 1980s. In the proceedings of an ACTFL National Conference on Professional Priorities, one contributor had the following to say about second language teaching: "With the exception of psychology, the rightful home of human measurement, there is probably no other academic field so heavily involved in testing" (Jones 1982:43). Agreeing with this observation are those who feel that tests have come to occupy all too important a place in L2 teaching and curriculum design. And yet the interrelatedness of teaching and tests is a fact that cannot be ignored. It is important, therefore, that every classroom teacher be aware of the issues involved and make informed choices regarding tests and how they are used.

In this chapter we shall look at second language tests of various kinds: Why were they developed? Who uses them? How are their results interpreted? Section 6.1 reviews basic psychometric concepts, such as *test, reliability, validity*, and *aptitude* and the distinction that is made between *criterion-referenced* and *norm-referenced* tests. Section 6.2 looks at the recent history of L2 testing with particular attention to the development in the 1960s of many large-scale test programs. Section 6.3 examines the characteristics of tests that attempt to measure the *integration* of components of communicative competence (grammatical competence, sociolinguistic competence, discourse competence, and strategic competence) in different specified contexts of language use. Section 6.4 provides descriptions of three well-known types of "integrative" tests,— *cloze, dictation*, and *oral interview*—with a discussion of formats and scoring procedures.

6.1. TESTING THEORY:
SOME BASIC CONCEPTS

Definition of a Test

A test is a *sample of behavior*. On the basis of the *observed performance* elicited on a test, inferences are made about the more general *underlying competence* of an individual to perform similar or related tasks. In order to make such inferences on the basis of limited observation, two important assumptions must first be made regarding the test itself:

1. The test score is an accurate and stable measure of individual performance. The same test given to the same person on another day, in another setting, or scored by a different rater is likely to yield the same or similar results. In other words, the test is *reliable*.

2. The sample test behavior is a true reflection of the underlying competence the test is designed to evaluate. For example, performance on a driving test in fact requires driving ability, performance on a reading test requires reading ability, etc. In other words, the test is *valid*.

The concepts of reliability and validity are central to any meaningful discussion of current language testing theory and practice and therefore merit examination in some detail.

Reliability

Reliability can be defined in terms of *accuracy, stability*, and *error of measurement*. Just as different bathroom scales may be more or less reliable measures of a person's weight, so different tests may be more or less reliable measures of some trait of a person's behavior. The first question one should ask about a test, then, before using it as a basis for making educational decisions is *"How accurately does it measure?"* Educational testing theory distinguishes three types of reliability, each pointing to a potential source of measurement error. One has to do with the *scoring procedure* used, a second with the nature of the *individual items* that make up a test, and a third with the *stability* of the measurement from one time and/or setting to another. We shall consider each in turn.

Rater reliability. Reliability of scoring procedure has to do with the extent to which the same test scored over and over again by the *same* scorer (*intrarater reliability*) or by *different* scorers (*interrater reliability*) yields the same or similar values. Rater reliability is of particular concern in tests sometimes referred to as "subjective"—essay tests and oral interviews, for example— where evaluation requires the evaluator to exercise individual judgment. In contrast, "objective" tests are true-false or multiple-choice tests in which there is little chance of score variation due to scorer error or difference of opinion.

As we have seen in Chapter 1, audiolingual claims of a "scientific" approach to language teaching were accompanied by so-called scientific tests of language proficiency. It was at this time that multiple-choice tests increased in popularity because they were seen to offer a maximum potential for reliability. The following quotation expresses well the enthusiasm for multiple-choice formats that was shared by many language testing specialists in the 1960s:

> With the aid of a simple scoring key or stencil, the teacher can very quickly and easily score a multiple-choice test or, where this possibility is available, assign the task to an electronic scoring device. Scoring reliability of multiple-choice tests is virtually absolute. . . . Viewed strictly from the standpoint of its scoring advantages, multiple choice format would be the response modality of preference for all types of foreign-language testing. [Clark 1972:40]

However, the *rater reliability* offered by a multiple-choice format is not sufficient to constitute the *whole* of test reliability, as we shall see.

Item reliability. Internal consistency, or *item reliability,* is a second type of test reliability. The internal consistency of a test is the extent to which all items consistently rank people the same. It has to do with the relationship of a person's performance on individual items to his or her performance on the test as a whole. For example, in a spelling test consisting of 25 words, one would expect the best spellers (those who correctly spell the greatest number of words) to misspell only the more difficult words, words that are misspelled by less able spellers as well. A word that is consistently misspelled by the best spellers but often spelled *correctly* by those with lower overall test scores would have a low item reliability and would therefore lower the internal consistency of the test. The test developers might decide to eliminate the item from the test for this reason. In multiple-choice tests an item may prove unreliable because it is ambiguous or because there is more than one correct response possible among the choices provided. For this reason extensive *pretesting* of items is an important step in the development of tests of this kind. A multiple-choice test may be easy to score, but a reliable one is very time-consuming to prepare.

Test-retest reliability. A third type of reliability has to do with the stability of a measurement procedure in different settings. Just as a person's body weight fluctuates from one day to another, individual performance on a behavior test may be expected to vary somewhat from one test administration to another. In both cases it is important to know to what extent the differences observed reflect *true variation* in the individual's underlying competence rather than variation due to the measurement procedure itself. For example, a change in a person's recorded weight from one weighing to another may reflect (1) a true change in body weight or (2) a failure to record weight consistently under the same conditions—one weighing taken perhaps following a morning shower and another taken fully dressed following a heavy meal. There are many potential sources of error in test administration that can reduce the stability of the measure. In a tape-recorded test of listening comprehension, for example, a faulty speaker or poor room acoustics may impede listening for some or all of the test takers. Lack of uniform administration procedures—for example, failure to give complete instructions or to monitor time properly—is another source of error. A common procedure for estimating test reliability of this kind is known as *test-retest*, which, as its name implies, involves the administration of the same test more than once with a comparison of the results.

All three kinds of test reliability we have considered—*intrarater/interrater*, *item*, and *test-retest*—are clearly defined and relatively easy to estimate. These estimates are stated in terms of the statistical relationship between two measures—the set of evaluations for each of two teachers, scores on an individual item and the test as a whole, etc.—or the *correlation* of measures. Correlations are often expressed by means of a statistic known as the *Pearson product-moment correlation coefficient*, or *Pearson r*, ranging from −1.0 to +1.0. The absence of a relationship is denoted by 0, whereas a perfectly consistent positive relationship (an increase in one measure is always accompanied by a corresponding increase in the other) is denoted by +1.0. A perfect *negative correlation* between two measures (−1.0), means that an *increase* in one measure corresponds to a *decrease* in the second measure. (It should be noted in passing that a common error in interpreting correlations is to assume a cause and effect relationship between the measures involved. This may be the case but is often not, as will be evident from the example that follows.)

Suppose, for example, that two teachers of Spanish decide to give the same final written examination to their first-year classes. Before they can make any meaningful comparison of the test scores for their respective classes, the teachers need to be sure that they are following uniform scoring procedures and that they are being consistent in their evaluations of the various sections of the test—for example, sentence completion, multiple-choice reading comprehension, short essay. That is, they need to be assured of a reasonably high interrater reliability. One way to estimate interrater reliability is to have both teachers *independently* rate a certain number of examinations and then compare the resulting sets of scores. Though perfect agreement between the two teachers (a correlation of +1.0) is unlikely, a correlation of 0.90 or above would be considered very good. The lower the correlation, the greater the margin of error in the reported scores.

CORRELATIONS

The boxes below show four different levels of relationship between two measures, the independent evaluations by teachers X and Y of a set of examination papers. In Box A the correlation is zero (r = 0), and the points scatter out in a pattern that is just about circular—illustrating the rather unlikely situation of no agreement whatsoever between the two teachers. Box B corresponds to a correlation of 0.30. You can see a barely perceptible trend for points to group along a diagonal from the lower left-hand corner to the upper right-hand corner. In Box C, representing a correlation of 0.90, the trend is much more marked; note, however, that even with this high a correlation, the scores spread out quite a bit and do not lie directly on the diagonal. Box D represents a perfect positive correlation of 1.0. All scores fall exactly on the diagonal going from the lower left-hand corner to the upper right-hand corner—showing the teachers to be in perfect agreement on all papers.

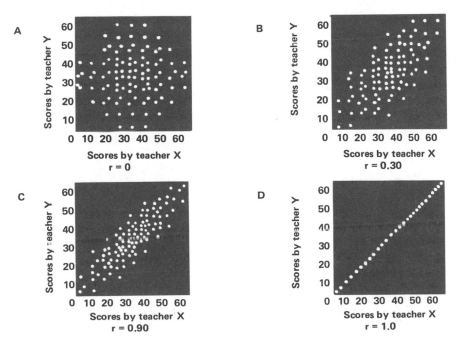

Source: Adapted from Thorndike and Hagen, *Measurement and Evaluation in Psychology and Education,* 1977.

Validity

If test reliability can be estimated in a relatively straightforward fashion, through the use of well-defined statistical procedures, test *validity* is a very different matter. Simply stated, the validity of a test is the *extent to which a test measures what it is supposed to measure and nothing else*. It matters little that a test is reliable if what it is measuring is unrelated or only peripherally related to the information sought. Regardless of how reliable it was, for example, few people would consider a bathroom scale a valid measure of a person's height. The need for validity in the use of an educational test is no different. To be valid, a test must first be reliable. However, a reliable test is not necessarily a valid one for a given purpose.

No fewer than five different kinds of validity are traditionally distinguished (Davies 1968, Cronbach 1971, Palmer and Groot 1981):

Face validity. The test *looks* as though it measures what it is supposed to measure. It is *perceived as a reasonable, fair, or appropriate test* by those who take it as well as by those who interpret the results.

Content validity. The tasks included are representative of the larger set of tasks of which the test is supposed to be a sample. For example, the test faithfully reflects the syllabus or instructional program on which it is based.

Predictive validity. The test predicts performance in some *subsequent* situation, such as job success, performance on another test, or grade in a course.

Concurrent validity. The test gives results similar to those obtained from another measure taken *concurrently*—for example, job success, performance on another test, grade in a course. Predictive and concurrent validity are both examples of what is sometimes referred to as criterion validity. The *criterion* in each case is performance in some other specified situation.

Construct validity. The test is an accurate reflection of an underlying theory of what it is supposed to measure. The question in this case is neither "How well does this test measure the attainment of course objectives?" nor "How well does this test predict performance on other tests?" but rather "What do scores on this test *mean*?" and "What is the nature of the trait it is intended to measure?" Palmer and Groot (1981:4) describe construct validity as follows:

> In construct validation, one validates a test not against a criterion or another test, but against a theory. To investigate construct validity, one develops or adopts a theory which one uses as a provisional explanation of test scores until during the procedure, the theory is either supported or falsified by the results of testing the hypotheses derived from it.

In other words, a test is developed to explore the adequacy of a theory, the construct, on which rests, in turn, the construct validity of the test. Examples of constructs are such things as "intelligence," "scholastic aptitude," "personality," or, to turn to examples of language proficiency, "reading ability," "pronunciation," and "communicative competence."

Of the five kinds of validity described above, face validity differs from the others in that it exists only with respect to the *impressions* of observers, casual or other, who may or may not know anything about testing theory. Face validity is certainly important to test takers, but it has no empirical basis and is of no value in evaluating test validity: "So-called 'face' validity, the mere appearance of validity, is not an acceptable basis for interpretive inferences from test scores" (American Psychological Association 1974:26).

Discussions of empirical procedures for estimating test validity focus therefore on the remaining kinds of validity. Of these, construct validity is by far the most important, as well as the most difficult to establish. As can be seen from the preceding definitions, content, predictive, and concurrent validity *exist only in terms of other specified criteria*. Thus although statistical techniques for estimating these kinds of validity have been developed to an impressive and sometimes even intimidating level of sophistication, their value as an indication of a presumed underlying construct rests, ultimately, on the validity of the criteria on which they are based.

To illustrate, a test that correlates highly with another accepted test of language ability—thereby demonstrating concurrent validity—will still be of limited validity as a measure of language proficiency if the L2 learning theory underlying both tests is itself inadequate. Similarly, a test may demonstrate content validity by faithfully reflecting the content of a textbook or instructional program. It will nonetheless be only as valid as the curriculum on which it is based. For example, a "speaking" test that evaluates the recitation of memorized dialogues may have content validity with reference to a particular instructional program without necessarily demonstrating the construct "speaking ability."

Predictive validity, as we have seen in the discussion of McClelland's views on aptitude tests in Chapter 1, may also be artificially introduced. Where language tests serve as a selection device, providing access to educational programs or jobs, their correlation with program or job success is misleading. In other words, if a minimum score on a language test is a prerequisite for employment or admission to graduate school, then those who do not meet the specified minimum will perforce be less successful as they are denied the opportunity to succeed in the first place. Thus the test can no longer be considered an independent measure of learner potential. It has become part of the validity criterion (that is, job or academic success) itself.

The circularity often inherent in estimates of test validity is summarized by Morrow (1979:147): "Starting from a certain set of assumptions about the nature of language and language learning will lead to language tests which are perfectly valid in terms of these assumptions, but whose value must inevitably

be called into question if the basic assumptions themselves are challenged."
Nor is the problem of circularity confined to language tests. To quote psychologist Elizabeth Ingram (1978:7): "The essential truth about nearly all kinds of
tests is that the only theory they are based on is *test construction theory*, which is
a kind of *applied statistics* [emphasis added]. Current intelligence tests are not
based on any coherent or explicit cognitive theory; language tests are not based
on any coherent or explicit psycholinguistic theory." In other words, language
tests and testing theory are a house of cards that may topple once its foundation
is shaken. The views of both Morrow and Ingram have been echoed by Messick
(1981:1) who gives the issue some historical perspective:

> "Since predictive, concurrent and content validities are all essentially *ad
> hoc*, construct validity is the whole of validity from a scientific point of
> view" [Loevinger 1957:636]. In the 25 years since these words were pub-
> lished, it has become increasingly clear that this seemingly radical doctrine
> is in actuality a central principle of educational and psychological mea-
> surement and that, if anything, it does not go far enough in stressing the
> fundamental role of construct validity—not just for scientific measurement
> but for applied measurement as well.

The construct validity of tests of L2 proficiency is thus a major issue in
current L2 test research (see, for example, Bachman and Palmer 1981, Oller
1981, Palmer, Groot, and Trosper 1981). Audiolingual methods of language
teaching have had a profound and far-reaching influence on classroom L2
programs around the world. The discrete-point structural approaches to language *testing* associated with these methods continue to dominate most large-
scale objective language tests in use today. As we have seen throughout the
earlier chapters of this book, behaviorist and structuralist theories underlying
both have proved inadequate. And though language teaching programs have
begun to reflect a more communicative, functional view of their goals, language tests in the main have not significantly changed to keep pace with these
developments. Attention is now being directed, however, to laying a sound
foundation on which to build a theory of communicative language testing and
to developing reliable measures of language proficiency that reflect the underlying construct of communicative competence. Before considering the progress
that has been made in this direction, it is important to understand the tradition
from which these efforts have emerged. We turn now, therefore, from a
general discussion of tests and testing theory to examples of L2 tests. We will
look first at tests of L2 *aptitude* and then at tests of L2 *achievement* and *proficiency*.

Aptitude Tests

Aptitude tests serve to estimate the degree of success a learner is likely to have
in a given educational setting. They may be said to have *predictive value* and
have been used in the past to select learners for L2 programs. Predictors of L2
achievement include the following:

past academic achievement—for example, grade point average, class rank, scores on standardized tests of achievement;

academic aptitude—for example, tests of general verbal or quantitative intelligence, reasoning ability or cognitive skills; and

aptitude for language learning as measured by tests of skills found to be related to *formal* L2 learning—for example, the Modern Language Aptitude Test (MLAT) (Carroll and Sapon 1959) and the Language Aptitude Battery (LAB) (Pimsleur 1966).

One can, of course, never predict with complete certainty the success a learner will experience in a particular L2 learning environment. Measures of any of the above factors alone or in combination can, however, provide an *estimate* of learner success in academic programs that emphasize grammatical competence and the conscious learning of rules of sentence-level structure. Measures of past academic achievement and academic aptitude are both useful in estimating the future achievement of learners in *academic programs in general*, whereas the Modern Language Aptitude Test is the best known example of a test designed to measure *second language learning aptitude in particular*. It was developed in response to the dissatisfaction with IQ tests (in U.S. military language programs, in particular) as a basis for selecting participants for intensive L2 training. There are five separate subtests: Number Learning, Phonetic Script, Spelling Clues, Words in Sentences, and Paired Associates. The MLAT is in most instances a better predictor of learner success than either IQ tests or prior academic achievement, but its value as a predictive measure is nonetheless limited. The MLAT and other L2 aptitude tests only begin to account for the wide differences in learner achievement in school programs (Jakobovits 1972, Gardner et al. 1976, Naiman et al. 1978, Clark 1978).

The predictive power of measures of any of the above factors may be increased by the addition of an evaluation of learner attitude toward the study of a particular language. The Pimsleur Language Aptitude Battery, for example, includes an opportunity for learners to express their interest in learning Spanish, German, French, etc. The Gardner and Lambert (1972) attitude and motivation test battery is a more elaborate set of scales that was developed to measure a wide range of attitudinal variables (see Chapter 3). This test battery was used, along with measures of all three predictive factors listed above, in the classroom study of communicative teaching and testing (Savignon 1972b) that is summarized in Section 2.2. The purpose in this instance was not to select learners for participation in the program but to see if the groups included in the experiment were equivalent with respect to factors known to be related to L2 achievement.

In immersion and other programs where the emphasis is on *acquisition* through language *use* rather than on the conscious learning of rules of usage, the predictive power of aptitude measures is even less than in traditional classroom programs (Krashen 1981). Learner *attitude*, on the other hand, takes on increased significance. In natural L2 environments it is learner attitude rather than aptitude that is related to both the *amount* and the *nature* of L2 interaction. As we have seen in Chapter 3, when measured in terms of *communicative language use* both inside and outside the classroom, attitude is probably the single most important predictor of learner achievement.

Criterion-referenced and Norm-referenced Tests

Scores on aptitude tests and other types of tests may or may not have an absolute meaning in themselves. Individual test scores may be reported in terms of an established *standard,* or *criterion,* of performance in a specific skill or in terms of a *comparison* with the results of others who have taken the same test. This is the difference between a criterion-referenced test and a norm-referenced test.

A *criterion-referenced* test is concerned with the completion of a defined task—the translation of a list of 20 sentences, the conjugation of 30 irregular verbs, the completion of a job application form, etc. It is theoretically possible for all who take the test to earn a perfect score. In an instructional setting, the more learners who earn high scores on a criterion-referenced test, the better, because this means that the educational goals of the program are being met.

A *norm-referenced* test, in contrast, reports individual scores—often in the form of percentile rank—in terms of their relationship to the performance of others who have taken the same test. Thus a score may place an individual at the 94th percentile rank, the 39th percentile rank, etc. depending on the percentage of test takers who received higher or lower scores at the time the test was normed. The purpose of a norm-referenced test is to spread people out, to make discriminations between them. (In an instructional program, the practice of "curving" grades, that is, basing a grade on the relationship of a test score to the total distribution of scores for a class by giving a predetermined percentage of A's, B's, etc., is a form of norm-referenced evaluation.)

For norm-referenced tests, the "meaning" of a grade or percentile rank remains relative and depends ultimately on the use that is made of a measurement in a given context. To illustrate with a familiar example drawn from outside the L2 testing field, most U.S. colleges and universities base admission decisions on a combination of secondary school class rank and a nationally normed achievement or aptitude test—for example, the American College Test (ACT) or the Scholastic Aptitude Test (SAT). The cutoff scores for admission to a particular university program may change from year to year with the number of openings available and the number of applicants seeking admission. The following published entrance requirements for the college of engineering at a major U.S. university for the years 1975 and 1982 are representative of a national trend.

TABLE 6.1 1975 COLLEGE OF ENGINEERING ADMISSIONS REQUIREMENTS

Applicants with the following minimum ACT/HSPR combinations will be considered for admission:

ACT composite score	18	20	22	24	26	28	30
High school percentile rank (HSPR)	*	*	*	65	65	65	65

* Applications will be reviewed with particular attention paid to mathematics ability.

TABLE 6.2 1982 COLLEGE OF ENGINEERING ADMISSIONS REQUIREMENTS

Applicants with the following minimum ACT/HSPR combinations will be considered for admission:

ACT composite score	25	26	27	28	29	30	31	32
High school percentile rank (HSPR)	99	97	94	92	89	86	84	81

As the tables show, the minimum ACT score and high school percentile rank (HSPR) required for admission have risen sharply in recent years. An applicant who would have qualified for admission in 1975 with an ACT score of 24 (providing the applicant's high school class rank was at the 65th percentile or higher) would have been inadmissible in 1982 even if he or she had been the class valedictorian! This rise in required minimum requirements is not because the curriculum itself has necessarily become any more demanding; there simply has been a marked increase in the number of applicants. Thus the cutoff scores and percentile ranks do not mean that a person who fails to meet a required minimum lacks the potential to succeed as an engineer. Faculty and facilities, rather, are no longer sufficient to train the many well-qualified applicants who seek admission. In this case, then, the adjustments of required minimum scores serve primarily to control the number of applicants declared admissible from year to year.

The validity of using test scores in this way—in effect to restrict the admission of intelligent and otherwise qualified applicants—is an issue of concern both *within* and *without* the engineering profession, as it is within and without other professions facing similar problems. Alternative procedures have been proposed and are being explored. For example, once minimum criteria of grade point and achievement test scores have been met, further selection of candidates may be based on a single factor or on multiple factors such as extracurricular activities, an oral interview, or a written essay. A lottery is sometimes used to make the final selection from among equally well-qualified applicants. The existence of these alternative procedures acknowledges that there is a point beyond which the discriminations yielded by a test of aptitude or achievement may cease to be meaningful for purposes of candidate selection. Beyond this point there are other, perhaps more appropriate, procedures that should be used to make final decisions. The issue of test validity thus extends beyond the test itself to the use that is made of the results.

In L2 programs in recent years the trend has been not to *exclude* learners but rather to make the benefits of second language learning available to an even wider population. Immersion, adult vocational, and other L2 programs that focus on the development of functional skills have proved successful with learners' from a wide range of academic ability. In most programs the *interests* and *needs* of learners have replaced past academic achievement or a specific language learning aptitude as criteria for acceptance.

On the other hand, evaluation of language achievement or proficiency, both L1 and L2, plays an important role in academic programs of all kinds. (The distinction that is sometimes made between *achievement* and *proficiency* will be discussed below.) The enactment of government policies having to do with language education for both minority and majority children in the United States, Canada, and many other countries around the world has assigned a heretofore unequalled importance to language tests. Major decisions concerning the future educational opportunities of countless learners are based on language test scores. All teachers need to be aware of the issues involved; what is more, they need to be prepared to raise an enlightened voice where these issues have a bearing on the formulation of educational policy. A brief review of the recent history of L2 test development will serve to further identify these issues and will provide a background for the discussion of tests of communicative competence to follow.

6.2 THE RECENT HISTORY OF L2 TEST DEVELOPMENT

The 1960s: A "Golden Age" of L2 Test Development

The recent history of L2 testing, which has been called the *psychometric-structuralist* period (Spolsky 1978), is characterized by a widespread interest in the use of *psychological measurement* techniques (hence the term *psychometric*) to evaluate learner mastery of discrete structural features of language. A concern with the "objective," "scientific" measurement of language proficiency began to grow in the 1950s and on into the 1960s, an impressive decade indeed for L2 testing in view of the number of large-scale standardized test programs that were initiated. John Clark, a former test consultant with Educational Testing Service (ETS), describes what he terms this "golden age" of standardized test development:

> The period extending roughly from 1960–67 may be considered the "golden age" of generally-available standardized test development in the foreign-language field. Under contracts from the U.S. Office of Education,

and using NDEA funds, two major standardized test batteries were developed through the collaborative effort of the Modern Language Association of America and Educational Testing Service. The first of these, the *MLA Foreign Language Proficiency Tests for Teachers and Advanced Students*, consisted of separate skills tests (listening comprehension, reading comprehension, speaking, and writing), each in two parallel forms, for five different languages: French, German, Italian, Russian, and Spanish. [1972:156–7]

The second of these was the *MLA Cooperative Foreign Language Tests*, a lower-level series of tests that was also developed with U.S. Office of Education funds and under MLA–ETS auspices. Never since has there been such a large-scale effort to establish tests and norms for L2 study in American schools.

It was during this same period that the *Test of English as a Foreign Language* (TOEFL) was launched. Developed to test the English proficiency of foreign students applying for admission to U.S. colleges and universities, the program was initially funded with grants from government and private agencies and attached administratively to the MLA. In 1965, ETS assumed responsibility for program operation, and its offices were moved to Princeton, New Jersey. In its present form the TOEFL test consists of three parts: listening comprehension, structure and written expression, and reading comprehension and vocabulary. An optional *Test of Spoken English* (TSE) was added in 1980 in response to an increasing demand for a measure of oral expression.

Some examples of the item types used in the standardized test batteries of this period will give a sense of what is meant by a psychometric-structuralist approach to testing. The attempt to isolate discrete structural features and the extensive use of a multiple-choice format are characteristic. The following items are from Clark (1972). The correct response is marked with an asterisk. Though they are labeled tests of "listening," "reading," "speaking," and "writing," respectively, all items shown are similar in that they reflect not the integrated skills involved in these activities so much as they do simple sound, spelling, vocabulary, or grammatical distinctions. The "reading" item, moreover, asks the test taker not to interpret meaning (the generally understood meaning of "reading") but rather to select the L2 vocabulary item that corresponds to the paraphrase given. In each case the restricted context (no more than a single sentence) is further reflection of an emphasis on sentence-level grammar as opposed to discourse.

DISCRETE-POINT TEST ITEMS

Listening (Tape-recorded instructions and items)

1. Identify the spoken word that is different from the other two.

   pero   *perro*   *pero*
    (a)   (b)   (c)

   a) ———————————— *b) ———————————— c) ————————————

2. Select the object described in the spoken sentence.

Voila un marteau.

*(a)   (b)   (c)   (d)

Reading (Written instructions and items)

3. Select the most appropriate completion of the sentence.

Es la primera vez que esta obra dramatica se presenta.
Es su

    a) *principio*
    b) *inicial*
    *c) *estrena*
    d) *origen*

Speaking (Tape-recorded instructions, items, and responses)

4. Say aloud the Spanish sentence that corresponds to the English sentence.

I see the moon.

    / beo la luna (yo beo la luna) /

5. Say what you see in the picture.

    * / lə myR /

Writing (Written instructions, items, and responses)

6. On the basis of the model, write in a single word that correctly completes the sentence. Study the sample item beforehand.

Salen temprano
Salian *temprano*
Son las once.
_____ *las once.*

The above items are but a sample, illustrative of item types commonly found on L2 tests developed during this period. The justification for this type of discrete-point item is examined further in the discussion that follows of the distinction between achievement and proficiency.

The Achievement/
Proficiency Distinction

Language test developers often make a distinction between *achievement* and *proficiency* testing. In his presentation of the item types illustrated above, Clark defines achievement testing as "any skills testing activities which are based on the instructional content of a particular language course." His explanation clearly reflects the audiolingual view of L2 acquisition he espouses in his well-known 1972 handbook, *Foreign Language Testing: Theory and Practice:* "In the beginning stages of instruction, the bulk of classroom activity usually involves the presentation of small linguistic units in rather artificial settings." Achievement tests at the beginning level are "necessarily and desirably of a detailed, highly structured type whose primary measurement purpose is to determine whether or not the student has learned specific discriminations, grammatical patterns, or other discrete instructional aspects of the course" (1972:25). The handbook reflects further the mood of the 1960s in devoting its major section to *achievement* with reference to "the four separate skill areas of listening, speaking, reading and writing." An 88-page chapter on achievement testing is followed by a brief 14-page discussion of proficiency testing with particular reference to the Foreign Service Institute (FSI) Language Proficiency Interview. There is no mention of reading proficiency.

The distinction made by Clark between achievement and proficiency appears to be as follows: Achievement tests are supposed to measure what learners do in the *classroom*, whereas proficiency tests measure what they do in the *real world*; achievement tests measure *grammatical competence*, whereas proficiency tests measure the use of that competence in somewhat more communicative settings. Achievement tests would therefore seem to be concerned primarily with *content validity*, and proficiency tests more with *construct validity*. Clark himself acknowledges that the two measures are not necessarily related. His observations parallel those of McClelland (cited in Chapter 1) concerning the selection criteria for policemen:

> Testing procedures based on a determination of the accuracy and extent of a student's linguistic command of the foreign language cannot serve to measure directly his communicative proficiency. Rather, what appear to be needed are work-sample tests of communicative proficiency in which the student's performance is evaluated not on the basis of extent of vocabulary, accuracy of morphology and syntax, excellence of pronunciation, and so forth, but rather in terms of the adequacy with which the student can communicate in specified language-use situations. [Clark 1972:120]

The development of "work-sample tests" and the specification of "language-use situations" is precisely what the evaluation of communicative competence is all about. Moreover, it is significant that one of the first tests to attempt to evaluate communicative competence, the FSI Oral Interview, was developed to meet *real-world L2 needs*. Used initially by the U.S. Department of State to evaluate the L2 proficiency of government personnel engaged in or being trained for foreign service, the FSI test has become familiar to many Americans through its use in Peace Corps Volunteer language training programs. The interview format and evaluation criteria it uses will be reviewed in more detail in Section 6.4.

The emphasis in L2 testing is now shifting. Discussions of language testing in recent years are giving more attention to the evaluation of language *proficiency* (see, for example, Oller 1979, B. Carroll 1980, Cohen 1980). It is perhaps noteworthy that in his statement of ACTFL testing priorities, R. Jones (1982) makes no mention of achievement tests, addressing simply the question "What is proficiency?" The achievement/proficiency distinction seems to fade, therefore, as the language profession becomes increasingly concerned with the development of functional skills for real-world use from the very beginning of classroom instruction.

This is not to say that a legitimate distinction cannot or should not be made between the objectives of a particular instructional program and L2 proficiency in a more general sense. With an emphasis on selected facets of language use and analysis, course or program goals will always be limited, and it is quite appropriate for course examinations to reflect course content. Analysis of linguistic or sociolinguistic rules of usage, business letter writing, informal conversational skills, minimum survival skills, reading novels for personal enjoyment, etc. all constitute valid curricular goals. Learner progress toward their achievement, however, should be measured in ways consistent with the proficiency construct underlying that goal. That is to say, *achievement tests should reflect the nature of the proficiency or competence toward which learners are supposed to be advancing.* Language proficiency *is* communicative competence and should be defined and evaluated as such. Failure to do so can only result in the distortion of instructional goals and dissatisfaction with learner achievement.

Teachers, Tests, and Learners

Whether standardized large-scale measures or teacher-made classroom tests, evaluation procedures are inextricably tied to teaching methods and goals. Teachers use tests of all kinds for a variety of purposes. They use tests to check on learner understanding and skill development, to encourage learners to prepare lessons and to stick to the tasks at hand. Tests serve to reward learners for excellence as well as to inform them of their failures. Tests administered at the end of an instructional program are used to evaluate learner achievement. The results are of interest not only to the learners themselves but to those who are paying for their training, whether a local school board, a government agency, or a private commercial firm. All want to know how well their time, money, and efforts have been spent.

The most important implication of the concept of communicative competence is undoubtedly the need for tests that measure an *ability to use language* effectively to attain communicative goals. Discrete-point tests of linguistic structures of the kind developed in the 1960s have not only failed to sufficiently take into account the complexity and dynamic quality of the communicative setting. In some cases, they also have served, in their emphasis on grammatical accuracy, to discourage the strategies needed for communicative competence and thus to hinder the development of more communicative curricula. A language course that sets out to "cover" all the points of grammar presented in a basic textbook, and then tests learners on their "mastery" of these points, has little time left for communication.

The importance of tests in shaping all that we do and think in the classroom is as great today as it has ever been. The following observations are summarized from Savignon (1977):

1. Tests serve first of all to measure student progress. If we teach for communicative competence, we have to test for communicative competence so that we and our students know how well we are doing what we claim to be doing.

2. Second, tests serve as a powerful motivating factor. They let learners know what is really important. We can talk all we want about language for communication, real-language activities, and spontaneous transactions, but if verb forms and dialogue recitation are what show up on the test, the learners quickly get the message that we do not mean what we say. The discrepancy between grammatical competence and communicative competence shows up nowhere more clearly than in the reactions of learners in an audiolingual type of program to a testing situation that required them for the first time to use what language they had learned in a variety of real-life encounters with native speakers (Savignon 1972b).

> If this is an easy test, I just found that I couldn't talk my way out of the airport if I flew to France.

> I thought it was fun, but very challenging. It doesn't seem as though we've had enough practice speaking off the top of our head. Until this evening I was never forced to say anything except answers to questions or substitute phrases . . . there was no need to search for words . . . they were supplied. I wish we were forced to do this more often. This is what a language should be.

> It seems very difficult but it is the first time I have had the chance to actually express myself in French. . . . I feel I have an "'A'' in beginning French writing, reading and grammar but an ''F'' in actually having a practical knowledge of the language.

> I felt that the whole test was difficult because I was told all semester not to think about what I was saying but rather to see patterns.

3. Third, to the extent they measure communicative language use, tests serve to tell us what learners can really do with the language they are learning. From performance on tests of communicative competence we as teachers and researchers can learn more about L2 learning strategies. L2 learning research has cast serious doubts on many commonly held assumptions of how a second language is learned or acquired. To the extent that the L2 classroom is tightly controlled in shaping or preventing L2 use, the situation is too artificial to provide any meaningful data on L2 acquisition strategies. Once we allow learners to use language for their own purposes, however, we will begin to see how they use what it is they have seen and heard, what meaningful organization they give to the L2 data presented. These insights will provide a basis from which to evaluate the instructional process and goals.

4. Fourth, tests of communicative competence offer the best assurance that we are preparing learners for the real world. Could a learner get simple directions from a francophone taxi driver in Montreal? coach a basketball team as a Peace Corps volunteer in Guatemala? serve as receptionist in a German-American firm? tutor Chicano children in mathematics?

As long as we look to traditional discrete-point tests of L2 grammatical competence for placement and evaluation, we are victims of what Marshall McLuhan has called the *rearview mirror syndrome* (Postman and Weingartner 1969). We are like drivers whose gaze is fixed not on where they are going but on where they have come from. It is not even a matter of seeing through the windshield but darkly. We are seeing clearly enough, but we are looking at the rearview mirror. We have not understood the message of communicative competence.

Placement Tests and Politics: The Example of Bilingual Education

Similar observations apply to testing that is done *outside* the classroom whether for placement of learners in an instructional sequence, program evaluation, or the assessment of language proficiency for purposes of employment or further training. Work abroad, teacher certification, and placement in bilingual education programs are among the many contexts calling on measurement of L2 skills. To focus on but one of these, Ellen Rosansky of the National Institute of Education has underscored the need to validate the oral proficiency measures used to determine the need or eligibility for bilingual education of non-English-speaking children in American schools. She cites a proposed federal regulation that sets as standards of test validity and reliability (a) the measurement of language skills necessary to make instructional or other educational decisions about those students and (b) the production of consistent results. In Rosansky's words,

> The standards specified in the regulation for validity and reliability are an example of good intentions gone awry. The intention was to avoid jargon; to explain validity and reliability in lay terms so that practitioners would know what was intended. The result, however, is a "standard" that stops short of providing real guidance to those who would have had to implement the regulation. More importantly, I believe, is the fact that such a validity standard is about as compromised as the available validity data on the commonly used language proficiency instruments themselves. [1981:5]

She goes on to point out the inadequacy of currently available tests as measures of communicative competence, the conflicting data they yield, and the consequences for the children involved—for example, placement in programs beyond or beneath their ability, denial of access to needed help, stigmatization as "slow learners." Among the problematic tests she includes in her analysis are the *Bilingual Syntax Measure* (BSM) (Burt, Dulay, and Hernandez-Chavez 1975), *Basic Inventory of Natural Language* (BINL) (Herbert 1975), and *Language Assessment Scales* (LAS) (DeAvila and Duncan 1977). (For further discussion of the consequences of language proficiency testing for school children see Cazden et al. 1977, Labov 1976, and Cummins 1980.)

The controversy over reliability and validity in language testing persists. Tests, especially multiple-choice tests that are machine scorable, may be remarkably reliable yet tell us very little about real-world L2 proficiency. On the other hand, a straightforward assessment by a teacher of a learner's day-to-day functional competence in classroom activities may be challenged as *subjective* or *unreliable*. A teacher may even *prefer* a reliable machine-scored test over a more valid observation of daily performance in an effort to avoid question or controversy. The dilemma is obvious. If communicative competence is the *expression*, *interpretation*, and *negotiation* of meaning involving *interaction* between two or more persons or between one person and a written or oral text, how can it be tested *objectively*, that is, without reference to human judgment?

6.3 TOWARD TESTS OF COMMUNICATIVE COMPETENCE

The terms *integrative* and *global* are sometimes used to describe tests that presumably involve the communicative use of language, whereas the term *discrete-point* is reserved for tests of isolated structural features of language. The distinctions are far from clear cut, however, and the terms are sometimes used in reference to test *format* as well as to test *content*. In this section we will consider, with examples of item types, the meaning of the terms *integrative*, *global*, and *discrete-point* as they have been used in discussions of L2 tests.

Discrete-point Versus Integrative Testing

The word "discrete" means *separate*, or *distinct* and has been used to describe two different aspects of language tests: (1) content, or *task*, and (2) *mode and scoring of response*. We shall consider each in turn.

A *discrete-point task* is one that focuses on an isolated bit of language, typically surface features of phonology, morphology, syntax, or lexicon, as in the sample items from Clark (1972) included in the preceding section. In their purest form, discrete-point items include but one *channel* (oral or written) and one *direction* (receptive or productive); that is, they test "separate" skills of listening, reading, speaking, and writing. In practice, however, this separation is difficult to achieve. A test of speaking may require the prior comprehension of a written or oral "stimulus," a test of listening may include the selection of a correct written response, etc. Context in discrete-point tasks is usually restricted to a sentence or phrase, but it may also be a longer oral or written text. So long as the criterion remains the recognition or use of a discrete structural feature, this kind of "contextualization," as it is sometimes called, does not alter the basic nature of the task.

In the test item below, for example, the task is discrete-point even though the context is that of a "conversation" in a Paris café. The *text* in this instance serves primarily as a *pretext* to test recognition of discrete points of French morphology. Learners are told to focus on form rather than on meaning (Valette 1977:8).

> Imagine you are sitting in a Paris cafe and are overhearing snatches of conversations. Can you tell whether the speakers are talking about present or past events? Listen carefully for the verb. If it is in the present tense, mark column A. If it is in the imperfect, mark column B.

In contrast, the following task may be said to be *integrative*, that is, several features combine to convey the *meaning* upon which a response is then based (Rumelhart, cited in Hunt 1982).

> Mary heard the ice-cream truck coming down the street. She remembered her birthday money and ran into the house.
> Answer the following based on the story above:

	True	False
1. Mary is a little girl.	X	☐
2. Mary wants some ice-cream.	X	☐
3. Mary goes into the house to get money.	X	☐

In another example of an integrative task, this one a listening comprehension item, learners are asked to identify the gist of an announcement. Alternatives are provided in advance to guide their listening (Ontario Assessment Instrument Pool, French as a Second Language, 1980).

> Listen to the following announcement to decide what the speaker is promoting. Then circle the letter of the correct answer. Look first at the possibilities on your page.
> The speaker is promoting:
>
> a) a taxi service.   *b) a hotel.   c) an airport.   d) a restaurant.
>
> *Text of tape*
> Idéalement situé. . . . Service de transport de l'aéroport international. . . . Quarante-deux chambres luxueuses, climatisées. . . . Elégant restaurant. . . . De réputation internationale.

The previous examples all involve connected sentences, or discourse, but the distinction between a discrete-point and an integrative task may be applied to single sentence contexts as well. Sentence-level grammar was in fact what Carroll had in mind when he first used the terms "integrative" and "discrete structure-point":

> I recommend tests in which there is less attention paid to specific structure-points or lexicon than to the total communicative effect of an utterance. For example, I have had excellent success in ascertaining levels of audio-lingual training by a listening comprehension test in which auditorily-presented sentences of increasing length and rapidity are to be matched with an appropriate picture out of four presented. The examinee is not concerned with specific structure-point or lexicon, but with the total meaning of the sentence, however he is able to grasp it. . . . Indeed, this "integrative" approach has several advantages over the "discrete structure-point" approach. [1961(1972:318)]

The *discussion, interview, reporting,* and *description* tasks described in Section 2.2 are examples of integrative tests, as are the test of text cohesion in Section 5.1 and most of the reading interpretation questions accompanying the Indian story, "Remembering," in Chapter 4. With the exception of those few Language Arts activities and exercises that focus exclusively on language form, most of the activities described in Chapter 5 are integrative in nature and could be used as test items as well. Essays, letters, story-telling, role playing (both prepared and improvised) are all examples of integrative tasks.

A *discrete-point* (or objective) *response mode*, on the other hand, is a matching, true-false, multiple-choice, or fill-in-the-blank format in which a response is either selected from among alternatives provided or otherwise restricted by the nature of the context provided. This type of response mode offers ease of scoring and, as we have seen, high rater reliability. In contrast, a *global response mode* might be an oral interview, a summary of a written or oral text, or a dictation. When a discrete-point mode of response is used, scoring involves the straightforward marking of correct responses. A global response, however, may be evaluated either *discretely*—that is, by looking for and counting distinct linguistic features—or *globally*—that is, by assigning an overall rating based on a combination of features, such as *effectiveness, appropriateness, coherence, comprehensibility, fluency,* etc. In practice a *combination* of these scoring methods is often used. Discrete features of pronunciation, spelling, syntax, etc. may be evaluated while at the same time a general impression of overall quality is established. A discrepancy in the results may be resolved by adjusting one or the other evaluation, or by adjusting both. Although test evaluation procedures may vary, in real-life communication it is, of course, always the general impression that prevails!

Generally speaking, the more integrative tasks will require a more global mode of response, whereas a *discrete-point mode of response can be used with both integrative and discrete-point tasks*. The learner's task may be integrative in that it requires inference, or *interpretation of meaning*, in a text while the response takes the form of a discrete-point selection of the best rejoinder, picture, map, summary, translation, etc. from among alternatives provided. This is apparent in the example on page 250 involving Mary and the ice-cream truck. Another example is the following item from a test to measure judgments of sociolinguistic style (Bachman and Palmer 1980). This particular item is provided as a model for test takers at the beginning of the test.

> This is a test of how well you can recognize natural written English. Each problem in the test is a short paragraph with five parts underlined. The whole paragraph is grammatically correct, but *one* of the five underlined parts is not natural for the style of English that is being used.

> *Example:* The bus to Chicago (1) *leaves at 5:15 p.m.* You (2) *may hop on board* at Gates 2 and 3. Be sure all your baggage is clearly marked (3) *with your name and address.* You may put only small items (4) *in the rack* (5) *above your seat.*

> In this paragraph, "may hop on board" is unnatural, so if this were part of the test you would darken circle (2) on your answer sheet.

Discrete-point/integrative or *discrete-point/global,* moreover, are not neat dichotomies but the *opposite ends of a continuum,* with most tests falling somewhere in between. This is illustrated in the chart on the next page. The horizontal axis shows the nature of the *task,* with the most discrete-point tasks (for example, the identification of isolated phonemes, completion of verb paradigms, recognition of verb tense, L1-L2 word translation, etc.) on the far left, and the most integrative tasks (for example, essay writing, the interpretation of a spoken or written text, conducting an interview, etc.) on the far right. The *response mode* is represented by the vertical axis with multiple-choice, true-false, and other discrete-point formats at the bottom. Response modes become increasingly global as they are placed along the continuum toward the top. The more global the mode of response, of course, the more integrative the task, so that there can be no item types in the extreme upper left-hand corner of the chart.

CLASSIFICATION OF SAMPLE TEST ITEMS ACCORDING TO TASK AND RESPONSE MODE

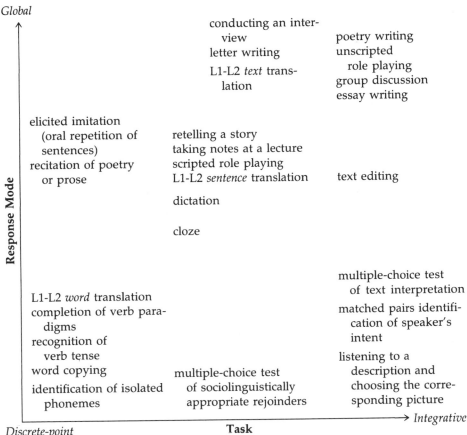

Global

conducting an interview
letter writing
L1-L2 *text* translation

poetry writing
unscripted role playing
group discussion
essay writing

elicited imitation
(oral repetition of sentences)
recitation of poetry or prose

retelling a story
taking notes at a lecture
scripted role playing
L1-L2 *sentence* translation

text editing

dictation

cloze

L1-L2 *word* translation
completion of verb paradigms
recognition of verb tense
word copying
identification of isolated phonemes

multiple-choice test of sociolinguistically appropriate rejoinders

multiple-choice test of text interpretation

matched pairs identification of speaker's intent

listening to a description and choosing the corresponding picture

Response Mode

Discrete-point **Task** *Integrative*

The placement of a particular item along the horizontal and vertical axes is relative, not absolute, and depends on many factors such as the scoring procedure, the test taker's understanding of scoring criteria, and the context in which the item occurs.

There is nothing absolute about the placement of a particular task along either the horizontal or the vertical continuum. Nor should the terms "integrative" and "global" be interpreted to mean necessarily "communicative" while "discrete-point" is "noncommunicative." The all too common use of the terms in this way is doubly misleading: Not only does it fail to reflect the *relative* nature of these attributes, it tends to perpetuate the false notion that somehow the communication process is one of "integrating" discrete points of linguistic knowledge (that is, the surface-form-to-meaning interpretation of communicative competence discussed in Chapter 1).

The position of various tasks, then, are ones that in all cases will be influenced by the nature of the evaluation criteria being used, as well as by what the learners understand these criteria to be. The form of a "letter" written as a test will in all likelihood differ from that of a letter written to a friend or business associate. The "conversation" between the *examinee* and the *examiners* in an FSI test will reflect the roles of the participants involved and will be shaped by the criteria of evaluation that have been predetermined. Learners who are aware of the structural features being observed may attempt to monitor their language accordingly at the expense of meaning. This strategy, whether in multiple-choice tests of sentence-level grammar or in oral interviews, is a part of a test-taking skill referred to as "test-wiseness"—that is, learner familiarity with test context and performance expectation. The functional nature of a test rests ultimately on the testing *context* itself and the *test takers' understanding of how their responses are being evaluated*. It is thus in the best interests of all involved to make overt and explicit statements of test objectives and criteria of evaluation. This kind of statement offers the best assurance that tests will measure what they are supposed to measure and, in turn, keeps teachers and learners working together toward these same goals.

Construct Validity of Tests of Communicative Competence

To return to our discussion of test validity in the preceding section, the construct validity of tests of communicative competence is the extent to which a test reflects an underlying theory of communicative competence. Tests of communicative competence, then, integrate the components of grammatical competence, sociolinguistic competence, discourse competence, and strategic competence to reflect the characteristics of communicative competence examined in Chapter 1. To summarize:

1. Tests of communicative competence assess the *dynamic negotiation of meaning* between two or more persons or between one person and an oral or written text.

2. They include *measures of both written and spoken language*, as well as paralinguistic and nonverbal features of communication.

3. Tests of communicative competence are *context specific*. The ability to write a scholarly essay on the poetry of Garcia Lorca is not a good measure of the ability to make small talk with a group of Mexican teenagers any more than the ability to interact socially with anglophone classmates is a good measure of a native Spanish-speaking child's ability to use English for academic purposes.

4. Although there is a theoretical difference between competence and performance, *only performance is observable* and therefore provides the basis for making inferences about a person's underlying competence.

In addition to the previous characteristics, tests of communicative competence in classroom settings should be ongoing (that is, not confined to the end-of-semester or end-of-year examination period) so as to reflect the evolving nature of a learner's communicative abilities. Moreover, they should emphasize what learners *can* do—the success they experience in limited communicative contexts rather than those features of native-speaker communication they have not yet acquired.

Setting Realistic Expectations for L2 Learners

This last-mentioned point brings up the issue of *realistic expectations for L2 learners* and the *native speaker myth*. It is often assumed that native speakers, or in some cases "educated" native speakers (see, for example, the FSI Oral Interview), are the model against which L2 learners are to be evaluated. Native speakers and even *educated* native speakers, however, differ widely in their communicative competence. In Chapter 1 we saw illustrations of the strategic competence of both native and nonnative speakers in response to a question "What is a 'redneck'?" to which neither knew the answer. The most significant difference between the native speaker and the nonnative speaker might well be that the latter is often *tested* for a competence the former is *assumed* to have. The implications for the construct validity of tests of communicative competence are enormous. Before we can judge the competence of nonnatives we need to better understand the competence of natives.

For beginning L2 learners, in any event, the emphasis should be not the discrimination or manipulation of discrete structural items but, rather, understanding the main point of the text, ascribing a general purpose or intent to language used in real-life settings—that is, the *antithesis* of the discrete-point achievement goals described by advocates of the psychometric-structuralist approach to testing. L2 learners should be evaluated on their ability to perform several language functions simply but appropriately rather than on their ability to manipulate a limited number of structural features perfectly. *Beginning-level tests, moreover, should emphasize receptive rather than productive skills of oral and written expression.* That is, learners should not be expected to express themselves and to negotiate meaning before they have been given the opportunity to develop the interpretive skills needed to do so.

A criticism of integrative tests is that they are too "vague" and insufficiently "diagnostic," that one cannot tell precisely what they measure. This, as Oller has pointed out, is no fault of the tests but reflects the underlying language proficiency construct they seek to measure. "Answering the question, 'How much language proficiency is necessary to understand what goes on in a college-level course?' is like answering the question, 'How much light is sufficient to find your way out of a forest?' It depends hardly at all on any particular discrete 'rays' of light, and the same sort of thing can be said about 'points' of grammar" (1978:55). In other words, proficiency is best determined not by how much language one knows but by how well one can communicate. A discrete-point approach fails to take into account the *interactive, compensatory* relations of the components of communicative competence. Though the problems of language testing are thus far more complex than most tests imply and may appear insurmountable, we should not lose heart or fall back on simple yet inadequate solutions. In the final analysis, the fact that human behavior is not so easily quantifiable is a state of affairs about which we should not be too unhappy.

6.4 THREE INTEGRATIVE TESTS

There is general agreement that the best test of functional language skills occurs in a real-life context. The ongoing evaluation of the *results* of L2 use in social encounters, on the job, or in the classroom provides the most valid measure of L2 proficiency. A salesman who makes his share or more of sales and a child who works at grade level or above have demonstrated their language proficiency in a convincing way. Problems in getting one's message across are often equally obvious. If someone orders a hamburger and gets a plate of spaghetti, something is clearly amiss!

Circumstances, however, most often require simulations or other less direct means of assessing communicative competence. Cohen (1980) describes three integrative tests used to estimate language ability that are gaining popularity in classroom use: *cloze, dictation*, and *dialogue*. Cloze and dictation have received attention in recent years through the research of Oller (1973) and Oller and Streiff (1975) who have documented their usefulness as tests of "general language proficiency." That is, scores on dictation and cloze tests correlate highly with total scores on batteries of tests supposedly measuring "separate" skills of reading, writing, listening, and speaking. (In other words, they show concurrent validity with reference to standardized L2 test batteries. The matter of construct validity with reference to communicative competence is yet another issue and will be addressed below.) These findings, along with the ease of preparing and scoring cloze and dictation tests, have resulted in their increased use as tests of placement as well as tests of both short-term and long-term instructional goals.

Dialogue in Cohen's (1980) discussion includes structured interviews such as the Ilyin Oral Interview (Ilyin 1976) and the Foreign Service Institute (FSI) Oral Interview, as well as the variety of communicative tasks described in Savignon (1972b). Teachers should be familiar enough with each of these formats to adapt them to their own program needs.

Cloze Procedure

Cloze is a term coined by W. Taylor (1953) who used it as a measure of the intelligibility or readability of texts by determining the percentage of systematic deletions that could be replaced by panels of readers. Inasmuch as the comprehensibility of a text depends as much on the world knowledge and reading skills of the *reader* as on the text itself, cloze readability scores have been proposed as equally good indices of individual differences in comprehension. A *high score* on a cloze test presumably indicates a *low level of uncertainty* on the part of the reader about the interpretation of the text. That is, the natural redundancy of discourse has enabled the reader to supply the missing items. A *low score*, on the other hand, indicates a *high degree of uncertainty* about overall meaning. The context is so unfamiliar that the reader needs all the contextual cues he or she can find.

A TYPICAL CLOZE PASSAGE

A typical cloze passage provides two or three lines of running text followed by the systematic deletion of every fifth or sixth word.

Publish and Perish

On Sunday, November 8, the Dallas Chronicle published an exclusive front-page

story about a 72-year-old retired oil engineer who had been a Soviet _____

and an FBI double _____ . Although the engineer, R.J., _____ admitted his

espionage activities _____ the Chronicle, he repeatedly _____ suicide if

exposed. Seven _____ before the presses were _____ roll, R.J. called the

_____ and learned the story _____ running.

"Well, I guess _____ know that leaves me _____ choice but to kill

_____ in the morning," he _____ the city editor. The _____ morning,

as the Chronicle _____ being tossed on Dallas _____ , R.J. went into the

_____ of his Wilmette, Ill., home _____ , according to police, shot _____ .

Replacements may be scored in one of two ways: (1) Replacements must correspond exactly to the word omitted, or (2) any word that fits the context is acceptable. (A replacement may be considered "acceptable" if judged by a linguist or language teacher to be both semantically and syntactically appropriate *or* if it is a replacement supplied with some frequency by native speakers.) In addition, a decision must be made in both (1) and (2) about whether to require the exact *spelling* of the word supplied. In terms of the *relative* performance of learners in most contexts it seems to make little difference if scoring method (1) or (2) is adopted. That is, even though there are a great many more incorrect responses when an exact-word method is used, the ranking of learners is about the same as when any appropriate response is accepted. The exact-word method (1) is far easier to score since no decisions of acceptability need be made, but method (2) increases the face validity of the test for learners who feel that any appropriate word should be accepted.

Presented and scored as described above, the cloze test may be considered an integrative task with a mode of response toward the discrete-point end of the continuum. Learners supply only single word items. The variety of contexts that can be used is as infinite as the needs and interests of learners. Anything from a newspaper article to the lyrics of a popular song can provide a text, provided it is related to the experience of those for whom it is intended.

Among the many adaptations of the cloze technique are (1) the deletion not of every *n*th word (fixed-ratio deletion) but of a certain *category* of words (rational deletion)—for example, prepositions, verbs, cohesive devices—and (2) the inclusion of a list of possible replacements for each deletion. Each of these adaptations changes the integrative nature of the task to some degree so that the continued use of the term *cloze* may be difficult to justify. The systematic deletion of cohesive devices (see example in Chapter 5, page 191) seems one of the better adaptations of the cloze procedure because it calls attention to features of discourse that extend beyond the boundaries of a single sentence. In this case, then, the task is still integrative. The response mode can be made even more discrete by supplying a list of all the deleted words at the bottom of the passage. This is a particularly good idea with beginning learners. For example, with the cloze passage *Publish and Perish* the following deleted words would be supplied:

agent	to	you	next	hours
myself	doorsteps	spy	to	me
himself	to	and	threatened	study
had	told	paper	was	

The deletion of prepositions, adverbs, or verb inflections, on the other hand, would not be the best use of cloze because the context needed for their replacement would be limited in most cases to a single sentence or less. To the extent that this is true, the text would then appear to be simply a *pretext* for the testing of discrete structural features.

In some tests a choice of replacements is provided in a multiple-choice format as shown below. Distractors are chosen to mislead the test takers or to test their recognition of particular structural or lexical items.

"Well I guess _____ know that leaves me _____ choice but to kill
                 (he, you, they)   (a, any, no)

_____ in the morning," he _____ the city editor.
(myself, me, you)   (said, told, threatened)

This format seems the least desirable because the presence of deliberately chosen distractors intermingled with the text seriously distorts the reading process and thus reduces the construct validity of the test.

In all cloze formats the matter of *face validity* must be carefully considered. There is some indication that learners tend to find the task difficult and artificial and unrelated to the skills they are seeking to acquire (Shohamy 1978). Where this is the case, other tests of a more functional nature are to be preferred.

AN EARLY EXAMPLE OF CLOZE

Cloze is not really a new idea. This page from a nineteenth-century reader entitled *Stories for Language Lessons* (Boston: D. Lothrop and Co., 1882) nicely illustrates the need in a cloze exercise to rely on real-world experience and knowledge. Even with the picture cues provided, children in *today's world* might have a difficult time filling in all the missing words! (Deletion here is *rational* rather than *fixed-ratio* since all the missing words are nouns selected at intervals of varying lengths.)

WHAT JENNIE DOES.

Jennie likes to wash. She has a little —— and a —— to hang the —— on, and some —— to pin them on with.

When her washing is done, Jennie takes the feather —— and puts the room in order. Mamma lets

Jennie roll out pie crust with the —— and taste the sauce for the —— ;

Dictation

Dictation is not new to language classrooms. It has had a long use in the teaching of French, in particular, as a test of spelling and grammar. In traditional French language classrooms, passages are often familiar to the learner and may be prepared in advance. The standard procedure is for the teacher to read the entire passage through once at a moderate rate, followed by dictation in short word groups with pauses long enough to allow learners to write what they hear. It is customary on this second reading to indicate all punctuation marks. The third and final reading is again given at a moderate rate with a slight pause at the end of each sentence to give learners time to check their spelling and punctuation. This procedure is still widespread in the teaching of French as both a first and a second language and is widely used as a measure of the language proficiency of foreign students seeking admission to French universities.

The procedure described above may be varied in a number of interesting ways to yield a test that is either *more* or *less* integrative. The following three basic features need to be considered in the development of a dictation test:

1. difficulty of the oral or written text(s) selected;
2. length of word groups, or *chunks*, on the second reading; and
3. scoring procedure.

The difficulty of the passage will depend on the topic or context of the text and its syntactic and lexical style or register.

When test developers are uncertain about the approximate proficiency level of learners (as in the initial placement of newcomers in an instructional program) it might be best to use *two or more* passages on different topics that reflect different styles of discourse (for example, newspaper, textbook, popular magazine, authentic dialogue, theater dialogue). If a passage is too difficult for a group of learners, scores will all cluster at the bottom of the scale and it will be impossible to discriminate meaningfully among them. Similarly, if a test is too easy, the cluster of scores at the upper end of the scale will obscure differences that may exist in individual proficiency. These same observations apply to the *cloze* procedure as well as to other tests of language proficiency. The *wider the spread of scores*, the *more discriminatory* the test may be said to be.

In order to qualify as an integrative test of language proficiency, the chunks dictated on the second reading of a dictation must be *sufficiently long* so as to challenge the test taker's short-term memory. That is, the test takers should have to *interpret* what they hear, to give the language some meaning in order to remember it long enough to write it down. For this reason, a passage read in chunks of two, three, or four words is not integrative to the same extent as a passage read in chunks of eight or nine words. The former may in fact be little more than a test of sound-spelling correspondences. In sum, to qualify as an integrative test a dictation passage must be (1) *unfamiliar* to test takers, (2) *read at moderate speed*, and (3) in *relatively long chunks*, that is, in chunks of eight or nine words. (In one experimental project (Cziko 1982) the number of words in each chunk was *progressively increased* from an initial two, four, and six words up to a total of twenty-two in what proved to be a successful attempt to make the transcription of chunks progressively more difficult.)

Scoring has traditionally been on an exact-word, exact-spelling basis, with one point awarded for each correct word. Alternatively, half points are sometimes awarded for words with errors in spelling or accent markings. The decision *not* to count errors in spelling is intuitively appealing to teachers concerned with communicative competence. If a dictation is to measure language proficiency more general than spelling ability, it seems unfair to penalize those who understand the passage but happen to be poor spellers. The decision to ignore errors in spelling leads, however, to difficulties in distinguishing between spelling errors and more "serious" errors. The attempt to define "mere spelling" errors as opposed to lexical and structural errors has led more than one researcher to conclude that in the final analysis the "decisions are somewhat arbitrary" (Cohen 1980:113). In practice, the numerous ambiguities that arise in attempting to distinguish error type, along with both the additional scoring time this requires and the risk of differences of opinion among scorers, have resulted more often than not in the continued use of an exact-word method of scoring.

An alternative method proposed by Cziko (1982) for dictation in English as a second language has been used successfully in French as a second language (Savignon 1982). It involves scoring by *chunks* (one point per chunk on an *all or nothing* basis) rather than by individual words. The three categories of evaluation that were established for experimental work with French dictation are as follows:

1. *Exact word:* For credit on this criterion a chunk has to be transcribed exactly in terms of spelling, including accent markings. Spelling of proper nouns, capitalization, and punctuation are disregarded. Hyphens and apostrophes are counted as spelling, not punctuation.

2. *Phonetic similarity/paraphrase:* The chunk has to be a phonetic rendering of the dictated chunk for credit on this criterion. Errors in accent and spelling not affecting pronunciation are disregarded. Paraphrases, including brief omissions, that do not alter the meaning of the chunk are also given credit on this criterion. (Instances of paraphrase in the test data for which these criteria of evaluation were established were rare, however, and occurred primarily in the dictations of native speakers. The decision to combine *paraphrase* with *phonetic similarity* rather than with *conveyance of meaning* was arbitrary.)

3. *Conveyance of meaning:* A chunk is awarded credit on this criterion if the scorer considers the subject to have understood the chunk. Chunks with clear cases of grapheme inversion, cognate spellings, and errors in gender are awarded credit on this criterion. Credit awarded on the *phonetic similarity* criterion automatically results in credit on the *conveyance of meaning* criterion.

In the Savignon (1982) study, chunks were scored on each of the three criteria, and scores were recorded on a prepared tally sheet. The examples below are all taken from actual data. A follow-up analysis of the *interrater*

EXAMPLES OF DICTATION SCORING

	EW	PS	CM
Model: *environ six centimètres cubes sur le disque*	1	1	1
environs six centimètres cube sur le disque	0	1	1
environs six cent mètres cube sur le disque	0	0	0
Model: *Une petite fille se regardait dans le miroir*	1	1	1
Une petite fille se regarder dans le miroir	0	1	1
Une petite fille se regarde dans le miroir	0	0	1
En principipe on se regardait dans le miroir	0	0	0
Une petite fille se regarde dans le noir	0	0	0
Une petite fille s'a regarde dans le mier wa	0	0	0
Model: *La campagne du sénateur du Massachusetts*	1	1	1
La campagne du sénateur du Massatchutes	1	1	1
La campagne du senateur du Massachusetts	0	1	1
La campaigne du senator de Mass.	0	0	1
La companions de senator de mal sussette	0	0	0
La campagne de senater a acheté	0	0	0
La compagnie de cette elector sur la sex	0	0	0

---

reliability for raters who had been given training in the use of the scoring procedures showed agreement to be as high on criterion (3) *conveyance of meaning* (CM) as on criterion (1) *exact word* (EW). (Criterion 2 was not included in the analysis of interrater reliability.) Scorers have found it faster and easier, moreover, to judge *conveyance of meaning* than to judge the *exact word* reproduction of a chunk. The former requires the scorer to focus on *meaning*, the latter on *form*, and as any newspaper or journal editor will attest, the nature of the two tasks is quite different. Proofreaders trained to look for errors in spelling and punctuation will, in fact, often read a text backwards so as not to be distracted by meaning.

Encouraging evidence of the value of the chunk scoring methods described above has been found both in the success of their use to evaluate the dictations of French *L1* learners—children are able to convey meaning long before they are able to spell all the words correctly—and in their usefulness as a classroom teaching and testing technique (Savignon, in preparation). The elaboration of alternative scoring methods has served to help teachers and learners alike focus on the differences between *conveyance of meaning* (comprehension) and *formal accuracy* (spelling and grammar). As a classroom teaching activity, short unprepared passages (for example, ten chunks) can be presented initially for general comprehension and scored using the *conveyance of meaning* criterion. The written text may then be distributed to learners as preparation for a *second* dictation on a subsequent day, this one to be scored on an *exact word* basis. This activity is particularly useful with learners who have acquired L2 *oral* skills with little practice in writing, as it is with those whose writing skills have decreased through lack of use. The initial scoring on an other than exact-word basis acknowledges the comprehension skills of these learners and at the same time gives them the opportunity to correct their spelling errors for a second, prepared dictation.

As an informal classroom test, a dictation may be prepared at a moment's notice using a text from the radio, daily newspaper, or some other source of interest to learners. More formal tests of placement and achievement, however, require additional preparation. The passage should be tape-recorded if possible to ensure a standard, high quality reading. The length of the pauses on the second reading may be calculated by having a small sample group of learners (or teacher volunteers if they are careful not to write too fast) write the passage as it is dictated. The following instructions and scoring sheet used in the Savignon 1982 study are included here as models for the development of large-scale dictation tests. The instructions were developed by Lyle Bachman for use with English Placement Test at the University of Illinois (Urbana-Champaign).

INSTRUCTIONS FOR DICTATION TEST

(Instructions are to be read aloud to test takers.)

Here are the instructions for the test.

You will hear the test passage *three* times.

First, the passage will be read at normal speed. You will not write anything on your paper: You will just listen carefully and try to understand as much as you can.

The *second* time, the passage will be dictated at a slower speed, and you must write down what you hear. For this, the passage will be divided into small parts. Each part will be read *only once*, so you must listen very carefully. You will be given enough time to write down each part before the next one is read. There are several sentences in the passage.

The *third* time, the passage will be read again at normal speed. There will be a short pause at the end of each sentence, to enable you to check your work. After the third reading, you will have exactly one minute to make any final corrections to your dictation before handing it in. You should make sure that what you have written is grammatically correct.

SCORING SHEET FOR DICTATION TEST

	EW	PS	CM
Passage No 1 SS No _____			
1. Une petite fille se regardait dans le miroir	___	___	___
2. pendant que sa mère la peignait	___	___	___

	EW	PS	CM
3. Maman dit-elle	___	___	___
4. est-ce que le bon Dieu a créé ma grand'mère	___	___	___
5. oui mon enfant dit la mère	___	___	___
6. est-ce que le bon Dieu a aussi créé mon grand-père	___	___	___
7. mais oui dit la mère	___	___	___
8. et mon père	___	___	___
9. oui	___	___	___
10. et toi aussi	___	___	___
11. certainement	___	___	___
12. la petite fille se regarde encore dans le miroir	___	___	___
13. puis	___	___	___
14. après quelques instants de réflexion	___	___	___
15. elle dit	___	___	___
16. Maman le bon Dieu a fait beaucoup de progrès n'est-ce pas	___	___	___

Limitations of cloze and dictation. In using both dictation and cloze formats one should keep in mind that an *integrative* task is not necessarily a *functional* task, that is, one involving the use of language for some communicative purpose, such as to report, to inquire, to greet, etc. Cloze procedures, for example, are integrative but not functional. Test makers may go to great lengths to make them *appear* functional by giving learners instructions such as "You have found a secret document. The ink has faded and some of the words are no longer legible." The excitement over the discovery of the "secret document" pales quickly, however, if learners find that the missing words are for the most part tricky irregular verb forms! Dictation is functional only to the extent that it corresponds to the task involved in recording what someone is saying, as in the dictation of a letter to a secretary. Both cloze and dictation are used because (1) performance on these tests has been shown to correlate highly with many other kinds of tests—that is, they have *concurrent validity*, (2) they are relatively easy to develop and score—that is, they are *practical*, and (3) they are relatively *reliable* in relation to other types of L2 tests, many of which require much more extensive preparation.

Face validity is only moderate for these types of tests, however, and their construct validity is a focus of ongoing research. Both formats should be used judiciously and not as a replacement for more functional reading and writing tasks such as following directions, letter writing, text interpretation, reporting, note taking, and summarizing. In the case of classroom tests in particular, the more functional they are the better.

Oral Interview

The Ilyin Oral Interview (1976) is a structured interview technique based on pictures with accompanying questions and is intended for use with upper elementary through adult learners. The pictures attempt to summarize activities in terms of a chronological sequence: *yesterday, today,* and *tomorrow* and given times of the day. They provide a framework for asking questions about what the people in the pictures *are doing, were doing, will do, did next,* and so on. The Bilingual Syntax Measure (BSM) (Burt, Dulay, and Hernanadez-Chavez 1975) has a somewhat similar format in that it uses pictures (cartoon figures in this case) to elicit grammatical structures. Both tests are discrete-point in their concern with grammatical structures as opposed to communicative intent. In this sense, then, they offer little improvement over earlier models of speaking tests that presented learners with a series of pictures to which they were expected to respond "The spoon is in the plate," "This is a wall," "I see a frog," etc. (For examples, see the discrete-point test items on pages 243–244.)

SAMPLE PICTURES FOR THE ILYIN ORAL INTERVIEW

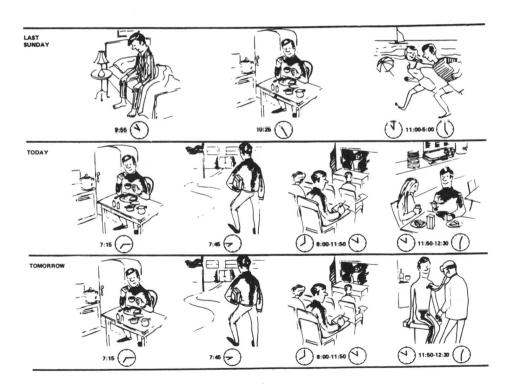

A more open-ended interview technique designed for use with adults is the FSI Oral Interview. Whereas the Ilyin Oral Interview and the BSM are commercially available tests designed for use by classroom teachers, the FSI

Oral Interview is a procedure developed for use by *trained interviewers* who are given extensive practice in its administration and interpretation. One member of a two-person team conducts the interview according to a prescribed sequence while the other observes and takes notes on the examinee's performance. On the basis of *separate, weighted scores* assigned to features of *accent, grammar, vocabulary, fluency,* and *comprehension* an FSI level of proficiency is assigned on a scale of 0 to 5. These proficiency levels correspond to capsule descriptions of overall proficiency:

FSI ABSOLUTE ORAL LANGUAGE PROFICIENCY RATINGS

All the ratings except the S-5 may be modified by a plus (+), indicating that proficiency substantially exceeds the minimum requirements for the level involved but falls short of those for the next higher level.

Elementary proficiency

S-1 *Able to satisfy routine travel needs and minimum courtesy requirements.* Can ask and answer questions on very familiar topics; within the scope of very limited language experience can understand simple questions and statements, allowing for slowed speech, repetition or paraphrase; speaking vocabulary inadequate to express anything but the most elementary needs; errors in pronunciation and grammar are frequent, but can be understood by a native speaker used to dealing with foreigners attempting to speak the language; while topics which are "very familiar" and elementary needs vary considerably from individual to individual, any person at the S-1 level should be able to order a simple meal, ask for shelter or lodging, ask for and give simple directions, make purchases, and tell time.

Limited working proficiency

S-2 *Able to satisfy routine social demands and limited work requirements.* Can handle with confidence but not with facility most social situations including introductions and casual conversations about current events, as well as work, family, and autobiographical information; can handle limited work requirements, needing help in handling any complications or difficulties; can get the gist of most conversations on nontechnical subjects (i.e. topics which require no specialized knowledge) and has a speaking vocabulary sufficient to respond simply with some circumlocutions; accent, though often quite faulty, is intelligible; can usually handle elementary constructions quite accurately but does not have thorough or confident control of the grammar.

Professional proficiency

S-3 *Able to speak the language with sufficient structural accuracy and vocabulary to participate effectively in most formal and informal conversations on practical, social, and professional topics.* Can discuss particular interests and special fields of competence with reasonable ease; comprehension is quite complete for a normal rate of speech, vocabulary is broad enough that he rarely has to grope for a word; accent may be obviously foreign; control of grammar good; errors never interfere with understanding and rarely disturb the native speaker.

Distinguished proficiency

S-4 *Able to use the language fluently and accurately on all levels normally pertinent to professional needs.* Can understand and participate in any conversation within the range of
own personal and professional experience with a high degree of fluency and
precision of vocabulary; would rarely be taken for a native speaker, but can respond
appropriately even in unfamiliar situations; errors of pronunciation and grammar
quite rare; can handle informal interpreting from and into the language.

Native or bilingual proficiency

S-5 *Speaking proficiency equivalent to that of an educated native speaker.* Has complete
fluency in the language such that speech on all levels is fully accepted by educated
native speakers in all of its features, including breadth of vocabulary and idiom,
colloquialisms, and pertinent cultural references.

Of the features evaluated, the grammar scale receives the heaviest weighting,
followed by vocabulary, comprehension, fluency, and, finally, accent, which
has the lowest weighting. Readers interested in a full description of the scales
and scoring procedures are referred to Adams and Firth (1979).

The FSI test was designed, as the descriptive categories suggest, with the
adult "educated native speaker" in mind as a standard of comparison. The test
has been used primarily with government personnel who need to demonstrate
a given level of L2 proficiency in order to qualify for certain jobs. As a model
of oral communicative competence, it is far from adequate. The need for
trained personnel and the 30 minutes or so required to test each candidate
(10–15 minutes for candidates with very low level proficiency) make the test
impractical, moreover, in most teaching situations.

There has been recent interest, however, in *adapting* the FSI interview
procedure and evaluation criteria for use in American school and college L2
programs. Efforts have been made to *expand* the lower end of the scale, (for
example, 0, 0A, 0B, 0C, 1A, 1B, 1C) so as to permit discrimination between,
say, first year, second year, and advanced undergraduate students of Spanish.
A working committee of teachers and testing specialists convened by ETS with
funds from the U.S. Department of Education has drafted preliminary descriptions of such a scale as a basis for further discussion (Woodford 1981). The
discussion that follows is not meant to detract from this important initiative
toward making the development of oral communication skills a more integral
part of school foreign language programs. It is intended, rather, to highlight
the issues of validity that must be taken into account.

One of the major shortcomings of the FSI system of evaluation as a more
general measure of communicative competence is the central role it assigns to
grammar. Examiners are trained to elicit and evaluate specific syntactic features and to assign proficiency levels accordingly. Examiner qualifications are
not unlike those summarized by Clark and Swinton (1979:7) in conjunction
with a research project to compare measures of speaking proficiency with
scores on the TOEFL. All interviewers were native speakers of English who

had an "excellent technical familiarity with English." This, Clark and Swinton go on to explain, means that the examiners had graduate degrees in English or English linguistics and experience teaching English as a second language. This approach recalls the observation of Cazden (1976:79–80) with which this chapter opened:

> Normally, in out-of-school conversations, our focal attention as speakers and listeners is on the meaning, the intention, of what someone is trying to say. Language forms are themselves transparent; we hear through them to the meaning intended. But teachers, over the decades if not centuries, have somehow gotten into the habit of hearing with different ears once they go through the classroom doors. Language forms assume an opaque quality. We cannot hear through them; we hear only the errors to be corrected.

The use of linguists trained in structural analysis to evaluate tests of speaking ability is bound to yield evaluations different from those that would result if native speakers with no language teaching experience were asked to develop criteria of evaluation (see, for example, Savignon 1972b). The quite natural tendency for structural linguists and language teachers alike is to evaluate performance in terms of the grammatical features that are typically presented in formal instructional programs, that is, in terms of grammatical competence.

The use of a relatively *limited scale* on the FSI Oral Interview to represent a *wide range* of proficiency reduces somewhat the importance of syntactic accuracy. The descriptive levels are broad enough so that a low score in grammar may be compensated for to some extent at the lower (1–2) levels by strengths in vocabulary and fluency. However, this same kind of compensation is not possible at the upper (3–5) levels. It could be argued, though, that the centrality of grammatical competence is of little *practical* significance in this upper range because a Level 3 rating in itself qualifies a person for most diplomatic, teaching, and other responsibilities requiring L2 use. There are many *native speakers* in fact who qualify for no more than a Level 3 rating. A Level 4 rating may be a goal for some learners, but it is not needed for most professional purposes.

In addition to the bias introduced by the evaluative categories and the training of the examiners, the FSI Oral Interview is limited in respect to *context of situation*. The roles of the participants are well-defined ones of *examiner* and *examinee*, and the activities in which they engage include but a few of the many uses of language that are a normal part of conversation—for example, to greet, to take leave, to explain, to describe, to commune, to report, to hide one's intention, to appear competent, to appear incompetent, etc. Serious questions have thus been raised concerning the *construct validity* of the test. To some, it may "look like" a good measure of speaking ability. Face validity alone, however, regardless of how reliable and widely respected a test may be, contributes nothing to the construct validity of a measure. (For a more detailed discussion of this important issue, see Bachman and Palmer 1980 and forthcoming, and Stevenson 1981.)

As more valid measures of communicative competence are sought, it seems particularly important that at the very beginning levels (those with which most classroom teachers are concerned) too much emphasis not be assigned to grammatical competence if the standard of accuracy is presumed to be that of an adult "educated native speaker." To expect or even to *suggest* an expectation of native grammatical accuracy in the spontaneous oral interaction of beginning and even intermediate L2 learners is inauthentic and bound to be a source of frustration for both learners and teachers. Tests designed to "test the subjunctive," or other such linguistic elements, are at this beginning level best confined to discrete-point modes of response where learners are given ample time to monitor their responses and to focus on form rather than meaning. This recommendation should not be interpreted to mean that grammar is unimportant. At issue, rather, is the appropriateness of adult native-speaker standards for beginners. Descriptions of oral proficiency at all levels, moreover, should be stated in terms of what learners *can do* in a functional sense rather than in terms of the structural features they have not yet mastered. (See Chapter 2, Sections 2.3 and 2.4 in particular, for illustrations of the distinction.)

Profile reporting. There is a tendency in testing, as in other forms of measurement, to want to summarize findings in terms of a global evaluation of overall qualifications. The resulting simplification can often be insufficient, however, if not misleading. To illustrate with an example from outside the language testing field, consumers interested in the "best buy" in automobiles will most likely look beyond global ratings of quality to the individual scales on which such ratings are typically based. They will take into account separate evaluations of cost, fuel, mileage, repair record, and handling, and then choose the model that *best suits their particular needs.* Judgments of language proficiency should be based on the same careful consideration of the many factors involved. In language use, moreover, as in other aspects of *human* behavior, the complex nature of proficiency makes the consideration of a profile of attributes all the more compelling.

For oral communication alone there are, as we have seen, many abilities that come into consideration depending on the setting, the roles of the participants, the nature of the task, and so forth. However, even within the confines of an FSI type of oral interview many of these abilities can be identified and evaluated to yield a report that is more detailed than an overall rating such as 1, 1+, 2, etc. The U.S. Central Intelligence Agency Language School, for example, now uses a performance profile reporting form that adds scales of "sociolinguistic performance" and "tasks" (defined as "functional language ability") to the traditional FSI categories of grammar, vocabulary, pronunciation, and fluency. This new format, which has replaced the FSI as a U.S. government test of oral language proficiency, is referred to as the ILR (Interagency Language Roundtable) Proficiency Test. Though not everyone would agree with the capsule definitions of "sociolinguistic performance" and "tasks" provided, the inclusion of these categories in the profile of speaking ability is an important recognition of the inadequacy of an evaluation based exclusively on surface structure accuracy. Learner profiles on the model of the one shown below (Higgs and Clifford 1982) may be useful to employers, school admissions committees, and others who want more information than that which is provided by a simple global rating of oral proficiency. In some contexts grammati-

INTERAGENCY LANGUAGE ROUNDTABLE PROFICIENCY TEST

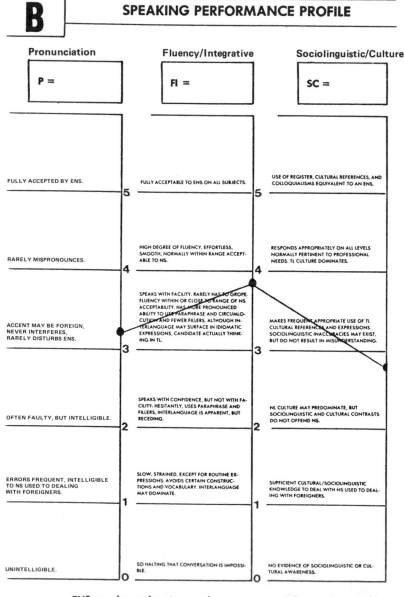

B   **SPEAKING PERFORMANCE PROFILE**

Pronunciation	Fluency/Integrative	Sociolinguistic/Culture
P =	FI =	SC =

Pronunciation

- **5** FULLY ACCEPTED BY ENS.
- **4** RARELY MISPRONOUNCES.
- **3** ACCENT MAY BE FOREIGN, NEVER INTERFERES, RARELY DISTURBS ENS.
- **2** OFTEN FAULTY, BUT INTELLIGIBLE.
- **1** ERRORS FREQUENT, INTELLIGIBLE TO NS USED TO DEALING WITH FOREIGNERS.
- **0** UNINTELLIGIBLE.

Fluency/Integrative

- **5** FULLY ACCEPTABLE TO ENS ON ALL SUBJECTS.
- **4** HIGH DEGREE OF FLUENCY. EFFORTLESS, SMOOTH, NORMALLY WITHIN RANGE ACCEPTABLE TO NS.
- **3** SPEAKS WITH FACILITY. RARELY HAS TO GROPE. FLUENCY WITHIN OR CLOSE TO RANGE OF NS ACCEPTABILITY. HAS MORE PRONOUNCED ABILITY TO USE PARAPHRASE AND CIRCUMLOCUTION AND FEWER FILLERS. ALTHOUGH INTERLANGUAGE MAY SURFACE IN IDIOMATIC EXPRESSIONS, CANDIDATE ACTUALLY THINKING IN TL.
- **2** SPEAKS WITH CONFIDENCE, BUT NOT WITH FACILITY. HESITANTLY, USES PARAPHRASE AND FILLERS, INTERLANGUAGE IS APPARENT, BUT RECEDING.
- **1** SLOW, STRAINED, EXCEPT FOR ROUTINE EXPRESSIONS. AVOIDS CERTAIN CONSTRUCTIONS AND VOCABULARY. INTERLANGUAGE MAY DOMINATE.
- **0** SO HALTING THAT CONVERSATION IS IMPOSSIBLE.

Sociolinguistic/Culture

- **5** USE OF REGISTER, CULTURAL REFERENCES, AND COLLOQUIALISMS EQUIVALENT TO AN ENS.
- **4** RESPONDS APPROPRIATELY ON ALL LEVELS NORMALLY PERTINENT TO PROFESSIONAL NEEDS. TL CULTURE DOMINATES.
- **3** MAKES FREQUENT APPROPRIATE USE OF TL CULTURAL REFERENCES AND EXPRESSIONS. SOCIOLINGUISTIC INACCURACIES MAY EXIST, BUT DO NOT RESULT IN MISUNDERSTANDING.
- **2** NL CULTURE MAY PREDOMINATE, BUT SOCIOLINGUISTIC AND CULTURAL CONTRASTS DO NOT OFFEND NS.
- **1** SUFFICIENT CULTURAL/SOCIOLINGUISTIC KNOWLEDGE TO DEAL WITH NS USED TO DEALING WITH FOREIGNERS.
- **0** NO EVIDENCE OF SOCIOLINGUISTIC OR CULTURAL AWARENESS.

ENS = educated native speaker   **NS = native speaker**

cal accuracy may be deemed very important, while in others sociocultural awareness and functional effectiveness is considered of greater value. A high value may or may not be placed on a nativelike pronunciation. A profile, in sum, allows greater discrimination among L2 speakers than is possible from a global score alone, thus ensuring that the selection criteria for a given context may be more accurately met.

Source: T. Higgs and R. Clifford, "The push toward communication." In T. Higgs (ed.) *Curriculum, Competence, and the Foreign Language Teacher* (Skokie, Ill.: National Textbook Co., 1982) p. 66.

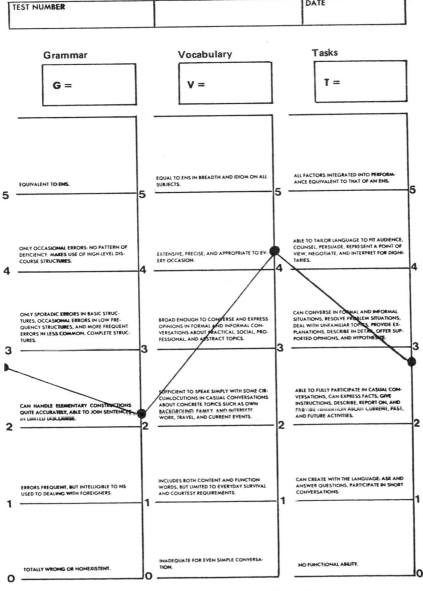

| TEST NUMBER | | DATE |

Grammar   **Vocabulary**   **Tasks**

G =   V =   T =

Grammar

5 — EQUIVALENT TO ENS.

4 — ONLY OCCASIONAL ERRORS; NO PATTERN OF DEFICIENCY. MAKES USE OF HIGH-LEVEL DISCOURSE STRUCTURES.

3 — ONLY SPORADIC ERRORS IN BASIC STRUCTURES, OCCASIONAL ERRORS IN LOW FREQUENCY STRUCTURES, AND MORE FREQUENT ERRORS IN LESS COMMON, COMPLETE STRUCTURES.

2 — CAN HANDLE ELEMENTARY CONSTRUCTIONS QUITE ACCURATELY, ABLE TO JOIN SENTENCES IN LIMITED DISCOURSE.

1 — ERRORS FREQUENT, BUT INTELLIGIBLE TO NS USED TO DEALING WITH FOREIGNERS.

0 — TOTALLY WRONG OR NONEXISTENT.

Vocabulary

5 — EQUAL TO ENS IN BREADTH AND IDIOM ON ALL SUBJECTS.

4 — EXTENSIVE, PRECISE, AND APPROPRIATE TO EVERY OCCASION.

3 — BROAD ENOUGH TO CONVERSE AND EXPRESS OPINIONS IN FORMAL AND INFORMAL CONVERSATIONS ABOUT PRACTICAL, SOCIAL, PROFESSIONAL, AND ABSTRACT TOPICS.

2 — SUFFICIENT TO SPEAK SIMPLY WITH SOME CIRCUMLOCUTIONS IN CASUAL CONVERSATIONS ABOUT CONCRETE TOPICS SUCH AS OWN BACKGROUND, FAMILY AND INTERESTS, WORK, TRAVEL, AND CURRENT EVENTS.

1 — INCLUDES BOTH CONTENT AND FUNCTION WORDS, BUT LIMITED TO EVERYDAY SURVIVAL AND COURTESY REQUIREMENTS.

0 — INADEQUATE FOR EVEN SIMPLE CONVERSATION.

Tasks

5 — ALL FACTORS INTEGRATED INTO PERFORMANCE EQUIVALENT TO THAT OF AN ENS.

4 — ABLE TO TAILOR LANGUAGE TO FIT AUDIENCE, COUNSEL, PERSUADE, REPRESENT A POINT OF VIEW, NEGOTIATE, AND INTERPRET FOR DIGNITARIES.

3 — CAN CONVERSE IN FORMAL AND INFORMAL SITUATIONS, RESOLVE PROBLEM SITUATIONS, DEAL WITH UNFAMILIAR TOPICS, PROVIDE EXPLANATIONS, DESCRIBE IN DETAIL, OFFER SUPPORTED OPINIONS, AND HYPOTHESIZE.

2 — ABLE TO FULLY PARTICIPATE IN CASUAL CONVERSATIONS, CAN EXPRESS FACTS, GIVE INSTRUCTIONS, DESCRIBE, REPORT ON, AND PROVIDE INFORMATION ABOUT CURRENT, PAST, AND FUTURE ACTIVITIES.

1 — CAN CREATE WITH THE LANGUAGE: ASK AND ANSWER QUESTIONS, PARTICIPATE IN SHORT CONVERSATIONS.

0 — NO FUNCTIONAL ABILITY.

TL = target language   **NL = native language**

ARELS ORAL EXAMINATION

Somewhat different from the evaluative categories of the FSI and ILR Oral Examinations are those of the British ARELS Oral Examinations (AOE), which describes "six major skills" of speaking ability that are tested "in situations encountered in everyday life." Two levels of proficiency are distinguished—Certificate (Intermediate) and Diploma (Advanced). The capsule descriptions of these skills for the Certificate examination are shown below to illustrate yet another approach to defining oral language proficiency.

Section	Certificate Examination Skills
1. Social responses	Test the candidate's ability to understand and be understood in everyday social situations: requests, invitations, thanks/apologies and reply, complaints, etc. Immediacy of reply is important.
2. Intelligible speech	The candidate reads aloud and speaks with intelligible intonation and pronunciation and accurate stress. Ability to deal with abbreviations, symbols, fractions, letters and spelling out, measurements, etc., and to read technical documents over the telephone, is assessed.
3. Audial comprehension	Ability to understand spoken English in context and possibly adverse conditions is tested; also specific intonational or lexical differences in meaning.
4. Sustained speaking	The candidate is required to sustain speech along predetermined lines by telling the story of a sequence of pictures (cartoon). Ability to hold listener's attention, use direct and reported speech, control tenses and to vary vocabulary, is expected.
5. Oral accuracy	A test in accuracy in the control of structures and words.
6. Free oral expression	The candidate has to show persuasiveness and clarity in speaking on a prepared subject of his choice.

Group testing. To best evaluate a wide range of language skills, formats for oral tests should be varied and should provide opportunity for group and individual testing. Most interviews are inadequate—at least as sole measures of communicative competence—because they are teacher-centered exchanges with learners who are put in the role of information givers, responding to questions put to them. As such, they are but *one kind* of communicative context. A comprehensive assessment of a person's ability to communicate in a second language should include situations where the learner is, alternately, *information-getter, describer, reporter*, etc., as is shown in the test models described in Section 2.2. Consider, as further examples, the following test items developed to accompany a beginning French textbook (Savignon 1974):

COMMUNICATIVE ORAL TEST ITEMS FOR BEGINNERS

I.   A.   Tell each student to pretend for a moment that he is an American visiting in Paris and you are a policeman (*agent de police*) who, finding him at the scene of a street demonstration, has stopped him for questioning. Ask him to give you as best he can and without interruption or assistance from you, the following information: (1) his name; (2) where he is from; (3) the name, (4) address, and (5) occupation of the person he is visiting in Paris. After he has finished, write down what you have understood and tell the student to write down, in English, the five items of information he was trying to give you. Scoring: Compare notes. Give 2 points for each item of information you understood correctly.

B. Reverse the procedure. This time the student plays an American policeman and the teacher a French visitor. The student tries to learn your name, address and occupation and the name, address and occupation of the person you are visiting.

II. To make this activity more realistic and, frankly, more fun, test students in groups of three. You will need a quiet room away from any distractions.

A. Have each student, in turn, give commands to one or both of the others. He scores 2 points for each different command correctly carried out in a time limit of one minute.

B. Give the students three minutes for a group discussion to find out all they can about each other's courses: what courses they are taking, teacher's names, likes and dislikes, etc. You can be available as a resource person to provide the words and expressions they ask for, but you should not participate otherwise in the discussion. At the conclusion of the three minutes have each student write down in English all he has learned about the other two students. Score 1 point for each correct item of information noted.

For advanced learners in an oral expression course one effective way to provide learners with feedback on their communicative successes and shortcomings is to have *other class members* evaluate them in a supportive way. The evaluation form below has worked well in classes for nonnative university teaching assistants. Class members give short presentations and then receive written reactions from their peers. All evaluation forms are completed as an in-class activity immediately following the presentation (Berns 1981).

IN-CLASS PEER EVALUATION FORM

Name:

Title of presentation:

1. Was the topic suitable to the ten minutes allowed? Why or why not?

2. List at least three facts or terms from the presentation which seem to be important to understanding the presentation.

3. Was the presentation well-organized? Was difficult vocabulary explained?

4. List three good aspects of the presentation.
   a)
   b)
   c)

5. List three aspects of the presentation which you think could be improved. Say why.
   a)
   b)
   c)

6. Did you understand the speaker's pronunciation?
   _____ all of the time

_____ most of the time
_____ some of the time
_____ not at all
Why do you think you had difficulty in understanding this person?

7. Does the speaker have any distracting gestures?
8. Did the presenter have good eye contact?
9. Did the presenter speak loudly and slowly enough?

Brendan Carroll (1981), a former test consultant for the British Council who has participated in the elaboration of evaluation criteria for the newer, more communicative language programs being developed in British schools, has emphasized the need to include measures of *group effectiveness*. Where *individual* performance is assessed by a single tester—or worse, by a *team* of testers—the social roles are necessarily antagonistic and noncohesive, with emphasis on the power dimension of the interaction. The assessment of individuals in the performance of a group task (for example, group discussion) contributes *some* element of social cohesion. However, the fact that *individuals* within a group are being evaluated rather than the group itself maintains a divisive force. Maximum social cohesion is achieved when the group as a whole is rewarded for its performance, much the same as a basketball or hockey team is rewarded for winning the game. Individuals are observed in terms of their *roles* within the group.

For those who would argue that this is unfair, that very good players might thus be penalized for the shortcomings of their teammates, the answer is that communicative competence is by definition a social rather than an individual trait. Differences in individual roles within a group are as desirable as they are inevitable. The simulation activities described in Chapter 5 illustrate the need for *group cohesion* and *differentiation of roles*—leaders, organizers, record keepers, negotiators, listeners, etc.—for maximum group effectiveness. Cooperation is best encouraged by rewarding the entire group for its success. Group composition can, of course, be rotated so that individuals will receive recognition for their contributions in more than one context.

The results of the communicative testing formats described in this and earlier chapters may not all be easily quantifiable. In many cases they do not lend themselves to neat statistical correlation, but they do emphasize the *qualitative* nature of communication, that is, the *human, interactive* nature of communicative competence. They are important not only for what they have achieved but for what they are striving for: the assessment of competence in terms of functional effectiveness rather than formal correctness. They offer the best assurance that learner progress and problems will be diagnosed in terms of *language use* rather than rules of usage and that the emphasis in teaching will be on *contexts of natural discourse* rather than on surface analysis of discrete linguistic features. This is the direction we must take if our profession is to remain vigorous and responsive in the years ahead and if we are to prepare learners for the real-life experiences that await them.

SUGGESTED READINGS

L. Bachman. 1982. "The Trait Structure of Cloze Test Scores." Discusses possible reasons for the differences that have been observed in native speakers' performance on cloze tests with reference to the types of skills presumably involved. Proposes a distinction between items that test "lower-level" sentence grammar and those that test "higher-order" discourse skills of cohesion.

L. Bachman and A. Palmer. 1981a. "Basic Concerns in Test Validity." Describes the process of construct validation in language testing and the need to distinguish between *trait* (what one is measuring) and *method* of measurement (how one is measuring it).

E. Brière et al. 1978. "A Look at Cloze Testing Across Languages and Levels." Reports on the successful use of cloze at the beginning levels of college instruction in German, Japanese, Russian, and Spanish.

A. Cohen. 1980. *Testing Language Ability in the Classroom*. Practical suggestions for more integrative teacher-made quizzes and tests.

R. Lado. 1961. *Language Testing*. The classic exposition of the psychometric-structuralist approach to testing. Reflects the structuralist/behaviorist model of language learning developed by Charles Fries, the author's doctoral dissertation director at the University of Michigan.

P. Lowe, Jr. 1981. "Structure of the Oral Interview and Content Validity." Describes the overall structure of the FSI Oral Interview with recommendations for improving the content validity of the test.

K. Morrow. 1979. "Communicative Language Testing: Revolution or Evolution?" Observes from a British perspective the imbalance that exists between the teaching materials now available and the kinds of tests or evaluation instruments that continue to prevail. Describes a *qualitative, synthetic* alternative to the *quantitative, analytic* tradition of language measurement.

J. Oller, Jr. 1979. *Language Tests at School*. Probably the most complete book on language testing available. This 492-page volume offers a detailed criticism of the theories and methods of discrete-point testing, and makes the point that as views of language change to ones concerned with *language in use*, our ways of evaluating learners' competence to communicate must also change. In addition, the author examines the extent to which the construct of language proficiency overlaps constructs of intelligence and academic ability. Extensive bibliography.

Ontario Assessment Instrument Pool, French as a Second Language. 1980. Based on the curriculum guideline, *French, Core Programs 1980* and the theoretical framework developed by Canale and Swain (1980), these testing materials represent an important attempt to develop items for large-scale public school programs that reflect the *human, interactive* nature of communicative competence. Of the items included, approximately half use a discrete-point mode of response and, therefore, can be machine scored. The remaining items must be scored manually, *"often by exercising individual, subjective judgment."*

M. Oskarsson. 1978. *Approaches to Self-Assessment in Foreign Language Learning*. Looks at the importance of involving learners in the evaluation of their progress according to their individual needs and objectives and offers possible forms of guided self-assessment in adult language learning.

A. Palmer, P. Groot, and G. Trosper (eds.). 1981. *The Construct Validation of Tests of Communicative Competence.* A collection of papers that provide an up-to-date discussion of issues of validity in oral proficiency testing. Among the authors included are Bachman, Canale and Swain, Hinofotis et al., Lowe, Palmer, and Stevenson.

R. Paul. 1981. "Needed: Stepladders of Foreign Language Learning." Reports the results of an ACTFL-sponsored survey of foreign language teachers and program coordinators at the elementary and secondary levels to determine interest in the creation of national proficiency goals and tests. Of those who responded, the majority reported that they were either not familiar with or "not very impressed" with tests that had been distributed nationally in the past (for example, the MLA Cooperative Tests), but that they agreed with the need to establish *oral* proficiency goals, in particular, as a guide to curriculum development.

S. Savignon. 1982. "Dictation as a Measure of Communicative Competence in French as a Second Language." Details of the alternative scoring methods for dictation described in this chapter along with sample passages.

D. Stevenson. 1981. "Beyond Faith and Face Validity: The Multitrait-Multimethod Matrix and the Convergent and Discriminant Validity of Oral Proficiency Tests." A technical discussion of the need for statistical validation of language proficiency measures with particular reference to the FSI Oral Interview, a well-known test that tends to be accepted largely on faith, that is, for its *face validity*.

M. Swain. 1981. "Linguistic Expectations: Core, Extended and Immersion Programs." Good discussion of the need for establishing realistic expectations or goals for L2 programs and then evaluating program success against these same criteria.

RESEARCH AND DISCUSSION

1. In a study to determine the effect of item disclosure on TOEFL scores there were significant increases in performance in proportion to the number of items made available to applicants (Hale et al. 1980). Discuss this finding in light of McClelland's view of proficiency testing in Chapter 1. Can you cite other examples of item disclosure for widely used tests of aptitude and proficiency? What have been the results?

2. The ARELS Oral Examination, a test of English language proficiency for foreign applicants to British universities, has been described by its developers as follows:

   > From the beginning the examination was regarded as a means as well as an end in itself. That is to say, it was considered no more important than the changes it would generate in language training by directing it towards modern and practical needs. A full-scale examination in spoken English would introduce new criteria, and influence beneficially classroom teaching and course planning. Its existence would encourage a shift from the purely academic to the more practical aspects of language as a means of communication.

   What is your reaction to this rationale for test development? Have you ever been a learner or a teacher in a situation where you felt that a test was dictating or strongly influencing the curriculum?

3. The face validity of a test is always relative and depends on a person's past experience and impressions of what a test should be. Compare the reactions of foreign students in an intensive English language institute with those of the learners in a beginning French program cited on pages 247.

> The Intensive English Institute (IEI) students are usually obsessed with the TOEFL and the necessary score that will get them admitted to an American university. They want no part of games, puzzles, role playing, etc. because these do not resemble *learning* to them. On one occasion I had a student refuse to finish a test constructed to test communicative competence because it didn't have face validity. If they are not filling in the oval-shaped marks on an answer sheet or completing a multiple-choice test, most students in the IEI feel they are being cheated and are not being adequately prepared to score a minimum of 500 on the TOEFL. [Kathleen Burke, personal communication]

   Have you ever had a similar experience? What strength does this observation give to the position of the ARELS test developers cited in Question 2 above?

4. If it is to be used, a test has to be not only *reliable* and *valid* but *practical* as well. In your view, what are the attributes of a practical teacher-made test?

5. If you were asked to recommend a procedure for evaluating the oral communicative competence of nonnative applicants for graduate teaching assistantships at an American university, which of the following would you choose:

   a) the written TOEFL,

   b) an FSI Oral Interview conducted by trained examiners, or

   c) an interview conducted jointly by one representative each from the ESL department, the graduate school, and the candidates' academic department?

   Defend your choice. What are the advantages and disadvantages of each in terms of (1) *reliability*, (2) *validity* (including *face validity*), and (3) *practicality*.

6. As a test *taker*, what kinds of language tests have you liked best? Why?

7. What emphasis do you feel should be placed on testing speaking ability early in an instructional program? Defend your views.

8. Collect a sample of L2 tests or test items and situate each with respect to the nature of the task and the response mode along the horizontal and vertical axes of the diagram on page 253.

9. Find some examples of functional language tests or test items that have high face validity. What *mode of response* do these tests tend to have—discrete-point or global?

10. Give a cloze test to a group of nonnative speakers as well as to a group of native speakers. What are the reactions of the two groups to the exercise? Experiment with the use of both *exact-word* and *any-acceptable-word* methods of scoring. Which do you prefer? Keep a list of replacements provided for each blank by natives and nonnatives and the number of times each appears. What differences do you observe?

11. Prepare and give a short dictation to a group of L2 learners following the guidelines in this chapter concerning chunk length and the number and nature of each reading. Score each chunk on each of three criteria: *exact word, phonetic similarity,*

and *conveyance of meaning*. What differences in results do you note? If possible, have one or more classmates or colleagues rate the same dictations and compare results. What kind of training is needed to ensure maximum interrater reliability on the various criteria?

12. Adapt one of the activities described in this or preceding chapters for use as a test of oral communication skills appropriate for a group of learners with which you are familiar. What scoring criteria will you use and why?

13. What are some ways in which test items can be developed to encourage group cooperation? Give examples for both oral and written communication and suggestions for scoring.

14. Describe ways in which oral testing can be done as a part of regular class activities so as to reduce the additional teacher time required.

15. Test validity is a matter of *degree* and depends on the purpose for which a test is being used. For example, a bathroom scale is a valid measure of weight, but not of height. Sometimes a measurement procedure is used for a purpose other than that for which it was intended because (1) it is readily available and offers a seemingly convenient solution to placement or selection needs or (2) test users are unfamiliar with psychometric concerns of test validity. Can you cite examples of situations in which you feel a test is being *misused* for one or both of the above reasons?

16. As a teacher who must provide students, parents, and others with information regarding learner achievement, what qualities do you or would you look for in a test or test program?

17. Public school students in Chicago have the widest choice of high school language instruction in the United States. Through a Proficiency Testing for Foreign Language Credit Program students may earn academic credit in 29 different languages for proficiency gained outside the classroom (FL Notes, *FL Annals* 1980, 13:423). Many students have learned languages in their homes, abroad, or in one of Chicago's many ethnic or "Saturday schools." Relate this testing program to the Beyond the Classroom component of L2 instruction discussed in Chapter 5. What do you think is the likely effect of such a program on learner and community attitudes toward L2 study? Do you know of other programs like it?

18. Piaget has made the following observation about tests and teaching (1970:7):

> All we have at our disposal as a basis for judging the productivity of our scholastic methods are the results of end-of-school examinations and, to some extent, certain competitive examinations. But the use of these data entails both a begging of the question and a vicious circle. A begging of the question, to begin with, because we are postulating that success in those examinations constitutes a proof of durability of the knowledge acquired, whereas the real problem, still in no way resolved, consists precisely in attempting to establish what remains after a lapse of several years of the knowledge whose existence has been proved once by success in those examinations, as well as trying to determine the exact composition of whatever still subsists independently of the detailed knowledge forgotten. On these two prime points, then, we still have almost no information.

Discuss Piaget's observation in general, as it relates to L2 learning and, in particular, as it relates to the context in which you teach.

Conclusion: A Letter To My Teacher

There is a well-known saying among teachers that the one way to really learn something is to try to teach it to others. The learner who becomes a teacher in turn becomes a better learner. With teaching comes a keener awareness of what one knows as well as of the many things one has yet to understand.

As a language teacher and methodologist of some twenty years experience, I can attest to the truth of the above observation. With each new academic term, with each new group of learners comes the challenge of adding to one's knowledge and of finding better ways to share what one knows. Moreover, many of what I consider my most valuable insights into the nature of learning and teaching have come from my students.

Perhaps my best lesson came when I moved, quite literally, to the other side of the desk and became a student in an elementary Spanish class taught by John Schmidt, a former methods student of mine who was at the time a graduate teaching assistant at the University of Illinois. Not only did I learn a good bit of Spanish in this particular class, I gained a renewed respect for the role of the classroom teacher. So important is this role that I can think of no more fitting way to conclude a book on the theory and practice of communicative language teaching than to give an account of my experience, a diary of sorts, written in the form of a letter to my teacher.

A LETTER TO MY TEACHER*

To my dear teacher,

You have been such a warm and enthusiastic teacher for me that I want to thank you for letting me join your class and let you know how much you have helped me. I am especially eager to thank you because, as a language teacher

---

* An earlier version of the following text was published in the *Canadian Modern Language Review* (1981). Permission to include it here is gratefully acknowledged.

myself, I have often wondered at the end of a term just how successful I had been in helping my students toward the competence they were seeking. Did I give them enough grammar? Was I too easygoing about errors? Should I have been more conscientious in sticking to the departmental syllabus? The opportunity you gave me to get on "the other side of the desk" has helped me to remember what it is like to be a language *learner*. The result is a renewed sense of direction as I resume my role as a language *teacher*.

I came into your second semester college class, Spanish 102, because I wanted to learn Spanish. A group of teachers of English as a second language had invited me to Barcelona to talk about ways of teaching for communicative competence. Inasmuch as I had been to Barcelona for the same purpose two years earlier, I thought it would be nice if I could show my hosts that in the meantime I had made some progress in Spanish. I wanted, at least, to be able to order my own *paëlla* and to ask my own directions. I further reasoned that with a better understanding of the basic structure of the Spanish language I would find it easier, once in Spain, to interact with native speakers and profit even more from my two-week stay.

I cannot begin to describe my anxiety as I walked into your class that first day. For one thing, I was plunging into a second semester course without having had the benefit of the first semester program. I chose your class, however, because I had heard from your supervisor what a very good teacher you were and because I planned to study hard and catch up on the grammar I had missed. Moreover, since I was already a fluent speaker of French and had spent a little time in Spain, I thought I could keep up. Another reason for my anxiety was that I was not only older than the other students—most of them undergraduates fulfilling the language requirement—I was a professor of French as well. You and the others might well expect me to excel in an elementary Spanish class.

The way the classroom was arranged on that first day of class did not help to put me at ease. We sat around tables arranged in a semicircle with our names spelled out on big cards in front of us. The idea was a good one, one I have often recommended myself. Sitting in a circle we could all see each other and begin to get acquainted. But seeing things now through the eyes of a student, it was clear to me that there was going to be no place to hide, no inconspicuous back row. I was going to have to speak Spanish!

What a relief it was, then, when, as our first task, you had us introduce ourselves to our neighbor. I was sitting next to a friendly young woman who helped me to say my name, my age, and what I was doing in life. She was patient and very encouraging, virtues I know we try to stress in teaching of all kinds but which suddenly took on a special significance for me. I had a friend on whom I could count in the weeks ahead.

It was also nice the way you, the teacher, walked about the room as we were conversing, giving us help in Spanish whenever we asked. You did this often, dividing us into groups of two or three to work on specific assignments—writing answers to questions, writing a little story to describe a picture you had put on the overhead projector, finding out about how the others had spent the weekend. This was one of the best parts of the class. At these times we could count on one another and on you for help in completing the task. I know the classroom became somewhat noisy at times with eight or so groups at work, but the noise never distracted me. It was at these times, rather, that I felt I was learning the most Spanish. I could try things out I wanted to say, find out how to say them, and get the feeling that everyone was there to help me rather than to see how much Spanish I remembered.

When it came time to introduce my neighbor to the rest of the class on that first day, however, I was far from comfortable. I rehearsed what I was going to say over and over in my head, much as I do when speaking out in a public forum in English. When my turn came, I made my introduction more or less as I had practiced it. When you corrected an error I had made, I repeated after you as best I could, but I was really too flustered to understand what I was doing. The experience was simply too intense to allow me to focus on the form you were trying to teach me. On the other hand, I gained many insights from your corrections of the other students' Spanish. Once out of the limelight, it was easier for me to rehearse forms and check them against the others' responses and your corrections. (From this personal experience I now have a much better understanding of learner reactions to error corrections.)

What I liked best was when you spoke Spanish to us. You explained grammar, told us stories about a funny drawing, talked about class activities, shared your slides of beautiful places to visit in Spain. These were all marvelous opportunities for the listening experiences I craved, and you made the most of them. I became anxious again, though, when you pointed on the map to Andorra and asked me what it was called. I know you were being nice and giving me a chance to speak, but I did not know the answer. When I could just relax and listen while you talked, without fear of being called on, so much vocabulary and points of grammar seemed to start coming together. At these times I could actually *feel* myself learning Spanish. It was at once a powerful and exhilarating feeling.

Then came our first written test. It was a rather typical test as language tests go, requiring us to complete sentences, conjugate verbs, and write answers to questions as they were read aloud. We did not do well as a class, and you were understandably disappointed. Seven out of seventeen of us had scored lower than 70%, and you explained to us all how important it was not to get behind, how miserable we would be in the semesters ahead if we did not get down to work. I was rather uncomfortable wondering how the seven in question must have felt. Your disappointment was inevitable—as a teacher myself I knew only too well what you were feeling!—but the sense of failure we experienced as learners certainly changed for a time the ambience of the class.

The unit test we took a week later went fairly well. I felt good about understanding the oral comprehension questions although the others had found that part particularly hard. The grammar part was hardest. I thought of all the things I had done wrong *after* I had handed in my paper and felt as though I had really put my ego on the line. As it turned out, I earned a grade of C (73%). Our scores were all rather low, and you were understandably frustrated because we continued to make so many errors. No doubt your departmental syllabus said that we were to have "covered" a certain amount of material by then. The textbook, after all, included all the basic features of Spanish grammar in a one year course. I was quite irritated, however, for having lost so many points for wrong spellings and missing accents. Where I thought I had done well because I was beginning to understand, I had missed points because of what looked to me like minor errors. As a result, and grown-up though I was, I was mad at you, mad at Spanish, . . . and feeling rejected by those I wanted to join. For me, the departmental exams we were required to take did much to destroy the productive, supportive atmosphere you had created in class.

Class discussions were always fun, but I had to concentrate hard on forms. One day you went around the table asking us questions so we would learn to change sentences from interrogative to declarative. The questions were no doubt interesting as you tried to ask things that related to us individually. I did not have time to listen to the questions asked of others, however, because I was busy counting the number of people ahead of me and rehearsing the forms silently to myself so as not to be caught off guard. When my turn came, you asked me "*Como se llama el presidente de Francia?*" (Who is the president of France?) I could not for the life of me fill in the name, so intent I was on the verb endings! Now I know what my students mean when they sometimes say they prefer not to talk about anything "heavy." At these times they are so busy concentrating on forms they do not want their intelligence to be put on the line as well.

The birthday surprise was marvelous! Enrico had a birthday, and you brought in a little cake with a candle. We sang a song you had written on the board, and you told us about birthday celebrations in Mexico. It was a nice relief of tension after an hour of verb and other structure drills. As teachers we perhaps forget that even adults in a second language classroom enjoy the frivolous. Songs, parties, and games that might seem unsophisticated to us in our native language are such a welcome way to relax in a second language. They also help to build the camaraderie we need in order to learn from one another.

I got bogged down in the subjunctive. We spent so much time learning the verb forms and examples of expressions requiring the subjunctive. Yet there were so few things I could say on my own in Spanish that I knew I did not yet have use for all those forms. I was sympathetic with your view that it would help if we got these "down pat"—you knew, after all, what was coming in the semester ahead—but that would have required a sheer memory feat. It was one to which, frankly, I simply could not push myself.

My own learning strategy was to prepare lots of vocabulary cards with Spanish verb infinitives. I then added some expressions I had heard that reminded me of verb endings, the use of subjunctive, various prepositions, and other vocabulary I liked. My best sources of expressions were (1) the things you said in class, (2) a magazine you had given me of current events in Barcelona, and (3) a book of poetry by Garcia Lorca. The Lorca poems were so beautiful I had a friend record them so that I could listen and practice them at home. It might seem curious that someone interested in Spanish for travel would want to spend time reading poetry. It certainly is not in step with the Language for Specific Purposes movement so popular now in our profession. The language was, however, beautifully simple and authentic. I could read the poems at home, silently or aloud, and feel I was in touch with something, with someone really Spanish. Many of my private vocabulary words came from these poems. I think that if we had *studied* them as a class it might have spoiled it for me.

Everyone told me I spoke with a French accent but that it sounded fine. This made me feel a part of the group. I could speak Spanish with my own accent and be accepted. I was happy you did not insist on the finer points of pronunciation. The pronunciation of *b* as /v/ was still a major hurdle, and I was also busy attending to all kinds of lexical and syntactical matters.

One of the nicest things you did for me was to introduce me to a Venezuelan woman of about my age who had recently arrived in the United States. She was looking for American contacts, and I needed someone with whom to practice my Spanish. Inasmuch as I was the hostess, it was up to me to take the initiative and arrange a meeting—*"a las cuatro y media, el diez y ocho julio, aqui."* I used lots of gestures and repeated myself frequently, but my Venezuelan guest was very gracious. I found I was able to listen to *her* Spanish as she spoke because we were working together to solve a problem. I did not have to be concerned with how to correct any errors in *my* Spanish. From this first and subsequent encounters I realized I was on my way. I could have some fun in Barcelona and show others I was eager to talk with them.

And talk I did. Once in Barcelona I even succeeded in phoning friends of yours to make a date to meet them. I spent hours in Spanish, listening mostly, but smiling and speaking up enough to let my companions know I enjoyed their company and was following the conversation. You could never have anticipated all of my needs. For example, how could you have known I would need to have a new heel put on my boot and would have to let the shoemaker know I wanted a rubber, not synthetic, heel? As it was, I enjoyed going into the shoemaker's shop and waiting my turn. This gave me a marvelous opportunity to eavesdrop. From the signs posted on the walls I was able eventually to figure out what I wanted and communicate it with some degree of self-assuredness. Joy!

I never earned above a B in our class exams, and my average was probably closer to a C. Errors in spelling and grammar kept down my marks. But you were my bridge to the Spanish-speaking world. In your classroom I was able to make friends with other learners and feel that together we were working and learning. You were my model. I trusted you and was grateful for your encouragement. You see, my dear Spanish teacher, for me test scores did not really matter. An A in Spanish was not what I wanted. I wanted Spanish speakers from Puerto Rico, Spain, Cuba, and Mexico to know that I respect them and their language, and that I am going to meet them halfway. Thank you for your help. You are a wonderful teacher!

*

Most language learners do not write books about language learning, of course. Nor do most language teachers for that matter. This fact does not make their experiences any less real, their observations any less valid. This book has examined issues in linguistic and communication theory in relation to the teaching of second and foreign languages. It has summarized avenues of inquiry and findings in the burgeoning new research field of second language acquisition. Just as important, it has sought to give collective voice to the insights of those many, many classroom learners and teachers who have been successful in making communication an integral part of their language programs. If, in so doing, it has brought encouragement and some practical know-how to those who seek to do likewise, then it will have served its purpose well. Books and research articles can do no more. But teachers and learners together can make the attainment of communication goals a reality in the L2 classrooms of today and tomorrow.

References

Adams, M. and J. Frith (eds.). 1979. *Testing kit: French and Spanish*. Washington, D.C.: Foreign Service Institute.

Allen, E. and R. Valette. 1977. *Classroom techniques: foreign languages and English as a second language*. New York: Harcourt Brace Jovanovich.

Allright, R. 1976. "Language learning through communication practice." *English Language Teaching Documents* (British Council). 3:2–14.

A-LM (Audio-Lingual Materials). French: level one. 1961. New York: Harcourt, Brace & World.

American Psychological Association, American Educational Research Association, and National Council on Measurement in Education. 1974. *Standards for educational and psychological tests*. Washington, D.C.: American Psychological Association.

Anderson, R. 1981. "Second language acquisition research in cross-linguistic perspective." Paper presented at the 1981 TESOL Conference.

ARELS oral examinations: rationale, development, and methods. London: ARELS Examination Trust.

Asher, J. 1969. "The total physical response approach to second language learning." *Modern Language Journal* 53:3–7.

––––––. 1977. *Learning another language through actions*. Los Gatos, Calif.: Sky Oaks Productions.

Ashton-Warner, S. 1963. *Teacher*. New York: Simon and Schuster.

Austin, J. 1962. *How to do things with words*. Oxford: Clarendon Press.

Ausubel, D. 1964. "Adults vs. children in second language learning: psychological considerations." *Modern Language Journal* 48:420–424.

Bachman, L. 1982. "The trait structure of cloze test scores." *TESOL Quarterly* 16.61–70.

Bachman, L. and A. Palmer. 1980. "Test of communicative competence: multiple-choice method." University of Illinois. Mimeograph.

––––––. 1981a. "Basic concerns in test validation." In J. Read (ed.) *Directions in language testing*. Singapore: University Press.

––––––. 1981b. "Validation of the FSI." *Language Learning* 31:67–86.

––––––. Forthcoming. *Basic concerns in language test validation*. Reading, Mass.: Addison-Wesley.

Bailey, A. 1980. *America, lost and found*. New York: Random House.

Barret, R., C. Gemignani, V. Kessling, and M. Sexton. 1978. *Horror. Issues 2.* Munich, West Germany: Langenscheidt-Longman.

Belasco, S. and A. Valdman. 1965. *College French in the new key.* Lexington, Mass.: D.C. Heath.

Berns, M. 1981. In-class peer evaluation form for oral presentations. Division of English as a Second Language, University of Illinois, Urbana.

Bettelheim, B. and K. Zelan. 1982. *On learning to read: the child's fascination with meaning.* New York: Knopf.

Bird, T. (ed.). 1968. *Foreign language learning: research and development.* Northeast Conference Working Committee Reports. Middlebury, Vt.: The Northeast Conference on the Teaching of Foreign Languages.

Birkmaier, E. (ed.). 1968. *Britannica review of foreign language education,* vol. 1. Chicago: Encyclopaedia Britannica, Inc.

Blatchford, C. and J. Schachter (eds.). 1978. *On TESOL '78.* Washington, D.C.: Teachers of English to Speakers of Other Languages.

Bloomfield, L. 1933. *Language.* New York: Holt, Rinehart.

Boyd, J. and M. Boyd. 1981. *Connections.* New York: Regents Publishing Company.

Braine, M. 1971. *"On two types of models of the internalization of grammars."* In D. Slobin (ed.).

Breen, M. and C. Candlin. 1980. "The essentials of a communicative curriculum in language teaching." *Applied Linguistics* 1:89–112.

Brenes, E. et al. 1963. *Learning Spanish the modern way.* New York: McGraw-Hill.

The Bridge: A Review of Cross-cultural Affairs and International Training. Chicago, Ill.: Systran Corporation.

Brière, E., G. Clausing, D. Senko, and E. Purcell. 1978. "A look at cloze testing across languages and levels." *Modern Language Journal* 62:23–26.

Brod, R. 1976. "Foreign language enrollments in United States colleges—fall 1974." *Modern Language Journal* 60:168–171.

Brooks, N. 1964. *Language and language learning: theory and practice.* New York: Harcourt, Brace & World. Second edition.

Brown, H. 1980a. *Principles of language learning and teaching.* Englewood Cliffs, N.J.: Prentice-Hall.

———. 1980b. "The optimal distance model of second language acquisition." *TESOL Quarterly* 14:157–164.

Brown, H., C. Yorio, R. Crymes. (eds.). 1977. *On TESOL '77.* Washington, D.C.: Teachers of English to Speakers of Other Languages.

Brown, R. 1973. *A first language: the early stages.* Cambridge, Mass.: Harvard University Press.

Brumfit, C. 1980. "From defining to designing: communicative specifications versus communicative methodology in foreign language teaching." *Studies in Second Language Acquisition* 3:1–9.

Brumfit, C. and K. Johnson (eds.). 1979. *The communicative approach to language teaching.* Oxford: Oxford University Press.

Bruner, J. 1975a. "From communication to language: a psychological perspective." *Cognition* 3:255–280.

———. 1975b. "The ontogenesis of speech acts." *Journal of Child Language* 2:1–20.

Burstall, C. 1975. "French in the primary school: the British experiment." *Canadian Modern Language Review* 31:388–402.

Burstall, C., M. Jamieson, S. Cohen, and M. Hargreaves. 1974. *Primary French in the balance.* Windsor, England: NFER Publishing Co.

Burt, M., H. Dulay, and E. Hernandez-Chavez. 1975. *Bilingual syntax measure.* New York: Harcourt Brace Jovanovich.

Campbell, R. 1978. "Notional-functional syllabuses: 1978. Part I." In C. Blatchford and J. Schachter (eds.).

Canale, M. Forthcoming. "From communicative competence to communicative language pedagogy." In J. Richards and R. Schmidt (eds.) *Language and communication.* London: Longman.

Canale, M. and M. Swain. 1980. "Theoretical bases of communicative approaches to second language teaching and testing." *Applied Linguistics* 1:1–47.

Carroll, B. 1980. *Testing communicative performance.* Oxford: Pergamon Press.

———. 1981. "The assessment of group oral communication." Paper presented at the Colloquium on Validation of Oral Proficiency Tests. Ann Arbor, Michigan.

Carroll, J. 1961. "Fundamental considerations in testing for English language proficiency of foreign students." In *Testing the English proficiency of foreign students.* Washington, D.C.: Center for Applied Linguistics. Reprinted in H. Allen and R. Campbell (eds.) 1972, *Teaching English as a second language.* New York: McGraw-Hill.

———. 1965. "The contributions of psychological theory and educational research to the teaching of foreign languages." *Modern Language Journal* 49:273–281.

———. 1969. "What does the Pennsylvania foreign language research project tell us?" *Foreign Language Annals,* 3:214–236.

———. 1981. "Conscious and automatic processes in language learning." *Canadian Modern Language Review* 37:462–475.

Carroll, J. and S. Sapon. 1959. *Modern language aptitude test.* New York: Psychological Corporation.

Cazden, C. 1976. "How knowledge about language helps the classroom teacher—or does it: a personal account." *Urban Review* 9:74–90.

Cazden, C., J. Bond, A. Epstein, R. Matz, and S. Savignon. 1977. "Language assessment: where, what and how." *Anthropology and Education* VIII:83–90.

Chomsky, N. 1965. *Aspects of the theory of syntax.* Cambridge, Mass.: MIT Press.

———. 1966. "Linguistic theory." In R. Mead (ed.) *Language teaching: broader contexts.* Northeast Conference Working Committee Reports. Menasha, Wis.: George Banta. Reprinted in J. Oller and J. Richards (eds.) 1973, *Focus on the learner: pragmatic perspectives for the language teacher.* Rowley, Mass.: Newbury House.

———. 1972. *Language and mind.* New York: Harcourt Brace Jovanovich. Enlarged edition.

Chun, J. 1980. "A survey of research in second language acquisition." *Modern Language Journal* 64:287–296.

Clark, J. 1972. *Foreign language testing: theory and practice.* Philadelphia: Center for Curriculum Development.

————. 1978. "Psychometric considerations in language testing." In B. Spolsky (ed.).

Clark, J. and S. Swinton. 1979. "An exploration of speaking proficiency measures in the TOEFL context." *TOEFL Research Report* 4, Princeton, N.J.: Educational Testing Service.

Cohen, A. 1980. *Testing language ability in the classroom.* Rowley, Mass.: Newbury House.

Corder, S.P. 1981. *Error analysis and interlanguage.* Oxford: Oxford University Press.

Coste, D., J. Courtillon, F. Ferenczi, M. Martins-Baltar, and E. Papo. 1976. *Un niveau-seuil.* Strasbourg: Council of Europe.

Coulombe, R., J. Barré, C. Fostle, N. Poulin, and S. Savignon. 1974. *Voix et visages de la France: level 1.* Chicago: Rand-McNally.

Coulthard, M. 1977. *Introduction to discourse analysis.* London: Longman.

Cronbach, L. 1971. "Test validation." In R. Thorndike (ed.) *Educational measurement.* Washington, D.C.: American Council on Education. Second edition.

Crymes, R. 1980. "Current trends in ESL instruction." *TESOL Newsletter* 14:1–4, 18.

Cummins, J. 1980. "The entry and exit fallacy in bilingual education." *National Association of Bilingual Education Journal* IV:25–59.

Curran, C. 1972. *Counseling-learning.* New York: Grune & Stratton.

————. 1976. *Counseling-learning in second languages.* Apple River, Ill.: Apple River Press.

————. 1978. "A linguistic model for learning and living in the new age of the person." In C. Blatchford and J. Schachter (eds.).

Cziko, G. 1982. "Improving the psychometric, criterion-referenced, and practical qualities of integrative language tests." *TESOL Quarterly* 16:367–379.

Davies, A. (ed.). 1968. *Language testing symposium: a psycholinguistic approach.* London: Oxford University Press.

————. 1981. "Review of *Communicative syllabus design.*" *TESOL Quarterly* 15:332–336.

DeAvila, E. and S. Duncan. 1977. *Language assessment scales.* Corte Madera, Calif.: Linguametrics Group, Inc.

De Garcia, R., S. Reynolds, and S. Savignon. 1976. "Foreign-language attitude survey." *Canadian Modern Language Review* 32:302–304.

De Sauzé, E. 1953. "Teaching French in the elementary schools of Cleveland." *French Review* 26:371–376.

Diller, K. 1978. *The language teaching controversy.* Rowley, Mass.: Newbury House.

Di Pietro, R. 1982. "The open-ended scenario: a new approach to conversation." *TESOL Quarterly* 16:15–20.

Dorian, N. 1981. *Language death.* Philadelphia: University of Pennsylvania Press.

Dubin, F. and E. Olshtain. 1981. *Reading by all means.* Reading, Mass.: Addison-Wesley.

Dulay, H. and M. Burt. 1972. "Goofing: an indicator of children's second language learning strategies." *Language Learning* 22:235–252.

———. 1974. "Errors and strategies in child second language acquisition." *TESOL Quarterly* 8:129–136.

Edwards, B. 1979. *Drawing on the right side of the brain*. Los Angeles: J.P. Tarcher, Inc. (Distributed by Houghton Mifflin Co., Boston).

Ervin, G. 1976. "So you're going to have a language camp?" *Foreign Language Annals* 9:109–116.

Ervin-Tripp, S. 1964. "Imitation and structural changes in children's language." In E. Lenneberg (ed.).

———. 1971. "An overview of theories of grammatical development." In D. Slobin (ed.).

Felix, S. 1981. "The effect of formal instruction on second language acquisition." *Language Learning* 31:87–112.

Ferguson, C. and S. Heath (eds.). 1981. *Language in the USA*. New York: Cambridge University Press.

Ferreira, L. 1981. *Notion by notion*. Rowley, Mass.: Newbury House.

Firth, J. 1964. *Tongues of men / Speech*. London: Oxford University Press. Reprint of works first published in 1937 and 1930, respectively.

Fish, S. 1980. *Is there a text in this class?* Cambridge, Mass.: Harvard University Press.

Flanders, N. 1970. *Analyzing teaching behavior*. Reading, Mass.: Addison-Wesley.

Fox, J. et al. 1980. *Telephone gambits*. Hull, Quebec: Canadian Government Publishing Center.

Fraser, B., F. Rintell, and J. Walters. 1980. "An approach to conducting research on the acquisition of pragmatic competence in a second language." In D. Larsen-Freeman (ed.).

Freed, B. 1981. "Foreigner talk, baby talk, native talk." *International Journal of the Sociology of Language* 28:19–39.

French, Core Programs 1980. Ontario, Canada: Ministry of Education.

Fries, C. 1945. *Teaching and learning English as a foreign language*. Ann Arbor: University of Michigan Press.

Galyean, B. 1977. "A confluent design for language teaching." *TESOL Quarterly* 11:142–156.

Gardner, R. 1980. "On the validity of affective variables in second language acquisition: conceptual, contextual and statistical considerations." *Language Learning* 30:255–270.

Gardner, R. and W. Lambert. 1972. *Attitudes and motivation in second-language learning*. Rowley, Mass.: Newbury House.

Gardner, R. and P. Smythe. 1981. "On the development of the attitude/motivation test battery." *Canadian Modern Language Review* 37:510–525.

Gardner, R., P. Smythe, R. Clément, and L. Gliksman. 1976. "Second language learning: a social psychological perspective." *Canadian Modern Language Review* 32:198–213.

Garrett, N. 1981. "In search of interlanguage: a study of second-language acquisition of German syntax." Dissertation. University of Illinois, Champaign-Urbana.

Gattegno, C. 1972. *Teaching foreign languages in schools: the silent way.* New York: Educational Solutions, Inc.

Gilgenast, T. and J. Binkley. 1981. "Student foreign language course interest and curriculum planning." *Unterrichtspraxis* 14:27–32.

Goodman, K. 1971. "Psycholinguistic universals in the reading process." In P. Pimsleur and T. Quinn (eds.).

———. 1976. "Reading: a psycholinguistic guessing game." In N. Johnson (ed.) *Current topics in language.* Cambridge, Mass.: Winthrop Publishers.

Gradisnik, A. 1980. *Helping parents learn a second language with their children.* Milwaukee, Wis.: Milwaukee Public Schools.

Graham, C. 1978. *Jazz chants.* New York: Oxford University Press.

Green, G. and J. Morgan. 1981. "Pragmatics, grammar and discourse." In P. Cole (ed.) *Radical pragmatics.* New York: Academic Press.

Gregory, A. and W. Shawn. 1981. *My dinner with André.* New Yorker Films and New York: Grove Press.

Grittner, F. 1974. "The teacher as co-learner." In F. Grittner (ed.) *Student motivation and the foreign language teacher.* Central States Conference Proceedings, 1973. Skokie, Ill.: National Textbook Co.

Guillaume, P. 1927. "Le développement des éléments formels dans le langage de l'enfant." *Journal de Psychologie* 24:1–25. "Les débuts de la phrase dans le langage de l'enfant." *Journal de Psychologie* 24:203–229. Translations in C. Ferguson and D. Slobin (eds.) 1973, *Studies of child language development.* New York: Holt, Rinehart, and Winston.

Hale, G., P. Angelis, and L. Thibodeau. 1980. "Effects of item disclosure on TOEFL performances." Princeton, N.J.: Educational Testing Service.

Hall, E. 1959. *The silent language.* New York: Doubleday and Co.

———. 1966. *The hidden dimension.* New York: Doubleday and Co.

Halliday, M. 1970. "Language structure and language function." In J. Lyons (ed.). *New horizons in linguistics.* Harmondsworth, England: Penguin.

———. 1973. *Explorations in the functions of language.* London: Edward Arnold Press.

———. 1978. *Language as a social semiotic: the social interpretation of language and meaning.* Baltimore: University Park Press.

Halliday, M. and R. Hasan. 1976. *Cohesion in English.* London: Longman.

Hancock, C. 1972. "Student aptitude, attitude, and motivation." In D. Lange and C. James (eds.) *Foreign language education: a reappraisal.* ACTFL Review, vol. 4. Skokie, Ill.: National Textbook Co.

Harbour, L. 1982. "Choosing a textbook: focus on communicative competence." Paper presented at the 1982 Central States Conference on the Teaching of Foreign Languages.

Harris, J. and A. Lévêque. 1968. *Basic conversational French.* New York: Holt, Rinehart and Winston. Fourth edition.

Hart, N., R. Walker, and B. Gray. 1977. *The language of children: a key to literacy.* Reading, Mass.: Addison-Wesley.

Hatch, E. (ed.). 1978. *Second language acquisition.* Rowley, Mass.: Newbury House.

———. 1979. "Apply with caution." *Studies in Second Language Acquisition* 2:123–143.

———. 1980. "Conversational analysis: an alternative methodology for second language acquisition research." In R. Shuy and A. Shnukal (eds.) *Language use and the uses of language.* Washington, D.C.: Georgetown University Press.

Hechinger, F. 1979. "U.S. alone in neglecting foreign languages." In *Information.* Wisconsin State Department of Public Instruction, Sept. 1979.

Hendrickson, J. 1978. "Error correction in foreign languages teaching: recent theory, research and practice." *Modern Language Journal* 62:387–398.

Herbert, C. 1975. *Basic inventory of natural language.* San Bernadino, Calif: Checkpoint Systems.

Higgs, T. and R. Clifford, 1982. "The push toward communication." In T. Higgs (ed.) *Curriculum, competence, and the foreign language teacher.* ACTFL Review, vol. 13. Skokie, Ill.: National Textbook Co.

Hinofotis, F., K. Bailey, and S. Stern. 1981. "Assessing the oral proficiency of prospective foreign teaching assistants: instrument evaluation." In A. Palmer, P. Groot, and G. Trosper (eds.).

Hinofotis, F., P. Lowe, and R. Clifford. 1981. "Native-speaker normative behavior on the FSI oral interview." Paper presented at the Colloquium on the Validation of Oral Proficiency Tests. Ann Arbor, Michigan.

Holland, N. 1975. *5 readers reading.* New Haven: Yale University Press.

Horwitz, E. and M. Horwitz. 1977. "Bridging individual differences: empathy and communicative competence." In R. Schulz (ed.) *Personalizing foreign language instruction.* Central States Conference Proceedings, 1977. Skokie, Ill.: National Textbook Co.

Hosenfeld, C. 1979. "Cindy: a learner in today's foreign language classroom." In W. Born (ed.) *The learner in today's classroom environment.* Northeast Conference Working Committee Reports. Montpelier, Vt.: Northeast Conference on the Teaching of Foreign Languages.

Hunt, M. 1982. "How the mind works." *New York Times Magazine.* January 24:31–33ff.

Hymes, D. 1967. "Why linguistics needs the sociologist." *Social Research* 34:632–647.

———. 1971. "Competence and performance in linguistic theory." In R. Huxley and E. Ingram (eds.) *Language acquisition: models and methods.* London: Academic Press.

Ilyin, D. 1976. *Ilyin oral interview.* Rowley, Mass.: Newbury House.

Ingram, E. 1978. "The psycholinguistic basis." In B. Spolsky (ed.).

Ionesco, E. 1950. *La cantatrice chauve.* First produced at the Théâtre des Noctambules, Paris, 11 May 1950.

Jakobovits, L. 1968. "The physiology and psychology of second language learning." In E. Birkmaier (ed.).

———. 1970. *Foreign language learning: a psycholinguistic analysis of the issues.* Rowley, Mass.: Newbury House.

James, C. 1980. *Contrastive analysis.* London: Longman.

Jesperson, O. 1904. *How to teach a foreign language.* London: Swan Sonnenschein and Co.

Johnson, C. 1979. "Choosing materials that do the job." *ACTFL Review* 10:67–92.

Johnson, K. and K. Morrow. 1981. *Communication in the classroom.* London: Longman.

Joiner, E. 1974. "Evaluating the cultural content of foreign language texts." *Modern Language Journal* 58:242–244.

Jones, K. 1974. *Nine graded simulations.* London: Inner London Education Authority Media Resources Centre. Reprinted 1980. Bedford: Management Games Ltd.

———. 1982. *Simulations in language teaching.* Cambridge, England: Cambridge University Press.

Jones, R. 1982. "Evaluation—proficiency goals, CBTE, national assessment: how do they interrelate?" In *Proceedings of the ACTFL National Conference on Professional Priorities.* Hastings-on-Hudson, New York.

Joos, M. 1967. *The five clocks.* New York: Harcourt, Brace & World.

Kachru, B. 1976. "Models of English for the third world: white man's linguistic burden or language pragmatics?" *TESOL Quarterly* 10:221–239.

———. 1981. "American English and other Englishes." In C. Ferguson and S. Heath (eds.).

Kalivoda, T. 1970. "Oral testing in secondary schools." *Modern Language Journal* 54:328–331.

Kaplan, R. 1966. "Cultural thought patterns in inter-cultural education." *Language Learning* 16:1–20.

Keller, E. and S. Warner. 1979. *Gambits: links.* Hull, Quebec: Canadian Government Publishing Center.

Kelly, L. 1969. *25 centuries of language teaching.* Rowley, Mass.: Newbury House.

Krashen, S. 1975. "The critical period for language acquisition and its possible bases." In D. Aaronson and R. Rieber (eds.) *Developmental psycholinguistics and communicative disorders.* New York: New York Academy of Sciences.

———. 1977. "Monitor model for adult second language performance." In M. Burt, H. Dulay and M. Finocchairo (eds.) *Viewpoints on English as a second language.* New York: Regents.

———. 1981. *Second language acquisition and second language learning.* Oxford: Pergamon Press.

Krashen, S., M. Long, and R. Scarcella. 1979. "Age, rate and eventual attainment in second language acquisition." *TESOL Quarterly* 13:573–582.

Kress, G. (ed.). 1976. *Halliday: system and function in language.* London: Oxford University Press.

Labov, W. 1965. "Stages in the acquisition of standard English." In R. Shuy (ed.) *Social dialects and language learning.* Champaign, Ill.: National Council of Teachers of English.

Labov, W.   1976.   "Systematically misleading data from test questions." *Urban Review* 9:146–171.

Lado, R.   1957.   *Linguistics across cultures: applied linguistics for language teachers.* Ann Arbor: University of Michigan Press.

———.   1961.   *Language testing.* New York: McGraw-Hill.

Lafayette, R.   1978.   "Coping with innovative overchoice: a curriculum model." *Foreign Language Annals* 11:247–256.

———.   1980.   "Formal and 'intake' informal second language classroom environments." Unpublished report. School of Education, Indiana University, Bloomington, Indiana.

Lambert, R. and B. Freed (eds.).   1982.   *The loss of language skills.* Rowley, Mass.: Newbury House.

Lambert, W.   1963.   "Psychological approaches to the study of languages: II. On second language learning and bilingualism." *Modern Language Journal* 47:114–121.

Larsen-Freeman, D. (ed.).   1980.   *Discourse analysis in second language research.* Rowley, Mass.: Newbury House.

———.   1981. "The WHAT of language acquisition." In M. Hines and W. Rutherford (eds.) *On TESOL '81.* Washington, D.C.: Teachers of English to Speakers of Other Languages.

Leemann, E.   1980.   "Teacher talk." Paper presented at the 1980 ACTFL Annual Meeting.

Lenneberg, E. (ed.).   1964.   *Directions in the study of language.* Cambridge, Mass.: MIT Press.

———.   1967.   *The biological foundations of language.* New York: Wiley.

Lett, J.   1977.   "Assessing attitudinal outcomes." In J. Phillips (ed.) *The language connection: from the classroom to the world.* ACTFL Review, vol. 9. Skokie, Ill.: National Textbook Co.

Lewis, F.   1982.   "Speaking in tongues." *New York Times.* February 4.

Lewis, R.   1977.   "The voices of La Salle: expedition II." Recording available from Reid Lewis, 616 Park Street, Elgin, Ill. 60120.

Loevinger, J.   1957.   "Objective tests as instruments of psychological theory." *Psychological Reports* 3:635–694.

Lowe, P.   1981.   "Structure of the oral interview and content validity." In A. Palmer, P. Groot, and G. Trosper (eds.).

Lozanov, G.   1979.   *Suggestology and outlines of suggestopedy.* New York: Gordon and Breach

Mackay, R. and J. Palmer.   1981.   *Languages for specific purposes.* Rowley, Mass.: Newbury House.

Madsen, H. and J. Bowen.   1978.   *Adaptation in language teaching.* Rowley, Mass.: Newbury House.

Maeroff, G.   1981.   "Educators' new worry: lack of reading insight by pupils." *New York Times.* April 30.

Malenfant-Loiselle, L. and J. Jones. 1978. "Recherche des centres d'intérêts et des besoins langagiers des élèves de 9 à 10 ans." Quebec, Canada: Ministère de l'Education.

Maley, A. and A. Duff. 1978. *Drama techniques in language learning*. Cambridge: Cambridge University Press.

Malinowski, B. 1923. "The problem of meaning in primitive languages." In C. Ogden and I. Richards (eds.) *The meaning of meaning*. London: Kegan Paul, Trench & Trubner.

———. 1935. *Coral gardens and their magic I, II*. New York: American Book Company.

Mallery, G. 1881. *Sign language among North American Indians*. The Hague: Mouton.

McClelland, D. 1973. "Testing for competence rather than for 'intelligence'." *American Psychologist* 28:1–14.

McConnell, G. et al. 1980. *Vive le français*. Don Mills, Ontario: Addison-Wesley.

McConochie, J. 1981. "Shopping for community contacts." *TESOL Newsletter* 15:31–35.

McGaw, C. 1980. *Acting is believing*. New York: Holt, Rinehart, and Winston. Fourth edition.

Messick, S. 1981. "Evidence and ethics in the evaluation of tests." Research Report. Princeton, N.J.: Educational Testing Service.

Micks, W. and O. Longi. 1953. *The new fundamental French*. Oxford: Oxford University Press.

Mollica, T. (ed.). 1976. "Attitude and motivation in language learning." *Canadian Modern Language Review* 32. Special issue.

Montaigne, M. 1580. *Essais*. Paris: Bibliothèque de la Pléiade, Editions Gallimard, 1962.

Morgan, J. 1981. "Discourse theory and the independence of sentence grammar." In B. Tannen (ed.) *Georgetown University round table on languages and linguistics 1981*. Washington, D.C.: Georgetown University Press.

Morrow, K. 1979. "Communicative language testing: revolution or evolution?" In C. Brumfit and K. Johnson (eds.).

Morrow, K. and K. Johnson. 1979. *Communicate 1*. London: Cambridge University Press.

Moscowitz, G. 1978. *Caring and sharing in the foreign language class: a sourcebook on humanistic techniques*. Rowley, Mass.: Newbury House.

Munby, J. 1978. *Communicative syllabus design*. Cambridge: Cambridge University Press.

Naiman, N., M. Frölich, H. Stern, and A. Todesco. 1978. *The good language learner*. Toronto: Ontario Institute for Studies in Education.

Nelson, R. 1972. "Electronic media in foreign language education: a report on applications." *French Review* 46:330–341.

Nelson, R. and R. Wood. 1975. *Radio in foreign language education*. ERIC/CAL Series in Applied Linguistics. Arlington, Va.: Center for Applied Linguistics.

Nemser, W. 1971. "Approximative systems of foreign language learners." *International Review of Applied Linguistics* 9:115–123.

Newmark, L. 1971. "A minimal language-teaching program." In P. Pimsleur and T. Quinn (eds.).

Nine-Curt, C. 1976. *Non-verbal communication.* Cambridge, Mass.: National Assessment and Dissemination Center for Bilingual Education.

Oller, J. 1973. "Cloze tests of second language proficiency or what they measure." *Language Learning* 23:105–118.

———. 1978. "Pragmatics and language testing." In B. Spolsky (ed.).

———. 1979. *Language tests at school.* London: Longman.

———. 1981. "Language testing research." In R. Kaplan (ed.) *Annual review of applied linguistics—1980.* Rowley, Mass.: Newbury House.

Oller, J. and V. Streiff. 1975. "Dictation: a test of grammar based expectancies." *English Language Teaching* 30:25–36.

Omaggio, A. 1979. *Games and simulations in the foreign language classroom.* Arlington, Va.: Center for Applied Linguistics.

Ontario Ministry of Education, *Ontario Assessment Instrument Pool: French as a second language.* 1980. Toronto: Ontario Ministry of Education.

———. 1977. "Teaching and learning French as a second language: a new program for Ontario students." Toronto: Ontario Ministry of Education.

Osgood, C., G. Suci, and P. Tannenbaum. 1957. *The measurement of meaning.* Urbana, Ill.: University of Illinois Press.

Oskarsson, M. 1978. *Approaches to self-assessment in foreign language learning.* Strasbourg: Council of Europe. Reprinted 1980. Oxford: Pergamon Press.

Palmer, A. and P. Groot. 1981. "Introduction." In A. Palmer, P. Groot, and G. Trosper (eds.).

Palmer, A., P. Groot and G. Trosper (eds.). 1981. *The construct validation of tests of communicative competence.* Washington, D.C.: Teachers of English to Speakers of Other Languages.

Paradis, M. 1977. "Bilingualism and aphasia." In H. Whitaker and H.A. Whitaker (eds.) *Studies in Neurolinguistics* 3:65–122.

Parker, D. 1970. "When should I individualize instruction?" In V. Howes (ed.) *Individualization of instruction.* New York: Macmillan.

Paul, R. 1981. "Needed: stepladders of foreign language learning." *Foreign Language Annals* 14:379–384.

Paulston, C. 1974. "Linguistic and communicative competence." *TESOL Quarterly* 0.347–362.

———. 1980. *Bilingual education: theories and issues.* Rowley, Mass.: Newbury House.

Penfield, W. 1953. "A consideration of the neuro-physiological mechanism of speech and some educational consequences." *Proceedings of the American Academy of Arts and Sciences* 82:201–214.

——— 1959. "Epilogue—the learning of languages." In W. Penfield and L. Roberts (eds.) *Speech and brain—mechanisms.* Princeton, N.J.: Princeton University Press.

Petersen, N.   1870.   *Sprogkundskab i norden.* Collected works. Copenhagen, Denmark.

Piaget, J.   1970.   *Science of education and the psychology of the child.* New York: Orion Press.

Piepho, H-E.   1976.   "Systematische lehrwerk—analyse als grundlage einer lerner-gerechten unterrichtsplanung." *Levende Talen*: 46–52. Groningen, the Netherlands: Wolters-Noordhoff.

Piepho, H-E. et al.   1979.   *Contacts.* Bochum, West Germany: Ferdinand Kamp.

Pimsleur, P.   1966.   *Pimsleur language aptitude battery.* New York: Psychological Corp.

Pimsleur, P. and T. Quinn (eds.).   1971.   *The psychology of second language learning.* Cambridge: Cambridge University Press.

Politzer, R. and L. Weiss.   1969.   *The successful foreign-language teacher.* Philadelphia: Center for Curriculum Development.

Postman, N. and C. Weingartner.   1969.   *Teaching as a subversive activity.* New York: Delacorte Press.

Preston, D.   1981.   "Ethnography of TESOL." *TESOL Quarterly* 15:105–116.

Purcell, E.   1981.   "Models of pronunciation accuracy." Paper presented at the Colloquium on the Validation of Oral Proficiency Tests. Ann Arbor, Michigan.

Purcell, E. and R. Suter.   1980.   "Predictors of pronunciation accuracy: a reexamination." *Language Learning* 30:271–287.

Purves, A. (ed.).   1981.   *Proceedings of the national seminar on the implementation of international schools.* Urbana, Ill.: University of Illinois.

Rhodes, M.   1981.   "Immersion and partial immersion language programs in U.S. elementary schools." Information compiled by the Center for Applied Linguistics, Washington, D.C.

Rivers, W.   1968.   *Teaching foreign language skills.* University of Chicago Press. First edition.

———.   1972.   *Speaking in many tongues.* Rowley, Mass.: Newbury House. First edition.

———.   1973.   "From linguistic competence to communicative competence." *TESOL Quarterly* 7:25–34.

———.   1975.   *A practical guide to the teaching of French.* New York: Oxford University Press.

Rogers, C.   1951.   *Client-centered therapy.* Boston: Houghton Mifflin.

———.   1961.   *On becoming a person.* Boston: Houghton Mifflin.

———.   1969.   *Freedom to learn.* Columbus, Ohio: Merrill.

Rosansky, E.   1981.   "Oral language proficiency assessment and the *Lau* regulation: on the need for validation of oral language proficiency assessments for use with children." Paper presented at the Colloquium on Validation of Oral Proficiency Tests. Ann Arbor, Michigan.

Ross, D.   1981.   "From theory to practice: some critical comments on the communicative approach to language teaching." *Language Learning* 31:223–242.

Sacco, M. 1979. *Has/had*. Hull, Quebec: Canadian Government Publishing Center.

Savignon, S. 1971. "A study of the effect of training in communicative skills as part of a beginning college French course on student attitude and achievement in linguistic and communicative competence." Dissertation. University of Illinois, Champaign-Urbana. Expanded and published as *Communicative competence: an experiment in foreign language teaching.* 1972.

―――. 1972a. "Teaching for communicative competence: a research report." *Audio-Visual Language Journal* 10:153–162.

―――. 1972b. *Communicative competence: an experiment in foreign language teaching.* Philadelphia: Center for Curriculum Development.

―――. 1972c. "A l'ecoute de France-Inter: the use of radio in a student-centered oral French class." *French Review* 46:342–349.

―――. 1973. "Other peoples' languages: a game everyone can play." Keynote address at the Indiana Foreign Language Teachers' Association Fall Meeting. ERIC Report ED 127 776.

―――. 1974. "Talking with my son: an example of communicative competence." In F. Grittner (ed.) *Careers, communication, and culture.* Central States Conference Proceedings, 1974. Skokie, Ill.: National Textbook Co.

―――. 1976. "On the other side of the desk: teacher attitudes and motivation in second language learning." *Canadian Modern Language Review* 32:295–304.

―――. 1977. "Communicative competence: theory and classroom practice." *SPEAQ* (Revue de la Société pour la Promotion de l'Enseignement de l'Anglais au Québec) 1:4–15.

―――. 1981a. "A letter to my Spanish teacher." *Canadian Modern Language Review* 37:746–750.

―――. 1981b. "Three Americans in Paris: a look at 'natural' second language acquisition." *Modern Language Journal* 65:241–247.

―――. 1982. "Dictation as a measure of communicative competence in French as a second language." *Language Learning* 32:33–51.

―――. In preparation. "Uses for dictation in communicative classrooms."

Saville-Troike, M. 1982. *The enthography of communication.* Oxford: Basil Blackwell & Mott.

Schegloff, E., G. Jefferson, and H. Sacks. 1977. "The preference for self-correction in the organization of repair in conversation." *Language* 53:361–382.

Scherer, G. and M. Wertheimer. 1964. *A psycholinguistic experiment in foreign language teaching.* New York: McGraw-Hill.

Schulz, R. 1980. "TA training, supervision, and evaluation: report of a survey." *ADFL (Association of Departments of Foreign Languages) Bulletin* 12:1–8.

Schulz, R. and W. Bartz. 1975. "Free to communicate." In G. Jarvis (ed.) *Perspective: a new freedom.* ACTFL Review, vol. 7. Skokie, Ill.: National Textbook Co.

Schumann, F. and J. Schumann. 1977. "Diary of a language learner." In H. Brown, C. Yorio, and R. Crymes (eds.).

Schumann, J. 1976. "Second language acquisition research: getting a more global look at the learner." *Language Learning* 4:15–28. Special issue.

Schwartz, J.   1980.   "The negotiation for meaning: repair in conversations between second language learners of English." In D. Larsen-Freeman (ed.).

Searle, J.   1970.   *Speech acts.* Cambridge, England: Cambridge University Press.

Seelye, H.   1974.   *Teaching culture: strategies for foreign language educators.* Skokie, Ill.: National Textbook Co.

Seliger, H.   1979.   "The nature and function of language rules in language teaching." *TESOL Quarterly* 13:359–369.

Selinker, L.   1972.   "Interlanguage." *International Review of Applied Linguistics* 10:201–231.

Selinker, L. and J. Lamendella.   1981.   "Updating the interlanguage hypothesis." *Studies in Second Language Acquisition* 3:201–220.

Shohamy, E.   1978.   "Investigation of the concurrent validity of the oral interview with cloze procedure for measuring proficiency in Hebrew as a second language." Dissertation. University of Minnesota.

Simon, P.   1980.   *The tongue-tied American: confronting the foreign language crisis.* New York: Continuum.

Simon, S., L. Howe, and H. Kirschenbaum.   1972.   *Values clarification.* New York: Hart.

Simon, S. and J. Clark.   1975.   *Beginning values clarification.* La Mesa, Calif.: Pennant Press.

Sims, W. and S. Hammond.   1981.   *Award-winning foreign language programs.* Skokie, Ill.: National Textbook Co.

Slagter, P.   1979.   *Un nivel umbral.* Strasbourg: Council of Europe.

Slobin, D.   1971a.   *Psycholinguistics.* Glenview, Ill.: Scott Foresman.

———. (ed.).   1971b.   *The ontogenesis of grammar.* New York: Academic Press.

Smith, F.   1971.   *Understanding reading.* New York: Holt, Rinehart, and Winston.

Smith, P.   1970.   *A comparison of the cognitive and audiolingual approaches to foreign language instruction: the Pennsylvania foreign language project.* Philadelphia: Center for Curriculum Development.

Smith, P. and E. Berger.   1968.   *An assessment of three foreign language teaching strategies using three language laboratory systems.* Washington, D.C.: U.S. Office of Education.

Smith, S.   Forthcoming.   *The theater arts and the teaching of second languages.* Reading, Mass.: Addison-Wesley.

Spolsky, B.   1968.   "Language testing: the problem of validation." *TESOL Quarterly* 2:88–94.

———. (ed.).   1978.   *Approaches to language testing.* Arlington, Va.: Center for Applied Linguistics.

———.   1978.   "Introduction: linguists and language testers." In B. Spolsky (ed.).

———.   1981.   "Bilingualism and biliteracy." *Canadian Modern Language Review* 37:475–485.

Stanford, G.   1977.   *Developing effective classroom groups.* New York: Hart.

Stanislawcxyk, I. and S. Yavener.   1976.   *Creativity in the language classroom.* Rowley, Mass.: Newbury House.

Starr, F. 1979. "America's schools: the frontier of language teaching." *ADFL (Association of Departments of Foreign Languages) Bulletin* 11:38–41.

Stern, H. 1976. "Optimal age: myth or reality?" *Canadian Modern Language Review* 32:283–294.

———. 1980. "Language learning on the spot: some thoughts on the language aspect of student exchange programs." *Canadian Modern Language Review* 36:659–669.

———. 1981. "Language teaching and the universities in the 1980's." *Canadian Modern Language Review* 37:212–225.

Stern, H. et al. 1980. *Module making: a study in the development and evaluation of learning materials for French as a second language.* Toronto: Ontario Ministry of Education.

Stern, R. 1976. "Sexism in foreign language textbooks." *Foreign Language Annals* 9:294–299.

Stevenson, D. 1981. "Beyond faith and face validity: the multitrait-multimethod matrix and the convergent and discriminant validity of oral proficiency tests." In A. Palmer, P. Groot, and G. Trosper (eds.).

Stevick, E. 1980. *Teaching languages: a way and ways.* Rowley, Mass.: Newbury House.

Stories for language lessons. 1882. Boston: N. Lothrop and Co.

Suzuki, S. 1969. *Nurtured by love.* New York: Exposition Press.

Swaffer, J. and M. Woodruff. 1978. "Language for comprehension: focus on reading." *Modern Language Journal* 62:27–32.

Swain, M. 1977. "Future directions in second language research." In C. Henning (ed.) *Proceedings of the Los Angeles second language research forum.* Los Angeles: University of California at Los Angeles.

———. 1981. "Linguistic expectations: core, extended and immersion programs." *The Canadian Modern Language Review* 37:486–497.

Tarone, E. 1981. "Some thoughts on the notion of communication strategy." *TESOL Quarterly* 15:285–295.

Tarone, E., M. Swain, and A. Fathman. 1976. "Some limitations to the classroom applications of current second language acquisition research." *TESOL Quarterly* 10:19–32.

Taylor, B. 1981. "Content and written form: a two-way street," *TESOL Quarterly* 15:5–13.

Taylor, H. 1981. "Learning to listen to English." *TESOL Quarterly* 15:41–50.

Taylor, H. and J. Sorensen. 1961. "Culture capsules." *Modern Language Journal* 45:350–354.

Taylor, W. 1953. "Cloze procedure: a new tool for measuring readability." *Journalism Quarterly* 33:42–48.

Terrell, T. 1977. "A natural approach to second language acquisition and learning." *Modern Language Journal* 61:325–337.

———. 1980. "A natural approach to the teaching of verb forms and function in Spanish." *Foreign Language Annals* 13:129–136.

Thorndike, R. and E. Hagen. 1977. *Measurement and evaluation in psychology and education.* New York: Wiley. Fourth edition.

Tucker, G. 1977. "Can a second language be taught?" In H. Brown, C. Yorio, and R. Crymes (eds.).

Upshur, J. 1968. "Four experiments on the relation between foreign language teaching and learning." *Language Learning* 18:111–124.

Valdman, A. 1978. "Communicative use of language and syllabus design." *Foreign Language Annals* 11:567–578.

———. 1980. "Communicative ability and syllabus design for global foreign language courses." *Studies in Second Language Acquisition* 3:81–96.

Valdman, A. and M. Moody. 1979. "Testing communicative ability." *French Review* 52:552–561.

Valdman, A. and H. Warriner-Burke. 1980. "Major surgery due: redesigning the syllabus and texts." *Foreign Language Annals* 13:261–270.

Valette, R. 1977. *Modern language testing.* New York: Harcourt Brace Jovanovich. Second edition.

Van Ek, J. (ed.). 1975. *Systems development in adult language learning: the threshold level in a European unit credit system for modern language learning by adults.* Strasbourg: Council of Europe. Republished 1980 as *Threshold level English.* Oxford: Pergamon Press.

Ventriglia, L. 1982. *Conversations of Miquel and Maria.* Reading, Mass.: Addison-Wesley.

Via, R. 1976. *English in three acts.* Honolulu: University of Hawaii Press.

Wattenmaker, B. and V. Wilson. 1980. *A guidebook for teaching foreign language.* Boston: Allyn and Bacon.

Watts, G. 1963. "The teaching of French in the United States." *French Review* 37:11–65.

Whitaker, H. et al. 1981. "Neurolinguistic aspects of language acquisition and bilingualism." *Annals of the New York Academy of Sciences* 379:59–74.

Widdowson, H. 1978. *Teaching language as communication.* Oxford: Oxford University Press.

Wilkins, D. 1974. "Notional syllabuses and the concept of a minimum adequate grammar." In S.P. Corder and E. Roulet (eds.) *Linguistic insights in applied linguistics.* Paris: Didier.

———. 1976. *Notional syllabuses.* Oxford: Oxford University Press.

Williams, F. 1976. *Explorations of the linguistic attitudes of teachers.* Rowley, Mass.: Newbury House.

Woodford, P. 1981. "A common metric for language proficiency." Princeton, N.J.: Educational Testing Service. Final project report.

World of the American Indian. 1974. Washington, D.C.: National Geographic Society.

Wright, A., D. Betteridge, and M. Buckby. 1979. *Games for language learning.* Cambridge: Cambridge University Press.

Wylie, L. and R. Stafford. 1977. *Beaux gestes: a guide to French body talk.* Cambridge, Mass.: The Undergraduate Press.

Glossary

ACHIEVEMENT TEST. A test that is based on the instructional content of a particular course or curriculum. Cf. PROFICIENCY TEST.

ACTFL. American Council on the Teaching of Foreign Languages, a professional organization.

AFFECTIVE (VARIABLES). Related to feelings and emotions; attitudinal, motivational, and personality factors in second language acquisition.

ALLOMORPH. A term used in structural linguistics to refer to a variant of an identified morpheme; that is, a morpheme may have two or more allomorphs, depending on the context in which it appears. The morpheme that expresses plurality in English, for example, appears in several variants: *hat-hats* /s/, *song-songs* /z/, *purse-purses* /əz/, etc.

ALLOPHONE. A term used in structural linguistics to refer to a variant of an identified phoneme; that is, a phoneme may have two or more allophones, depending on the particular phonetic shape it takes in a given context. The English phoneme /t/, for example, includes the variants that occur in *eight* and *eighth*. Cf. PHONEME.

A-LM. *Audio-Lingual Materials* and, by extension, the audiolingual methods these materials promoted. Cf. AUDIOLINGUALISM.

ANOMIE. A feeling of social alienation, of not belonging to a cultural group.

APHASIA. Impairment or loss of the ability to use or understand spoken or written language as a result of brain injury or disease.

APPROACH. A set of assumptions about the nature of language and the nature of language teaching and learning; a philosophy or point of view. Cf. METHOD (OF TEACHING).

APTITUDE. Capability; innate or acquired capacity for something; an indication of the degree of success a learner is likely to have in a given educational setting.

ARELS. Association of Recognised English Language Schools, a British association of government approved private language schools.

ASTP. Army Specialized Training Program, an intensive language training program established in the United States during World War II.

ATTITUDE. A position that may be either physical, mental, or emotional; in relation to L2 learning, includes conscious mental position as well as a full range of often subconscious feelings or emotions.

AUDIOLINGUALISM. A language teaching approach based on structural linguistic theory and behaviorist psychology; methods of teaching language that emphasize habit formation and the production of error-free utterances.

BEHAVIORISM. A psychological theory that regards objective and observable facts of behavior or activity as the only proper subject for psychological study. An example is the stimulus-response theory of animal and human behavior elaborated in particular by B.F. Skinner and criticized subsequently by cognitive psychologists. Cf. COGNITIVE PSYCHOLOGY.

BILINGUAL EDUCATION. An educational program in which two or more languages are used in instruction.

BILINGUALISM. The use of two languages by an individual or by a social group. Cf. MULTILINGUALISM.

BODY LANGUAGE. *See* KINESICS.

CAPITAL-C CULTURE. The literary and artistic masterpieces of a civilization; major historical events. Cf. SMALL-C CULTURE.

CHANNEL. The form of communication, for example, spoken or written language, telegraphic signals, gestures (sign language).

CLOZE. The replacement of systematic deletions in a passage, proposed as a measure of the intelligibility or readability of texts (W. Taylor 1953) and, subsequently, as a test of language proficiency (Oller 1973).

CODE. A system of signs and/or signals used in communication.

CODE MIXING. The systemic mixing of linguistic units (words, idioms, and clauses) from two or more languages or language varieties in the course of a speech act or language activity.

CODE SIMPLIFICATION. Deviation from standard adult linguistic norms by a speaker or writer in an attempt to facilitate communication with a listener or reader presumed to be unfamiliar with these norms (e.g., a child, a foreigner).

CODE SWITCHING. Changing from one language or language variety to another in the course of a language activity.

COGNITIVE. Pertaining to the mental functions involved in perceiving, knowing, and understanding.

COGNITIVE PSYCHOLOGY. The study of mental states through inference from behavior. Cf. BEHAVIORISM.

COHERENCE. Ideas within a text; semantic links provided by meaning.

COHESION. The relationship of one linguistic item to another in a text; relations of meaning that exist within a text and that define it as a text; a means of achieving textual coherence. Cf. COHERENCE.

COMMEDIA DELL'ARTE. Italian popular comedy, developed during the sixteenth to eighteenth centuries, in which actors improvised from a basic plot outline; improvisation on a theme.

COMMUNICATIVE COMPETENCE.   Functional language proficiency; the expression, interpretation, and negotiation of meaning involving interaction between two or more persons belonging to the same (or different) speech community (communities), or between one person and a written or oral text. Cf. LINGUISTIC COMPETENCE.

COMPETENCE/PERFORMANCE.   A dichotomy proposed by Chomsky to distinguish between what an ideal hearer or speaker knows about the structure of his or her native language (competence) and the manifestation of this knowledge in actual language use (performance).

CONCEPTUAL LEVEL.   A measure of an individual's cognitive complexity and interpersonal maturity.

CONSTRUCT.   A mental ability, trait, or competence that is part of a theory of what it is that a test is supposed to measure. Cf. TRAIT.

CONTEXT OF SITUATION.   Establishes the rules of appropriateness for the behavior of participants in a language event on the basis of who they are, where they are, and why they have come together, and gives meaning to that behavior.

CONTRASTIVE ANALYSIS (CA).   The systematic comparison of structural features of two or more languages or language varieties.

CORRELATION.   A systematic relationship between two or more observed variables without necessarily implying a cause and effect relationship.

CRITERION-REFERENCED TEST.   Goal-referenced test; the evaluation of test takers in relation to their ability to achieve a particular level of performance, that is, a criterion; results are often expressed in terms of the percentage of correct answers in relation to the total number of items on the test. Cf. NORM-REFERENCED TEST.

CROSS-SECTIONAL (STUDIES OF L1/L2 ACQUISITION).   Observation and comparison at a given time of the language performance of different groups representing different levels of development and/or contexts of acquisition. Cf. LONGITUDINAL.

CULTURE.   See CAPITAL-C CULTURE and SMALL-C CULTURE.

CURRICULUM.   A statement of both the content and process of teaching for a course or sequence of courses; a guide to selection of items and activities (British: syllabus); all educational experiences for which the school is responsible. Cf. SYLLABUS.

DEDUCTIVE.   Refers to a method or approach to language teaching that reasons from general rules to particular cases; exposition of rules or principles. Cf. INDUCTIVE.

DEEP STRUCTURE.   A term used in transformational-generative linguistic theory to refer to the sentence-level grammatical interpretation of surface structures. Cf. SURFACE STRUCTURE.

DIACHRONIC.   *See* LONGITUDINAL.

DIALECT.   A regional or social variety of a language distinguished from other varieties by features of pronunciation, grammar, or vocabulary; a variety of language defined in terms of the *user* (e.g., social class, caste, religion). Cf. REGISTER, VARIETY.

DIRECT METHOD.   A language teaching method that makes exclusive use of the L2 without recourse to the learner's native language; inspired by the Natural Method but with claims for a more systematic approach to problems of L2 learning, particularly phonological; an American adaptation of this method is known as the "Cleveland Plan" (de Sauzé 1953). Cf. NATURAL METHOD.

DISCOURSE.   Connected speech or writing that extends beyond a single sentence or utterance.

DISCOURSE ANALYSIS.   Analysis of connected speech or writing that extends beyond a single sentence or utterance; study of the pragmatic functions of language.

DISCOURSE COMPETENCE.   The ability to recognize different patterns of discourse, to connect sentences or utterances to an overall theme or topic; the ability to infer the meaning of large units of spoken or written texts.

DISCRETE-POINT LANGUAGE TESTING.   Separate assessment of isolated formal features of language; use of discrete-point response types (multiple choice, true-false, etc.). Cf. INTEGRATIVE LANGUAGE TESTING.

EGO PERMEABILITY.   The permeability of a person's ego boundaries; the ease with which a person is able to acquire a new self-identification.

EMPATHY.   A capacity for participation in another's feelings or ideas.

ETHNOGRAPHY.   A field of study concerned with the description and analysis of culture.

ETHNOGRAPHY OF COMMUNICATION.   A field of study that looks at the norms of communicative conduct in different communities from a multidisciplinary perspective as well as methods for studying these norms.

ERROR.   A form that deviates from some selected norm of adult language performance; deviation from a prescriptive norm. Cf. GRAMMAR.

ERROR ANALYSIS.   A listing or classification of learner errors.

ESL.   English as a second language; teaching of English to nonnative speakers.

ESP.   English for Specific (Special) Purposes, (e.g., academic purposes, science and technology); a component of ESL.

ETHNOMETHODOLOGY.   A concentration on strategies of discourse interpretation.

ETS.   Educational Testing Service, a developer and distributor of many large-scale standardized tests of aptitude, achievement, and proficiency, including the TOEFL.

FIELD DEPENDENCE/INDEPENDENCE.   A measure of perceptual functioning indicating the extent to which a person is able to isolate elements from the context in which it appears.

FIRST LANGUAGE (L1).   A language acquired in early childhood prior to, or simultaneously with, another language; native language; mother tongue; primary language.

FLES.   Foreign languages in the elementary schools, a curricular development that gained momentum in the United States in the 1960s.

FOREIGNER TALK.   Modifications (or simplifications) made in the speech of native speakers when conversing with nonnative speakers. Cf. CODE SIMPLIFICATION.

FOSSILIZATION.   The process of stabilization in L2 acquisition whereby nonnative forms become a permanent feature of an individual's (or a group's) performance; the resistance of interlanguage features to further change. Cf. INTERLANGUAGE.

FSI.   Foreign Service Institute, a U.S. government agency whose test of oral proficiency has been widely used in the Peace Corps and other language learning programs.

FUNCTION.   The purpose of an utterance; the use to which a particular grammatical form is put (e.g., to request, to permit, to describe). Cf. ILLOCUTIONARY ACT, SPEECH ACT.

GLOBAL LANGUAGE TESTING.   *See* INTEGRATIVE LANGUAGE TESTING.

GRAMMAR.   A theory of language competence; rule-governed language behavior; any explicit characterization of language behavior (e.g., phrase-structure grammar, transformational grammar, functional grammar); prescriptive norms, that is, a set of rules for "correct" or "proper" language usage, intended to preserve imagined standards and typically critical of socially stigmatized forms of the standard dialect. A PEDAGOGICAL GRAMMAR is a grammar intended for language teaching.

GRAMMATICAL COMPETENCE.   Knowledge of the sentence structure of a language.

IDIOLECT.   The linguistic system of an individual speaker.

ILLOCUTIONARY ACT.   An act performed in saying something; function; speech act.

ILR.   Interagency Language Roundtable, an association of U.S. governmental agencies (including the FSI) concerned with language training and testing.

IMMERSION.   Use of the L2 as a means of communication with members of a surrounding community; participation in an L2 community as opposed to the classroom study of an L2 as a foreign language.

IMMERSION PROGRAM.   An educational program for language acquisition in which the L2 is the medium of instruction; exclusive use of the L2 as a means of communication within the classroom or school.

INDUCTIVE.   Refers to a method or approach to language teaching that proceeds from particular facts or examples to a general rule or principle; discovery learning. Cf. DEDUCTIVE.

INSTRUMENTAL ORIENTATION.   An orientation to L2 learning that emphasizes the utilitarian value of L2 proficiency such as getting a pay raise, a better job, or a good grade in school; the use of language as a tool for a specific goal (e.g., science, technology).

INTEGRATIVE ORIENTATION.   An orientation to L2 learning that reflects an openness toward another culture group and that may include a desire to be accepted as a member of that group.

INTERLANGUAGE.   The knowledge of an L2 that a language learner (user) has that approximates, but is not identical to, the knowledge of adult native speakers of the language; approximative system; a language system in transition; transitional competence.

INTEGRATIVE LANGUAGE TESTING.   Global assessment of effectiveness in terms of functional (semantic) criteria; use of an integrative response type (e.g., essay, interview, etc.). Cf. DISCRETE-POINT LANGUAGE TESTING.

INFERENCE.   Interpretation of meaning based on assumptions regarding the context of a speech act.

INTERFERENCE.   Presence of features of pronunciation, grammar, vocabulary that may be attributed to one's knowledge of another language. Cf. TRANSFER.

KINESICS.   The study of body movements of all kinds including facial gestures, hand motions, leg movements, and shifts in overall posture; body language.

L1.   *See* FIRST LANGUAGE.

L2.   *See* SECOND LANGUAGE.

LANGUAGE FOR SPECIFIC PURPOSES (LSP).   Instructional programs developed in response to specific adult professional, occupational or social needs, for example, English for Academic Purposes (EAP), English for Science and Technology (EST).

LANGUAGE LOSS.   Attrition of language skills; forgetting a language through lack of use.

LATERALIZATION.   Specialization of language function by one side (right or left) of the brain; cerebral dominance; loss of brain plasticity.

LEP.   Limited English Proficiency, a classification used in the description of the language skills of nonnative speakers of English in U.S. schools.

LEXICON.   The vocabulary of a language; a dictionary.

LINGUA FRANCA.   A language used for communication among speakers of different native languages.

LINGUISTIC COMPETENCE.   *See* GRAMMATICAL COMPETENCE.

LONGITUDINAL (STUDIES OF L1/L2 ACQUISITION). Observation over time of the language performance of a single person or a group of persons with attention to changes that may occur. Cf. CROSS-SECTIONAL (STUDIES OF L1/L2 ACQUISITION).

MEAN. Arithmetic average of a given set of values found by dividing the sum of the set by the number of values.

METALANGUAGE. Language used to talk about language, (e.g., noun, verb, phoneme, speech act, cohesion).

METHOD (OF TEACHING). Overall plan for the grading and presentation of material to be taught, based on an approach. Cf. APPROACH.

METHOD (OF MEASUREMENT). In testing, the technique used to measure a trait (e.g., multiple choice, interview, cloze). Cf. TRAIT.

METHOD ACTING. A theory and technique of acting in which the performer identifies with the character to be portrayed and renders the part in a naturalistic, individualized manner; the Stanislavski Method.

MLAT. Modern Language Aptitude Test, best known example of a test designed to measure language learning aptitude.

MINIMAL PAIR. Two words that sound alike in all but one distinguishing feature, denoting a difference in meaning, (e.g., *ship-sheep, cup-cop, watching-washing*). Cf. PHONEME.

MONITOR. To give conscious attention to the form of linguistic production.

MORPHEME. The smallest meaningful unit of a language; the smallest functioning unit in the composition of words. In English, for example, *unclaimed* consists of three morphemes: *un, claim,* and *ed.*

MORPHOLOGY. The system of the word structure of a language; the study of the structure of words or word formation.

MULTILINGUALISM. The use of three or more languages by an individual or by a social group.

MOTIVATION. Incentive, need, or desire.

NATURAL METHOD. A language teaching method advocated in the nineteenth century, so called because its proponents claimed to follow the way in which children learn their native language, through conversation; characterized by a repudiation of books and grammar rules and the active demonstration of meaning through mime, gestures, and physical objects. Cf. DIRECT METHOD.

NDEA. National Defense Education Act, legislation passed in 1958 that gave support to foreign language study in U.S. secondary schools.

NEEDS ASSESSMENT. A survey of learner needs and interests as a basis for L2 curriculum and/or materials development.

NEGOTIATION. A process whereby a participant in a speech event uses various sources of information—prior experience, the context, another participant—

to achieve understanding; the reciprocal efforts of conversational partners to maintain the flow of conversation; cooperation.

NEUROLINGUISTICS.　Area of physiological research concerned with the relationship between human language and neural, or nerve, systems.

NEW KEY.　A term used in the 1960s to refer to audiolingual methods of language teaching. Cf. AUDIOLINGUALISM.

NORMED-REFERENCED TEST.　A standardized test that compares the performance of a test taker with the performance of a normative group and is designed to maximize individual differences. Results may be expressed in terms of a percentile rank. Cf. CRITERION-REFERENCED TEST.

NORMATIVE GROUP.　A representative sample of the population for whom a test was developed (e.g., foreign student applicants, elementary school immersion students, native speakers).

NORMS.　(1) In testing, the distribution of scores on a test; a descriptive framework for test score interpretation with reference to the characteristics of the normative group (e.g., age, grade level, sex, L1, etc.). Cf. NORMATIVE GROUP. (2) In linguistic theory, the standard practice in speech or writing with reference to a given speech community or a group within that community.

NOTION.　A unit of meaning (e.g., time, space, quantity); a semantic unit.

NOTIONAL-FUNCTIONAL SYLLABUS.　Organizes language content by semantic and functional categories within a general consideration of the communicative functions of language. Cf. SYLLABUS, SITUATIONAL SYLLABUS, STRUCTURAL SYLLABUS.

PARALINGUISTIC.　Pertaining to vocal signals or features outside the conventional linguistic channels (e.g., pitch, rate, volume, and nonspeech vocalizations such as laughter and coughs).

PHONETICS.　The science that studies human vocal sounds and the way they are produced (articulated) by the vocal organs.

PHONOLOGY.　The sound system of a language.

PHONEME.　A minimum unit of speech sound that manifests differences in meaning, most often identified and represented through the contrast of words, or minimal pairs. In English, for example, the minimal pair *ship* and *sheep* may be used to demonstrate the distinction between the phonemes /ɪ/ and /i/. Cf. MINIMAL PAIR.

PRAGMATICS.　Concerned with the relationships between expressions in the formal system of language and anything else outside it; an interdisciplinary field of inquiry concerned with relations between linguistic units, speakers, and extralinguistic facts; roles and uses of language in social contexts; the science of language use.

PROFICIENCY TEST.　Any test that is based on a theory of the abilities required to use language. Cf. ACHIEVEMENT TEST.

PROXEMICS.   Interpersonal space; the distance individuals stand or sit from one another.

PSYCHOMETRIC.   Having to do with the measurement of psychological abilities or attributes and the statistical properties of such measurments.

RP.   Received Pronunciation, the pronunciation traditionally characteristic of British public schools and the universities of Oxford and Cambridge.

REDUNDANCY.   Repetition of subject matter already familiar to learners; availability of information from more than one source.

REGISTER.   A special variety of language defined in terms of its use in various professional contexts or settings (e.g., classroom, courtroom, pub, hospital); a variety of language defined in terms of its *use*. Cf. DIALECT, VARIETY.

RELIABILITY.   The accuracy, consistency, or stability of the results (scores) of a test measurement.

SECOND LANGUAGE (L2).   A language learned after the basics of a first or primary language have been acquired; foreign language; "target" language.

SECOND LANGUAGE ACQUISITION.   All nonnative language acquisition.

SEMANTIC(S).   Pertaining to meaning in language; meaning; content.

SEMANTIC DIFFERENTIAL SCALE.   A technique of attitude measurement in which respondents react to a concept or experience by placing an X along a series of bipolar response continuums, for example:

Father

happy ___: ___: _X_: ___: ___ sad
hard ___: _X_: ___: ___: ___ soft

SEMIOTICS.   The study of both human and nonhuman signaling systems.

SIMULATION.   Simplification of a real-world situation; a language learning activity that places learners in a situation or environment in which events and outcomes depend on their collective communicative competence.

SITUATIONAL SYLLABUS.   Organizes language content according to situations or settings. Cf. SYLLABUS, STRUCTURAL SYLLABUS, NOTIONAL-FUNCTIONAL SYLLABUS.

SMALL-C CULTURE.   Culture in an anthropological sense; the day-to-day living patterns of a group of people. Cf. CAPITAL-CULTURE.

SOCIOLINGUISTIC COMPETENCE.   The ability to use language appropriate to a given communicative context, taking into account the roles of the participants, the setting, and the purpose of the interaction.

SPEECH ACT.   A functional unit of speech that derives its meaning not from grammatical form but from the rules of interpretation in a given speech community. Cf. FUNCTION, ILLOCUTIONARY ACT, INFERENCE.

STANDARD DEVIATION.   A statistic that indicates the variability present in a group of measures (scores), based on the deviations of individual measures (scores) from the mean.

STRATEGIC COMPETENCE.   The ability to compensate for imperfect knowledge of linguistic, sociolinguistic, and discourse rules or limiting factors in their application such as fatigue, distraction, inattention; the effective use of coping strategies to sustain or enhance communication.

STRATEGY.   A particular method of approaching a problem or task; a mode of operation for achieving a particular goal.

STRUCTURALISM.   An approach for the analysis and description of language; emphasizes the procedures by which linguistic items can be described as *structures* and *systems*. In the United States, this term is used with special reference to Bloomfield's emphasis on segmenting and classifying physical features of an utterance.

STRUCTURAL SYLLABUS.   Organizes instructional material according to discrete structural, or formal, features of language. Cf. SYLLABUS, SITUATIONAL SYLLABUS, NOTIONAL-FUNCTIONAL SYLLABUS.

STYLE.   Refers to the linguistic choices made by participants in a language activity, especially the level of formality (e.g., informal, formal).

SURFACE STRUCTURE.   The surface representation of a word or sound sequence with no reference to meaning or semantic value. Cf. DEEP STRUCTURE.

STYLISTICS.   A linguistically oriented approach to the analysis and description of situationally distinctive uses (varieties) of language; establishes principles and generalizations for the choices made by groups and individuals in their use of language; a school of literary criticism that attempts to go from a formal description of style to an interpretation of an author's personality or way of organizing experiences.

SYLLABUS.   (1) British: specification of the content of language teaching; a structuring or ordering of that content in terms of grading and presentation. (2) American: A schedule of items or units to be taught; a daily or weekly program of material to be presented. Cf. CURRICULUM.

SYNCHRONIC.   *See* CROSS-SECTIONAL.

SYNTAX.   That part of grammar that is concerned with the arrangement of words in sentences, the distribution of words in constructions, and the systematic structural relations between sentences.

SYSTEM(IC).   A network of patterned relationships constituting the organization of language.

TARGET LANGUAGE.   The L2 being learned or taught.

TECHNIQUE.   A particular device, strategy, activity used to accomplish an immediate goal. Cf. APPROACH, METHOD (OF TEACHING).

TESOL.   Teachers of English to Speakers of Other Languages, a professional organization.

TEST.   A sample of behavior; on the basis of observed performance on a test, inferences are made about the more general underlying competence of an individual to perform similar or related tasks.

TEXT. A "piece" of language relevant to a specific context; language in setting; transactions of various kinds such as tasks, games, discussions, etc.; a spoken or written passage that forms a unified whole.

THEORY. A formulation of basic principles supported by empirical evidence and open to confirmation or refutation by evidence yet to be discovered.

TOEFL. Test of English as a Foreign Language, a written test designed to test the English proficiency of foreign students applying for admission to U.S. colleges and universities, prepared and administered by Educational Testing Service.

TRAIT. In testing theory, the ability or attribute one is measuring. Cf. METHOD (OF MEASUREMENT).

TRANSFER. The carry-over into learner performance in a new language of features of pronunciation, grammar, and vocabulary, or discourse strategies that have previously been learned for another language. POSITIVE TRANSFER results when the two languages have features in common. NEGATIVE TRANSFER occurs when features do not coincide. Cf. INTERFERENCE.

TRANSFORMATIONAL-GENERATIVE (GRAMMAR). A linguistic theory concerned with the relation between the grammatical interpretation of sentences and surface structure as a means of discovering universal categories of grammar; Chomskyan linguistic theory. Cf. SURFACE STRUCTURE, DEEP STRUCTURE.

VALIDITY. The extent to which a test measures what it is supposed to measure and nothing else.

VARIETY (OF LANGUAGE). A situationally distinctive use of language (e.g., social, religious, professional). Cf. DIALECT, REGISTER.

Index